Die Abenteuer des Grafen Friedrich Reinhard von Rechteren-Limpurg im Mittelmeer und im Amerikanischen Unabhängigkeitskrieg 1770 bis 1782

The adventures of Friedrich Reinhard count of Rechteren-Limpurg in the Mediterranean and the American War of Independence 1770 – 1782

herausgegeben von/edited by

Jane A. Baum, Hans-Peter Baum, Jesko Graf zu Dohna

Die Abenteuer des Grafen Friedrich Reinhard von Rechteren-Limpurg im Mittelmeer und im Amerikanischen Unabhängigkeitskrieg 1770 bis 1782

The Adventures of Friedrich Reinhard count of Rechteren-Limpurg in the Mediterranean and the American War of Independence 1770 – 1782

herausgegeben von/edited by

Jane A. Baum, Hans-Peter Baum, Jesko Graf zu Dohna

Mainfränkische Hefte, Heft 115

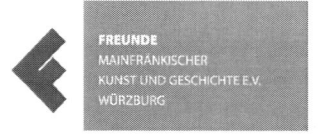

Bibliografische Information der Deutschen Nationalbibliothek

Die Deutsche Nationalbibliothek verzeichnet diese Publikation in der Deutschen Nationalbibliografie; detaillierte bibliografische Daten sind im Internet über http://dnb.dnb.de abrufbar.

Bibliographic information published by the Deutsche Nationalbibliothek

The Deutsche Nationalbibliothek lists this publication in the Deutsche Nationalbibliografie; detailed bibliographic data are available on the Internet at http://dnb.dnb.de.

Mainfränkische Hefte, Heft 115
„Freunde Mainfränkischer Kunst und Geschichte e.V.", Würzburg

1. Auflage, November 2016
© Spurbuchverlag, 96148 Baunach,
info@spurbuch.de; www.spurbuch.de
© Verein der „Freunde Mainfränkischer Kunst und Geschichte e.V."
Ausführung: pth-mediaberatung GmbH, Würzburg
Umschlaglayout: Monika Glück

ISBN 978-3-88778-484-3

Inhaltsverzeichnis / Contents

Vorwort der Herausgeber / Editors' Preface 7

Einleitung / Introduction

Friedrich Reinhard Graf von Rechteren-Limpurg-Speckfeld, ein fränkischer Standesherr. 9
von Hans-Peter Baum

Friedrich Reinhard count of Rechteren-Limpurg-Speckfeld, a Franconian nobleman 9
by Hans-Peter Baum

Die Abenteuer des Grafen Friedrich Reinhard von Rechteren-Limpurg im Mittelmeer
und im Amerikanischen Unabhängigkeitskrieg 1770 bis 1782 45
bearbeitet von Jane A. Baum, Hans-Peter Baum und Jesko Graf zu Dohna

The adventures of Friedrich Reinhard count of Rechteren-Limpurg in the Mediterranean
and the American War of Independence 1770 – 1782 45
edited by Jane A. Baum, Hans-Peter Baum, and Jesko Graf zu Dohna

Bildanhang / Illustrations 119

Quellen und Literatur / Bibliography 137

Register / Index 143

Vorwort der Herausgeber

Das vorliegende Buch hat eine längere Entstehungsgeschichte. Das Editionsprojekt begann Mitte der 1990er Jahre, als Graf Dohna das Ehepaar Baum mit den Erinnerungen von Friedrich Reinhard Graf von Rechteren-Limpurg bekannt machte, die er bereits vollständig transkribiert hatte. Es war insbesondere der auf Rechterens Teilnahme am Amerikanischen Unabhängigkeitskrieg bezügliche Teil dieser Memoiren, der eine Herausgabe des Textes für die fränkische Landesgeschichte wichtig erscheinen ließ, denn zwar haben die meisten Deutschen und Amerikaner von den hessischen (und – nicht zu vergessen – auch braunschweigischen und ansbach-bayreuthischen) Söldnern gehört, die mehr oder weniger zwangsweise in der britischen Armee gegen die aufständischen Kolonisten in Amerika kämpften. Dass aber auch zahlreiche Deutsche auf Seiten der Amerikaner in den Krieg um die Unabhängigkeit der Kolonien eingriffen, ist in der Öffentlichkeit kaum bekannt, noch viel weniger, dass auch Männer aus Franken daran beteiligt waren. Dies ließ auch eine zweisprachige Edition sinnvoll erscheinen, um diese historischen Fakten auf beiden Seiten des Atlantiks bekannt zu machen (Spezialisten für die Geschichte des Unabhängigkeitskriegs sind sie natürlich längst bekannt gewesen).

Zunächst wurde der Text mit Fußnoten versehen, um die zahlreichen Orts- und Personennamen im Text zu erläutern. Dabei übernahm Graf Dohna allein die Fußnoten zu dem auf die Mittelmeerreise Rechterens bezüglichen Teil der Memoiren, H.P. Baum diejenigen für den Textteil, der Rechterens Teilnahme am Unabhängigkeitskrieg beschreibt. Jane Baum übersetzte unterdessen den Text ins Englische. Mehrere Korrekturgänge schlossen sich an. All dies nahm viel Zeit in Anspruch, weil die Herausgeber in Vollzeit berufstätig waren und daher größere zeitliche Pausen eintraten. Schließlich verfasste H.P.Baum einen biographischen Abriss und eine vergleichende Bewertung Rechterens als Memoirenschreiber; letzteres v.a. deswegen, weil zum Amerikanischen Unabhängigkeitskrieg viele solcher Texte vorliegen und weil nicht zuletzt zwei sehr lebendig geschriebene Memoiren von Kriegsteilnehmern bekannt sind, die auf demselben Schiff nach Amerika reisten wie Rechteren. Zu betonen ist an dieser Stelle, dass der biographische Abriss keineswegs als vollständige Biographie Rechterens gelten kann, dass auch die darin enthaltenen Ausführungen zur Grafschaft Rechteren-Limpurg nicht im Entferntesten eine abgerundete Geschichte dieses Territoriums in Friedrich Reinhards Lebenszeit darstellen; sie sollen dem Leser nur eine Vorstellung von den Problemen geben, mit denen sich ein fränkischer Standesherr wie Rechteren um die Wende vom

Editors' Preface

This book has been quite a while in the making. The project of an edition took off in the mid-1990s when Jesko count zu Dohna introduced the Baums to the memoirs of Friedrich Reinhard count of Rechteren-Limpurg which had already been completely transcribed by him. It was Rechteren's part in the War of American Independence as described in these memoirs which made an edition of his text appear of great interest for the regional history of Franconia. Most Germans and Americans have heard of the Hessian soldiers (and – not to forget – those from Brunswick and Ansbach-Bayreuth as well) who were more or less coerced to fight in British service against the insurgent colonists in America, but neither the average German nor the average American knows that many Germans fought on the side of these colonists, and even fewer have heard of the fact that men from Franconia were among them. This seemed to call for a bilingual edition in order to make these historical facts known on both sides of the Atlantic (experts of the history of the American War of Independence have been familiar with them for a long time, of course).

The text was then thoroughly annotated to explain the many personal and place names to the reader. Count Dohna wrote the footnotes for the part of Rechteren's memoirs which describes his voyage in the Mediterranean, H.P.Baum those pertaining to the American campaign. Simultaneously, Jane Baum translated the text into English. Repeated corrections were made. All this took a lot of time as the editors were working full time jobs and there were several long pauses between stages of activity. Finally, H.P.Baum wrote a biographical outline and a comparative assessment of Rechteren as an author of memoirs; this seemed necessary as there are quite a few such texts from the American War of Independence, and in particular, two very vivid memoirs written by soldiers who travelled to America on the same ship as Rechteren. It is essential to emphasize here that this biographical outline should not be considered as a complete history of Rechteren's life nor that the brief remarks on some events in and the finances of the county of Rechteren-Limpurg to be found here constitute a comprehensive history of that territory; they are just meant to give the reader an idea of the problems with which a Franconian nobleman like Rechteren saw himself confronted at the transition from the 18th to the 19th century. It has to remarked here as

18. zum 19. Jahrhundert konfrontiert sah. An dieser Stelle sei auch darauf hingewiesen, dass Rechterens Text wohl zum Lesen für jüngere Generationen seiner Familie gedacht war und kontroversen Urteilen oder Bewertungen ausweicht, so etwa bei Phänomenen wie der Sklaverei in den amerikanischen Kolonien; auch kommen Begegnungen mit Frauen nicht vor, obwohl einer der auf seinem Schiff mitreisenden Kriegsteilnehmer sich sehr gern an Tanzabende mit „schönen Maiden" in Amerika erinnert, die auf dem Marsch der Truppe von Neuengland nach Virginia immer wieder veranstaltet wurden.

Es ist vielen dafür zu danken, dass das Projekt schließlich doch zu einem guten Abschluss gekommen ist. Für guten Rat und die Bereitstellung von Quellen zu Rechterens Biographie ist zunächst Herrn Dr. Robert Selig in Holland/Michigan zu danken; er gehört nicht nur zu den bereits angesprochenen Kennern und Spezialisten der Geschichte des Unabhängigkeitskriegs, sondern hat auch maßgeblich zur Geschichte der Grafschaft Limpurg-Speckfeld geforscht. Zu danken ist sodann den Freunden mainfränkischer Kunst und Geschichte unter ihrem Vorsitzenden Prof. Dr. Helmut Flachenecker, dem Bezirk Unterfranken, hier besonders Herrn Kulturdirektor Professor Dr. Klaus Reder, der Gemeinde Sommerhausen, vertreten durch ihren ersten Bürgermeister, Herrn Fritz Steinmann, für ihre großzügig gewährten Druckkostenzuschüsse, last, but not least Dr. Icho Graf von Rechteren für seine Unterstützung sowie dem Verlag pth-mediaberatung für die professionelle Ausführung von Satz und Druck.

Würzburg/Castell, im Frühherbst 2016

well that Rechteren's memoirs seem to have been written for the younger generations of his own family as they do not go into controversial subjects such as the slavery in the American colonies. It is striking as well that there are no mentions of meeting women anywhere in the whole text even though one of the memorialists mentioned above who travelled on the same ship and served in the same unit as Rechteren is very fond of remembering evening dances with "pretty maidens" in America; such dances were organized quite a few times on the march of the French and German troops from New England to Virginia.

The editors would like to give thanks to all who contributed with helpful advice or financial support to complete the project. We thank Dr. Robert Selig of Holland/MI for useful information and source material on Rechteren; he is one of the experts on the history of the American Revolution mentioned above as well as one of the history of the county of Limpurg-Speckfeld. We should like to give thanks to the "Freunde mainfränkischer Kunst und Geschichte" and their president Professor Dr. Helmut Flachenecker, to the Bezirk Unterfranken, especially Kulturdirektor Professor Dr. Klaus Reder, and to the town of Sommerhausen, represented by First Bürgermeister Fritz Steinmann, for their financial support. Last, but not least, we should like to thank Dr. Icho Graf von Rechteren for his support as well as the staff of pth-mediaberatung for the professional work they did on the layout and typesetting of this book.

Würzburg/Castell, in the fall of 2016

Einleitung

Friedrich Reinhard Graf von Rechteren-Limpurg-Speckfeld,

ein fränkischer Standesherr

von Hans-Peter Baum

Friedrich Reinhard Burkhard Rudolph von Rechteren wurde am 22. September 1751 auf Schloss Rechteren in der niederländischen Provinz Overijssel geboren.[1] Seine Eltern waren Johann Eberhard Adolph, Graf von Rechteren zu Rechteren, Schulenburg und Ehse, und Sophia Carolina Florentina, geb. Gräfin von Rechteren zu Almelo. Friedrich Reinhard war ihr jüngster Sohn. Johann Eberhard starb schon 1754, Sophia Carolina heiratete später einen entfernten Verwandten.[2]

Friedrich Reinhard lebte in seiner frühesten Kindheit, und zwar vom Jahresende 1752 bis 1757, mit seiner Familie in Sommerhausen.[3] Sein Vater hatte einen Teil der Grafschaft Limpurg-Speckfeld geerbt, wozu Sommerhausen gehörte, und die Reichsstandschaft erworben[4] und hielt sich mit seinen Angehörigen daher abwechselnd in den Niederlanden und in Franken auf. Nach seinem Tod kehrte die Familie in die Niederlande zurück und lebte in Almelo.[5] Die Kinder erhielten Privatunterricht, erst durch einen Herrn Schwab aus Ansbach, dann durch den Advokaten

---

1. Geburtsanzeige vom 23.09.1751 in FCA HA IV 55. Schloss Rechteren liegt fast am Ufer der Overijsselsche Vecht, etwa 1 km südöstlich von Dalfsen, dieses wiederum ca. 8 km östlich von Zwolle, der Provinzhauptstadt von Overijssel. – Das Wort „Standesherr" wird in seiner engeren Bedeutung gebraucht, für einen Adligen, der im Zuge der Mediatisierung seine Stellung als immediater Reichsstand verloren, aber persönliche Vorrechte behalten hatte.

2. Die Darstellung von Rechterens Kindheit und Jugend folgt zum großen Teil seinen eigenen Mitteilungen in seinen hier veröffentlichten Memoiren, ergänzt durch Angaben in einem sehr ausführlichen Nachruf, der ohne Nennung eines Autors in seinem Todesjahr in Würzburg im Druck erschien; FCA HA IV 118. Unter FCHA XIVc 51 liegt im Fürstlich Castell'schen Archiv eine umfangreiche Geschichte des Hauses Rechteren vor.

3. Etwa 14 km südöstlich von Würzburg am rechten Mainufer gelegen.

4. Der Vater Johann Eberhards hatte durch Heirat die Grafschaft Limpurg-Speckfeld erworben, Johann Eberhard selbst durch Aufnahme in das fränkische Reichsgrafen-Kollegium die Reichsstandschaft; s. Kneschke, Adelslexikon, Bd. 7., S. 379 f.; Siebmacher, Wappenbuch, Bd. I, Abt. 3, Reihe II, S. 12; Prescher, Reichsgrafschaft Limpurg, 2. Teil, 1790, S. 71 – 73, und Wunder/Schefold/Beutter, Schenken von Limpurg, 1982, S. 54 ff.

5. Sicher in dem heute noch bestehenden und im Besitz der Familie Rechteren-Limpurg befindlichen „Huis Almelo" am Rande der Innenstadt; vgl. Wikipedia unter „Almelo".

Introduction

Friedrich Reinhard count of Rechteren-Limpurg-Speckfeld,

a Franconian nobleman

by Hans-Peter Baum

Friedrich Reinhard Burkhard Rudolph of Rechteren was born on September 22, 1751, at Rechteren castle in the Dutch province of Overijssel.[1] His parents were Johann Eberhard Adolph, count of Rechteren in Rechteren, Schulenburg, and Ehse, and Sophia Carolina Florentina, countess of Rechteren in Almelo. Friedrich Reinhard was their youngest son. Johann Eberhard died in 1754, Sophia Carolina later married a distant relative.[2]

In his earliest childhood, i.e. from the end of 1752 until 1757, Friedrich Reinhard and his family lived in Sommerhausen.[3] His father had inherited part of the county of Limpurg-Speckfeld which Sommerhausen belonged to and had become a count of the Holy Roman Empire;[4] that is why he and his family alternately lived in the Netherlands and in Franconia. After his death the family returned to the Netherlands and lived in Almelo.[5] The children had private tutors, first a Mr. Schwab of Ansbach (in Bavaria), then the lawyer and later judge Düll of Almelo. At the age of 16,

---

1. Birth announcement of Sept. 23rd, 1751, in: FCA HA IV 55. R. castle is situated close to the the Overijsselsche Vecht river, about 1 km southeast of Dalfsen which lies about 8 km east of Zwolle, the provincial capital of Overijssel. – The precise definition of the German term "Standesherr" is used here, i.e. of a nobleman who had lost his status as an immediate estate of the Holy Roman Empire by mediatisation, but retained some personal prerogatives.

2. The description of Rechteren's childhood and youth mostly follows his own memoirs published here; it is completed by a detailed obituary, printed in Würzburg in the year of his death without an author's name; cf. FCA HA IV 118. The Fürstlich Castell'sche archive keeps an extensive history of the house of Rechteren under FCHA XIVc 51.

3. Situated on the right bank of the Main river about 14 km southeast of Würzburg, Bavaria.

4. Johann Eberhard's father had acquired the county of Limpurg-Speckfeld by marriage; Johann Eberhard had been formally received into the college of Franconian counts of the Empire; cf. Kneschke, Adelslexikon, vol. 7, p. 379 f.; Siebmacher, Wappenbuch, vol. 1, part 3, series II, p. 12; also H. Prescher, Reichsgrafschaft Limpurg, Part 2, 1790, p. 71 – 73; G.Wunder/M. Schefold/H. Beutter, Schenken von Limpurg, 1982, p. 54 ff.

5. Most certainly at "Huis Almelo", a palace at the edge of the city centre of Almelo, which is still owned and lived in by the Rechteren-Limpurg family; cf. Wikipedia under "Almelo".

und späteren Richter Düll in Almelo. Im 16. Lebensjahr ging Friedrich Reinhard ein Jahr auf die Lateinschule in Ijsselstein[6] und besuchte dann zwei Jahre lang die Universität Utrecht. Seine Bildung, nicht nur in den alten und modernen Sprachen, sondern auch in der Mathematik, dürfte recht umfassend gewesen sein.[7]

Im Jahre 1770 nahm Rechteren eine Ausbildung zum Seeoffizier auf, um so zugleich mehr von der Welt kennenzulernen. Nach zweijähriger Reise als Seekadett durch das Mittelmeer kehrte er zurück nach Almelo. Er trat dann als Fähnrich in das Rechterensche Regiment, später in ein Garderegiment der niederländischen Armee ein, wo er den Rang eines „Kapitäns" (Hauptmanns) erreichte.[8] Da ihm das Leben in der Garnison nicht zusagte, wollte er mit einem anderen niederländischen Regiment nach Surinam gehen, was sich allerdings nicht verwirklichen ließ.[9] Dann unternahm Rechteren einige längere Reisen in Frankreich, im Benelux-Raum und nach Franken, die teils dem Versuch dienten, eine Offiziersstelle in einer Armee zu finden, teils auch dem Besuch von Verwandten.[10] Der Bayerische Erbfolgekrieg,[11] an dem er in preußischen Diensten teilzunehmen gehofft hatte, endete, bevor er eine Anstellung erlangen konnte. 1780 gelang es ihm endlich nach mehrmonatigem „Sollicitieren" (persönlichem Vorsprechen) in Paris, als

---

6. Provinz Utrecht, etwa 8 km südlich der Stadt Utrecht.

7. Vgl. den erwähnten (o. Anm. 2) Nachruf, S. 4. S.; auch BHStA, Abt. IV: Kriegsarchiv, OP 81367 (Schreiben eines kgl. Hofbeamten in Würzburg an den Kriegsminister vom 25.10.1815), wonach Rechteren „dermalen die Mathematik mit viel Liebe" betreibt, also im Alter von 64 Jahren. Dass Rechteren talentiert und gebildet war und mehrere Sprachen beherrschte, wird auch in seiner Personalakte im französischen Militärarchiv (Yb 346) bestätigt, hier: Vorlage für den König vom 24.06.1780 betr. Beförderung R.s zum Hauptmann.

8. Lt. der o. Anm. 7 zitierten Personalakte trat Rechteren am 29.08.1770 in den Dienst der niederländischen Marine; am 17.07.1775 wurde er zum Leutnant mit Hauptmannsrang im 2. niederländischen Garderegiment zu Fuß ernannt, s. Bericht des Vicomte de Tryon-Montalembert an den Kriegsminister; insgesamt diente R. danach 9 ½ Jahre im niederländischen Militär und schied dort erst kurz vor seinem Dienstantritt in der französischen Armee aus.

9. Das war vermutlich ein Glück für Rechteren, denn die aufständischen, an das Leben im Regenwald viel besser als die Kolonisten und ihr Militär angepassten Sklaven brachten den niederländischen Truppen mehrfach hohe Verluste und empfindliche Niederlagen bei. S. dazu im kurzen Überblick Encyclopaedia Britannica, 15. Aufl., 1974, Macropaedia, Bd. 17, S. 825 (Artikel „Surinam").

10. Hierzu Nachruf, S. 4, sowie die hier vorliegende Textausgabe von Rechterens Memoiren, Mskr., S. 53 – 58.

11. Weitestgehend unblutig verlaufene Auseinandersetzung zwischen Österreich und Preußen um das bayerische Erbe nach dem Aussterben der bayerischen Linie der Wittelsbacher 1777. Der wegen der schlechten Versorgung der Truppen mit Lebensmitteln auch als „Kartoffelkrieg" bezeichnete Streit begann im Juli 1778 und endete im Mai 1779 mit dem Teschener Frieden; s. dazu Gebhardt, Deutsche Geschichte, Bd. II, S. 291 f.

Friedrich Reinhard attended the "Latin school" at Ijsselstein for one year,[6] then Utrecht university for two years. His education, both in the classics and modern languages, but also in mathematics seems to have been quite thorough.[7]

In 1770, Rechteren joined the Dutch navy in order to become a naval officer and to see more of the world. After a two-year voyage in the Mediterranean as a naval cadet he returned to Almelo. He then joined the Dutch army, first as an ensign in the Rechteren regiment, later in a Guards regiment where he reached the rank of captain.[8] As he did not enjoy life in the garrison he tried to go to Surinam with another Dutch regiment, a plan which could not be realized, however.[9] Then, he took several extended trips to France, the Netherlands and Belgium as well as to Franconia attempting to find employment in an army or navy, sometimes simply visiting relatives.[10] The War of the Bavarian Succession[11] in which he had hoped to serve in the Prussian army ended before he was able to obtain a commission. In 1780, after several months' of "soliciting" (contacting influential persons) in Paris he finally succeeded to secure a place in the French army's German regiment "Royal Deux-Ponts" as an unpaid volunteer (cadet

---

6. Small town in Utrecht province, about 8 km south of the city of Utrecht.

7. Cf. Obituary (fn. 2); cf. also BHStA, dep. IV: War Archive, OP 81367 (court official's letter to the Bavarian minister of war, Oct. 25, 1815): according to this letter, Rechteren loved to practise mathematics even at the age of 64. His personal file at the French military archive (Yb 346) attests his talents, good education, and mastery of several languages; see: nomination of promotion to the rank of captain submitted to the king on June 24th, 1780.

8. According to the French file quoted above (fn. 7) Rechteren entered into the service of the Dutch navy on Aug. 29th, 1770; on July 17th, 1775, he was promoted to Lieutenant with a captain's rank in the 2nd Dutch regiment of Guards, see: report of Vicomte de Tryon-Montalembert to the minister of war. In sum, Rechteren served in the Dutch military for 9 ½ years and only left that service immediately before joining the French army.

9. Rechteren was probably lucky in that as the rebellious slaves who were much better adapted to life in the rain forest than the Dutch colonists and their army repeatedly inflicted severe defeats and heavy losses on the Dutch troops; cf. Encyclopedia Britannica (Macropedia), vol. 17, p. 825 (article on Surinam).

10. Cf. Obituary, p. 4, as well as Rechteren's memoirs published here; mscr., p. 53 – 58.

11. A conflict between Austria and Prussia over the inheritance of Bavaria after the extinction of the Bavarian line of the house of Wittelsbach. War began in July of 1778 and ended in May 1779 with the Teschen Peace; it did not lead to any major bloodshed. Because of the especially poor supply of victuals to the troops of both sides it was nicknamed the "potato war"; cf. Gebhardt, Deutsche Geschichte, vol. II, p. 291 f.

zunächst unbesoldeter Freiwilliger in das deutsche Regiment „Royal Deux-Ponts" der französischen Armee aufgenommen zu werden. Mit dieser Einheit nahm er vom Frühjahr 1780 bis zur Kapitulation der Briten bei Yorktown im Herbst 1781 am Amerikanischen Unabhängigkeitskrieg teil. Er stieg dabei zum Hauptmann à la suite auf, d.h. zu einem Offizier, der keine eigene Einheit befehligte, sondern zum unmittelbaren Stab des Regimentskommandeurs gehörte. Er wurde mit Belobigung aus dem Regiment entlassen.[12] Die Jahre 1770 bis 1782 stellen den wesentlichen Inhalt von Rechterens Lebenserinnerungen dar, die hier ediert werden; deshalb wird an dieser Stelle nicht näher auf diese für ihn sehr ereignisreichen Jahre eingegangen.

Im Lauf des Jahres 1782 ließ Rechteren sich in Franken nieder; am 13. November 1783 heiratete er in Thurnau (Lk Kulmbach), also in der Heimat seiner Braut, Friederika Antoinetta Carolina, Gräfin von Giech. Aus dieser Ehe gingen zwischen 1785 und 1794 vier Söhne und vier Töchter hervor, doch überlebten nur zwei Söhne und zwei Töchter das Kindesalter. Im Juni 1798 starb seine Frau, deren Gesundheit seit ihrer letzten Schwangerschaft stark beeinträchtigt gewesen war.[13] Im Jahre 1787 trat Rechteren zusammen mit seinem älteren Bruder Friedrich Ludwig Christian, ehemals Oberst in britischen Diensten und österreichischem Kammerherrn, die Herrschaft in der Grafschaft Limpurg-Speckfeld an. Die Besitzübernahme wurde durch das Reichskammergericht in Wetzlar und den würzburgischen Lehenhof bestätigt. 1790 besuchte Rechteren in seiner Eigenschaft als Reichsgraf die Kaiserkrönung Leopolds II. in Frankfurt a.M. Er dürfte dort dieselbe Aufgabe wahrgenommen haben wie sein Vater bei der Krönung Franz' I. am 4.10.1745, nämlich Speisen oder wohl eher – als Rechtsnachfolger der Reichserbschenken von Limpurg – Wein auf die kaiserliche Tafel aufzutragen.[14] Im selben Jahr gewann er einen intensiv betriebenen Prozess um die Herrschaft Adelmannsfelden, die

gentilhomme). With this unit, he took part in the American War of Independence from the spring of 1780 up to the British capitulation at Yorktown in the fall of 1781. Early in the campaign he reached the rank of a "captain à la suite", i.e. a commissioned officer who did not command a unit of his own, but belonged to the immediate staff of the regiment's commander. He left the regiment with a military commendation.[12] The years 1770 to 1782 constitute the main part of Rechteren's memoirs which are published here; that is why these eventful years are not described in greater detail in this introductory chapter.

In 1782, Rechteren settled in Franconia. On November 13th, 1783, he married Friederika Antoinetta Carolina, countess of Giech, in Thurnau (close to Kulmbach, Bavaria), his bride's home town. Between 1785 and 1794, the couple had four sons and four daughters, but only two of the sons and two of the daughters survived their infancy. In June 1798, Rechteren's wife died; she had been in poor health since her last pregnancy.[13] In 1787, Rechteren, together with his elder brother Friedrich Ludwig Christian, formerly a colonel in British service and an Austrian chamberlain, assumed possession of the county of Limpurg-Speckfeld. This was confirmed by the Court of the Imperial Chamber at Wetzlar and by the feudal court of the principality of Würzburg. In 1790, Rechteren, as a count of the Holy Roman Empire, attended the Imperial coronation of Leopold II. Most probably, he carried out the same duty there as his father had at the coronation of Francis I. on Oct. 4th, 1745, i.e. serving food or rather – as successor to the Reichserbschenken (hereditary Imperial butlers) of Limpurg – wine at the Emperor's table.[14] In the same year, he won a law-suit concerning the manorial estate of Adelmannsfelden which was part of the county of Limpurg-Speckfeld; he later

---

12. Die Ernennung zum Hauptmann à la suite erfolgte schon im Juni 1780, kurz vor der Landung in Newport; s. Selig, Wenn die Katze ..., S. 47. Die Erhebung zum Ritter des französischen Militär-Verdienstordens durch den französischen König in BHStA, Abt. IV: Kriegsarchiv, OP 81367 (Schreiben vom 18.12.1817).

13. Die Nachrichten über seine Ehe, Frau und Kinder sind dem mehrfach zitierten Nachruf entnommen, dem auch für den folgenden Abschnitt gefolgt wird.

14. Der Nachruf, S. 7, nennt nur 1790 als Jahr der von Rechteren besuchten Kaiserkrönung, also der Leopolds II; ob er auch 1792 an der Franz' II teilnahm, wissen wir nicht. BHStA, MInn 47717 enthält (in Abschrift) ein Schreiben des kgl. Staatsministeriums des kgl. Hauses und des Aeussern von 1896, verfasst von Frhrn. von Crailsheim, in dem aus Möser, Deutsches Staatsrecht, 38. Teil, 1749, zitiert wird; er berichtet, dass Johann Eberhard Adolph von R. „bei der jetzigen Kaiserkrönung", also der von 1745, als Mitglied des fränkischen Grafenkollegiums diesen Dienst leistete.

12. Actually, Rechteren was promoted to the rank of captain a few days before landing at Newport, R.I.; cf. Selig, When the Cat ..., p.47. The royal letter conferring the honour of a knight of the French order of merit to him is kept in: BHStA, dept. IV: War Archive, OP 81367 (letter of Dec. 12th, 1817.)

13. The information on his marriage and children is taken from Obituary (cf. fn. 2) which we'll follow for the next paragraph as well.

14. As Obituary, p. 7, names the coronation of 1790 as the only one at which Rechteren was present, it must have been Leopold's II; we don't know whether he attended that of Franz II in 1792. A letter (in: BHStA, MInn 47717) of the Royal Bavarian Department of the Royal House and Foreign Affairs of 1896, written by a baron Crailsheim (quoting Möser, Deutsches Staatsrecht, pt. 38, 1749) tells us that Johann Eberhard Adolph von Rechteren, as a member of the college of Franconian counts, had done this service "at the current coronation" which must refer to the one of 1745.

Teil der Grafschaft Limpurg-Speckfeld war, später aber von ihm an Württemberg verkauft wurde.[15] Während des Reichskriegs gegen das revolutionäre Frankreich führte er 1793 eine Kompanie des limpurgischen Kontingents ins Feldlager bei Fürth, legte aber wegen der gravierenden Organisationsmängel bei den Reichstruppen das Kommando nieder, ohne in den Krieg einzugreifen.[16] Stattdessen unternahm er mit seinem Schwager Graf von Giech eine Reise nach Mainz, das zu der Zeit von den französischen Revolutionstruppen besetzt war und von den Truppen der gegen Frankreich gerichteten Koalition, insbesondere Preußen und Österreich, belagert wurde. Rechteren hätte als strikter Anhänger des „Legitimitätsprinzips", also der hergebrachten Herrschaftsordnung, wohl keine prinzipiellen Bedenken gehabt, gegen das Land zu den Waffen zu greifen, dessen Armee er in Amerika gedient hatte, scheint aber gravierende Zweifel an der Legitimität der Politik auch anderer europäischer Mächte gehabt zu haben; jedenfalls nahm er an den Koalitionskriegen gegen die französische Republik und das napoleonische Kaiserreich nicht teil.[17]

Im Jahre 1795 reiste Rechteren nach Wien, um am Kaiserhof Belange seiner Landesherrschaft zu vertreten. Als Frankreich 1796 die Niederlande erobert hatte, und Rechteren vernahm, dass seine Mutter sich deswegen in einer schwierigen Lage befand, eilte er zu ihr und ging, um die Grenze leichter, d. h. wohl unter Umgehung der Grenzkontrollen, überschreiten zu können, streckenweise sogar zu Fuß. 1797 empfing er als gemeinschaftlicher Lehensträger für alle Teilhaber der Grafschaft Limpurg-Speckfeld in Würzburg erneut die Belehnung, die durch den „Herrenfall", den 1795 erfolgten Tod des Würzburger Bischofs und Lehensherrn Franz Ludwig von Erthal, notwendig geworden war; im selben Jahr erwarben die Brüder Rechteren für immerhin

---

15. Der Prozess wird im Nachruf, S. 7, erwähnt; die Beschreibung des Oberamts Aalen von 1838 teilt S. 211 mit, dass die limburgischen [sic] Erben in der Regelung der Erbschaft ihrer im Oberamt gelegenen Herrschaftsteile, wozu auch Adelmannsfelden gehört, ein „günstiges Schlussurtheil des Reichshofraths" erwirkten (wohl aufgrund von Rechterens Bemühungen), ihr Besitz aber 1806 an das Königreich Württemberg ging; vgl. Siebmacher, Wappenbuch, Bd. I, Abt. 3, Reihe 2, S. 12, sowie http://de.wikipedia/org/Wiki/Adelmannsfelden und http://de.wikisource.org/wiki/Beschreibung_des_Oberamts_Aalen; auch Prescher, Reichsgrafschaft Limpurg, 2. Teil, 1790, S. 393 – 401.

16. Gemäß seines eigenen Schreibens an den französischen König von 1816 war Rechteren so unzufrieden mit dem Mangel an Organisation und Effizienz bei den Reichstruppen, dass er dort nicht weiter dienen wollte; Personalakte Rechterens im frz. Militärarchiv, Bitte an den König um Verleihung des Verdienstkreuzes, 1816.

17. Zu diesen Nachrichten wiederum Nachruf, S. 7; als Verfechter der „Legitimität" tritt er in dem o. Anm. 16 zitierten Schreiben hervor, wo er sich auch zu den Herrschern Europas äußert.

---

sold it to the kingdom of Württemberg.[15] In the Imperial war against revolutionary France in 1793, Rechteren led a company of the Limpurg contingent into the military camp at Fürth, but then renounced his command and did not join in the war.[16] Together with his brother-in-law count Giech he took a trip to Mainz instead. That city, occupied by French revolutionary forces at the time, was besieged by the armies of the coalition allied against France, Prussia and Austria in particular. As a champion of the principle of legitimacy, Rechteren probably would not have had any qualms about taking up arms against the country in whose army he had served in America, but he seems to have had grave doubts about the legitimacy of many other Europeans powers' politics as well. As far as we can tell he did not take part in any of the coalition wars against the new French republic or the Napoleonic empire.[17]

In 1795, Rechteren went to the Imperial court at Vienna to look after matters concerning his county. When France had conquered the Netherlands in 1796 and Rechteren found out that his mother was in a difficult situation he hurried to see her; in order to cross the border more easily (which probably means: evading the border controls) he even walked part of the way. In 1797, Rechteren was invested again with the county of Limpurg-Speckfeld personally and as the representative for all of his associates. This enfeoffment was occasioned by the death of their lord Franz Ludwig von Erthal, the prince-bishop of Würzburg. In the same year, the Rechteren brothers spent the considerable sum of

---

15. The law-suit is mentioned in Obituary, p. 7. A description of the "Oberamt Aalen" of 1838, p. 211, mentions the fact that the "Limburg [sic] heirs" had – probably because of Rechteren's endeavours – gained a favourable decision of the Imperial Court Council concerning the inheritance of their property in the "Oberamt" which Adelmannsfelden manor was a part of. Adelmannsfelden became part of the kingdom of Württemberg in 1806. Cf. Siebmacher, Wappenbuch, vol. I, part 3, series 2, p. 12 as well as http://de.wikipedia/org/Wiki/Adelmannsfelden and http://de.wikisource.org/wiki/Beschreibung_des_Oberamts_Aalen. S. also Prescher, Reichsgrafschaft Limpurg, part 2, 1790, p. 393 – 401.

16. Rechteren told the French king in a letter (written in 1816, asking to have the Medal of Military Merit bestowed on him) that he was so discontented with the lack of organization and efficiency of the Imperial troops that he refused to serve with them any more; see his file (Yb 346) in the French military archive.

17. Again cf. Obituary, p. 7; Rechteren emerges as a champion of legitimacy in the letter quoted above (fn. 16) where he also touches on his opinions on other European powers.

4 000 fl. den Castell'schen Teil einer großen Jagdgerechtigkeit.[18] Trotz der Kriegswirren jener Jahre fand Rechteren 1800 die Zeit für eine Bildungsreise nach Breslau und Dresden. Im Jahre 1802 war er einige Zeit in den Niederlanden, 1805 nach dem Tode seiner Mutter ebenfalls, nicht zuletzt zur Übernahme seines Teils der Herrschaft Almelo.[19] Im Mai 1809 unternahm er wieder eine Reise dorthin; die darüber im Bayerischen Hauptstaatsarchiv vorliegende Akte gibt interessante Einblicke in die Umstände einer solchen Reise. Kurze Auszüge daraus seien deshalb im Wortlaut zitiert. Am 14.05.1809 richtete Rechteren mit der Bitte um Ausstellung eines Passes ein Schreiben an den bayerischen König, eigenhändig unterzeichnet als dessen „allerunterthänigst treugehorsamster Unterthan und Vasall", eine Formulierung, die ihm angesichts der nachfolgend geschilderten Vorgänge von 1803 trotz des zeitlichen Abstands noch immer nicht ganz leicht gefallen sein dürfte. So wird der Zweck der Reise beschrieben: „Graf Friedrich Reinhard Burkhard Rudolph von Rechteren und Limpurg ist gesonnen, mit seiner Gemahlin und ältesten Tochter, dann einem männlichen Bedienten und einer Kammerjungfer, von Sommerhausen bey Würzburg nach Holland […] nach Almeloo in der Provinz Ober Issel, Familienangelegenheiten wegen zu verreisen und wird 2 bis 3 Monate ausbleiben. Ist übrigens von 57 Jahren, großer Statur, runden Angesicht, etwas tiefer Stirne, blauen Augen, hoher eingebogener Nase, proportionirtem Mund, braunen Haaren, und wird den Weeg von hier durch Westphalen über Kassel nehmen […]". Der Pass wurde bewilligt, doch sollte er sich nach der Ankunft in Holland bei der königlich-bayerischen Gesandtschaft melden.[20] Vom Standpunkt des 21. Jahrhunderts ist neben der selbst gelieferten, recht vagen Personenbeschreibung von Interesse, dass die Begleitpersonen offensichtlich gar nicht beschrieben werden mussten, sondern auf Treu und Glauben mitreisen konnten und in den Pass mit eingeschlossen waren.

Im Jahre 1803 war es in Sommerhausen zu Ereignissen gekommen, die in der Ortschronik unter der Überschrift „Der Sommerhäuser Krieg 1803" beschrieben werden; sie können einen guten Einblick in Rechterens Charakter, Selbstverständnis

4000 fl. to buy the counts of Castell's part of a large chase.[18] In spite of the wartime disorders of those years, Rechteren found the time for an art and culture trip to Breslau and Dresden in 1800. In 1802, he spent some time in the Netherlands as well as in 1805, after his mother's death, not least to take possession of the county of Almelo of which he had become a part-owner.[19] In May 1809, he took another trip there; a file of the "Bayerische Hauptstaatsarchiv" in Munich allows some interesting glimpses into the circumstances of such a trip at that time. That is why a few short excerpts shall be quoted verbatim (in translation). Rechteren applied to the Bavarian king for the issuance of a passport in a letter of May 14th, 1809, signed in his own hand with the words "Your majesty's most obedient and most loyal vassal and subject", a choice of words which – even after the passage of several years – cannot have been easy for him in the light of the events to be subsequently described. This was the purpose of the trip: "Count Friedrich Reinhard Burkhard Rudolph of Rechteren and Limpurg intends to take a trip from Sommerhausen near Würzburg to Almeloo in the province of Ober Issel on family business and will stay away for about 2 or 3 months. He will be accompanied by his wife and eldest daughter as well as a male servant and a chambermaid. He is 57 years of age, of tall stature, has a round face, a somewhat low forehead, blue eyes, a high curved nose, a well-proportioned mouth, and brown hair and will take the route from here through Westphalia by way of Kassel [...]". The passport was issued with the injunction that Rechteren was to contact the Bavarian envoy after his arrival in the Netherlands.[20] From the point of view of the early 21st century it is interesting to note that the applicant could describe his physical appearance himself, and rather vaguely at that, and that the people in his company did not have to be described at all; they seem to have been included on good faith in the applicant's passport.

In 1803, incidents had occurred in Sommerhausen which have been described under the title "The Sommerhausen war of 1803" in a local chronicle. These incidents and Rechteren's reaction to them can give us a good idea of Rechteren's character, the way he saw himself and his

---

18. Die Neubelehnung innerhalb von Jahr und Tag nach dem Tod des Lehensherrn oder Lehensmanns, war in den meisten süddeutschen Lehenhöfen vorgeschrieben, doch wurden die Fristen oft großzügig ausgelegt; vgl. z.B. Baum, Lehenswesen. Zum Erwerb der Jagd s. FCWA FK 90/135.

19. Auch dieser Absatz nach dem Nachruf, S. 7.

20. BHStA, MA 74554.

---

18. In Southern Germany, a new enfeoffment within "a year and a day" was expected after the death either of the lord or of the man, but this timespan could usually be extended; cf. Baum, Lehnswesen. For the acquisition of the chase see FCWA FK 90/135.

19. Again according to Obituary, p. 7.

20. BHStA, MA 74554.

und politische Haltung geben.[21] Rechteren und sein Bruder sahen sich veranlasst, noch im selben Jahr eine „Beurkundete Darstellung" der dem Hause Rechteren-Limpurg von Seiten des kurbayerischen Fürstentums Würzburg „widerfahrenen Eingriffe und harten Kränkungen in ihren reichständischen landesherrlichen Rechten" und der erlittenen „unerhörten Vergewaltigungen und Mißhandlungen ... Schäden und Kosten" aus ihrem Blickwinkel im Druck herauszubringen.[22] Nachdem mit dem Frieden von Lunéville vom Februar 1801 die Säkularisierung der geistlichen Territorien und die Mediatisierung zunächst der Reichsstädte im rechtsrheinischen Deutschland eingeleitet worden war – die linksrheinischen Territorien fielen an die Republik Frankreich –, hatte der bayerische Kurfürst im September 1802 Stadt und Hochstift Würzburg mit seinen Truppen besetzt. Am 28. November 1802 dankte der letzte Würzburger Fürstbischof ab und Bayern übernahm die Herrschaft im Hochstift, obwohl das erst durch den am 27. April 1803 in Kraft getretenen „Reichsdeputationshauptschluss" und, was die Mediatisierung der meisten weltlichen Reichsstände betrifft, sogar erst durch die Rheinbundakte vom 12. Juli 1806 und den Pariser Vertrag vom 28. Februar 1810 sanktioniert wurde.[23] Aber schon am 14. Dez. 1802 erschien ein Trupp von sechs bayerischen Soldaten mit dem Ochsenfurter Stadtschultheissen[24] an der Spitze in Sommerhausen und schlug das bayerische Besitzergreifungspatent an der Rathaustür an; dasselbe geschah in Winterhausen und Lindelbach,[25] einen Tag später auch in Gollhofen. Rechteren, der sich in Markt Einersheim[26] aufhielt, wurde davon unterrichtet und ritt unverzüglich zum kurbayerischen Landeskommissär Freiherrn von Hompesch nach Würzburg. Dieser beruhigte ihn mit der Auskunft, es handle sich bei der bayerischen Besitzer-

---

21. Der Bericht über diese Ereignisse folgt der Darstellung bei Gutmann/Furkel, Sommerhausen, S. 68 – 75, sowie StAW, Reg.v.Ufr., 1943/45, 12563, Nr. 4 (Protokoll über die Vorgänge in Sommerhausen am 14. Juli 1803).

22. Die Druckschrift liegt vollständig vor in BHStA, MA 5783; sie wird ergänzend herangezogen.

23. Über diese für die deutsche Geschichte wichtigen Verträge informieren alle größeren Konversationslexika, historischen Lexika und Handbücher sowie die Wikipedia.

24. Ochsenfurt, ca. 6 km südlich von Sommerhausen, war die nächst gelegene würzburgische Amtsstadt; daher wurde wohl der dortige Schultheiß mit der Sache beauftragt.

25. Diese beiden Dörfer gehörten zum limpurg-speckfeldischen Amt Sommerhausen; Winterhausen liegt unmittelbar gegenüber von Sommerhausen auf dem linken Mainufer; Lindelbach liegt auf der Gäuhochfläche ca. 5 km nördlich.

26. Markt E. liegt etwa 4 km südöstlich Iphofen an der Straße nach Nürnberg (B 8), Gollhofen 5 km nordwestlich von Uffenheim an der Straße nach Ansbach (B 13); beide Orte gehörten zum limpurg-speckfeldischen Amt Einersheim.

---

position in the world, and his political standpoint.[21] Rechteren and his brother (his co-regent) felt called upon to publish a printed "Documentary Record" of the "drastic interference and severe molestation of the house of Rechteren-Limpurg's traditional rights and privileges as independent lords of their lands and free estates of the empire" suffered at the hands of the Bavarian principality of Würzburg as well as the "unheard-of violence and ill-treatment, damages and costs" inflicted on them and their subjects; the booklet appeared some time after the events and described them from the Rechterens' point of view.[22] The peace of Lunéville of February 1801 had set in motion the secularization (dissolution) of the ecclesiastical territories and the mediatisation of the minor lay estates of the Empire. At first, mediatisation only concerned some of the Free Imperial cities. At the same time, the German territories on the left bank of (west of) the Rhine were ceded to the French republic. As early as September 1802, the elector of Bavaria's troops had occupied the ecclesiastical principality and the city of Würzburg. On November 28th, 1802, the last prince-bishop of Würzburg resigned and Bavaria took full dominion of the principality even though that step was only sanctioned by the enactment of the "Reichsdeputationshauptschluss" (the treaty dealing with the dissolution of these principalities) on April 27th, 1803. The mediatisation of most of the secular estates was not legally sanctioned before the Confederation of the Rhine had been founded by act of July 12th, 1806, in some cases only after the signing of the Treaty of Paris on February 28th, 1810.[23] In spite of that, the mayor of Ochsenfurt[24] appeared in Sommerhausen at the head of a detail of six Bavarian soldiers on December 14th, 1802, posting the Bavarian declarations of taking possession on the door of the town hall; this happened in Winterhausen and Lindelbach on that same day,[25] one day later in Gollhofen. Rech-

---

21. The account given here follows the description by Gutmann/Furkel, Sommerhausen, p. 68 – 75, as well as StAW, Reg.v.Ufr. 1943/45, 12563 (records of the events in Sommerhausen on July 14th, 1803).

22. The complete booklet is extant in BHStA, MA 5783; it will be used in this account as well.

23. Information on these treaties which are important for German history can be found in any large general or historical encyclopedia or in Wikipedia.

24. Ochsenfurt, about 6 km south of Sommerhausen, was the closest town of the principality of Würzburg where ducal officials resided; that is probably why its mayor was given the job.

25. Both villages belong to the County of Limpurg's district of Sommerhausen; Winterhausen is situated right across the river from Sommerhausen, Lindelbach about 5 km to the north up on the higher plain.

greifung nur um die Errichtung einer lockeren Oberherrschaft, die – wie die würzburgische Lehensherrschaft – seine Landeshoheit nicht weiter beeinträchtigen werde.²⁷ Damit gab Rechteren sich zunächst zufrieden und kehrte nach Markt Einersheim zurück.

Bald sollte es sich aber erweisen, dass die bayerische Oberhoheit doch einen merklichen Eingriff in Rechterens Landesherrschaft darstellte. Er hatte nämlich einem kaiserlichen und einem preußischen Werber die Tätigkeit in seinen Orten gestattet. Pfalzbayern, das schon seit dem Friedens- und Freundschaftsvertrag vom 24. August 1801 mit Frankreich in einem engen Bündnisverhältnis²⁸ und kurz vor dem Eintritt in den französisch dominierten Rheinbund stand, dem weiter in Art. 26 der Rheinbundakte die Aufstellung von Truppen als Merkmal der vollen Souveränität zugestanden werden sollte, konnte die Werbung für fremde, Frankreich nicht freundlich gesinnte Staaten auf seinem Gebiet aus politischen Gründen nicht zulassen. Und so wurden die beiden Werbeoffiziere am 11. Januar 1803 aus Lindelbach ausgewiesen. Am frühen Morgen des 2. Februar wurde der kaiserliche Werbeoffizier, dem Rechteren den weiteren Aufenthalt in Sommerhausen erlaubt hatte, nachdem er sich gerade noch hatte ankleiden dürfen, von einem bayerischen Korporal mit vier Mann über die Grenze des limpurgischen Gebiets geführt; die Rückkehr wurde ihm verboten. Auf Befragen erklärte der Korporal, dass da, wo das kurbayerische Patent angeschlagen sei, der bayerische Kurfürst die alleinige Landeshoheit habe und fremde Werbungen nicht dulde.²⁹

Dies sah Rechteren, dessen Herrschaft ja bis dahin noch nicht mediatisiert worden war, zu Recht als einen schweren Eingriff in seine Hoheitsrechte an. Er war im März 1803 bei einem seiner gewohnheitsmäßigen Wohnsitzwechsel nach Sommerhausen gezogen und hatte dabei 25 Männer seines Markt Einersheimer Kreiskontingents mitgenommen, die dort die üblichen Wachdienste leisten sollten. Kurz darauf kam aus Würzburg die amtliche Verlautbarung, dass

teren who was living in Markt Einersheim²⁶ at the time was told of this and immediately rode to Würzburg to see baron Hompesch, the administrative head of the – now Bavarian – principality of Würzburg. Hompesch quieted him down by suggesting that Bavarian possession only meant the establishment of a loose jurisdiction comparable to the prince-bishop's former feudal suzerainty which would not impair the status of Rechteren's own dominion.²⁷ Rechteren was satisfied with this information and returned to Markt Einersheim.

But it did not take long before it became clear that the Bavarian "suzerainty" actually did mean a noticeable interference with the Rechterens' territorial dominion. They had given permits to an Imperial and a Prussian recruiting officer to be active in their territory. But Bavaria which, first of all, had been closely allied with France following their treaty of peace and amity of August 24th, 1801,²⁸ which, secondly, expected to be included in the French-dominated Confederation of the Rhine very soon, and which, thirdly, hoped to be given the exclusive right of levying troops within its own borders by art. 26 of the Confederation Treaty as a symbol of its full sovereignty could not tolerate the recruitment of soldiers for foreign armies, especially armies of states inimical to France within its area of influence. And thus, the two recruiting officers were expelled from Lindelbach on January 11th, 1803. The Imperial recruiting officer who had been given a new permit by Rechteren to continue with his job in Sommerhausen, was apprehended by a Bavarian corporal at the head of four soldiers in the early morning of February 2nd, 1803, and – having barely been allowed to get dressed – was taken across the border of Rechteren's land and ordered not to come back. Upon questioning the corporal stated that wherever the Bavarian patent letters of possession had been posted the elector of Bavaria was the

---

27. So jedenfalls verstand Rechteren die Aussagen des Kommissärs; vgl. StAW, Reg.v.Ufr. 1943/45, 12563, Nr. 4 (Protokoll über die Vorgänge in Sommerhausen am 14. Juli 1803); nach der o. Anm. 22 zitierten „Beurkundeten Darstellung", S. 7, entschuldigte sich Hompesch sogar wegen des Vorgehens der bayerischen Verwaltung, die die fränkischen Verhältnisse noch nicht genügend kenne.

28. Zu diesem Vertrag Spindler, Handbuch, Bd. III, 1, S. 254. Zur Werbung für Reichstruppen 1801 – 1806 s. Napoleon und Bayern, S. 63 – 65; die kaiserliche Werbung war aber in Bayern zu dem Zeitpunkt eigentlich erlaubt!

29. So die o. Anm. 22 zitierte „Beurkundete Darstellung", S. 8.

---

26. Markt E. is situated about 4 km southeast of Iphofen on the Nürnberg road (B 8), Gollhofen 5 km northwest of Uffenheim on the Ansbach road (B 13); both villages are part of the County of Limpurg's district of Einersheim.

27. At least that is what Rechteren thought Hompesch had told him; cf. StAW, Reg.v.Ufr. 1943/45, 12563; no. 4 (record of the events in Sommerhausen of July 14th, 1803); according to Documentary Record, p. 7, Hompesch tried to excuse the actions of the new Bavarian administration as not being familiar with conditions in Franconia yet.

28. For information about this treaty cf. Spindler, Handbuch, vol. III, p. 254. According to: Napoleon und Bayern, p. 63- 65, recruitment for the Imperial army should have been permitted in Bavaria at that moment, however.

überall dort, wo kurfürstliche Patente angebracht worden seien, bewaffnete fremde Truppen nicht geduldet würden; Rechteren solle zur Vermeidung von „Unannehmlichkeiten" seine Truppe sofort entlassen.[30] Er ließ daraufhin in Sommerhausen, Winterhausen und Lindelbach Gegenpatente des Inhalts an die Rathaustüren nageln, dass er immer noch die Landeshoheit in seinen Dörfern innehabe. Die Tore wurden besetzt und Wachtposten auf den Höhen postiert, die das Nahen bayerischen Militärs sofort melden sollten; dann sollte Sturm geläutet werden, die Sommerhäuser Bürgerwehr sich bewaffnet versammeln.[31] Der inzwischen neu ernannte Landeskommissär Heffner forderte nun Rechteren nochmals in sehr höflichem, und als das nichts fruchtete, in scharfem Ton auf, seine Gegenpatente sofort zu entfernen, stattdessen die bayerischen Patente wieder anzubringen. Der Ochsenfurter Schultheiss brachte sodann auf festen Pappendeckel aufgezogene Patente, die – so wurde Rechteren erklärt – ein Jahr und sechs Wochen an den Rathaustoren ausgehängt, zudem in allen öffentlichen Wirtshäusern ausgelegt werden müssten. Rechterens Militärkontingent sei – wie bereits angemahnt – umgehend zu entlassen.

Rechteren reagierte auf diese Anordnungen nicht, eben so wenig auf die Drohung des Einsatzes von Militär, und so befahl endlich der Würzburger Stadtkommandant Graf Ysenburg, Sommerhausen nunmehr, wenn nötig, mit Waffengewalt einzunehmen und Rechteren zur Raison zu bringen.[32] Nach Weisung der „königlichen Landes-Direction" sollte das Militär sich nach Sommerhausen begeben und dort auf Kosten von Rechteren solange bleiben, „bis von dem gedachten Grafen selbst Parition [Gehorsam] geleistet oder die von ihm beabsichtigte Renitenz vereitelt", die bürgerliche Ordnung wiederhergestellt sei. Am Morgen des 14. Juli 1803 marschierte ein Trupp von 172 Mann Infanterie und 32 Kavalleristen nach Sommerhausen.[33] Um 8 Uhr früh war Regierungskommissär Heffner dort bereits eingetroffen, das Militär folgte im Abstand von einer halben

---

30. Ebd., S. 17.

31. Dies und das Folgende nach Gutmann/Furkel, Sommerhausen (wie Anm. 21).

32. So nach Gutmann/Furkel, Sommerhausen, S. 72; nach StAW, Reg.v.Ufr., 1943/45, 12563, Nr. 2, ging der Befehl vom Regierungspräsidenten aus. Der Bericht bei Furkel/Gutmann stützt sich anscheinend auf den gräflichen Notar Übel; die Regierungsakte enthält einige deutliche Abweichungen zu dieser Darstellung.

33. Nach der zitierten Regierungsakte bestand das Détachement aus 200 Mann, ohne Unterscheidung von Infanterie und Kavallerie. Neben den Soldaten begab sich zugleich auch der Regierungskommissär Heffner nach Sommerhausen.

---

sole sovereign of the land who would not tolerate recruitment for foreign armies.[29]

Rechteren whose possessions had not actually been mediatised so far considered this a grave interference with his prerogatives. He had moved to Sommerhausen in March of 1803 in the course of one of his regular changes of residence and had taken with him 25 men of his Markt Einersheim militia contingent; the men were supposed to do the usual guard duties. Shortly afterwards, an official letter arrived from Würzburg stating that wherever the Bavarian letters of possession had been posted, armed non-Bavarian troops would not be tolerated; Rechteren was told to dismiss his contingent immediately to avoid "trouble".[30] In reply, Rechteren had counter-declarations nailed to the town hall doors in Sommerhausen, Winterhausen, and Lindelbach stating that he and his family still had the full dominion over their lands. The town gates were manned and guards who were told to give alarm at the sight of Bavarian troops approaching were stationed in the surrounding hills. In that case, the church bells were to be rung and the militia of Sommerhausen was to assemble fully armed.[31] Meanwhile, commissary Heffner had replaced baron Hompesch as administrative head in the principality of Würzburg; he asked Rechteren very politely at first, and sharply when there was no reaction, to immediately remove his counter-declarations and to affix the Bavarian patent letters again. The mayor of Ochsenfurt then appeared with new patent letters mounted on solid cardboard which – as he explained to Rechteren – were to remain posted on the town hall doors for a year and six weeks and to be displayed openly in every public inn. He should dismiss his military contingent at once as he had been told before.

Rechteren did not follow this instruction and did not react to the threat of military action against him, so the military commander of Würzburg, count Ysenburg, finally gave the order to take Sommerhausen by force, if necessary, and to bring Rechteren to submission.[32] According to the order of the "Electoral Territorial Administration" the

---

29. Thus the Documentary Record, p. 8.

30. Loc.cit., p. 17.

31. This and the subsequent information in this paragraph according to Gutmann/Furkel, Sommerhausen (cf. fn. 21).

32. Thus according to Gutmann/Furkel, Sommerhausen, p. 72; according to StAW, Reg.v.Ufr. 1943/45, 12563, no. 2, the order was issued by the civilian district commissary. Gutmann/Furkel's account seems to rely on the report given by Mr. Übel, Rechterens' notary; the district government's file differs from that account in several instances.

Stunde. Heffner wurde von der Torwache eingelassen und führte zunächst ein längeres Gespräch mit Rechteren. Man konnte sich dabei nicht ganz einigen. Inzwischen war, wie befohlen, Sturm geläutet worden, Bürgerwehr und die 25 Männer des Kreiskontingents versammelten sich unter Waffen.[34] Rechteren war aber klar, dass seine Männer gegen eine größere Militäreinheit nicht würden bestehen können, er wollte vor allem die Anwendung von Gewalt verhindern. Er schärfte seinen Leuten daher ein, keinesfalls von der Schusswaffe Gebrauch zu machen; sein Bruder[35] ging zu dem ihm bekannten befehlshabenden Offizier vor das Maintor, um zu verhandeln. Die bayerischen Soldaten, die höchst verärgert darüber waren, dass sie anderthalb Stunden vor dem Tor hatten warten müssen, nutzten die Gelegenheit, um dieses gewaltsam zu öffnen. Sie drangen gegen 10 Uhr in Sommerhausen ein, wobei sich hässliche, auch gewalttätige Szenen abspielten, es aber zumindest ohne Blutvergießen abging. Sie besetzten das ganze Dorf, entwaffneten die Bürger und die übrigen Männer von Rechterens Kontingent und ließen sich dann vor allem mit Essen und Trinken geradezu fürstlich bedienen.[36] Das Gelage dauerte bis zum nächsten Morgen; die ganze Aktion verursachte Kosten von fast 3000 Gulden, davon allein 1200 für die Zehrung, was alles dem Hause Rechteren in Rechnung gestellt wurde. Die Hälfte der bayerischen Soldaten kehrte am Folgetag mit den beschlagnahmten Waffen nach Würzburg zurück; 53 Mann Infanterie und die Kavallerie blieben noch drei Tage dort.

Die Brüder Rechteren erhoben im August 1803 Klage gegen Bayern am Kaiserhof und bekamen im Januar 1804 Recht: das Kurfürstentum Bayern wurde bei Androhung einer Strafe von zehn Pfund lötigen Goldes zur Unterlassung aller Drohungen und Gewaltmaßnahmen gegen die Grafschaft Rechteren-Limpurg, zur Zurückziehung seiner Besitzergreifungspatente, zum Ersatz aller beim Militäreinsatz 1803 entstandenen Schäden und zur Rückerstattung der beschlagnahmten Waffen verurteilt.[37] Dass die kleine Grafschaft Limpurg-Speckfeld gegen das mächtige Bayern ein solches Urteil erwirken konnte, zeigt exemplarisch die zuletzt in der angelsächsischen Historiographie betonte Wirksamkeit des rechtlichen Systems der Friedenswahrung

---

34. So nach der Regierungsakte, insbes. 12563, Nr. 4 (Protokoll der Vorgänge, von dem Heffner begleitenden Aktuar Valentin Hofmann erstellt).

35. So die Beurkundete Darstellung, S. 23.

36. So nach Gutmann/Furkel, Sommerhausen, S. 72 f., auch für den Rest des Abschnitts; zur Gewaltanwendung detailliert auch die Beurkundete Darstellung, S. 23 ff.

37. Auch dies nach Gutmann/Furkel, Sommerhausen, S. 74.

troops were to proceed to Sommerhausen and stay there at Rechteren's cost until "the said count [Rechteren] will have shown obedience and his intended resistance will have been thwarted" and public order was restored. In the morning of July 14th, 1803, an infantry unit of 172 men as well as 32 cavalry marched to Sommerhausen.[33] The government commissary, Mr. Heffner, had arrived there at about 8 o'clock, the military arrived half an hour later. Heffner was admitted by the gatekeepers and first had a lengthy conversation with Rechteren. They could not quite come to an agreement. In the meantime, the bells had been rung, the Sommerhausen militia and Rechteren's 25 guardsmen from Markt Einersheim had assembled fully armed.[34] Rechteren clearly saw that his men would have no good chance of success against a military unit which outnumbered them by far. Most of all, he wanted to prevent the use of force. Therefore, he urged his men not to start firing in any event; his brother went outside the town gate to negotiate with the commanding officer with whom he was acquainted.[35] The Bavarian soldiers – irate for having been kept waiting outside the walls for an hour and a half – used that moment to open the gate forcibly. Around 10 o'clock, they entered the town where ugly and violent scenes took place, but where at least no blood was shed. The soldiers occupied the whole town, disarmed the citizens and Rechteren's contingent and then proceeded to gorge themselves with food and drink in a princely style.[36] The carousing lasted into the following morning; the costs of the whole military action amounted to 3,000 fl., the bill for food and drink alone came to 1,200 fl. All of this was charged to the house of Rechteren-Limpurg. About half of the troops returned to Würzburg on the following day, taking with them the seized arms; 53 infantry men and all the cavalry stayed at Sommerhausen for three more days.

The Rechteren brothers filed a suit against the electorate of Bavaria at the Imperial Court in August of 1803. In January, 1804, they had a favourable decision in hand: the electorate of Bavaria was condemned to abstain from any threat or

---

33. The government file just mentions a unit of 200 men without differentiating between the infantry and the cavalry; Heffner is mentioned there, too.

34. According to the government file, especially 12563, no. 4 (record of the events in Sommerhausen as relayed by the secretary Valentin Hofmann who accompanied Heffner).

35. Cf. Documentary Record, p. 23.

36. Thus Gutmann/Furkel, Sommerhausen, p. 72 f., whose account will be followed for the rest of this paragraph; the violent scenes are described in great detail in Documentary Record, p. 23 ff.

im Alten Reich vor 1806.³⁸ Politisch war das Urteil – so kurz vor dem Ende des Alten Reichs – letztlich doch bedeutungslos, denn nur zwei Jahre später sollte Rechteren trotz hartnäckigen Widerstands seine Landeshoheit verlieren. War sein Verhalten nun Zeichen einer uneinsichtigen Halsstarrigkeit von geradezu kohlhaasischem Zuschnitt?³⁹ Er musste doch wissen, dass kleinere Adelsherrschaften wie die seine überall in Deutschland über kurz oder lang mediatisiert würden und dass er mit seinen Machtmitteln nicht in der Lage war, dagegen etwas Ernsthaftes zu unternehmen. Wozu sein trotzig-verzweifeltes Aufbegehren, das schließlich in einer Art „Operettenkrieg" endete?

Um die Vorgänge des „Sommerhäuser Kriegs" besser zu verstehen, müssen die Handlungsmotive und -zwänge der beteiligten Parteien berücksichtigt werden. Der bayerische Kurfürst konnte es nach der reichsrechtlich sanktionierten Übernahme der Herrschaft im Hochstift Würzburg kaum dulden, dass seine Souveränität an der wichtigen Verkehrsstraße des Mains durch ein autonomes, von ihm nicht beherrschtes Gebiet durchbrochen wurde. Die rechteren-limpurgischen Dörfer Sommer- und Winterhausen hätten aber eine solche, nicht tolerierbare Durchbrechung der bayerischen Herrschaft dargestellt.⁴⁰ Man hätte ja hier die Schifffahrt auf dem Main und den Verkehr auf der wichtigen parallel laufenden Landstraße von Ansbach nach Würzburg mit Zöllen belasten oder unterbrechen können. Hinzu kam, dass es im Zuge der Zeit lag, von kleinstaatlichen Zuständen wegzukommen und größere einheitliche Staatsgebiete zu schaffen.

Andererseits war Rechteren formal im Recht: seine Herrschaft war bis dahin de jure noch nicht mediatisiert worden, und ob der Kurfürst von Pfalzbayern auf Dauer sein Souverän werden würde, konnte 1802/03 zweifelhaft erscheinen. Tatsächlich musste Bayern ja schon 1806 das Hochstift Würzburg wieder aufgeben, das für die nächsten acht Jahre als habsburgische Sekundogenitur zum Großherzogtum Würzburg erhoben wurde. Rechteren musste es so erscheinen, dass Bayern sich ohne Rücksicht auf die Rechtslage sein Territorium aneignen wolle, und dass er sich zur Bewahrung seiner eigenen, zumindest annähernd souveränen Herrschaft mit allen zur Verfügung stehenden Mitteln

---

38. So speziell Kissinger, Weltordnung, 2014 und Whaley, Das Hl. Röm. Reich 1493 – 1806, 2014 (engl. Originalausgabe 2012).

39. Der Titelheld von Heinrich von Kleists berühmter Novelle wird im Zuge des Versuchs, eine Erstattung von ihm zugefügtem Schaden zu erlangen, wegen seiner Kompromisslosigkeit selbst zum gefährlichen Rechtsbrecher.

40. Dies wird auch gleich einleitend in der Beurkundeten Darstellung, S. 3 betont.

---

use of violence against the county of Rechteren-Limpurg, to retract its patent letters of possession, to compensate the house of Rechteren for all damages wrought by the use of military force in 1803, and to return all seized arms to their rightful owners; any contravention would be fined with 10 pounds of pure gold.³⁷ That the small county of Rechteren-Limpurg could succeed in getting such a favourable legal decision against the powerful electorate of Bavaria seems to prove the effectiveness of the legal system for keeping the peace in the Holy Roman Empire before 1806 praised in recent Anglo-Saxon historiography.³⁸ From a political point of view, however, the decision was meaningless so close to the end of the Holy Roman Empire; only 2½ years later, Rechteren lost the full dominion over his county in spite of his stiff-necked resistance. Did his behaviour indicate a pattern of reckless defiance in the spirit of a Michael Kohlhaas?³⁹ He certainly should have known that, in the long run, minor estates of the Empire like his own would be mediatised, i.e. incorporated into a larger principality, and that this was going on all over Germany. He would not be able to put up a decisive resistance to this process with the very limited powers at his disposal. Why this desperate defiance which finally culminated in a kind of "comic-opera war"?

To better understand the events of the "Sommerhausen war" we have to look at the motives and constraints underlying the actions of the opposing parties. After his full sovereignty over the principality of Würzburg had been sanctioned by Imperial law the elector of Bavaria could hardly tolerate an interruption of his territorial dominion by an autonomous district outside his control, least of all on the important traffic route of the Main valley. If the little towns of Sommerhausen and Winterhausen had remained under the dominion of Rechteren-Limpurg they would have constituted such a disturbance of Bavarian sovereignty; it would have been possible to stop traffic on the Main or the busy roads on the river banks connecting the district capitals of Würzburg and Ansbach or to levy new

---

37. According to Gutmann/Furkel, Sommerhausen, p. 74, and Documentary Record, appendix 2.

38. Cf. Henry Kissinger, World Order (2014) or J. Whaley, The Holy Roman Empire 1493 – 1806 (2012).

39. Michael Kohlhaas is the protagonist of the eponymous German short novel by Heinrich von Kleist. Kohlhaas suffers damages and in the course of seeking reparations by any means becomes a dangerous criminal himself.

dagegen zur Wehr setzen müsse, wie es einem adligen Landesherrn gebührte. Die Gründe für diese Haltung werden in dem Gespräch, das Rechteren mit dem Regierungskommissär Heffner führte, auch ganz klar genannt:[41] Während Heffner ihn auf seine Pflichten als bayerischer Vasall hinwies, entgegnete Rechteren, dass der bayerische Kurfürst als Lehnsherr gegenüber seinem Vasallen auch eine Verpflichtung habe. Aus dem ganzen Vorgehen sei für Rechteren ersichtlich, dass man das in Franken bisher unbekannte „Landsassiat" einführen wolle, d.h. dass man ihn zu einem bayerischen Landsassen und Untertan machen wolle. Der kaiserliche Werber sei ohne sein Wissen vertrieben worden, auch dies sei ein unerhörtes Vorgehen. Rechteren fragte weiter, warum man nur ihn so behandle, nicht aber Castell, Schwarzenberg und andere Herren seines Stands. Wenn die bayerischen Patente wirklich nur auf die Beibehaltung des Lehnsnexus im bisherigen Umfang abzielten, wie es ihm der vorige Landeskommissär zugesichert habe, und nicht auf die Einforderung neuer, weiterer Rechte, sei nicht einzusehen, warum man so scharf gegen seine Gegenpatente vorgehe. Nach Reichsrecht sei er befugt, sich dem zu widersetzen. Rechteren erkannte also richtig, dass man seine bisherige Rechtsstellung mindern wollte. Der fränkische Adel hatte bis dahin nach dem Rechtsgrundsatz „Lehensmann nicht Untertan" gelebt; dies schloss zwar nicht aus, dass ein Vasall auch Untertan sein konnte, machte aber einen Vasallen nicht automatisch dazu.[42]

Zudem stellte die Art und Weise des bayerischen Vorgehens – dies klingt deutlich in Rechterens Einlassungen an – einen Affront gegen den ausgeprägten Höflichkeitscodex des alten europäischen Adels dar, denn der bayerische Kurfürst hatte es nicht für nötig befunden, Rechteren als den Inhaber einer der seinen nahezu gleichrangigen Landesherrschaft persönlich und in aller Form davon in Kenntnis zu setzen, dass die Landeshoheit infolge einer Entscheidung der hohen Politik an ihn übergehen werde und sich dadurch für Standesherren wie Rechteren einschneidende rechtliche Änderungen ergeben würden. Vielmehr hatte er dies nur durch Subalterne wie den Ochsenfurter Schultheiss oder einen Korporal indirekt bekannt machen lassen. Vieles spricht dafür, dass es neben dem eklatanten bayerischen Rechtsbruch dieser gravierende Formfehler gewesen sein dürfte, der Rechteren zu so kräftigen Formen des

customs duties here.[40] Moreover, contemporary trends favoured the creation of larger, more uniform states over the preservation of tiny territories and their limitations.

On the other hand, Rechteren was within his rights: his dominion had not been mediatised *de jure* yet, and whether the elector of Bavaria would finally become his sovereign lord must have appeared highly dubious in 1802/03. Sure enough, in 1806 Bavaria had to renounce its dominion over the principality of Würzburg which, for the next 8 years, was raised to the rank of a grand-duchy under the second-born prince of the house of Habsburg. Rechteren thus had good reasons to conclude that Bavaria was out to take possession of his lands under mere legal pretences and that he was called upon to defend his own quasi-autonomous position as an immediate estate of the empire by all available means like a noble territorial lord should. The underlying reasons for this attitude were clearly stated in Rechteren's conversation with commissary Heffner.[41] While Heffner reminded Rechteren of his duties as a Bavarian vassal Rechteren replied that the elector of Bavaria as lord had some obligations to his vassal as well. Rechteren viewed the whole procedure as evidence of the elector's intention to introduce the Bavarian "Landsassiat" into Franconia, i.e. the elector wanted to turn him into a mere subject. The Imperial recruiting officer had been expelled without Rechteren's knowledge; this was an outrage. Rechteren further asked why only he was treated this way, but the Castells, Schwarzenbergs and other nobles of his rank were not. If the Bavarian declarations of taking possession did not mean any more than the maintenance of a loose feudal suzerainty like before – as the former commissary [Hompesch] had assured him – why did Bavaria then proceed so sharply against his counter-declarations? By Imperial law he was entitled to resist. Rechteren understood quite correctly that his traditional status was to be diminished. The Franconian nobility had so far lived by the maxim "a vassal, but not a subject"; a vassal could, of course, be the subject of his lord as well, but being a vassal did not automatically make him that.[42]

Moreover, it had been the Bavarian modus operandi – as Rechteren's injunctions clearly show – which had struck

---

41. In StAW, Reg.v.Ufr., 1943/45, 12563, Nr. 4 (Protokoll des Gesprächs) aufgeführt; durchgängig auch in der Beurkundeten Darstellung.

42. Dazu Baum, Lehnswesen.

40. This consideration is mentioned at the very beginning of the Documentary Record, p. 3.

41. These reasons are mentioned in StAW, Reg.v.Ufr. 1943/45, 12563, no. 4 (minutes of the conversation) and in the Documentary Record as well.

42. Cf. Baum, Lehnswesen.

politischen Widerstands greifen ließ.[43] Dass er bei seinem Vorgehen einen kühlen Kopf bewahrte, Schaden für und Gewalt gegen seine „Landeskinder" auf jeden Fall vermeiden wollte, zeigt seine strikte Anweisung hinsichtlich des Waffengebrauchs. Rechteren zeigte sich in dieser ganzen Angelegenheit als ein selbstbewusster, altadliger Standesherr, der energisch seine Rechte zu wahren bereit war, aber die politischen Realitäten und insbesondere das Wohlergehen seiner Untertanen nicht aus dem Auge verlor; letzteres erklärt auch, dass seine Herrschaft von diesen anscheinend über viele Jahre hinweg anerkannt und geschätzt wurde. Angesichts der geschichtlichen Entwicklungen erscheint Rechterens Haltung allerdings als Versuch einer Bewahrung überlebter Verhältnisse.

Rechterens Herrschaft fand vor allem in ihren ersten Jahren und bis in die 1820er Jahre hinein Anklang bei der Bevölkerung, weil er nach seiner festen Ansiedlung in Franken 1783 sofort begann, gegen die infolge langer Herrschaftsvakanz eingerissenen üblen Zustände in seinem Land einzuschreiten, d. h. gegen Korruption, Schlendrian, Vetternwirtschaft in der Verwaltung, was oft genug mit krasser Ausbeutung der Untertanen, Unterschleifen gegenüber der Herrschaft und sittlicher Dekadenz einherging. Es war ein sehr mühsamer Prozess, diese Reformen gegen den zähen Widerstand der Beamtenschaft und „Honoratioren" seiner Dörfer durchzusetzen, und nicht immer hatte er dabei vollen Erfolg.[44] Aber seine Untertanen schätzten seine ernsthaften Bemühungen, die zwar nicht zuletzt seinen eigenen, doch zugleich auch ihren Interessen dienten. Ebenso waren sie sicher dankbar dafür, dass Rechteren, wohl wegen seiner guten Beziehungen zur französischen Armee, bei der ersten französischen Besetzung Frankens 1796 eine Sauvegarde, einen Schutzbrief, für sein Territorium erwirken konnte, das dieses weitgehend vor den Folgen der Besetzung bewahrte.[45] Nach 1820 könnte allerdings eine fühlbare Änderung in diesem guten Verhältnis eingetreten sein.[46]

him as a grave insult to the punctilious courtesy of the European nobility of the ancien régime. The Bavarian elector had not seen fit to inform Rechteren as a territorial lord and an immediate estate of the empire – thus almost his peer – personally and politely of the fact that his dominion would be incorporated into the electorate of Bavaria by a decision made at the level of international politics and that, therefore, a nobleman of Rechteren's position would suffer noticeable legal and constitutional restrictions. Instead, he had made these changes known by subalterns like the mayor of Ochsenfurt or a corporal. It seems that it was this lack of polite form almost as much as Bavaria's brazen breach of the law which led to Rechteren's massive acts of political resistance.[43] That he remained cool-headed and acted circumspectly, striving to avoid damage to and violence against his subjects, is evidenced by his strict order concerning the use of firearms. In this whole affair, Rechteren comes across as a self-respecting nobleman of the ancien régime ready to fight for his rights energetically, but not about to lose sight of the political realities and the well-being of his subjects; this explains the fact that his reign was – as far as we know – respected and esteemed by them for many years. Seen from the point of view of long-term historical developments Rechteren's attitude has to be viewed as an attempt to preserve by-gone conditions, however.

Rechteren's reign was held in esteem by his subjects from its beginnings at least until the 1820s. The reason was that – right after permanently settling in Franconia – he energetically engaged in improving the bad state which he had found his county in after long years of absence of a legitimate regent, fighting corruption, sloppiness, and cronyism in its administration which was often enough combined with crass exploitation of the subjects, embezzlement of taxes and dues, and moral decadence. It was laborious work to prevail against the tough resistance of his officials and the local dignitaries and he wasn't completely successful all the time.[44] But his subjects appreciated his earnest endeavours because they were not only in his, but also in their interest. They were certainly grateful that – probably because of his good relations with the French army – he was able to obtain a "sauvegarde", a letter of protection, for his territories at the time of the first French occupation of

---

43. Auch dies macht die Beurkundete Darstellung mehrfach deutlich.
44. Dazu mit treffenden Beispielen Selig, Wenn die Katze … . Rechteren hatte als Erwachsener nur 1777 mehrere Monate in seinen fränkischen Besitzungen gelebt; erst nach der Heirat 1783 zog er auf Dauer hierher.
45. Dazu Selig, Vier Herren in 27 Jahren, S. 33.
46. Dazu u. S. 26.

---

43. Several passages of the Documentary Record hint at that.
44. Vivid examples of corruption and decay in Selig, When the Cat … . Before 1777, Rechteren had lived in his county as an adult just for a few months; he moved there permanently only after his marriage.

Trotz ihres kräftigen Widerstands konnten Rechteren und sein Bruder es nicht verhindern, dass mit dem Vollzug der rheinischen Bundesakte das nunmehrige Königreich Bayern am 26. September 1806 von der Grafschaft Limpurg-Speckfeld Besitz ergriff.[47] Rechteren war so „unter k[önigliche] Souverainität" gekommen und – wie sein bereits zitierter Passantrag von 1809 erweist – nun doch ein bayerischer Vasall und Untertan geworden. Auf Einzelheiten der bayerischen Besitzergreifung wird weiter unten näher eingegangen.[48]

Am 11. August 1807 heiratete Rechteren zum zweiten Mal, und zwar Auguste Eleonore, Prinzessin zu Hohenlohe-Kirchberg. Aus dieser Ehe gingen zwischen 1808 und 1818 sieben Kinder hervor, von denen nur drei das Erwachsenenalter erreichten. Seine zweite Frau, die viel jünger war als er, überlebte ihn um einige Jahre. Zwei seiner erwachsenen Kinder starben noch vor ihm, nämlich sein 1792 geborener ältester Sohn aus erster Ehe, der 1812 als Fahnenjunker eines bayerischen Kavallerieregiments aus Napoleons Feldzug nach Russland nicht wiederkehrte, und sein 1794 geborener zweiter Sohn aus erster Ehe, der 1821 als „Accessist" (Referendar) des bayerischen Innen- und Finanzministeriums in München verstarb. Er erlebte aber auch einige Eheschließungen seiner Kinder und die Geburt mehrerer Enkel.[49]

Als nach dem Ende der napoleonischen Zeit und des Großherzogtums Würzburg Unterfranken im Juni 1814 erneut an Bayern überging, bemühten sich die bayerische Regierung und der bayerische König, die Fehler der ersten Regierungsübernahme zu vermeiden. Für Rechteren bedeutete dies, dass er – vielleicht gerade wegen seines mannhaften Auftretens in der Sommerhäuser Affäre – vom König am 29. Juni 1815 zum Kreiskommandanten der „Nationalgarde" (später „Landwehr") im Großherzogtum Würzburg ernannt wurde.[50] Zwei Wochen später dankte Rechteren dem König für diese Ernennung und bat zugleich um die Verleihung des Rangs eines Generalmajors. Das

47. Dazu der am 14.12.1806 von Graf Thürheim nach München gesandte Bericht in BHStA, MInn 47716.
48. S. u. S. 24f.
49. Zu den familiären Ereignissen s. Nachruf, S. 6; s. auch den Lebenslauf seines Sohnes und Nachfolgers Ludwig (Louis) von Rechteren-Limpurg-Speckfeld (1811-1909), FCA HA IV 118; lebhafte Beschreibung der Familie Rechteren nach 1850 in: J. Graf zu Dohna (Hg.): Emma Fürstin Castell-Rüdenhausen, 2014, passim.
50. Dazu, zur Ernennung zum Generalmajor à la suite und zu Rechterens Karriere in der Nationalgarde s. BHStA, Abt. IV: Kriegsarchiv, OP 81367.

Franconia in 1796 which sheltered them from the worst abuses of the occupation.[45] After 1820, however, these good feelings may have been disturbed somewhat.[46]

In spite of their energetic resistance, the Rechteren brothers could not avoid being incorporated into the kingdom of Bavaria together with their whole county of Limpurg-Speckfeld on September 26th, 1806, as a consequence of the creation of the Confederation of the Rhine in that year.[47] Thus, they had come under "royal sovereignty" and had become Bavarian vassals and subjects after all, as we have seen in Rechteren's application for a passport in 1809. A more detailed description of what the Bavarians found when they took possession of their new territory will be given below.[48]

On August 11th, 1807, Rechteren married for the second time. His bride was Auguste Eleonore, princess of Hohenlohe-Kirchberg. Seven children were born to the couple between 1808 and 1818, only three of whom reached adulthood. His second wife who was many years his junior survived him by a number of years. Two of Rechteren's grown-up children also preceded him in death, thus his eldest son, born 1792 into his first marriage, who was an ensign in a Bavarian cavalry regiment and did not return from Napoleon's campaign in Russia 1812, and the second son of that marriage, born 1794, who died in Munich in 1821 as an "Accessist" (official) of the Bavarian Department of the Interior and Finance. But Rechteren also lived to see a number of his children's marriages and the births of several grandchildren.[49]

When Lower Franconia passed to Bavaria again in June 1814 at the end of Napoleon's rule and of the Grand-Duchy of Würzburg, the Bavarian king and his government took pains to avoid the mistakes of the first takeover. That may be the reason why Rechteren – perhaps even because of his manly resistance in the "Sommerhausen war" – was appointed district commander of the "National Guard" (later "Landwehr", i.e. militia) in the principality (later only a

45. See Selig, Four Masters in 27 Years, p. 35.
46. See below, p. 26.
47. The procedure is described in the report sent to Munich on December 14th, 1806, by count Thürheim; in BHStA, MInn 47716.
48. See below p. 24-25.
49. These details of his family history are taken from Obituary, p. 6; also cf. the CV of his son and successor Ludwig (Louis) count of Rechteren-Limpurg-Speckfeld (1811 – 1909), in: FCA HA IV 118 and the lively description of the Rechteren family's history after 1850 in: J. Graf zu Dohna (ed.): Emma Fürstin zu Castell-Rüdenhausen, 2014.

Gesuch wurde aus drei Gründen vom Ministerium des Äußeren und des königlichen Hauses unterstützt: erstens habe Rechteren in Würzburg bei der Nationalgarde einen Oberst unter sich und könne ohne höheren Rang dort nichts bewirken; zweitens habe er zusammen mit Generalleutnant von Zollern und General von Verger in Nordamerika gedient und von beiden gute Zeugnisse als Militär bekommen; drittens habe man ihm auch entsprechende Hoffnungen gemacht, eine Verzögerung der Genehmigung werde „auf den dortigen [d.h. unterfränkischen] Adel einen nachtheiligen Einfluß bezüglich der Stimmung" haben. Letztere Bemerkung zeigt deutlich, dass man in München nun viel mehr Rücksicht auf die Stimmung der Bevölkerung in den neu erworbenen Landesteilen nahm als 1802/03. 1816 lagen die Verleihung des „Charakters" eines Generalmajors der Infanterie und die Erlaubnis zum Tragen der Uniform à la suite vor. 1817 und nochmals 1820 wurde Rechteren sogar in Vertretung zum Oberkommandanten der gesamten bayerischen Reservearmee ernannt. Er erhielt auf Antrag 1817 die Erlaubnis zur Annahme des französischen Militär-Verdienstordens, den er erst 1816 – wohl im Hinblick auf seine neue Position in der Landwehr – als Gnadenerweis vom französischen König erbeten hatte, obwohl sein Militärdienst für diese hohe Auszeichnung an sich nicht ausreichte; dies war ihm selbst auch bekannt und daher stützte er sein Gesuch nicht zuletzt auf die Nähe der Familie seiner Frau, der Hohenlohe, zum Hause Bourbon.[51] 1817 wurde er auch zum Ritter des Civil-Verdienstordens der bayerischen Krone ernannt. Per Dekret vom 5. Dez. 1818 wurden Rechteren und das jeweils folgende Haupt seiner Familie – wie andere Standesherren – zu erblichen Reichsräten der Krone Bayern, damit auch Mitgliedern der Kammer der Reichsräte, gewissermaßen des Oberhauses des Bayerischen Landtags, erhoben.[52] Allerdings änderte auch dies nichts an der 1806 vollzogenen Mediatisierung seiner Herrschaft.

Für mehrere Jahre zog er nach Würzburg, wo er einen der säkularisierten Domherrnhöfe, den Hof „Weinsberg" (Herrngasse 2, heute: Kardinal-Döpfner-Platz 8 – 9) schräg gegenüber vom Hof „Conti", dem nunmehrigen Wohnsitz der Würzburger Bischöfe, erworben hatte. 1833 verkaufte er diesen Besitz an eine Palastdame der kronprinzlichen Hofhaltung

---

51. Das Gesuch um diese Auszeichnung und der damit verbundene Schriftverkehr füllen einen Großteil von Rechterens Personalakte bei der französischen Armee. Er konnte den Ludwigs-Orden nicht bekommen, weil er Protestant war.

52. BHStA, MInn 47246.

district) of Würzburg on June 29th, 1815.[50] A fortnight later, Rechteren sent a letter of thanks to the king, with the request of having the rank of major general conferred on him. The "Department of Foreign Affairs and of the Royal House" supported his request citing three reasons: first of all, Rechteren would have at least one colonel under him in the staff of the National Guard and would need higher rank to be effective as commander, secondly, he had served with Lt. General von Zollern and General von Verger in North America and had been recommended by both as a military officer, thirdly, he had been given hope to expect this appointment and any delay of the king's consent would "have a detrimental influence on the mood of the regional nobility". This clearly shows that, in 1815, the Bavarian government paid more heed to the prevailing mood of the population in the newly acquired regions than it had in 1802/03. In 1816, Rechteren received his appointment as a major general of the infantry and the permit to wear the army uniform à la suite. In 1817 and again in 1820, he was even appointed head of the whole Bavarian army reserves at a time of absence of their actual commander-in-chief. In 1817, his request to accept the French military order of merit was granted. He had asked the French king for this honour in 1816 – probably with his new position in the militia in mind – although his military service for France was not sufficient for this high decoration; he was aware of that himself and, therefore, stressed the close connections of the Hohenlohes (his wife's family) with the house of Bourbon.[51] In 1817, he was also made a knight of the Bavarian civil-merit order. By decree of Dec. 5th, 1818, Rechteren and his legal heirs as heads of the house of Rechteren-Limpurg were appointed hereditary Councillors of the Bavarian Crown, i.e. members of the Chamber of Crown Councillors, the upper house, so to speak, of the Bavarian diet, together with all families of equal rank.[52] But this did not undo the incorporation of his territory into the kingdom of Bavaria in 1806, either.

For several years, so it seems, Rechteren moved to Würzburg where he had acquired one of the secularized canon's houses, the "curia Weinsberg" (then: Herrngasse 2, today: Kardinal-Döpfner-Platz 8/9), diagonally across from "curia

---

50. On the new Bavarian policy, Rechteren's appointment as commander and his further career in the National Guard cf. BHStA, dept. IV: War Archive, OP 81367.

51. The request for this decoration and the concomitant correspondence constitute a large part of Rechteren's personal file in the French military archive. As he was a Protestant he could not apply for the Order of St. Louis.

52. BHStA, MInn 47246.

in der Residenz.⁵³ Die Stadt Würzburg ernannte ihn 1819 zum Ehrenbürger.⁵⁴ Die Begründung für diese Ehrung ist aufgrund ihrer auffällig vagen Formulierung bemerkenswert. Rechteren wurde zum Ehrenbürger ernannt „wegen seines wohltätigen Einflusses als Reichsrat auf das Allgemeine", im Widmungsgedicht ist von dem „mutigen Krieger für eines fremden Volkes Freiheit" von dem „gefälligen Dichter schöner, sanfter Lieder" und dem „kraftvollen Redner für Völkerrecht und Staatenwohl" die Rede. Man ehrte Rechteren also wohl, weil er sich kräftig für die bayerische Verfassung eingesetzt haben dürfte – er gehörte 1821 zu den Gästen bei der Einweihung der Gaibacher Konstitutionssäule⁵⁵ – und die Verfassung war bei den Würzburger Bürgern populär. Man ehrte ihn wegen seiner Beteiligung am Amerikanischen Unabhängigkeitskrieg und seiner – heute nicht mehr bekannten – literarischen Werke. Tatsächlich dürften jedoch die Bürger, denen die erste bayerische Besitzergreifung sehr widerstrebt hatte,⁵⁶ seine mannhafte Haltung gegen Bayern im Jahre 1803 gewürdigt haben, was selbstverständlich so nicht ausgesprochen werden konnte. In Würzburg war er anscheinend mit Oberbürgermeister von Brock und dem bedeutenden Theologen Prof. Dr. Franz Oberthür befreundet.⁵⁷

Im Jahre 1819 traf Rechteren eine wichtige Entscheidung, die seine Herrschaft betraf: er einigte sich mit seinem Neffen, dem Sohn seines inzwischen verstorbenen älteren Bruders, dahingehend, dass die Grafschaft Limpurg-Speckfeld allein auf ihn und seine Nachkommen, die Herrschaft Almelo und die zugehörigen Besitzungen in den Niederlanden hingegen auf jenen und dessen Nachkommen übergehen sollte; damit wurde er zugleich zum Begründer der jüngeren Linie des Hauses

Conti", which had become the residence of the bishops of Würzburg after 1808. In 1833, he sold it to a lady of the Bavarian crown prince's household which was located in the "Residenz" palace (the former prince-bishop's seat).⁵³ The city of Würzburg conferred the title of "honorary citizen" on him in 1819.⁵⁴ The reasons given for this honour are remarkable for their extreme vagueness. Rechteren was made an honorary citizen because of "the beneficial influence he took on general affairs in his capacity as Councillor of the Crown", the dedicatory poem speaks of the "courageous fighter for a foreign nation's liberty", the "agreeable poet of soft, beautiful songs", the "forceful speaker for the rights of the people and public welfare". This means that Rechteren was honoured for his stand in favour of the Bavarian constitution – in 1821, he was among the guests of the inauguration of the "constitution obelisk" at Gaibach⁵⁵ – and the constitution was popular with the citizens of Würzburg; he was honoured for his participation in the War of American Independence and for his literary works which have not come down to us. But it seems very likely that the citizens – who had been strongly opposed to the first Bavarian takeover of their principality⁵⁶ – wanted to honour his manly stand against the Bavarian elector in 1803; this could not be uttered publicly, of course. In Würzburg, he seems to have had friendly relations with mayor von Brock and with the distinguished theologian Professor Franz Oberthür.⁵⁷

In 1819, Rechteren came to an important agreement concerning his possessions. He settled with his nephew, the son of his deceased elder brother, in this way: the county of Limpurg-Speckfeld was to remain in his and his rightful heirs' possession whereas the county of Almelo and its appurtenances in the Netherlands were to fall to his nephew and his descendants; thus he also became the

---

53. Dazu StadtAW, Grundliste „Herrngasse 2" sowie die Würzburger Adressbücher von 1806, S. 44; 1829, S. 32; 1833, S. 18; 1838, S. 117, jeweils unter II. District, Herrngasse.

54. Alle Vorgänge zum Ehrenbürgerrecht der Stadt Würzburg publiziert bei Kann, Ehrenbürger, S. 11 – 13. Die Ehrenbürger-Urkunde vom 20.12.1819 wurde am 8.03.1997 beim Auktionshaus Bergmann in Erlangen versteigert (Nr. 1156 der März-Auktion).

55. Das Ölbild von Peter von Hess, 1822/23, in: von Freeden, Schätze, Nr. 55, zeigt Rechteren als Gast der Einweihungsveranstaltung.

56. S. dazu etwa Weiß, Übergang an Bayern, 2004, S. 217.

57. Allerdings wird dies in der Literatur ohne eindeutige Quellenbelege behauptet; dazu Kann, Ehrenbürger, S. 12, und „Fränkisches Volksblatt", Nr. 265 vom 8.11.1963.

---

53. Cf. StadtAW, Grundliste "Herrngasse 2" as well as the Würzburg city directories of 1806, p. 44, 1829, p. 32, 1833, p. 18, and 1838, p. 117, always under "II. District, Herrngasse".

54. All relevant information connected with the conferring of this title was published by Kann, Ehrenbürger, p. 11 – 13. The charter on the bestowal of this title of Dec. 20Th, 1819, was auctioned off at the Bergmann auction house in Erlangen on March 8th, 1997 (No. 1156 of the March auction).

55. The painting by Peter von Hess (1822/23), cf. von Freeden, Schätze, 1972, No. 55, shows Rechteren present there.

56. Cf. Weiß, Übergang an Bayern, p. 217.

57. This, however, is only asserted in secondary texts, no clear evidence for it was found in primary sources; cf. Kann; Ehrenbürger, p. 12, and "Fränkisches Volksblatt", Nr. 256, Nov. 8th, 1963.

Rechteren-Limpurg.⁵⁸ Drei Jahre später, 1822, führte er durch Familienstatut in seinem Hause die Primogenitur ein.⁵⁹

Welche Besitzungen umfasste die Standesherrschaft des Hauses Rechteren-Limpurg am Anfang des 19. Jahrhunderts, worüber hatte Bayern im September 1806 die Souveränität erworben? Die Grafschaft Limpurg-Speckfeld, von der Bayern durch den Direktionsrat Stupp am 26.09.1806 Besitz ergriff, umfasste die beiden Ämter Einersheim [heute: Markt E.] und Sommerhausen.⁶⁰ Zum Amt Einersheim gehörten der speckfeldische Anteil an Gollhofen, dann die Orte Einersheim, Possenheim, „Hellmigheim" [Hellmitzheim] und Neundorf. Das Amt Sommerhausen umfasste die Orte Sommerhausen, Winterhausen und Lindelbach. Weiter gehörten wohl Teile des Ritterguts Oberlaimbach zur Grafschaft Limpurg. Davon und von dem zum Fürstentum Ansbach zu rechnenden Gollhofen abgesehen, zählte die Herrschaft Speckfeld im September 1806

im Amt Einersheim	266 Häuser	339 Familien	1446 Seelen
im Amt Sommerhausen	464 Häuser	572 Familien	2226 Seelen
zusammen	730 Häuser	911 Familien	3672 Seelen.

Die Besitznahmeakte geht in der Folge recht genau auf die die neuen Souveräne sicherlich nicht zuletzt interessierenden Einnahmen und Ausgaben dieser Herrschaften ein; sie können hier nicht im Detail wiedergegeben werden. Direktionsrat Stupp stellte versuchsweise einen „General-Etat" auf; danach hatte die „Kammerkasse"

Einnahmen von ca. 4.709 fl, Ausgaben von ca. 119 fl, einen Überschuss von ca. 4.590 fl;

die „Landschaftskasse"

---

58. Nachruf, S. 7, sowie Siebmacher, Wappenbuch, 1. Bd., 3. Abt., II. R., S. 12. Die umfangreichen weiteren Verhandlungen zur Umsetzung des Teilungsvertrags vom 6.11.1819 mit den bayerischen Behörden und dem dem Hause Castell angehörenden Vormund einiger minorenner Vertragspartner 1820 – 1822 in FCA HA I d II 7.

59. Nachruf, ebd.

60. Die nachfolgende Beschreibung der Zugehörigkeiten und Einkünfte der Grafschaft Limpurg-Speckfeld zum Zeitpunkt des Übergangs an Bayern nach BHStA, MInn 47716; Geldsummen mit „ca." zitiert, weil nur die Gulden-, nicht die Kreuzer- und Pfennigsummen aufgeführt werden; deren Addition könnte die Guldensummen geringfügig ändern; für Gulden wird hier die übliche Kurzform „fl." verwendet. 1 fl. war unterteilt in 60 Kreuzer (kr) zu 4 Pfennig (d).

---

founder of the younger line of the house of Rechteren-Limpurg.⁵⁸ Three years later, in 1822, he introduced the right of primogeniture in his line by family statute.⁵⁹

What were the house of Rechteren-Limpurg's possessions at the beginning of the 19th century, what did the kingdom of Bavaria incorporate into its sovereignty in September 1806? The county of Limpurg-Speckfeld of which Bavaria took possession by its agent, councillor Stupp, on Sept. 26th, 1806, consisted of the districts of Einersheim [today: Markt E.] and Sommerhausen.⁶⁰ Einersheim district included the county's share of the village of Gollhofen, then the villages of Einersheim, Possenheim, "Hellmigheim" [Hellmitzheim], and Neundorf. Sommerhausen district was composed of the villages of Sommerhausen, Winterhausen, and Lindelbach. Moreover, the county had a small share of the manor of Oberlaimbach. Omitting this manor and the county's share of Gollhofen which pertained to the principality of Ansbach, in September of 1806, the county of Speckfeld had

in Einersheim district	266 houses	339 families	1446 souls
in Sommerhausen district	464 houses	572 families	2226 souls
in sum	730 houses	911 families	3672 souls.

The file on Bavaria's takeover of these possessions then goes on to list their revenues and expenses, a topic of great interest to the new sovereigns, no doubt; a detailed reproduction of these lists is not feasible here. Councillor Stupp tried to draw up a "general budget"; according to this the "Kammerkasse" ("chamber receipts") amounted to

revenues of ca. 4.709 fl, expenses of ca. 119 fl, leaving a surplus of ca. 4.590 fl;

the "district receipts" consisted of

---

58. Cf. Obituary, p. 7, and Siebmacher, Wappenbuch, vol. 1, 3. dept., II. series, p. 12. For the lengthy negotiations concerning the enactment of the partition agreement with Bavarian officials and the guardian (a member of the house of Castell) of some partners of the contract who were minors, in 1820 – 1822, cf. FCA HA I d II 7.

59. Cf. Obituary, p. 7.

60. The subsequent description of the appurtenances and the revenue of the county of Limpurg-Speckfeld at the time of its acquisition by Bavaria follows BHStA, MInn 47716. All sums given are qualified by "ca." because only the sums in Gulden (fl.) are listed whereas the amounts of kreutzer (kr) and pennies (d) are neglected. Their addition could lead to a minor change of the fl.-sums. The Gulden was partitioned into 60 kreutzer of 4 pennies each.

Einnahmen von ca. 11.639 fl, Ausgaben von ca. 3.832 fl, einen Überschuss von ca. 7.807 fl.

Der speckfeldische Anteil an Gollhofen hatte

Einnahmen von ca. 1.714 fl, Ausgaben von ca. 23 fl, einen Überschuss von ca. 1.690 fl.

Die sehr beträchtlichen Schulden der Herrschaft Speckfeld beliefen sich auf ca. 48.185 fl, die jährlichen Zinszahlungen auf ca. 1.887 fl.[61]

Thürheim berichtete nach München, dass Rechteren noch bei der Besitzergreifung seiner Herrschaft durch Bayern erklärt habe, dass er nicht gewillt sei, seine Rechte aufzugeben, diese vielmehr für sein Haus und seine Nachfahren auf immer bewahren zu wollen. Speziell erklärte er – obwohl ihm bekannt war, dass nach der Rheinischen Bundesakte die neuen Souveräne Teile der Landesschulden der neu erworbenen Territorien übernehmen sollten – sich auf diese Weise nicht seiner Schulden entledigen zu wollen, sich dafür aber einen erheblichen Teil der bisherigen Steuern und Abgaben vorzubehalten. Nach Thürheims Meinung verlor Rechteren durch die Mediatisierung relativ viel; er werde insbesondere sein bisheriges Regierungskollegium von einem Direktor, zwei Assessoren und einem Sekretär auf Dauer nicht halten können.

Außerdem besaß Rechteren in Sommerhausen und Markt Einersheim je ein – recht bescheidenes – Schloss, weiter von ca. 1815 bis 1833 den erwähnten Domherrnhof in Würzburg; sie dienten der Familie als wechselnde Wohnsitze. Andere Besitzungen waren, wie berichtet, verkauft worden.[62] Auf die Verwaltung dieser Ortschaften hatte Rechteren trotz der Mediatisierung – durch die in allen grundsätzlichen politischen Fragen an die Stelle seiner früheren Herrschaft die Regierungen in Würzburg oder München als entscheidende Instanzen getreten waren – einen erheblichen Einfluss behalten. Er erhielt weiterhin die meisten grundherrlichen Abgaben von den Einwohnern und war Polizeichef und Herr des „Herrschaftsgerichts", über dessen Tätigkeit jedoch regelmäßige Berichte an die Bezirksregierung in Würzburg zu liefern waren.[63]

revenues of ca. 11.639 fl, expenses of ca. 3.832 fl, leaving a surplus of ca. 7.807 fl.

The county's share of Gollhofen had

revenues of ca. 1.714 fl, expenses of ca. 23 fl, and a surplus of ca. 1.690 fl.

The rather heavy debts of the county of Speckfeld amounted to ca. 48.185 fl, the annual interest payments to ca. 1.887 fl.[61]

Count Thürheim, Stupp's superior, reported to Munich that even at the very moment of losing his sovereign rights Rechteren had declared that he did not want to give them up, but intended to retain them for himself and his descendants for the future. More specifically he declared – even though he knew that, by the Treaty of the Confederation of the Rhine, the new sovereigns were supposed to assume some of the debts of their new territories – that he did not want to rid himself of his debts that way, but would prefer to retain a large number of his accustomed revenue titles. In Thürheim's view, Rechteren stood to lose a relatively large part of his revenues by the Bavarian takeover and would not be able to retain his "government office" consisting of one director, two assessors, and one secretary in the long run.

Beyond the possessions listed above, Rechteren owned – rather modest – castles in Einersheim and Sommerhausen; from about 1815 to 1833 he also owned the former canon's house in Würzburg. All of these were used in turn as residences of his family. Other possessions had been sold as mentioned before.[62] In spite of the Bavarian sovereignty, Rechteren retained quite a bit of influence on the administration of his possessions. To be sure, all fundamental political decisions were made by the central government in Munich or the district government in Würzburg now, not by himself any more. But he had retained much of his revenue, especially most of the manorial ones, and was still chief of police and lord of the "patrimonial court" even though he now had to send regular reports about its activities and decisions to the district government in Würzburg.[63]

---

61. Die Schuld wurde also zu ca. 3,9% verzinst.

62. Insbesondere die Herrschaft Adelmannsfelden; s. dazu S. 11.

63. Die vollständige Ablösung der grundherrschaftlichen Abgaben erfolgte in Bayern erst 1849 ff.; zum Gericht und zum Folgenden Redelberger, Herrschaftsgericht, 1965, S. 59 f. Ein Bericht über die Tätigkeit des Gerichts liegt z.B. vor in StAW, Reg.v.Ufr., 1943/45, 1871, Nr. 5.

---

61. The interest rate thus was 3,9% on average.

62. This means the manor of Adelmannsfelden; cf. above, p. 11.

63. In Bavaria, the manorial taxes were fully abolished (on payment of a redemption sum by the farmers) only after 1849; for the patrimonial court and the economic situation in the court district, see Redelberger, Herrschaftsgericht, 1965, p. 59 f. One of the reports mentioned above in StAW, Reg.v.Ufr. 1943/45, 1871, no. 5.

Es wurde oben bereits erwähnt,[64] dass Rechterens Wertschätzung durch die Bevölkerung nach 1818 einen Rückschlag erfahren haben dürfte. Das hing mit den unklaren Reformen der bäuerlichen Abgaben und Frondienste in den Jahren zwischen dem Erlass der bayerischen Verfassung 1818 und den endgültigen Regelungen 1849/51 zusammen. Die Untertanen hatten natürlich angenommen, dass mit der Verfassung auch überlebte und lästige Abgaben und Dienste sowie adlige Vorrechte, wie etwa der Zehnt, Jagd- und Weiderechte, Gerichtsrechte oder Dienstleistungen wie Botengänge und Erntearbeit u. dgl. abgeschafft worden seien; dies war aber nicht der Fall. Die Standesherren wie Rechteren hatten die meisten dieser Rechte noch inne und waren im eigenen Interesse bestrebt, sie unvermindert beizubehalten. Jedoch war es nun möglich geworden, zumindest gegen einen Teil dieser Beschwernisse auf dem Rechtswege vorzugehen, und die Bevölkerung machte von dieser Möglichkeit auch z.B. in Sommer- und Winterhausen regen Gebrauch, sodass Rechteren sich mit zahlreichen solcher Klagen konfrontiert sah. Die endgültige Regelung all dieser Missstände erfolgte aber erst ein Jahrzehnt nach seinem Tode.[65]

Im Herrschaftsgericht Sommerhausen, dem wichtigsten Teil seiner Besitzungen, lebten um 1820/30 schon ca. 2500 Einwohner – die Bevölkerung war also seit 1806 gewachsen. Sie erwarb ihren Lebensunterhalt teils in dem damals zurückgehenden Weinbau, teils im Getreide-, Gemüse- und dem zunehmenden Obstanbau. Beim Weinbau gab es Qualitätsprobleme, und nur Rechteren selbst hatte sich um die Anpflanzung neuer, qualitativ besserer Rebsorten wie Riesling und Burgunder bemüht. Um 1840 wurden jährlich nur noch ca. 60 Fuder[66] Wein aus Sommerhausen ausgeführt; der Winterhäuser Wein, der einen weniger guten Ruf genoss, blieb ganz überwiegend im Lande. Neben Wein wurde in größerem Umfang auch Essig ausgeführt. Es gab daneben diverse Handwerke; so waren im Bezirk 24 Posamentierer (Bortenmacher) tätig, von denen die zwei bedeutendsten jährlich italienische Seide im Wert von 17 000 Gulden verarbeiteten. Daneben wurde die Weberei betrieben, die nicht nur Leinentuch, sondern als Spezialprodukt auch Wasserschläuche aus Hanf herstellte; 1817 waren ein Webermeister und sein Sohn vom bayerischen König für diese Produkte mit einer Medaille ausgezeichnet worden. Von Bedeutung waren die Gerber mit einer Lederproduktion im Wert von ca. 9 000

We have already mentioned the fact that Rechteren may not have been held in as much esteem as before by his subjects after 1818.[64] This came about as a consequence of the unclear legislation concerning the reform of manorial rights between the promulgation of the Bavarian constitution in 1818 and the final settlement of these questions in 1849/51. Rechteren's subjects had assumed, of course, that the manorial rights and the often onerous duties and levies connected with them had been abolished with the constitution, especially the tithe, chase and pasture reservations, and judicial prerogatives of the nobility as well as labour services and errands for the lord. But it wasn't so. The nobles, such as Rechteren, still held most of these rights and – in their own interest – strove to maintain them. At least, it was now possible to proceed against some of these burdens in the courts of law, and the population of Sommerhausen and Winterhausen availed itself of these new possibilities, so Rechteren was confronted with quite a number of such court cases against himself. These problems were finally settled about a decade after his death.[65]

Sommerhausen district, the most important part of Rechteren's possessions, had about 2.500 inhabitants around 1820/30 which means that the population had grown somewhat since 1806. These people made their living by viticulture – in decline then – or by growing grains, vegetables, and fruit; fruit production was on the upswing. There were quality problems in wine growing; only Rechteren himself had taken pains to introduce new and better varieties of vines, such as Burgundy and Riesling. Around 1840, only about 60 "Fuder"[66] of wine were exported from Sommerhausen annually; the Winterhausen wine with an even lesser reputation mostly remained in the district. Vinegar had become a major export product next to the wine. There were several major crafts; thus, about 24 loop makers (employed in passementerie) worked in the district, the two most important ones of whom annually processed Italian silk worth 17.000 fl. There was some weaving which not only produced linen cloth, but also hose made from hemp as a specialty; in 1817, a master weaver and his son were awarded a medal for these products by the

---

64. S. o. S. 20.

65. Dazu ausführlich und mit erhellenden Beispielen Selig, Unruhige Tage.

66. Ein Fuder entsprach in Franken meist knapp 900 Litern, sodass 60 Fuder etwa 54 Hektoliter bedeuteten.

---

64. See above, p. 20.

65. A more detailed discussion of these questions with some elucidating examples in Selig, Restless Days.

66. On average, the Franconian Fuder equalled almost exactly 900 Liters (or 237.8 US-gallons, 198.2 Imp. Gallons); 60 Fuder thus correspond to about 54 Hektoliters.

Gulden im Jahr, dann die Kammmacher, die Hörner im Wert von 6 000 Gulden als Rohstoff bezogen und ihre Produkte bis nach Frankfurt, Nürnberg und Ansbach vertrieben. Schließlich erzielten die Korbmacher Jahresumsätze von etwa 8 000 Gulden. Inwieweit Rechteren diese Handwerke förderte, ist nicht bekannt. Der Zustand der Landwehr, für den Rechteren ja selbst verantwortlich war, wird als sehr erfreulich bezeichnet; der König belohnte dies durch die Umbenennung des Landwehr-Bataillons „Ochsenfurt" in „Sommerhausen". Allerdings nahm die Landwehr im Wesentlichen nur die Aufgaben der Feuerwehr und der staatlichen Repräsentation bei öffentlichen Festen wahr.

Zu Anfang des 19. Jahrhunderts unterstand das Gesundheitswesen im Gerichtsbezirk einem fähigen Arzt, Dr. Windeck, der „wegen seiner glücklichen Kuren" sogar auswärtige Patienten nach Sommerhausen zog und der auch – wahrscheinlich mit Rechterens Unterstützung – die Kinder des Orts mit Erfolg gegen die Pocken impfte. Rechteren bemühte sich seit etwa 1820 darum, einen Apotheker in Sommerhausen anzusiedeln und erteilte einem befähigten Bewerber, der auch von vielen Bürgern in seinem Gerichtsbezirk und in Eibelstadt (das ja nicht dazugehörte) unterstützt wurde, eine Konzession. Dagegen legten die Apotheker in Ochsenfurt, Kitzingen und Marktbreit Widerspruch ein, dem die Regierung von Unterfranken stattgab. So gelang die Ansiedlung eines Apothekers erst im Jahre 1828; es handelte sich um einen Mann, der in Bamberg und Würzburg studiert hatte und eine Approbationsurkunde vorweisen konnte. Nicht ganz sicher belegt, aber aufgrund von Rechterens persönlichen Erfahrungen leicht glaubhaft, ist sein besonderes Bemühen um den Mutterschutz, das sich in fürsorglichen Verordnungen niederschlug.[67]

Rechteren war anscheinend nicht nur ein politischer Realist, der für seine Rechte energisch eintrat, sondern hatte auch einen Sinn für seinen finanziellen Vorteil. In Winterhausen gab es eine von den Gemeinden Winter- und Sommerhausen gemeinsam genutzte Mühle, die – wie überall in Franken – ursprünglich eine herrschaftliche Einrichtung war. 1526 hatte Karl Schenk von Limpurg diese Mühle für 1 000 Gulden auf Wiederkauf an die beiden Gemeinden verkauft. 1789 machte Rechteren von seinem Wiederkaufsrecht Gebrauch und erwarb die Mühle zu diesem Preis zurück. Schon 1794 verkaufte er sie für 2 000 Gulden und die jährliche Abgabe von vier Maltern Korngült erneut an die beiden Gemeinden, ohne

king of Bavaria. The tanners were of some importance with a leather production worth about 9.000 fl annually, as well as the comb makers who processed horn worth about 6.000 fl and sold their products as far as Frankfurt, Nuremberg, and Ansbach. Lastly, there were the basket weavers who had annual sales of about 8.000 fl. We don't know whether Rechteren promoted these crafts. The state of the "Landwehr" (militia) which Rechteren was directly responsible for was excellent; the king rewarded him by renaming the "Ochsenfurt" battalion "Sommerhausen". But its main tasks were only fire fighting and official representation on festive occasions.

At the beginning of the 19th century, public health in the district was in the hands of a Dr. Windeck who – because of his "fortunate cures" – attracted patients even from outside of the district and who – most likely with Rechteren's support – inoculated the children in town against smallpox with good success. Around 1820, Rechteren tried to establish an apothecary in Sommerhausen and issued a licence to a well-qualified applicant who was supported by many inhabitants of Sommerhausen and Eibelstadt (which did not belong to the county). But the apothecaries of Ochsenfurt, Kitzingen, and Marktbreit opposed that and the government in Würzburg yielded to their petitions of protest. That is why the first apothecary could not be established in Sommerhausen before 1828; the licensee had studied in Bamberg and Würzburg and had an official approbation. Not proven, but easily credible in view of Rechteren's personal experience is his keen engagement for the protection of mothers, as shown in protective ordinances.[67]

It seems that Rechteren was not only a political realist who vigorously defended his rights, but also a man with a clear head for his financial gain. In Winterhausen, there was a mill used communally by the towns of Sommer- and Winterhausen. Originally it had been a seigneurial installation as everywhere in Franconia. In 1526, Karl Schenk von Limpurg had sold this mill to the two villages for the price of 1.000 fl stipulating the right of repurchase for this sum. In 1789, Rechteren made use of this clause and repurchased the mill for the original price. But in 1794, he resold it to the two villages for

---

67. Dazu der biographische Artikel über Rechteren in „Fränkisches Volksblatt", Nr. 265 vom 8.11.1963.

67. Cf. the biographical article on him in "Fränkisches Volksblatt", Nr. 265 of Nov. 11th, 1963; the attitude is credible since more than half of his children died in childhood, and his first wife died after her last pregnancy.

Vorbehalt des Rückkaufs.⁶⁸ 1804 verkaufte die Gemeinde Sommerhausen ihren hälftigen Anteil für 2 000 Gulden an Winterhausen, dem nun die Mühle ganz gehörte, und schließlich überließ Winterhausen 1812 den ganzen Betrieb für 4 085 Gulden einem Privatmann.⁶⁹

Seinem mehrfach zitierten Nachruf zufolge pflegte Rechteren eine sehr schlichte, regelmäßige Lebensweise und hatte vielleicht deswegen bis ans Ende seines langen Lebens nur wenig unter Krankheiten zu leiden. Bis ins hohe Alter schätzte er die Beschäftigung mit den großen Autoren des griechischen und römischen Altertums, mit der Mathematik, mit geschichtlichen Themen und hatte Interesse an neuen Entwicklungen von Kunst und Technik. Anscheinend war er selbst bis ins Alter hinein literarisch tätig. Er begegnete den Menschen mit Wohlwollen und hörte ihm vorgetragene Anliegen mit Sorgfalt an; wenn es ihm möglich war, unterstützte er Bitten und Vorschläge, die ihm sinnvoll und berechtigt erschienen.⁷⁰ Auch darauf beruhte wohl die Wertschätzung, die ihm – wie oben berichtet – entgegen gebracht wurde. Rechteren starb am 20. Juni 1842, im 91. Lebensjahr, in Sommerhausen und wurde am 23. Juni 1842 in der rechterenschen Gruft in Markt Einersheim beigesetzt.⁷¹

In den Beständen des Fürstlich Castell'schen Archivs befindet sich ein Manuskript aus dem Jahre 1835, das Rechterens Lebenserinnerungen, zumindest Teile davon, enthält.⁷² Entgegen der auf dem Titelblatt genannten Jahreszahl ist anzunehmen, dass Teile des Manuskripts, bis etwa zur Seite 58, bereits in den

2.000 fl plus an annual duty of two "Malter" of "corn",⁶⁸ now without reserving the repurchase right. In 1804, Sommerhausen sold its half share of the mill to Winterhausen for the price of 2.000 fl. Winterhausen thus had become the sole owner; in 1812, it sold the whole mill to a private buyer for 4.085 fl.⁶⁹

According to the much-quoted obituary Rechteren led a very modest and regular life; this may be one of the reasons why he didn't much suffer from diseases up to the end of his long life. Even at a very old age, he enjoyed studying the famous authors of Greek and Roman antiquity, mathematics, historical topics, and kept an interest in new developments in art and technology. It seems that he wrote poetry and works of belles-lettres into his old age as well. He treated people benevolently and carefully listened to pleas and suggestions proposed to him. If possible, he supported those which seemed justified and meaningful to him.⁷⁰ That was the main reason for the esteem in which he was apparently held. Rechteren died in Sommerhausen on June 20th, 1842, in his 91st year and was buried in the Rechteren family grave in Markt Einersheim on June 23rd, 1842.⁷¹

Among the documents kept at the Fürstlich Castell'sche Archive there is a manuscript dated to the year 1835 containing Rechteren's memoirs or at least part of these.⁷² In spite of the year given on the title page we have to assume that parts of the manuscript, up to page 58, were

---

68. „Korn" meint normalerweise Roggen; ein Malter entsprach in Franken meist etwa 173,3 Litern.

69. S. Winterhäuser Kalenderblatt 2012 unter der Überschrift „Vor 200 Jahren: Winterhäuser Mühlenkapitalismus". Dabei unterstellt der Artikel Rechteren eine rücksichtslose Ausnutzung des Wiederkaufrechts zum Preis von 1526 und erneute Abtretung an die Gemeinden zu nunmehr verdoppeltem Preis, übersieht aber, dass die Gemeinde Sommerhausen beim Verkauf ihrer Hälfte an Winterhausen sich genau so verhielt.

70. Nachruf, S. 8; s. auch „Fränkisches Volksblatt", Nr. 265 vom 8.11.1963.

71. S. Nachruf, S. 10.

72. Dass Rechteren noch weitere Erinnerungen niedergeschrieben hat, ist relativ unwahrscheinlich, da die vorliegenden Erinnerungen nur sieben Jahre vor seinem Tod abgeschlossen wurden. Allerdings findet sich auch auf der ersten Manuskriptseite die Notiz „ … geschrieben 17 … " (wie auf S. 58; dazu u. Anm. 73), die auf einen früheren Entwurf hinweist; die Archivsignatur lautet FCA HA XIV c 138, in der Folge mit „Mskr." zitiert; dazu weiter u. Anm. 76.

68. "Corn" usually means rye in Franconia; a "malter" is a measure containing, on average in Franconia, 173.3 Liters.

69. These business transactions are described in Winterhäuser Kalenderblatt 2012 under the heading (in translation) "200 years ago: mill capitalism in Winterhausen". The article reproaches Rechteren for ruthlessly taking advantage of the repurchase clause, buying the mill back for a price set in 1526 and then reselling it at double the price, but it overlooks the fact that Sommerhausen did exactly the same with the sale of its share to Winterhausen.

70. Cf. Obituary, p. 8, and "Fränkisches Volksblatt", Nr. 265 of Nov. 11th, 1963.

71. Obituary, p. 10.

72. It is not likely that Rechteren wrote additional memoirs as the ones published here were completed only seven years before he died. However, there is an incomplete date given on the first page of the manuscript "written in 17 …", indicating an earlier draft (cf. below fn. 73); the manuscript's archive signature is FCA HA XIV c 138, it is quoted here as "mscr.".

1790er Jahren niedergeschrieben wurden.[73] Der Rest muss später entstanden sein, weil mehrfach Ereignisse aus dem frühen 19. Jahrhundert erwähnt werden.[74] Da die Handschrift des Manuskripts einheitlich von derselben Hand stammt, sind also wohl Teile eines früheren Entwurfs hier abgeschrieben worden. Der Text berichtet über Rechterens Jugendjahre 1751 bis 1782, speziell seine große Seereise durch das Mittelmeer auf einem niederländischen Kriegsschiff 1770 bis 1772[75] und seine Teilnahme am Amerikanischen Unabhängigkeitskrieg 1780/81. Rechteren wollte wohl in hohem Lebensalter, gestützt auf frühere Aufzeichnungen, die Erinnerungen an seine Jugendjahre festhalten. Im Folgenden sollen diese Memoiren näher betrachtet und im Vergleich mit denen anderer Autoren eingeordnet werden.

Rechterens Manuskript umfasst 125 kleinformatige handschriftliche Seiten;[76] es kann thematisch in vier größere Abschnitte unterteilt werden: erstens die Beschreibung der Seereise im Mittelmeer, der auch die ganz kurzen Bemerkungen über seine Kindheit und Schulzeit – nicht mehr als zwei Seiten umfassend – zuzuordnen sind; dieser Teil reicht bis zur Seite 52. Der folgende kürzere Abschnitt hat Rechterens Bemühungen zum Inhalt, in den Jahren 1772 bis 1780 eine Anstellung als Marine- oder Heeresoffizier zu finden; er endet mit der Seite 58. Dann folgt erneut ein langer Abschnitt, nämlich der über seine Beteiligung am Amerikanischen Unabhängigkeitskrieg, der die Seiten 59 bis 110 umfasst. Dieser Teil des Textes ist aus zwei Gründen der wichtigste: zum einen berichtet der Autor hier als Augenzeuge über Ereignisse von weltgeschichtlicher Bedeutung, zum zweiten liegen hierzu zahlreiche andere Zeitzeugenberichte vor, die es ermöglichen, Rechterens Memoiren vergleichend einzuordnen und zu bewerten. Der Rest des Manuskripts beschreibt auf den Seiten 111 bis 123 Rechterens Heimreise. Sie gehört nicht mehr zu seinem Kriegseinsatz, da er unmittelbar nach der Entscheidung von Yorktown im Herbst 1781 seinen Abschied von der französischen Armee nahm und unabhängig von dieser, auch auf eigene Kosten, nach Europa zurückkehrte. Mit der Ankunft in Paris im Januar 1782 endet seine Erzählung.

Das gesamte Manuskript ist in unkomplizierter Sprache und Erzählweise gehalten; es treten kaum Verständnisprobleme auf. Der Verfasser ist bemüht, die erzählten Ereignisse exakt zu

written as early as the 1790s.[73] The rest of it must have been completed later as mention is made of events which happened in the early 19th century.[74] As the whole text was written by the same hand it seems that parts of a former draft were copied here. The booklet describes Rechteren's youth from 1751 until 1782, particularly his great voyage in the Mediterranean sea in a Dutch man-of-war 1770 to 1772[75] and his participation in the American War of Independence 1780/81. Rechteren probably wanted to record the memories of his youth in his old age, partly relying on earlier records. Subsequently, these memoirs shall be looked at more closely and compared to those of other authors.

Rechteren's manuscript comprises 125 handwritten pages in a small format;[76] it may be subdivided into four large sections: the first one contains the description of the voyage mentioned above which includes the very short account of his childhood and school years – no more than two pages long – as well; it extends from page 1 to page 52. The short subsequent section tells us about Rechteren's attempts from 1772 to 1780 to find employment as a navy or army officer; it ends with page 58. Another long section, the one about his participation in the American War of Independence, follows from page 59 to 110. For two reasons, this part of the text is the most important one: first of all, the author describes events of major importance in world history as an eye-witness here; secondly, there are many other contemporary eye-witness reports describing the same events which enable us to compare and evaluate Rechteren's memoirs. The rest of the manuscript, page 111 to 123, covers Rechteren's return voyage. This was not part of his military service any more as he left the French army right after the victory at Yorktown in the fall of 1781 and returned to Europe independently and at his own expense. The story ends with his arrival in Paris in January of 1782.

The whole manuscript is written in a plain and straightforward style; there are hardly any problems understanding it. The author takes pains to report the exact times and

---

73. Vgl. dazu Anm. 149 der Textausgabe, wonach das Manuskript „im Jahre 179 …" [letzte Ziffer fehlt] entstand.

74. Z.B. trifft er 1811 einen Bekannten aus Amerika in Würzburg, s. Mskr. S. 104.

75. S. dazu u. S. 30-32, 45-71.

76. Die nachfolgend genannten Seitenzahlen beziehen sich stets auf die Seitenzählung des Manuskripts, die in der vorliegenden Textausgabe in eckigen Klammern angegeben wird.

---

73. According to fn. 149 of the edition the manuscript was produced "in the year 179…" [the last digit is missing].

74. Cf. mscr., p. 104, where Rechteren meets an acquaintance from America in Würzburg in 1811.

75. See below, p. 30-32, 45-71.

76. The page numbers given here always mean the page numbers of the manuscript which are printed out in the edition.

datieren und zu lokalisieren, die Personen und Orte, die er kennenlernte, genau und vollständig aufzuführen, zumal wenn es sich um solche von größerer Bedeutung handelt. Die Erzählung folgt dabei, ohne Vor- oder Rückgriffe, dem zeitlichen Ablauf; die Abfolge der berichteten Ereignisse ist in sich stimmig. Jedoch könnte man wegen der falschen Datierung einer bedeutenden Seeschlacht und des Zusammenhangs, in dem sie erwähnt wird, die Frage stellen, ob sich der Autor bei der Datierung der gesamten Seereise geirrt habe. Am 16. Juni 1771, so schreibt er, habe sein Geschwader auf der Reede von Livorno einige der russischen Kriegsschiffe angetroffen, die in der Folge, am 7. Juli 1771, vor Tschesme die türkische Flotte vernichtet hätten.[77] Allerdings fand die Seeschlacht bei Tschesme am 5./6. Juli 1770 statt. Begann also Rechterens Seereise tatsächlich im November 1770, wie er sagt, und nicht schon im November 1769? Die nachfolgend beschriebenen Umstände zeigen, dass seine Reise wirklich im Spätherbst 1770 begann, er die russischen Schiffe im Juni 1771 sah, sich aber bei der Datierung der Seeschlacht irrte. Solche Irrtümer sind bei Erinnerungen, die in größerem zeitlichen Abstand zu den dargestellten Ereignissen und vielleicht ohne genaue Überprüfung des Niedergeschriebenen zu Papier gebracht wurden, nicht auszuschließen.

Die niederländische Marine beteiligte sich im 18. Jahrhundert noch an den Patrouillenfahrten europäischer Seemächte im Mittelmeer, die einerseits der Unterdrückung der Piraterie, zumal an den nordafrikanischen Küsten, andererseits der Diplomatie dienten, wobei Staatsgeschenke mit den Herrschern der Barbareskenstaaten ausgetauscht wurden. Dies galt, obwohl die Flotte in der zweiten Hälfte des 18. Jahrhunderts nur noch ein Schatten ihres früheren bedeutenden Selbst war: die Zahl der Schiffe war stark reduziert worden, die Schiffe selbst waren schlecht gewartet und ausgerüstet, viele Offiziere inkompetent, die Mannschaften ungenügend ausgebildet.[78] Im Frühjahr 1770 beschlossen die Generalstaaten aber angesichts andauernder Konflikte mit den Barbareskenfürsten, ein Geschwader von sechs Linienschiffen, nicht, wie zuvor, bloß von Fregatten auszurüsten und ins Mittelmeer zu entsenden, um politisch Eindruck

places of the events he relates, and to name the people he met and the places he saw completely and correctly, especially when these were of some importance. The narrative follows the chronological sequence of events without any previews or flashbacks. There is no reason to question the sequence of events as given here as there are no contradictions. But as the author gives us a wrong date for an important naval battle the dates given for the voyage as a whole may appear dubious. On June 16th, 1771, so he tells us, the Dutch "escadre" (squadron) he travelled with had met, in the roadstead of Leghorn, some of the Russian battleships which had later destroyed the Turkish fleet at Cesme on July 7th, 1771.[77] But the battle of Cesme actually took place on July 5/6, 1770; did, therefore, Rechteren's voyage really start in November of 1770 as he states or rather in November of 1769? The circumstances related in the paragraph below will show that Rechteren's voyage really started in the late fall of 1770, that he saw the Russian ships on the date that he tells us, but made a mistake about the date of the battle. Such errors cannot be precluded in a text written about 20 years after the event and maybe without a very intensive check on mistakes in the draft.

Throughout the 18th century, the Dutch navy still joined the other European naval powers in their patrols of the Mediterranean; the objectives of these were the suppression of piracy, especially on the North African coasts, as well as diplomacy, which mostly meant the exchange of official gifts with the rulers of the Barbary states. This was kept up even though the Dutch fleet had become a mere shadow of its impressive former self: the number of ships had been much reduced, the ships themselves were badly kept up and equipped, many officers were incompetent, most crews poorly trained.[78] But in the spring of 1770, the Dutch government – in view of continuing conflicts with the Barbary princes – decided to raise a squadron of six ships-of-the-line, not merely frigates, as before, and dispatch it to the Mediterranean in order to make a show of

---

77. Mskr., S. 30.

78. Dazu van der Horst, Kinckel, S. 171 – 174; zur unzureichenden Ausrüstung und Bemannung der Schiffe s. Mskr., S. 2 (kein Schiff führt die an sich mögliche Zahl von Geschützen; die Mannschaft von Rechterens Schiff ist für große Gefechte zu schwach, dazu u. Anm. 92). Mskr., S. 3, berichtet z.B. von dänischen Schiffen, die einen Kriegszug gegen Algier unternahmen; s. auch Mskr., S. 44.

77. Mscr., p. 30.

78. See van der Horst, Kinckel, p. 171 – 174; the poor equipment and manning of the ships is evident in mscr., p.2 (no ship has the number of guns it is built for, the crew is too small for major battles; see below fn. 92); mscr., p. 3, mentions Danish ships on an expedition against Algiers; see also mscr., p. 44.

strength.[79] The squadron's itinerary and ports of call seem to indicate that the expedition was meant to let not just the Barbary pirates, but also the European powers know that the Dutch navy was still to be reckoned with. It was this expedition, then, that Rechteren joined – indubitably in 1770. The ships left port on different dates because they belonged to two or three of the several Dutch admiralties of the time and later met at pre-ordained places in the Mediterranean.[80]

Rechteren gives a detailed description of the voyage with all the ports of call and the dates of these calls, he also reports on encountering other naval squadrons, both Dutch and foreign, with the place and date of these encounters.[81] He also mentions quite a few coastal cities which his squadron passed without stopping and doesn't forget to tell about the traditional portolanos, naval handbooks describing these coastlines and harbours.[82] Rechteren gives us rather brief and unemotional accounts of storms at sea,[83] and mentions the observation of marine animals only a few times; this topic is treated more extensively in the memoirs of other contemporary witnesses.[84] At least, his narrative can be quite lively then, e.g. in a section where he describes their passage through the straits of Gibraltar, sailing at a remarkably high speed when "it was quite a beautiful spectacle to observe the huge number of dolphins, tunas, and 'brownfish' accompanying our ship which were rolling about as if they regarded our ship as an especially large fish which they wanted to show their respect to."[85] But he hardly goes into the uncomfortable

---

79. That a mere show of strength and no serious military action against the Barbary pirates was intended is evidenced by the report in mscr., p. 34, where Rechteren's ship fires once (!) on the city of Algiers and then immediately turns back. The pirates' actions, by the way, were just as unimpressive.

80. Van der Horst, Kinckel, p. 176, mentions the ship "Zierikzee" just like mscr., p. 36 f., does (the spelling is wrong in the mscr.!); it had left the Netherlands in January 1771. Rechteren's text also talks of several admiralties.

81. See mscr., p. 28, 36, 50 etc.

82. Mscr., p. 31 or 41; for the portolanos whose tradition goes back to the Middle Ages see LexMA, vol. VII, col. 122 ff.

83. Cf. mscr., p.3, where he barely mentions "a lot of stormy weather" in the bay of Biscay, or p. 26 where he describes the appropriate sailor's reaction to heavy storms, the taking in of reefs etc. and just incidentally reports the fact that his squadron traversed an archipelago in severe weather which was certainly quite dangerous.

84. Cf., e.g., the memoirs of Georg Flohr who went to America in the same ship as Rechteren; Tröss, Regiment, p. 117.

85. Mscr., p. 42; "brownfish" means the smallest kind of dolphins.

auf das beengte und wenig komfortable Leben an Bord ein, das bei der Überfahrt nach Amerika so viele bittere Kommentare anderer Zeitzeugen hervorrief.[86] So hört man bei ihm auch nichts über Eintönigkeit der Verpflegung und Mangel an Trinkwasser. Rechterens Mittelmeerreise war allerdings dadurch gekennzeichnet, dass der Verband viele Häfen anlief, sodass sich öfters Gelegenheit zu kürzeren Landgängen und sogar größeren, mehrtägigen Ausflügen ergab. Wahrscheinlich wurden auch frische Lebensmittel eingekauft – auch wenn Rechteren das nicht ausdrücklich erwähnt, vielmehr ein- oder zweimal von niederländischen Proviantschiffen berichtet, die sein Verband in südlichen Häfen traf, die jedoch nur der Versorgung der „Escadre" mit dauerhaft haltbaren Lebensmitteln gedient haben können[87] –, sodass räumliche Enge, Langeweile und Verpflegungsmängel wohl weniger deutlich hervortraten als bei der 70-tägigen Überfahrt nach Amerika. Die niederländische Marine stand im Übrigen in dem Ruf, auf gute Ordnung und Sauberkeit auf ihren Schiffen zu halten,[88] sodass die erwähnten Probleme vielleicht auch deswegen weniger bemerkbar waren. Dass man beim Anlaufen von Häfen frisches Wasser beschaffte, berichtet der Verfasser gleich bei der Ankunft in Spanien, der ersten Station der Mittelmeerreise. Dabei fällt es Rechteren auf – eine für seine Memoiren fast typische Bemerkung zu Dingen, die ihm von seinen mitteleuropäischen Erfahrungen her ungewöhnlich erschienen –, dass das Schöpfwerk am Brunnen keine ledernen oder hölzernen Gefäße hatte, sondern irdene Töpfe.[89] Auf der Mittelmeerreise hören wir auch direkt nichts vom Auftreten des gefürchteten Skorbuts, der auf der Reise nach Amerika so viele der transportierten Soldaten befiel.[90] Allerdings berichtet Rechteren, dass etwa sechs Monate nach Beginn der Reise das Linienschiff „Rotterdam" mit 150 Kranken in Neapel zurückgelassen wurde; wir wissen aber nicht, ob es sich hier um Kranke des ganzen Geschwaders oder nur der „Rotterdam" handelte, ebenso wenig, ob sie an Skorbut erkrankt waren.[91]

living conditions on board the ship which caused many bitter commentaries of other contemporary travellers.[86] We don't hear anything about monotonous food, lack of drinking water, or cramped accommodations. Rechteren's voyage in the Mediterranean was characterised by the fact that his squadron called at many ports giving the crew numerous chances to go ashore for shorter or even longer excursions lasting several days. We may assume that fresh food was bought then, too. True, Rechteren does not explicitly mention that, but rather tells about meeting Dutch supply ships in these southern ports; these, however, can only have supplied the squadron with non-perishable foods.[87] Such diversions may have contributed to the fact that cramped conditions, monotony, and defects in the provisioning were a lot less conspicuous on this voyage than on the 70-day trip to America. The Dutch navy was known for keeping good order and cleanliness on board of its ships;[88] this may also have contributed to make the problems mentioned above less noticeable. That ships replenished their water supply at most ports of call is something that the author informs us about right after their arrival in Spain at their first port of call. Rechteren was struck by the fact that the bucket elevator at the well did not have leather or wooden buckets, but earthen pots instead.[89] This remark is typical for Rechteren's way of observing things which struck him as unusual from his central European background. In the course of the voyage in the Mediterranean no mention is made of the dreaded scurvy either which befell many of the soldiers transported to America.[90] Rechteren, it is true, lets us know that, six months after the beginning of the voyage, the ship-of-the-line "Rotterdam" was left behind in Naples with 150 sick persons on board, but we can't tell whether these were crew members of the "Rotterdam" only or men from the whole squadron and whether they were suffering from scurvy.[91]

---

86. Zur räumlichen Enge etwa Flohr, in: Tröss, Regiment, S. 116 – 120, oder – sehr lebhaft – die Memoiren von Ludwig von Closen (ebenfalls Passagier auf Rechterens Transportschiff), in: Acomb, Journal, S. 10 f.

87. S. Mskr. S. 31 und 35. Diese Nachschubschiffe kamen aus den Niederlanden und können, da es ja noch keine Kühlung oder Einfrieren von Lebensmitteln gab, nur Pökelfleisch, Mehl, Bier u.ä. gebracht haben.

88. So z.B. Israel, Dutch Republic, S. 679. Dies galt wohl trotz der von van der Horst (s. o. Anm. 70) beschriebenen Wartungsmängel im späteren 18. Jahrhundert.

89. Mskr., S. 5.

90. Dazu auch u. S. 33.

91. S. Mskr. S. 25; die „Rotterdam" gehörte anfänglich nicht zu Rechterens Geschwader; s. Mskr. S. 2.

---

86. For cramped conditions see Flohr's complaints, in: Tröss, Regiment, p. 116 – 120, or, even more lively L. von Closen's (who travelled in Rechteren's ship) in: Acomb, Journal, p. 10 f.

87. Cf. mscr., p. 31 or 35. These supply ships came straight from the Netherlands and can only have brought salted meat, flour, beer etc. as there was no refrigeration or freezing of fresh foods then.

88. See Israel, Dutch Republic, p. 679; this was probably true even then in spite of the poor maintenance of the ships towards the end of the 18th century (cf. above fn. 78).

89. Mscr., p. 5.

90. See below, p. 33.

91. See mscr., p. 25; the "Rotterdam" wasn't one of the three ships which had sailed in Nov. 1770 (cf. mscr., p.2).

Manches spricht dafür, dass sich, was das Fehlen von Klagen über räumliche Beengtheit angeht, die Größe des Linienschiffs „Nassau", auf dem Rechteren während seiner Mittelmeerreise als Seekadett diente, als Erklärung dienen kann; das Schiff dürfte über 65 Meter lang gewesen sein und neben dem offenen Hauptdeck zwei darunter liegende, geschlossene Artilleriedecks gehabt haben; seine Verdrängung belief sich vielleicht auf 2.000 Tonnen. Auf der Reise waren 360 Mann Besatzung an Bord.[92] Das bedeutet übrigens, dass die „Nassau" kaum für größere Gefechte ausgerüstet war, denn dazu wäre eine deutlich größere Besatzung nötig gewesen.[93] Demgegenüber war „La Comtesse de Noailles", auf der Rechteren nach Amerika fuhr,[94] fast als Nussschale zu bezeichnen; das Schiff hatte eine Länge von ca. 35, eine Breite von ca. 9 Metern und war mit rund 300 Tonnen vermessen; jedoch wurden auf ihm 350 Soldaten transportiert, und zusätzlich war eine Stammbesatzung von ca. 50 Mann an Bord.[95] Die 70-tägige Reise über den Atlantik forderte aufgrund der mangelhaften Ernährung und der Enge an Bord neun Todesopfer bei dem auf drei solcher Schiffe verteilten Regiment „Royal Deux-Ponts" und rief bei der Hälfte der Soldaten – nicht aber bei den Offizieren – eine Skorbuterkrankung hervor.[96] Zwar war die Menge der ausgegebenen Fleisch-, Zwieback- und Suppenrationen ausreichend, doch fehlten frisches Gemüse und Obst völlig, und das Fleisch war sehr stark gesalzen; zudem klagten die Soldaten über die zwar qualitativ sehr guten, von der Menge her aber unzureichenden Getränkerationen: 1 ½ Schoppen Wein, d.h. etwa 0,75 Liter, ersatzweise sogar nur ¼ Schoppen Branntwein, mussten zusammen mit einem halben Schoppen schlechten Wassers und einer Portion noch schlechterer Suppe – wenn man diese zu den Getränken rechnen will – für den Tag ausreichen.[97]

The lack of complaints about cramped conditions on board may also be explained by the size of the ship-of-the-line "Nassau" where Rechteren served as a cadet on his voyage in the Mediterranean; the ship probably had an overall length of more than 65 meters (about 210 feet), two closed artillery decks under the open main deck and a displacement of about 2.000 tons; it carried 360 officers and crewmen.[92] This incidentally shows us that the "Nassau" wasn't manned for major battles as a much larger crew would have been needed for that.[93] In contrast, the "Comtesse de Noailles", Rechteren's transport on the voyage to America,[94] could be called a mere tub; the ship had an overall length of about 35 meters (115 feet), a width of about 9 meters (30 feet), and a displacement of ca. 300 tons; yet, 350 soldiers were taken to America on it and in addition to them, there was a regular crew of almost 50 men on board.[95] Because of the poor food and the cramped conditions on board, the 70-day voyage across the Atlantic claimed the lives of nine soldiers of the "Royal Deux-Ponts" regiment which were distributed on three such ships and caused scurvy in almost half of the soldiers – not with the officers, however.[96] The meat, hard tack, and soup rations were sufficient, but fresh vegetables and fruit were completely lacking and the meat was very heavily salted. Most of all, the soldiers complained about the insufficient quantity of the drink rations even if they praised the quality of the wine and brandy: they had to make do with 1 ½ "Schoppen" of wine (about ¾ of a litre/quart), sometimes replaced by only ¼ "Schoppen" of brandy, plus ½ "Schoppen" of bad water, and a portion of rather dubious soup – if that is included in the drinks – for the whole day.[97]

---

92. Nach Mskr., S. 2, hatte die „Nassau" 70 Stückpforten, führte aber nur 60 Geschütze. Nach Mskr., S. 3, waren 10 Offiziere und Kadetten sowie 350 Mann Besatzung an Bord. Die Länge des Schiffs ist hier nur geschätzt.

93. Dazu http://de.wikipedia.org/wiki/Rangeinteilung_der_Kriegsschiffe (22.04.2014). Danach war die „Nassau" ein Linienschiff 3. Ranges von ca. 1.300 – 2.000 Tonnen und 64 – 80 Kanonen; die übliche Besatzungsstärke solcher Schiffe betrug 490 – 720 Mann.

94. Mskr., S. 63.

95. Dazu Selig, German Allies, 2. Teil, S. 48.

96. Vgl. Troess, Regiment, S. 44. Die Offiziere waren wohl besser über die Gefahren des Skorbuts und über die Gegenmittel (Vitamin C-reiche Früchte) informiert, s. Acomb, Journal, S. 6 u. 10.

97. Die Mengenangaben nach Flohrs Bericht, in: Troess, Regiment, S. 119 f.; ein Schoppen dürfte im 18. Jahrhundert in Deutschland meist mit ca. 0,5 Liter anzusetzen sein, vgl. http://de.wikipedia.org/wiki/Schoppen (29.07.2014).

---

92. According to mscr., p. 2 f., the "Nassau" had 70 gunports, but only 60 guns, 10 officers and cadets and a crew of approximately 350 men. The ship's length could only be estimated here.

93. Cf. http://de.wikipedia.org/wiki/Rangeinteilung_der_Kriegsschiffe (22.04.2014). According to this, the "Nassau" would have been a ship-of-the-line of the third rank, displacing about 1.400 – 2.000 tons and armed with 64 – 80 guns; the usual crew size would have been 490 – 720 men.

94. Mscr., p. 63.

95. See Selig, German Allies, part 2, p. 48.

96. Cf. Tröss, Regiment, p. 44, or Acomb, Journal, p. 6 and 10: The officers may have had better information about the disease and how to prevent it (eating fruit rich in vitamin C).

97. The amounts are taken from Tröss, Regiment, p. 119 f. In the 18th century, a "Schoppen" would have been equal to about ½ litre (approx. 1 pint), cf. http://de.wikipedia.org/wiki/Schoppen (29.07.2014).

It is interesting to observe how differently conditions were described by the three witnesses whose memoirs we are comparing: Georg Daniel Flohr[98] who went to America as a simple infantryman gives us some detailed information about the food and drink rations, also about the very unpopular hammocks – two men had to use one, sleeping in turns – and the large number of men who had to sleep on the floorboards; he vividly and accusingly reports on the effects of the scurvy and makes the reader familiar with the experience of severe storms at sea and the amazement of seeing unheard-of marine animals.[99] Baron Ludwig von Closen,[100] one of General Rochambeau's, the commander-in-chief's, aides-de-camp and staff officer, mostly complains about the cramped living conditions on board which demanded that 22 persons eat together at one table in a cabin only 5 meters (17 feet) long, 4 meters (14 feet) wide and no more than 1,3 meters (4 feet!) high; he very much dislikes the tight seating, the noise and the smells of the many people and dogs (!) in there. He had to sleep in a very narrow bed in an ever narrower cabin together with nine other men, some of whom slept in hammocks.[101] On the other hand, food and drink were plentiful for the officers and they even had fresh eggs and milk as there were hens and cows on board. He clearly understood that the soldiers suffered from heat, extremely cramped living conditions, bad drinking water and monotonous food and he had even expected more people to get sick of scurvy than actually did – he thought that a third of the soldiers were afflicted with it.[102] The large number of scurvy cases in the fleet did not evade Rechteren either, of course, but he summed up his impressions in three rather dry sentences: "After a voyage of 70 days, the fleet arrived at Newport in Rhode Island on July 12th, 1780. There were many cases of scurvy, and

---

98. Georg Daniel Flohr was born in Sarnstall close to Annweiler in the Palatinate in 1756, joined the Royal Deux-Ponts regiment in 1776; after 8 years' service, he went to Strasbourg, then to Paris and emigrated to the U.S. around 1798. He died in Wytheville, VA, in 1826, having served that community as a Lutheran pastor; cf. Selig, German Allies, part 2, p. 47 with fn. 19.

99. See Tröss, Regiment, p. 117 and 119 on storms, p. 120 on sleeping accommodation on board, p. 124 and 126 on scurvy.

100. Ludwig, baron of Closen, born 1752 or 1755 in Monheim close to Worms, joined the Royal Deux-Ponts regiment as a "seconde-lieutenant", in 1780; he became Rochambeau's aide-de-camp, was a major general by 1792, and served as sous-prefect of the département Rhin-et-Moselle in 1806; he left French services in 1813 and died in Mannheim in 1830; see Acomb, Journal, p. XXII – XXXV.

101. Loc. cit., p. 10.

102. On the differences in the food and drink of officers and men and the number of scurvy cases in the fleet, see Acomb, Journal, p. 26.

immer oben auf dem Schiff in freier Luft und Bewegung, und mäßig im Essen ist."[103]

Beim Auslaufen aus dem französischen Kriegshafen Brest hatte das Schiff, auf dem unsere drei Zeitzeugen reisten, eine Havarie, und zwar kollidierte die „Comtesse de Noailles" mit einem der großen Linienschiffe, die den Konvoi über den Atlantik begleiten sollten, der „Conquérant". Zwei der drei Memoiren berichten darüber, jedoch mit deutlichen Unterschieden. Flohrs Text liegt bisher noch nicht vollständig ediert vor; anscheinend hat er aber den Vorfall gar nicht erwähnt.[104] Closens Erinnerungen daran sind etwas ausführlicher als die Rechterens, jedoch weniger genau; Closen teilt zwar – in ziemlich spöttischem Ton – mit, dass sein Schiff aufgrund von fehlerhaften Anweisungen der Führung die „Conquérant" rammte, aber allein Rechteren benennt das ursprüngliche Problem, dass nämlich das Schiff – von der Schiffsführung unbeachtet – an einem schwimmenden Ponton festgemacht war und das Festmachtau, als das Schiff Fahrt aufgenommen hatte, unter Lebensgefahr für alle an Deck gekappt werden musste. Dann kann er deutlicher als Closen die Kommandos des Kapitäns – dem er die Schuld an der Havarie gibt – und des 2. Offiziers beschreiben; dass größere Schäden verhindert wurden, schreibt er den schnellen Ankerkommandos des 2. Offiziers zu. Beide befürchteten, dass sie wegen dieses Unfalls zurückgelassen würden, weil ihr Schiff ohne Begleitung eines Kriegsschiffs nicht auf die Reise gehen werde, die Konvoischiffe aber nicht auf ein einziges Transportschiff warten würden. Beide berichten – Closen etwas genauer – über die überraschend schnelle Reparatur innerhalb von 24 Stunden. Closen zählt auch etwas ausführlicher die Tage auf, die man anschließend noch auf guten Wind warten musste.[105] Die Beschreibung des Vorfalls lässt erkennen, dass Rechterens Urteil in seemännischen Dingen genauer war; es hatte schon auf der Mittelmeerreise Vorfälle gegeben, bei denen er sich ein Urteil über seemännische Fragen erlaubte;[106] es ist anzunehmen, dass er sich selbst in erheblichem Maße als Seemann sah und über manche Erscheinungen des Bordlebens deshalb weniger aussagte, weil sie ihm selbstverständlich waren.

---

103. Mskr., S. 68.
104. Dazu Tröss, Regiment, S. 115 f.; Selig, German Allies, Teil II, S. 47 f.
105. Vgl. Mskr., S. 63 – 65, und Acomb, Journal, S. 7 – 10.
106. Dazu bes. Mskr., S. 51, wo er einen ähnlichen Vorfall auf der Reede von Cowes beschreibt und auch einen höheren Offizier und dessen Kommandos negativ beurteilt. Mskr., S. 81 eine weitere ähnliche Havarie bei dem vergeblichen Unternehmen, die Truppen per Schiff von Rhode Island nach Virginia zu bringen.

most of them in the German regiment. The reason for this may be that the French soldiers are mostly on deck, move about in fresh air and are moderate in their food intake."[103]

When leaving the French naval port of Brest the ship that our three witnesses travelled on had an accident; the "Comtesse de Noailles" collided with the "Conquérant", one of the big ships-of-the-line which were meant to convoy the transport ships across the Atlantic. Two of our three memoirs mention it, but with marked differences. Flohr's memoirs have not been edited completely so far, but it seems that he didn't report the incident at all.[104] Closen's memoirs are somewhat longer on this point than Rechteren's, but less precise; Closen tells us – in a rather sneering tone – that his ship rammed the "Conquérant" because of the incompetent orders given by its commander, but it is only Rechteren who informs us about the basic mistake made by that officer: the "Comtesse de Noailles" had been moored to a floating wooden platform which the commander overlooked and after the ship had started to move under sail the rope with which it was moored had to be cut quickly, putting the life of everyone on deck at that time in jeopardy. Rechteren describes the commands given by the ship's captain – whom he blames for the accident – and of the second officer more clearly than Closen; he ascribes the fact that major damage could be averted to the second officer's rapid order to drop anchor. Both Rechteren and Closen tell us about being afraid that they would be left behind because of this accident as their ship would not go on its voyage without being escorted by a man-of-war, but the battleships would not wait for just one transport ship. Both authors report on the surprisingly fast repair work done on their ship which was completed within 24 hours. In this and in describing the days spent waiting for a fair wind Closen is somewhat more detailed than Rechteren.[105] The description of the accident lets us see that Rechteren's assessment of nautical matters was more precise; there had been incidents in the course of his voyage in the Mediterranean where he had ventured some decided opinions on nautical matters.[106] We may assume that Rechteren saw himself mostly as a sailor at that time, and that may also be why he doesn't tell us more

---

103. Mscr., p. 68.
104. See Tröss, Regiment, p. 115 f., Selig, German Allies, part 2, p. 47 f.
105. Cf. mscr., p. 63, and Acomb, Journal, p. 7 – 10.
106. Mscr., p. 51, describes a similar incident in Cowes roadstead where he also blames a ship's officer; mscr., p. 81, tells of another similar incident in connection with the futile attempt to take troops from Rhode Island to Virginia by ship.

Dass seemännische Dinge Rechteren beschäftigten, zeigt im ersten Teil der Memoiren sein Interesse an den tragischen Unfällen von Seeleuten, die bei Arbeiten an Deck oder in der Takelage über Bord gingen, und die, zumal bei schneller Fahrt des Schiffes, bewegter See und schlechter Sicht kaum gerettet werden konnten. Er verteidigt die niederländische Marine, der damals vorgeworfen wurde, in solchen Fällen besonders wenig Hilfsbereitschaft zu zeigen, gegen solche Vorwürfe. Sehr interessant ist, dass er dabei auf religiöse Einstellungen zu sprechen kommt, die im 18. Jahrhundert wohl als typisch niederländisch galten, nämlich den Glauben an die Prädestination, wonach das Schicksal der Menschen von Gott vorherbestimmt sei, weswegen man nicht eingreifen müsse. Die Holländer seien darin den Türken [gemeint: den Moslems] ähnlich. Dagegen wendet Rechteren sich entschieden; er führt zu Recht praktische seemännische Probleme als Begründung dafür an, dass den verunglückten Seeleuten meist nicht geholfen werden konnte.[107] Intensiver als es dem heutigen Leser nötig erscheinen dürfte, berichtet Rechteren über Protokollfragen im Seeverkehr, speziell über die korrekte Zahl von Salutschüssen beim Anlaufen eines Hafens und deren Erwiderung. Offensichtlich war ihm das wichtig, aber den heutigen Leser dürfte die häufige Wiederholung von Passagen wie „der Vicekönig wurde mit 15 und die Stadt mit 9 Schüssen salutiert, worauf sie mit 13 und 7 dankten" eher irritieren.[108] Häufig spricht er auch davon, dass Schiffe zum Einlaufen in einen Hafen eine Erlaubnis, genannt „Pratica", einholen mussten, und dass diese auch verweigert werden konnte; dann blieb das Schiff in Quarantäne auf der Reede außerhalb des Hafens.[109]

Sehr bezeichnend für Rechterens Erzählstil ist, dass er eine Anekdote zu dem erwähnten Vorfall im Hafen von Brest anhängt, wonach der Graf de Noailles in einer Gesellschaft gewitzelt habe, dass seine Frau (die Comtesse de Noailles) den „Conquérant" habe vergewaltigen wollen.[110] Rechteren schätzt nämlich Anekdoten, Zitate aus der klassischen Antike oder Vergleiche mit Vorfällen aus der neuzeitlichen Geschichte zur Erläuterung selbst erlebter Vorgänge oder Szenen, auch besonders ungewöhnliche und erstaunliche Phänomene, die ihm offensichtlich nach vielen Jahren noch

explicitly about some aspects on life aboard a ship; they were just more obvious to him than to others.

That nautical matters were something that Rechteren occupied a lot can be seen from the interest he takes in the tragic accidents of sailors who fell overboard while working on deck or in the rigging and who could hardly ever be saved, especially when the ship was moving fast, the sea was rough or the visibility was bad. He defends the Dutch navy which was reproached at that time of being especially callous in such cases against these accusations. It is particularly interesting for us to see that he then goes into some religious attitudes which must have been considered to be typically Dutch in the 18th century, i.e. the idea of predestination; according to this, the fate of all humans was predestined by god and therefore it was unnecessary to try to help in such accidents. The Dutch supposedly resembled the Turks (i.e. the Muslims) in this respect. Rechteren resolutely rejects this opinion and is certainly right with invoking practical nautical problems as reasons for the fact that, in such accidents, sailors could not be saved.[107] Rechteren informs us much more intensively than most present-day readers would think necessary about questions of nautical etiquette, particularly about the correct number of salute guns to be fired when calling at a port and the correct number of answering shots. Evidently, this was a question of great interest to him, but today's readers might be rather vexed by the frequent repetition of phrases like this: "The viceroy was saluted with 15 guns and the city with 9 whereupon they replied with 13 and seven guns."[108] He often tells about the necessity to get a permission named "pratica" to call at a port; if it wasn't given, the ship had to stay quarantined in the roadstead outside the harbour.[109]

It is quite characteristic of Rechteren's narrative style that he adds an anecdote to the incident in Brest harbour according to which the count of Noailles had joked at a party that his wife (the comtesse de Noailles) had tried to rape the "Conquérant".[110] Rechteren highly esteems anecdotes, quotations from classical antiquity, and comparisons with incidents of modern history in order to further elucidate

---

107. S. Mskr., S. 15 f., 31.
108. Zitat zum Einlaufen in Cágliari/Sardinien, s. Mskr., S. 28; Erläuterung zum Usus Mskr., S. 17; u. ö.
109. Ausführliche Erklärung zur Pratica Mskr., S. 32; Erwähnung auch S. 34 u. ö.
110. Mskr., S. 65.

107. See mscr., p. 15 f., 31.
108. When his ship called at Cágliari/Sardinia, mscr., p. 28; an explanation given for the idea behind it, mscr., p. 17 et al.
109. Long explanation of the "pratica" in mscr., p. 32; also mentioned p. 34 et al.
110. Mscr., p. 65.

klar und lebhaft vor Augen stehen. Dazu weiter unten andere Beispiele.

Deutlich unterscheiden sich die drei Memoiren beim Bericht über den Fortgang der Seereise nach Amerika. Closen, der mit dem Kapitän und den Offizieren des Schiffs sicherlich täglich sprach, ist am ausführlichsten, da er fast zu jedem Tag die bis dahin erreichte geographische Länge und Breite nennt; Flohr ist nicht ganz so gut informiert, teilt aber auch mehrfach mit, wo man sich an welchem Tag befand.[111] Rechteren verzichtet gänzlich auf solche Angaben; die gesamte Seereise nimmt bei ihm nicht mehr als sieben Manuskriptseiten (etwa zwei Druckseiten) ein,[112] wovon zwei besondere Vorfälle und eine Beschreibung der Eigenarten des Kapitäns den meisten Raum einnehmen. Auch auf der Mittelmeerreise nannte er zwar alle angelaufenen Häfen, aber fast nie die Tagespositionen des Schiffs. Der erste der Vorfälle auf der Amerikareise war die oben erwähnte Havarie zu Beginn, der zweite die Begegnung mit einem englischen Flottenverband in der Höhe der Bermudas. Hier beschreibt Closen eingehend die Manöver der beiden Flottenverbände, obwohl sich letztlich keine Seeschlacht daraus entwickelte; auch Flohr ist relativ ausführlich.[113] Rechterens Darstellung ist auch hier der kürzeste, doch erwähnt er zumindest den einzigen Schusswechsel als spektakuläre Aktion; man hört bei ihm mehr als bei den beiden anderen von der Missstimmung unter den Offizieren, weil man dem englischen Verband überlegen war und gute Beute hätte machen können. Deswegen solle – und dies Wortspiel ist nur bei Rechteren überliefert – der Kommandant der Flotte zukünftig statt de Ternay „terni", d.h. blind, trüb heißen. Doch fügt er sofort an, dass de Ternay von Rochambeau gelobt wurde, weil es seine Aufgabe war, die Truppe sicher nach Amerika zu bringen und Risiken aus dem Wege zu gehen.[114] Dies wird auch von Closen so bestätigt, ohne dass er das Wortspiel erwähnt. Auffällig ist hier Rechterens Vorliebe nicht nur für Anekdoten, sondern auch für lehrhafte Bemerkungen, diesmal aus der Zeitgeschichte. Er schließt nämlich gleich danach an, dass zwei Jahre danach eine Seeschlacht in ähnlicher Konstellation für die Franzosen unglücklich endete, wobei fünf Linienschiffe, darunter die „Ville de Paris" von 104 Kanonen,

scenes or events at which he had been present; he also likes to mention especially unusual or surprising phenomena which he evidently remembers very clearly and vividly many years afterwards. More examples will follow.

The three memoirs differ very clearly in the way they report about the progress of the voyage to America. Closen who certainly had daily conversations with the captain and officers of the ship is the most detailed one as he gives us the exact geographical position reached every day; Flohr wasn't quite as well informed, but also often reports on this point.[111] Rechteren almost completely does without such information; the whole voyage only covers seven manuscript pages (maybe two pages in print);[112] he concentrates on two particular events and the ship's captain's idiosyncrasies. When describing the Mediterranean voyage he named every port of call, but hardly ever the geographical position reached on any given day. The first event on the voyage to America was the accident at its very beginning, the second one was meeting a British naval squadron off the Bermuda islands. Closen goes into a very detailed description of the two fleets' manoeuvres even though no naval battle developed out of this; Flohr is quite exhaustive as well.[113] Rechteren's report is the shortest by far in this case, too, but he also mentions the one exchange of shots which occurred as the only notable action. More than the other two he reports about the angry mood among the officers as the French squadron was superior to the British one and much booty could have been taken. Because of his failure to attack the fleet commander, de Ternay, should be called "terni" (blind, dull) from now on – only Rechteren relates this pun. But he immediately adds that Rochambeau praised de Ternay because it was his job to take the army units safely to America and to avoid any risks.[114] This is confirmed by Closen, but he does not know about the pun. What is conspicuous again is Rechteren's predilection for anecdotes or, in this case, an educational remark taken from contemporary history: he goes on to tell us about a naval battle in a very similar constellation which was fought two years later and which ended in defeat for the French who lost five ships-of-the-line, among them the

---

111. Dazu Acomb, Journal, z.B. S. 11 – 13, 18 f.; Tröss, Regiment, S. 116 f.
112. Mskr., S. 63 – 70.
113. Acomb, Journal, S. 21 – 23; Tröss, Regiment, S. 121 f.
114. Mskr., S. 66 f.

111. See, e.g., Acomb, Journal, p. 11 – 13, 18 f. et al.; Tröss, Regiment, p. 116 f.
112. Mscr., p. 63 – 70.
113. Acomb, Journal, p. 21 – 23; Tröss, Regiment, p. 121 f.
114. Mscr., p. 66 f.

den Engländern in die Hände fielen.[115] Dies ist den anderen beiden Autoren nicht bekannt.

Neben Anekdoten, von denen bereits einige erwähnt wurden, schätzte Rechteren die Verbindung von eigenen Beobachtungen mit historischen Parallelen oder auch Zitaten aus klassischen Autoren.

So beschreibt er, wie Washington und Rochambeau mit ihrer Entourage Stellungen bei New York rekognoszierten und diese Gruppe dann von den Engländern beschossen wurde. Zwar kam niemand dabei zu Schaden, doch bemerkte Rechteren, dass Washington trotz seines großen persönlichen Muts sich aus Vorsichtsgrundsätzen stets so stellte, dass er eine schmale Front bot. Als ein solches Verhalten rechtfertigende historische Parallele nennt er das Schicksal des französischen Marschalls Turenne, der am 27. Juli 1675 vor der Schlacht von Sasbach beim Rekognoszieren des Geländes erschossen wurde.[116] Nach der lebhaften Beschreibung eines Hurrikans, der das Lager der Truppen zerstörte, sodass Baracken gebaut und leer stehende Häuser zu ihrer Unterbringung genutzt wurden, spricht Rechteren ein Phänomen an, das viele europäische Teilnehmer des Feldzugs beschäftigte, dass nämlich „das Eigenthum hier so heilig gehalten wurde, dass Washington's Armee im Sommer nie anders als unter Zelten und im Winter in Baraquen wohnte".[117] Hierzu fällt Rechteren der germanische König Ariovist ein, der Caesar sagen ließ, dass seine tapferen Krieger seit 14 Jahren nie unter ein festes Dach gekommen seien, und fügt das wörtliche Zitat aus „De bello Gallico" an. Bei dieser historischen Parallele lässt er es bewenden. Anders viele andere Feldzugsteilnehmer, die erhebliche Anpassungsprobleme an die amerikanischen Grundsätze in Betreff des Eigentums hatten. So beschwerte sich ein französischer Offizier darüber, dass – anders als in Europa – Truppen auf dem Marsch keineswegs Pferde, Wagen und anderes requirieren oder Soldaten zur Unterbringung über Nacht auf Privatunterkünfte verteilen könnten, wobei der Ortsgendarm in Europa in der Lage sei, eventuelle Schwierigkeiten mit den Hauseigentümern zu regeln. Hier sei es aber so, dass die Menschen frei seien und ein Hauseigentümer, dem das Gesicht eines Soldaten nicht passe, die Unterkunft verweigern könne; die Worte „I don't want to" seien dann das Ende

104-gun "Ville de Paris" which was taken by the British.[115] Our other two memoir authors don't know about this.

Next to anecdotes – some of which have already been presented – Rechteren had a predilection for illustrating his own observations with historical parallels or quotations from the classics. Thus he tells us how Washington and Rochambeau, with their entourage, reconnoitred positions around New York City and how this group of people then came under British fire. Nobody was hurt, but our narrator remarks on the fact that Washington – in spite of his great valour which Rechteren does not put into doubt – always followed caution and sought to present a narrow profile. Rechteren justifies this behaviour by informing the reader about the fate of the famous French marshal Turenne who was killed by a cannonball on July 27th, 1675, when reconnoitring the battlefield before the battle of Sasbach.[116] After giving us a lively description of a hurricane which destroyed the army camp so that barracks had to be built and empty houses had to be used to put up the troops, Rechteren touches upon a subject that preoccupied many other European participants of the campaign which was "that property was so sacrosanct in America that Washington's army always lived in tents in the summer and in barracks in the winter". Here, Rechteren remembers the Germanic king Ariovist who let it be known to Caesar that his valiant warriors had never lived under a firm roof for the last 14 years and then quotes the relevant passage from "De bello Gallico".[117] The matter is finished for Rechteren with this historic comparison. Not so for many other participants of the campaign who had trouble adjusting to American principles concerning private property. Thus, a French officer complained that – unlike in Europe – troops on the march could not requisition horses, wagons, and other necessities and could not simply distribute their soldiers into private lodgings for the night. In Europe, the local police officer would be able to settle any disputes with the house owners. But here, all citizens were free and a house owner who did not like the looks of a soldier to be quartered in his house could decline the lodging; the words "I don't want to" were the end of the discussion then and there was no appeal

---

115. Mskr., S. 67 f. Rechteren schreibt hier irrtümlich „im Jahr danach"; s. dazu Edition, Anm. 237; die „Ville de Paris" hatte 104 Kanonen, nicht 100, wie Rechteren schreibt.

116. Mskr., S. 92 f.

117. Zum Hurrikan Mskr., S. 71; zum Zitat und zum folgenden lateinischen Zitat s. Mskr., S. 72.

115. Mscr., p. 67 f. Rechteren mistakenly places the incident "in the following year"; cf. text edition, fn 237. The "Ville de Paris" was a ship of 104 guns, Rechteren's number of "100" is an approximation.

116. Mscr., p. 92 f.

117. Description of the hurricane in mscr., p. 71; Ariovist's boast and the quotation, mscr., p. 72.

der Verhandlung, gegen die man nicht appellieren könne.[118] Noch deutlicher wurden die Unterschiede bei einem allgemeineren Vergleich der Gesellschaften; französische Reisende in Amerika bemerkten, dass die Amerikaner viele alte Vorurteile hinter sich gelassen hätten und auch keine Veranlassung zu besonderer Ehrerbietung sahen, nur weil ihr Gegenüber einen Adelstitel oder Offizierspauletten trug; dies war für viele adlige Offiziere des Feldzugs nur schwer verständlich.[119]

Es könnte sein, dass auch Rechteren in dieser Hinsicht nicht alles gefiel, was er in Amerika sah. Auffällig ist jedenfalls – und darin liegt eine gewisse Schwäche seiner Memoiren gegenüber den von Closen und Flohr –, dass er sich in seinem Bericht über Amerika relativ eng an die Ereignisse des Feldzugs und seine persönlichen Erlebnisse dabei hält, ohne in größerem Umfang auf eine Beschreibung von Land und Leuten auszugreifen. So sagt er z.B. nichts zur Sklaverei in Amerika, einem besonders in Virginia doch sehr auffälligen sozialen Phänomen, oder zum aufwändigen Lebensstil der Oberschicht. Sklaven erwähnt er nur als Hilfstruppen von Cornwallis nach der Kapitulation von Yorktown, von denen viele an den Blattern gestorben seien.[120] Auch in Europa, nämlich in Marseille, hatte er auf seiner früheren Reise Sklaven gesehen; aufgefallen war ihm dabei, dass sie zwar Sklavenkleidung trugen, aber zugleich kleine Geschäfte in der Stadt besaßen.[121]

Es ist kaum anzunehmen, dass Rechteren rassische Vorurteile gegenüber den schwarzen Sklaven hatte, denn beim Bericht über den Besuch von Indianern im Feldlager beurteilt er diese – anders als bspw. Closen – interessiert und wohlwollend.[122] Die zahlreichen deutschen Einwohner, insbesondere von Pennsylvania, sind ihm keine Erwähnung wert; gerade dass er auf wenigen Zeilen von seinem Ausritt nach Germantown berichtet, das von Franz Daniel Pastorius aus Sommerhausen gegründet wurde. Auch erfahren wir nichts über die Bewohner des Orts.[123] Ebenso werden holländische Siedler – Rechteren dürfte sich 1780/81 noch eher als Holländer denn als Deutscher empfunden haben – in Amerika nur beiläufig erwähnt, so als er bei einem holländischen Bauern im Hudson-Tal ein Pferd unterstellt, das – als trainiertes altes Militärpferd – nach einem Alarm sofort selbständig zu ihm ins Lager gelaufen kommt, während er es schon aufgegeben

against them.[118] Differences were even more conspicuous when the societies were compared in a more general way; French travellers in America noticed that the Americans had left many old prejudices behind and did not see any need for special deference just because the other person was a titled nobleman or had an officer's rank; quite a few of the noble officers participating in the campaign found this hard to understand.[119]

Rechteren may not have liked everything that he saw in America in this respect, either. It can't be overlooked that Rechteren – and this may constitute a certain deficit of his memoirs as compared to those of Closen and Flohr – stuck rather closely to the events of the campaign and his personal experiences in his report on America; he did not describe the country and its inhabitants in a more comprehensive way. For example, he doesn't mention slavery in America at all – a very striking social phenomenon in places like Virginia – nor the conspicuous consumption of the upper classes. He only mentions slaves as Cornwallis' auxiliary troops after the latter's capitulation at Yorktown, many of whom had died of small-pox as he tells it.[120] He had seen slaves earlier, though, in Marseilles on his Mediterranean voyage and had been struck by the fact that they wore slaves' clothes but, on the other hand, owned small shops in the city.[121]

It seems unlikely that Rechteren had racial prejudices against the black slaves as he reports in a friendly and interested manner – unlike Closen – about Native Americans visiting the military camp.[122] But the many German inhabitants, especially in Pennsylvania, aren't mentioned at all, he barely tells us about riding to Germantown which had been founded by Franz Daniel Pastorius of Sommerhausen. Again, we don't find out anything about its inhabitants.[123] In the same way, Dutch settlers in America – in 1780/81, Rechteren probably saw himself more as a Dutchman than as a German – are mentioned only incidentally. He had, e.g., given a horse he had acquired into the care of a Dutch farmer in the Hudson valley which – as a trained warhorse – came running to the camp on

---

118. Dazu Selig, German Allies, Teil II, S. 50.
119. Ebd.
120. Mskr., S. 109 a.
121. Mskr., S. 7.
122. Dazu Mskr., S. 76 – 78; demgegenüber Closens recht unfreundliche Beschreibung der Indianer, in Acomb, Journal, S. 37 – 39.
123. Mskr., S. 94 f.

118. See Selig, German Allies, part II, p. 50.
119. Loc. cit.
120. Mscr., p. 109 a.
121. Mscr., p.7.
122. Cf. mscr., p. 76 – 78, with Closen's rather negative view of Indians, in: Acomb, Journal, p. 37 – 39.
123. Mscr., p. 94 f.

hatte.[124] Die Geschichte mit dem Pferd ist lebhaft erzählt, gehört aber auch zu seinen persönlichen Feldzugserlebnissen.

Interessiert ist Rechteren stets an Neuerungen in der französischen Armee, so z.B. an der in jenen Jahren sehr kontrovers diskutierten, vom französischen Kriegsminister Graf Saint-Germain aus der preußischen Armee übernommen neuen Disziplinarstrafe des „Fuchtelns", die in den französischen Regimentern in Amerika zu tragischen Ereignissen führte; er berichtet dazu ausführlich, obwohl ihm die tieferen Gründe für die Ablehnung – die Ausdehnung körperlicher Strafen auch auf adlige Offiziersanwärter bei gleichzeitiger Verminderung der Zahl der mehr oder weniger dem Adel allein vorbehaltenen hohen Offiziersstellen – wohl nicht klar geworden sind; für Rechteren war das Fuchteln einfach mit dem „ächten" alten französischen Volksempfinden nicht vereinbar.[125]

Was die Rolle seines Regiments und seine eigene bei der siegreichen Belagerung von Yorktown angeht, ist Rechterens Darstellung etwas zu bescheiden. Er teilt dem Leser zwar – zutreffend – mit, dass bei dem entscheidenden Sturm auf die Bastionen[126] 9 und 10 sein Regiment zusammen mit einem anderen den Sieg herbeiführte, dann aber, dass es – hier spricht sozusagen der abgeklärte Veteran aus ihm, der eher die Beschwerlichkeiten als das Hochgefühl von Ehrungen sieht – 52 Stunden in der Stellung unter freiem Himmel verbringen musste.[127] Er beschreibt den Angriff außerdem zuerst vom Standpunkt eines bloßen Beobachters aus und lässt nur nebenbei erkennen, dass er selbst bei den Kämpfen mit im Schützengraben stand.[128] Er wurde in der Nacht von Oberst Christian von Zweibrücken, dem Regimentskommandeur, dem er ja speziell zugeordnet war, noch ausgesandt, um dessen jüngeren Bruder, Oberstleutnant Wilhelm von Zweibrücken, der den Sturm als Kommandeur befehligt hatte, auf dem Schlachtfeld zu finden. Wir erfahren dann nur, dass ihm dies in der Dunkelheit nicht gelang, dass Wilhelm zwar verwundet war, aber keine bleibenden Schäden davontrug.[129] Nicht von Rechteren erwähnt wird, dass Wilhelm von Zweibrücken als

---

124. Mskr., S. 89 f.

125. S. Mskr., S. 73 f., sowie Deflers, Militärreformen, bes. auch zu der öffentlichen Diskussion dieser Neuerung.

126. Mskr. verwendet den Begriff „Redoute" (engl. „redoubt"), der aber heute für ein Festungswerk kaum noch üblich und verständlich ist; deswegen wird hier der bekanntere Begriff „Bastion" benutzt.

127. Mskr., S. 107.

128. Dazu Mskr., S. 101 – 102 und 104.

129. Mskr., S. 104 f.

---

its own after an alarm had been sounded when he had expected to have lost it.[124] The story about this horse is told in a lively way, but it does not go beyond his personal experiences in the campaign, either.

Rechteren shows a lot of interest in new developments in the French army, most of all in the newly introduced corporal punishment of "Fuchteln" (beating soldiers on their backs with the flat side of the sabre). The French minister of war, count Saint-Germain, had adopted it from the Prussian army after the devastating French defeat in the battle of Roßbach. As Rechteren tells it, this led to tragic events in the French regiments in America; he probably did not fully understand the underlying reasons for the sharp disapproval it met with in the French officer corps – the punishment was extended to the (mostly noble) cadets while, at the same time, the number of high officer positions (reserved for the nobility) was sharply reduced – and describes it as simply unacceptable to innate French popular sentiments.[125]

As far as his regiment's and his own role in the successful siege of Yorktown are concerned Rechteren's description is a little too unassuming. The reader is told – truthfully – that his regiment together with another one stormed redoubts 9 and 10 which led to the final victory at Yorktown, but then – here, it seems, the veteran soldier in him is speaking who emphasizes inconveniences over the emotional high of receiving honours – he mostly tells us that as victors the men now had to stay in their conquered positions in the open air for 52 hours.[126] Also, he first describes the attack from the point of view of an outside observer and only later lets on that he was fighting in the trenches himself.[127] Later that night, he was sent out on the battlefield by Col. Christian von Zweibrücken, the regiment's commander, to try and find his younger brother, Lt.-Col. Wilhelm von Zweibrücken, who had led the storm on those redoubts. We then learn that he couldn't find him because of the darkness and that Wilhelm had been wounded, without lasting injuries.[128] But our author does not inform us that Wilhelm von Zweibrücken was greatly honoured as the victorious hero of the battle by Washington and Rochambeau as well as later

---

124. Mscr., p. 89 f.

125. See mscr., p. 73 f., and Deflers, Militärreformen, especially for the subsequent public debate about it.

126. Mscr., p. 107.

127. See mscr., p. 101 f. and 104.

128. Mscr., p. 104 f.

Held des Tages, dessen Angriff die Entscheidung brachte, von Washington und Rochambeau und in der Folge am französischen Hof, wohin er die erbeuteten Fahnen überbringen durfte, hoch geehrt wurde und dass das Regiment die in der Bastion erbeuteten Haubitzen danach als besonderes Ehrenzeichen auf Dauer behalten durfte.[130]

Anders als Rechteren ist der einfache Soldat Flohr entsetzt über die Sklaverei und besonders über die unzureichende und anstößige Bekleidung der Sklaven; er weiß auch, dass die Besitzer der Sklaven aus Sparsamkeitsgründen so mit ihren Plantagenarbeitern umgehen. Er sieht nicht nur die riesigen „Plantaschen" [Plantagen] der „Schändelmänner" [Gentlemen] mit ihren bis zu 200 Sklaven, sondern auch, dass sie Menschen verachten, die von ihrer Hände Arbeit leben; sie sind wie die Aristokraten in Europa, nur noch „staatsmäßiger" [reicher].[131] Er berichtet von der freundlichen Aufnahme, die die deutschen Soldaten überall erfahren[132] – anders als die französischen – und den vielen wohlhabend gewordenen pfälzischen Auswanderern, zumal in Pennsylvania.[133] Flohr sieht den Reichtum des Landes und der meisten seiner Bewohner sehr deutlich. Seine Darstellung des Feldzugs und der Erlebnisse der einfachen Soldaten ist teilweise ausführlicher als die Rechterens;[134] er nennt bei der Belagerung von Yorktown z.B. Tag für Tag die Verluste bei den Belagerern,[135] was Rechteren verschweigt. Flohr beschreibt auch Besonderheiten von Fauna und Flora in Amerika,[136] worüber Rechteren nichts sagt, außer dass er bei dem berühmten Botaniker Bartram in Philadelphia zwei Kisten Pflanzenschösslinge und -samen für den Schlossgarten erwirbt.[137] Er hat also durchaus erkannt, dass es in Europa damals kaum bekannte Pflanzen in Amerika gibt, sagt aber nichts dazu.

Auch von Ludwig von Closens Memoiren unterscheiden sich die Rechterens deutlich, allein schon vom Umfang her, denn Closens Text dürfte mehr als zehnmal so lang sein wie der von Rechteren.[138] Closen blieb länger in Amerika als Rech-

at the French court; he was chosen to take the conquered flags to France, and the regiment received the howitzers which it had taken in redoubt 9 as permanent badges of honour.[129]

The plain infantryman Flohr, unlike Rechteren, is horrified by slavery and particularly by the insufficient and indecent clothes that the slaves have to wear; he knows that the owners treat their plantation workers in this way because of their stinginess. He does not only observe the huge size of the "Schändelmänner's Plantaschen" [gentlemen's plantations] with up to 200 slaves working there, but also that they look down on people who live by manual work; they are just like European aristocrats, but even "staatsmäßiger" [wealthier].[130] He reports on the friendly reception that the German soldiers of the "Royal Deux-Ponts" regiment find everywhere[131] – unlike their French comrades – and on the many immigrants from the Palatinate who have become quite wealthy, most of all in Pennsylvania.[132] Flohr clearly sees the wealth of the land and its inhabitants. His description of the campaign and the experiences of rank and file soldiers is not inferior to Rechteren's, on the contrary, it is more extensive;[133] thus, he reports, day by day, the number of soldiers who were killed in the siege of Yorktown,[134] something that is not found in Rechteren's story. Flohr tells us about the peculiarities of America's flora and fauna,[135] a topic which is also lacking in Rechteren's memoirs except that he tells us about buying two large casks of seeds and sprouts for his castle gardens from the famous botanist Bartram in Philadelphia.[136] This shows that Rechteren, too, took notice of the existence of exotic American plants unknown in Europe then, but his memoirs are silent about this.

Rechteren's memoirs differ considerably from Closen's as well, not least by their volume; Closen's text probably is ten times as long as Rechteren's.[137] Closen also staid in America much longer, he only returned to Europe in 1783. As

---

130. Dazu Tröss, Regiment, S. 46 – 49.
131. Tröss, Regiment, S. 138, S. 194 f.
132. Ebd., S. 127, 129 u.a.m.
133. Ebd., S. 149 f.
134. Ebd., bes. S. 157 – 186 (Belagerung und Einnahme von Yorktown).
135. Ebd., S. 166, 172 f., 183 u.a.
136. Ebd., S. 196 f., 199 u.a.
137. Mskr., S. 112.
138. Closens Memoiren umfassen etwa 300 Druckseiten, Rechterens Text zu Amerika würde in vergleichbarem Satz vielleicht 25 Seiten Umfang haben.

---

129. See Tröss, Regiment, p. 46 – 49.
130. Tröss, Regiment, p. 138, 194 f.
131. Loc.cit., p. 127, 129 et al.
132. Loc. cit., p. 149 f.
133. Loc.cit., pp. 157 – 186 which deal with the siege and conquest of Yorktown.
134. Loc.cit., pp. 166, 172 f., 183 et al.
135. Loc.cit., p. 196 f., 188 et al.
136. Mscr., p. 112.
137. Closen's text comes to 300 printed pages, Rechteren's would cover about 25 pages in comparable type-setting.

teren und kehrte erst 1783 nach Europa zurück. Als einer der Adjutanten von Rochambeau hatte er bessere Möglichkeiten, den Feldzug zu überblicken, und dies zeigt sich in seiner erheblich ausführlicheren Darstellung der militärischen Abläufe.[139] Er hatte aber auch mehr Gelegenheit als Rechteren, Land und Leute kennenzulernen. Er berichtet denn auch sehr detailliert über die amerikanische Gesellschaft, über wichtige Treffen, Bälle, Festlichkeiten, an denen er teilnahm, über bedeutende Persönlichkeiten wie Jefferson und Washington, die er auf ihren Landsitzen besuchte, über das Land und seine Flora und Fauna, über religiöse Toleranz und die verschiedenen Konfessionen und vieles mehr, stets Vergleiche zu den Verhältnissen in Europa ziehend.[140] Wie Flohr lehnt er die Sklavenhaltung scharf ab[141] (er stellte zwar einen Afroamerikaner als Diener an – im 18. Jahrhundert in Europa ein adliges Statussymbol –, der ihm nach Europa folgt, betont aber dessen freie Abkunft),[142] beurteilt andererseits, wie erwähnt, die Indianer recht negativ. Eigentlich gibt es nur einen Teil des Feldzugs, der bei Rechteren genauer beschrieben wird, und das ist der fehlgeschlagene Versuch im Frühjahr 1781, mit einer Flotte in Virginia zu landen;[143] der Grund dafür ist, dass Rechteren sich freiwillig zur Teilnahme an dieser Unternehmung meldete – die dann auch einen erheblichen Teil seines Berichts ausmacht – während Closen und ebenso Flohr nur aus zweiter Hand davon berichten können.

Ist nun aus dieser vergleichenden Betrachtung zu schließen, dass Rechterens Memoiren weniger wertvoll und beachtenswert sind als die seines Standesgenossen, des Freiherrn von Closen, und des aus tieferer sozialer Perspektive dieselben Ereignisse beobachtenden Georg Daniel Flohr? Man muss hier wohl beachten, dass sowohl Closen als auch Flohr ihre – ohnehin viel umfangreicheren – Memoiren speziell und ausschließlich auf die Beschreibung des Feldzugs in Amerika und auf die Beschreibung von Land und Leuten dort abgestellt haben, während Rechterens kleinerer Text der Vergegenwärtigung von und Erinnerung an seine Jugendjahre dient. Von daher ist sein Text enger auf ihn selbst, seine eigenen Erlebnisse und Beobachtungen beschränkt und konzentriert.

mentioned before, he was Rochambeau's aide-de-camp and in this position had much better information about the whole campaign; this shows in his much more detailed description of the planning and actual events.[138] He also had more chances to get to know the land and the people, and therefore he is able to give us very detailed information on American society, important meetings, festivities, and dances which he attended, on eminent persons like Washington and Jefferson at whose plantations he stayed as a house guest, on the geography of the country, the flora and fauna, on religious tolerance and the numerous religious denominations and many other topics, always comparing conditions in America with those in Europe and commenting on circumstances and developments in America.[139] Like Flohr, he sharply disapproves of slavery[140] (although he employed a black American as his servant – something of a status symbol in 18th century Europe – who accompanied him to Europe, but Closen emphasized the fact that he was freeborn);[141] on the other hand, has a rather negative opinion of Native Americans. There is only one part of the campaign which is described with more detail by Rechteren, and that is the failed attempt to take part of the troops to Virginia by ship in the spring of 1781.[142] The reason for this is that Rechteren volunteered for this naval operation – which, because of that, figures prominently in his memoirs – whereas Closen and Flohr have only second-hand information on it.

Do we have to conclude from these comparisons that Rechteren's memoirs are less remarkable or valuable than those of his peer, baron Closen, or those of Georg Daniel Flohr who observed things from a lower social perspective? We have to remember that both Closen and Flohr aimed at a special and exclusive description of the American campaign and of the country and its inhabitants and that their memoirs are much more extensive than Rechteren's whose shorter text is just meant to remind the author – let him visualize, so to speak – an important part of his life, basically the years of his youth. Because of this underlying intention the text concentrates much more on the author himself, on his own

---

139. S. z.B. seine Darstellung der Belagerung von Yorktown, in Acomb, Journal, S. 138 – 163; allein dieser Teil ist also so lang wie Rechterens ganzer Text zum Krieg in Amerika.

140. Dazu bspw. ebd., S. 165 – 265 zum Winterquartier in Virginia und zur Rückkehr des Regiments nach Neu-England.

141. Ebd., S. XII.

142. Dazu Selig, German Allies, Teil III, S. 30.

143. Mskr., S. 80 – 86.

138. Thus, his description of the siege of Yorktown covers pages 138 to 163 in Acomb, Journal, i.e. about as many pages as Rechteren's description of his whole stay in America.

139. Cf. Acomb, Journal, p. 165 – 265 with his report on the regiment's winter quarters in Virginia and its return march to New England.

140. Loc.cit., p. XII.

141. See Selig, German Allies, part III, p. 30.

142. Cf. mscr., p. 80 – 86.

Rechteren ist ein guter Beobachter, der in der Lage ist, mit wenigen Sätzen ein treffendes, lebendiges Bild von Situationen oder gesellschaftlichen Umständen zu zeichnen, den schlichten Lebensstil sardischer Hirten ebenso wie das zeitaufwendige, mühe- und ränkevolle „Sollicitieren" um eine Verwendung bei der Armee am Hof und in hohen Adelskreisen des vorrevolutionären Paris, den gefährlichen Unfall in der Kalesche des Herrn von der Wisch, mit dem zusammen er von Paris nach Brest reiste, den entscheidenden Sturm auf die Redoute Nr. 9 vor Yorktown, wobei er selbst im Schützengraben stand, oder den schweren Sturm auf der Rückreise von Amerika vor der bretonischen Küste, bei dem er leicht mit dem Schiff hätte untergehen können.[144] Rechteren schildert fast exemplarisch die Lebensweise eines mitteleuropäischen Adligen in der zweiten Hälfte des 18. Jahrhunderts, bei der eben der militärische Aspekt in den Jugendjahren weithin dominierte. Ergänzend kann man die Seereise im Mittelmeer mit ihren vielen Besuchen „Baedeker-würdiger" Stätten, gesellschaftlichen Unternehmungen wie Gottesdienst-, Ball-, Theater- und Museumsbesuchen – bei denen der Autor trotz seiner Jugend und relativ subalternen Stellung als Kadett offensichtlich weder finanziell noch sozial eingeschränkt war – als einen Ersatz für die so zeittypische „Kavalierstour" ansehen, die Rechteren anscheinend nicht absolvierte. Wenn dann die treffenden Beobachtungen des Autors noch gewürzt werden mit durchaus unterhaltenden Berichten über Ungewöhnliches und Absonderliches, mit Abenteuer und Gefahr und mit lehrreichen Parallelen zu historischen Ereignissen, ist eine Quelle von erheblichem Wert entstanden, die zugleich noch fesselnd zu lesen ist.

experiences and observations. And Rechteren is a very good observer who is able to sketch a vivid and true-to-life picture of situations or social conditions with just a few apt sentences. In this way, he informs us about the simple lifestyle of Sardinian shepherds as well as about the time-consuming, troublesome and rich-in-intrigue "solicitation" for a position in the army at the pre-revolutionary French court and in the circles of the high nobility in Paris, about the dangerous accident in the calash of baron Wisch with whom he travelled from Paris to Brest, about the decisive storming of redoubt no. 9 at Yorktown where he personally fought in the trenches or the severe storm off the coast of Brittany on his way back home from America where he could very easily have been drowned in a foundering ship.[143] In his text, Rechteren depicts in an almost exemplary fashion the way of life of a central European nobleman in the second half of the 18th century when a military career tended to be the dominant aspect in the years of adolescence and early adulthood. Moreover, the Mediterranean voyage with its many sightseeing tours of places worthy of a mention in Baedeker, its social events such as the attendance at religious services, dances, plays, and visits to museums – where we see our author unencumbered by his youth and his subaltern position as a cadet, and unimpeded by social or financial constraints – can be viewed as a replacement of the "grand tour" which he did not do. And as the author's vivid observations are spiced with entertaining reports about strange and unusual events and things, with a whiff of danger and adventure, and with educational comparisons to historical events we have source material on hand which is of high intrinsic value and makes for captivating reading as well.

---

144. Dazu (in dieser Folge) Mskr., S. 29, 55 – 58, 59 – 61, 100 – 103, 115 – 120.

143. See, in this sequence, mscr., p. 29, 55 – 58, 59 – 61, 100 – 103, 115 – 120.

The adventures of

Friedrich Reinhard count of Rechteren-Limpurg in the Mediterranean and the American War of Independence

1770 – 1782

based on the manuscript of July, 1835, in the Fürstlich Castell'sche Archive at Castell, Bavaria

edited by Jane A. Baum, Hans-Peter Baum, and Jesko Graf zu Dohna

[The edition follows the German manuscript word for word, in the author's or copyist's orthography and punctuation which could not be transferred to the English translation.]

I was born September 22nd, 1751 in the castle of Rechtern[1], Over-Ijssel. When I was 1&1/4 years old, I moved to Sommerhausen[2], Franconia, with my parents[3], and my brothers and sister[4]. In 1754 my father died.[5] In 1757 we moved back to Almelo[6] in Over-Ijssel. We had a teacher named Schwab from Ansbach[7]. After he left, I was instructed in Latin by a lawyer named Dull.

---

1. See fn. 1 of the introduction.

2. Cf. fn. 3 of the introduction.

3. Johann Eberhard count von Rechteren-Limpurg (1714 – 1754) and Sophia Karolina Florentina, née countess von Rechteren-Almelo (1725 – 1805), heiress of Almelo.

4. He had an elder sister, Josina Elisabeth (1738 – 1804), from his father's first marriage, who, in 1754, married count August Wilhelm zu Hohenlohe-Ingelfingen (†1769), and two elder brothers, Joachim Adolf (1747 – 1775) and Friedrich Ludwig Christian (1748 – 1814).

5. Count Johann Eberhard von Rechteren-Limpurg died on March 15th, 1754.

6. The town of Almelo (province of Overijssel/Netherlands) is situated close to the Dutch-German border between Enschede and Zwolle.

7. Ansbach (Middle Franconia, Bavaria) was the capital of the principality of Brandenburg-Ansbach.

When I was 16, I left Almelo to attend the Latin school in Ijsselstein[8], and stayed there for one year. Then I was sent to Utrecht[9], to finish my studies.[2] But I wanted to join the Navy, and after spending 2 years in Utrecht, I signed on the ship "Nassau" as a cadet (Adelborst in Dutch) when I was 19. Since November 12th, 1770 was the sailing date, I travelled from Almelo to Amsterdam and met my cousin[10] there, who was the commander of the ship "Nassau". Together we went by way of Alkmar[11] to Helder[12], where the ships lay; namely first the "Nassau", which was bored for 70 cannon, but actually carried only 60; second the "Nassau-Weilburg", Captain Zoutmann[13] (later Admiral); third the "Kennemerland", Capt. Dedel[14]. The last 2 ships could carry 60 cannon, but had only 50 then. The ship "Nassau" had as Captain van Goor Hinlopen who commanded the Escadre (fleet).[15] Under him were three commanders on the same ship [3]: van Loo, Reintjes, and Count von Rechtern. Lieutenants were: Kroon, Spengler, Boreel de Moregneau, van Haren, de Bas, de Vries: Cadets: Binker, Rechtern, Wenlerswyk, van Son. The crew consisted of 350 men.

On November 18th we weighed anchor and the Escadre set sail. On the 19th we saw the high hills around Calais[16]; on the 20th Bevesier[17]; after much bad weather, Cape St.

---

8. Cf. Introduction, fn. 6.

9. Utrecht (province of Utrecht), seat of an important university (since 1326), episcopal see.

10. Probably baron Joachim Philipp Adolf von Rechteren zu Mennighave (1715 – 1796) , cf. Europäische Stammtafeln, N. F., ed. by Detlev Schwennicke, vol. IV: Standesherrliche Häuser I, Marburg 1981, table 88.

11. Alkmaar (province of Noordholland/Netherlands), approx. 25 miles north of Amsterdam.

12. Den Helder (province of Noordholland), then and today the largest Dutch naval base at the northern tip of West Friesland, opposite the island of Texel.

13. Johan Arnold Zoutman (1724 – 1793) was made vice-admiral of Holland and West Friesland after the battle of the Doggerbank (August 1781), cf. www.maritiemdigitaal.nl, or Wikipedia.

14. Captain Salomon Dedel (1736 – 1800), later „schout-bij-nacht" (commodore), received the newly created Doggerbank medal for his valour in that battle (August 1781), www.maritiemdigitaal.nl, or Wikipedia.

15. Captain Jan van Goor Hinlopen was the scion of a highly respected Amsterdam family; he is also named as commander of the whole squadron by van der Horst, Kinckel, p. 176.

16. French harbour town surrounded by the hill range of the Collines de l'Artois.

17. Cap Béveziers is the French name of Beachy Head, East Sussex, close to Eastbourne, where on July 10th, 1690, the French beat the English and Dutch navies in a naval battle.

stümen Wetter am 6ten Dezember Cap St. Vincent[18], am 8ten den Affenberg auf der Africanischen Küste. Wir segelten nahe an der africanischen Küste, welche sicherer ist, bei Ceuta[19] vorbei, und kamen am 9ten auf der Rhede[20] von Malaga[21] vor Anker. Hier trafen wir 2 dänische Kriegsschiffe, commandiert von Admiral Kaas[22] und Capitain Juel an, welche auf einer Expedition gegen Algier[23] begriffen waren.

[4] Es ist eine angenehme Empfindung, im Winter aus einem nördlichen Clima nach wenigen Wochen in ein so warmes Land sich versetzt zu sehen. Ich fuhr mit der Chaloupe in den Hafen. Beim Aussteigen wurde ich durch den Anblick eines Knaben von etwa 15 Jahren überrascht, der um ein Almosen bat. Er war ohne Arme geboren, übrigens aber wohlaussehend und behende. Man warf ihm das Almosen auf die Erde, und er hob es mit dem Fuße, den er so gut wie eine Hand brauchte, auf, steckte es in den Mund, und ließ es von da in seine Westentasche fallen, die dazu eingerichtet war. Ein zweiter Bettler, welcher da saß, hatte die ganze untere Kinnlade verloren, so daß die Zunge frey herunter hing. Unter einem großen Zusammenfluß von Menschen ging ein spanischer Hidalgo[24] mit einem gro- [5] ßen Degen unterm Arm, dessen Spitze unter seinem Mantel hervorguckte, ohne auf Jemanden zu achten, auf und ab spazieren. Ein paar französische Seefahrer warfen einen Ball mitten unter die Leute, und ein Pudelhund mußte ihn suchen und apportiren. Von diesem allen nahm der Hidalgo keine Notiz.

Das Wasser, womit die Fässer gefüllt wurden, wurde in einer ziemlichen Entfernung von der Stadt bei einem Bauernhof geholt. Ein Schöpfwerk an einem Brunnen wurde von Ochsen getrieben; anstatt der Eimer oder Kasten waren irdne Töpfe daran.

Ich ging in die Comoedie, wo das Stück „Tobias" gespielt wurde. Da wurde ein Wunderwerk vorgestellt: Ein elender Lahmer, dessen Fuß mit einer Menge [6] Bandagen umwickelt war, wurde von einem Heiligen berührt; die Bandagen wurden

Vincent[18] on December 6th; on the 8th, Gibraltar, the "monkey rock" on the coast of Africa. We sailed close to the African coast, which was safer, past Ceuta[19], and cast anchor in the roadstead[20] of Malaga[21]. Here we met two Danish war-ships, commanded by Admiral Kaas[22] and Capt. Juel, who were in the middle of a campaign against Algiers.[23] [4]

It is a very pleasant feeling to leave the cold northern winter behind, and after just a few weeks to find yourself in such a warm climate. Getting out of the sloop, which I had taken into the harbor, I was surprised to see a lad of about 15, who was begging there. He was born without arms, but otherwise good-looking and lively. People dropped coins on the ground in front of him, he picked them up with his feet, which he used like hands, put the coin in his mouth, and then let it fall into his vest pocket, which was arranged to catch it. A second beggar, who sat there too, had lost his whole lower jaw, so that his tongue was hanging out. In the middle of a large crowd, a Spanish hidalgo[24] was promenading with the tip of his huge sword [5] looking out from under his coat. He was oblivious to the whole scene. A couple of French sailors were throwing a ball into the crowd, and a poodle dog had to retrieve it. The hidalgo was above noticing any of this.

The fresh water which was stored in barrels on our ship had to be drawn up at a farm, rather far out from the city. The bucket elevator at the well was powered by oxen; instead of buckets or wooden boxes, clay pots were attached here.

I went to a comedy theatre where I saw the play "Tobias". It was a story about a miracle: a poor lame man, whose foot was wrapped up in lots of bandages,[6] was touched by a saint; then the bandages were taken off – one by one

---

18. Das Cabo de Sao Vicente bildet die süd-westliche Spitze von Portugal.
19. Ceuta, spanische Hafenstadt in Marokko, östlich von Tanger, gegenüber von Gibraltar.
20. Reede, geschützter Ankerplatz vor einem Hafen.
21. Malaga, Hafenstadt in Südspanien, Hauptstadt der Provinz Malaga.
22. Frederik Christian Kaas (1725-1803), 1768 Kontreadmiral, 1772 Vizeadmiral, 1775 Admiral (Dansk Biografisk Leksikon Band IX, S.53-55).
23. Algier (Al Dschesair), im 18. Jahrhundert Hauptstadt eines von unabhängigen „Deis" regierten Soldatenstaats, der wegen seiner ständigen Seeräuberei von den europäischen Seemächten vom 16. bis ins 18. Jahrhundert erfolglos bekämpft wurde; s. auch Einleitung, S. 29.
24. „Edler", Titel des niederen Adels in Spanien.

18. Cabo S. Vicente forms the southwestern tip of Portugal.
19. Spanish harbour in Morocco, east of Tangier, opposite Gibraltar.
20. Protected anchorage outside of a harbour.
21. Harbour in Southern Spain, capital of Malaga province.
22. Frederik Christian Kaas (1727 – 1804), 1768 rear admiral, 1772 vice admiral, 1775 admiral (Dansk biografisk Leksikon, vol. IX, p. 53-55).
23. Algiers (Al Dschesair), in the 18th century the capital of a military state governed by independent „deis". The European maritime powers fought this pirate state unsuccessfully from the the 16th to the 18th centuries, cf. Introduction, p. 29.
24. "Nobleman", title of the lower nobility in Spain.

nach einander abgenommen, und der Fuß zeigte sich vollkommen gesund, welches sehr natürlich zuging.

Den 21ten segelten wir von Malaga ab, und kamen den 1. Januar nach Marseille[25]. Da die Schiffe, die im Hafen liegen, alles Pulver ausladen müssen, so blieben wir bei der Insel Chateau d'If.[26] Der Erzbischof von Aix[27] besuchte unser Schiff, welcher 2 sehr artige Cousine[n] bei sich hatte.

Ich fuhr mit einigen Officieren in einer Chaloupe, die an's Land geschickt wurde. Als wir vom Schiffe abgefahren waren, wurde der Wind sehr heftig und die Wellen gingen sehr hoch. Rechterhand von uns hatten wir das Ufer, welches eine steile Wand von lauter Felsen ist, und gerade [7] dahin trieb uns der Wind. Das Schiff wieder zu erreichen war nicht möglich, und eben so wenig zu landen, ohne zu scheitern. Zuletzt entdeckten wir eine kleine Oefnung in dem Felsen. Wir fuhren da hinein, und waren auf einmal in einem kleinen Bassin gegen allen Wind geschützt. Die Oberfläche des Wassers war wie ein Spiegel. Wir kletterten die Felsen hinan bis oben zum Fort Notre-Dame-de la Garde[28], und gingen von da in die Stadt.

Wir blieben etliche Tage in derselben. Ich sah die Galeeren im Hafen, wo die Galeeren[s]claven angeschlossen sind und arbeiten müssen. Verschiedene hatten jedoch Boutiquen und trieben kleine Gewerbe am Hafen, nur hatten sie die Sclavenkleidung an.

Auf dem Rathhause sah ich ein [8] großes Gemählde, welches die Straßen von Marseille vorstellte, als anno 1720 und 1721 die Pest, die durch ein Schiff aus der Levante[29] dahingebracht worden war, achtzigtausend Menschen wegraf[f]te.

In der Comoedie sah ich das Stück „Le Roi de Cocagne"[30], welches lauter Possen enthält. Einen so lauten Ausbruch

and the foot was completely healed: which all happened quite naturally.

December 21st, we set sail from Malaga, and arrived at Marseilles[25] on January 1st. Since the ships which want to lie in port have to unload all gun-powder we stayed close to the island, Chateau d'If[26]. The Archbishop of Aix[27] visited our ship; he had two very courteous cousins (female) in tow.

I went with some officers in a sloop which was sent to shore. After we left the ship, the wind came up and the waves were very high. On our right hand we had the shore, which is a steep wall of sheer rock [7] and the wind was blowing us over that way. We could not get back to our ship, neither could we land without being shipwrecked. Finally we discovered a tiny opening in the rocks. We turned in there, and suddenly found ourselves in a little basin protected from the wind. The surface of the water looked like a mirror. We climbed up the rocks, on top was the fort Notre Dame de la Garde[28], and from there we went into the city.

We stayed there for several days. I saw some galleys in port and the chained galley-slaves who are forced to work and row them. Some of them, however, ran boutiques and little shops in town, but they were forced to wear slave's clothing.

In the city hall, I saw a huge painting,[8] showing the streets of Marseilles anno 1720, when the plague, brought there on a ship from the Levantine coast[29], killed 80,000 souls.

At the comedy theatre I saw the play "Le Roi de Cocagne"[30], which was very silly. Such loud bursts of laughter, as these jolly Provençal people crown the jokes with,

---

25. Marseille, Hafenstadt in Südfrankreich, nahe der Rhonemündung, zweitgrößte Stadt Frankreichs.

26. 1524 zum Schutz gegen die Spanier erbaute Festungsinsel, später in ein Gefängnis umgewandelt; verdankt ihre Berühmtheit dem Roman „Der Graf von Monte Christo" von Alexandre Dumas.

27. Lt. Liste der Erzbischöfe von Aix-en-Provence (Wikipedia) war seit 4.11.1770 Jean-de-Dieu-Raymond de Boisgelin de Cucé im Amt. Da Rechteren im Januar 1771 dort war, müsste es sich um ihn gehandelt haben. Aix-en-Provence liegt ca. 35 km nördlich von Marseille.

28. Wallfahrtskapelle.

29. „Morgenland", ital., alle von Italien aus nach Osten liegenden Länder am Mittelmeer, vor allem die Küsten von Kleinasien, Syrien und Ägypten.

30. „Der König von Schlaraffenland", Komödie von Marc-Antoine Legrand (Paris 1719).

25. Harbour in Southern France, close to the delta of the Rhone river, 2nd largest city of France.

26. Island fortified in 1524 against the Spaniards; the fortress later became a prison and owes its fame to Alexandre Dumas' novel "The count of Monte Christo".

27. According to the catalog of the archbishops of Aix (Wikipedia), Jean-de-Dieu-Raymond de Boisgelin de Cucé had become archbishop on Nov. 4th, 1770. As our author was at Marseille in January 1771, he must have seen him. Aix-en-Provence is approx. 22 miles north of Marseille.

28. Votive church, place of pilgrimage which the fort is named for.

29. "The East" (Italian), all the Eastern coasts of the Mediterranean, esp. Asia Minor, Syria, and Egypt.

30. "The King of Cockaigne", comedy by Marc-Antoine Legrand, Paris 1719 (C. is a mythical land of idleness and luxury).

von Fröhlichkeit, wie ihn diese munteren Provençalen bei solchen Späßen äußern, habe ich sonst nirgends gefunden. Auch besuchte ich einen öffentlichen Ball, wo nach einer wie gewöhnlich besetzten Musik getanzt wurde. Doch war hievon abgesondert noch die provençalische Volksmusik, welche in einem Tambourin und einer Pfeiffe besteht, anzutreffen, wonach auch getanzt wurde. Die Promenade, der Cours genannt, ist wegen der vielen Spaziergänger sehr angenehm.

Am 20. Januar 1771 segelte die Escadre von Marseille ab, und [9] kam am 23ten in der Bei von Toulon[31] an. Wir ankerten außerhalb des Ford Grande Tour. Am 25ten Morgens besah ich die Stadt, den Hafen und das Arsenal. Man sagte mit Recht, daß wenn man die Macht und Größe des Königs von Frankreich sehen wolle, man nicht sowohl Versailles, Compiègne und Fontainebleau, sondern seine Kriegshäfen und Hauptfestungen sehen müsse.

An dem obbenannten Grande Tour wurde täglich um Mittag mit Canonen nach der Scheibe geschossen. Alsdann wurde da eine rothe Flagge aufgezogen, welches bedeutete, daß Niemand da passiren sollte, weil die Kugeln, die daneben flogen, diese Passage bestrichen. Jetzt da wir in der Stadt waren, sahen wir unvermuthet, daß unser Schiff das Zeichen zum Absegeln gab. Es war jetzt nicht zu wählen, [10] wir mußten fort. Sobald wir dahin kamen, hörten wir die Kugeln über uns wegschnurren und sahen sie auf dem Meere hüpfen. Den Ruderern wurde Brandwein versprochen, wenn sie alle ihre Kräfte anstrengten, um bald hinauszukommen. Am Lande waren sie vielleicht gewiß, uns nicht zu treffen. Wir sahen, wie sie mit Ferngläsern nach uns schauten und sich vielleicht an unserer Contenance belustigten. Denn wenn es einem neu ist, glaubt man beinahe getroffen zu werden, wenn es auch in einer ziemlichen Höhe über einen weggeht.

Am 29. kamen wir nach Genua.[32] Ein Pilot brachte unser Schiff in den Molo bei dem Leuchtthurme. Der Doge von Genua war gestorben, und eine zeitlang wurde in jeder Minute eine Canone abgefeuert. Dies macht eine besondere Wirkung. Da Ge- [11] nua von der Landseite mit sehr hohen Bergen und Felsen umgeben und gegen dieselbe angebaut ist, so giebt jeder Schuß ein so vielfältiges Echo, als wenn eine ganze Artillerie nacheinander abgefeuert würde.

I'd never heard anywhere else. Also I attended a public ball, where one danced to normally instrumented music. They played their own Provençal folkmusic as well, with tambourine and pipe, and they danced to this, too. The Promenade, called the "Cours", was a pleasant spot to watch the many passers-by.

January 20th, 1771, the Escadre set sail from Marseilles[9] and arrived in the bay of Toulon[31] on the 23rd. We cast anchor outside the Fort Grande Tour. On the morning of the 25th, I visited the city, harbor and arsenal. It is true as they say, that if you want to see the power and stature of the King of France you should not so much visit Versailles, Compiègne and Fontainebleau, but rather his naval harbors and main fortresses.

Every day at noon, at the above-mentioned Grande Tour, they had cannon target practice. A red flag was then hoisted, which meant that no one should pass that way because the cannonballs were flying around thick and fast. Now when we were in the city, we saw, unexpectedly, that our ship gave the sign for departure. We had no choice,[10] we had to get going. As soon as we arrived, we heard the cannonballs rushing over our heads and saw them dancing on the water. We promised the rowers brandy to exert themselves to the utmost and get us out of there. On land they may have been sure of not hitting us. We saw them lifting their field glasses to watch us, and they were probably laughing at our deportment. Because when you are new at this game, you think you have been hit, even when things are flying by pretty far above you.

On the 29th we reached Genoa[32]. A pilot brought our ship to the pier by the light-house. The Doge of Genoa had just died, and for a while they fired a cannon a minute, which was very impressive.[11] Genoa is surrounded by high rocks and mountains, and the city is also built on these, so that every shot has a tremendous echo, as if a whole artillery battalion were firing one after the other.

---

31. Französische Stadt mit Kriegshafen am Mittelmeer, südöstlich von Marseille.

32. Genua, Stadtrepublik an der ligurischen Küste, Hauptstadt der gleichnamigen Provinz in der Region Ligurien, im 16. Jahrhundert führender Geldmarkt des katholischen Europa, im 18. Jahrhundert mehrfach unter französischer Herrschaft.

---

31. French naval base on the Mediterranean, southeast of Marseilles.

32. Genoa, an important port city, capital of the eponymous province in the Ligurian region of northern Italy. In the 16th century, Genoa became the leading money market of catholic Europe. The 17th century saw its economic decline, in the 18th century, it came under French dominion several times.

Am Ufer des Meeres, außer dem Thor, ist der Palast Doria[33]. Innerhalb desselben ist der berühmte Admiral Andreas Doria[34] auf einem Springbrunnen, seltsam genug, nackt als Neptun in Marmor vorgestellt.

Genua hat sehr enge Straßen und dabei die höchsten Häuser in Europa (viele von 7 Stock) und da die Stadt gegen den Berg gebaut ist, steigt man zuweilen von einer Strasse auf 80 Stufen hinauf in die andere. Nur 2 Straßen sind breit, nämlich die Strada nuova und die Strada Balbi[35], in welcher lauter Paläste, einige ganz von Marmor, stehen.

[12] Die Bank ist ein freier Platz. Allda sah man die Nobili, welche zum Theil Kaufleute waren, wie Abbées gekleidet.[36] Denn die Familie Doria allein durfte Degen tragen und in einer Kutsche in der Stadt fahren. Die andern bedienten sich der Sänften.

Im Palaste des Doge[n], im Versammlungssaale des Senats, steht die marmorne Bildsäule des Marschalls Richelieu[37], welcher in den 40er Jahren als französischer Bevollmächtigter und General in Genua war. Man zeigt da unter Anderem auch das Modell einer hölzernen Brücke, die in einem Bogen ohne Pfeiler über einen breiten Fluß gehen soll; – ferner einen Koffer, der mit vielen kleinen Pistol-Läufen versehen und so eingerichtet ist, daß sie zu bestimmter Zeit losgehen und nach allen Seiten treffen, wodurch man einst den Senat hatte meuchelmörderisch tödten [13] wollen – ferner alte Gewehre und Waffen, welche Columbus (der ein Genueser war) bei der Entdeckung Amerikas auf seinem Schiffe hatte.

Down by the water, outside the city-gate is the Doria palace.[33] In the palace courtyard, in the middle of a fountain, the famous Admiral Andrea Doria[34], is immortalized as a marble Neptune, oddly enough, completely naked.

Genoa has very narrow streets and, at the same time, the tallest buildings in Europe (many have 7 stories). Since the city is built up against a mountain, you must often walk up 80 steps to reach the next street; only two streets are wide, namely the Strada nuova and the Strada Balbi[35], the latter seems to be filled with palaces, some completely built of marble.[12]

The Bank is an open space. There you can see the "Nobili" (nobility) dressed like "Abbées"[36] but some of them were certainly merchants. For only the Doria family are permitted to bear swords and drive round the city with horse and carriage. All others use sedan-chairs.

In the Doges' Palace, in the Senate Meeting Hall, stands a marble column depicting Duke Richelieu[37], the marshal of France, who in the 1740s was a French chargé d'affaires and general in Genoa. Many interesting things are displayed there; for one, a model of a wooden bridge, said to span a wide river in one arch without any pillars supporting it. I also saw a suitcase outfitted with many small pistol barrels and arranged with a timer to go off one after the other and shoot in all directions. Someone had planned to assassinate the whole Senate that way.[13] Moreover I saw old guns and weapons which Columbus (who was Genoese) had on board his ships when he discovered America.

---

33. Die Doria waren spätestens seit dem 12. Jahrhundert die führende Familie innerhalb der Handels-Aristokratie der Republik Genua. Seit der Mitte des 17. Jahrhunderts aus der Reihe der Dogen-Kandidaten ausgeschlossen, widmeten sie sich vornehmlich kirchlichen Laufbahnen und diplomatischen Aufgaben.

34. Andrea Doria (1468-1560), bedeutender Condottiere, Großadmiral Kaiser Karls V., löste Genua aus der Abhängigkeit von Frankreich, machte es wieder zur unbestrittenen Vormacht in Ligurien. Er kämpfte gegen die Türken und die Piraten Nordafrikas. Er wurde nie Doge, errichtete aber ein aristokratisch-republikanisches Regiment und führte Genua an die Seite Spaniens.

35. Heute: Via Garibaldi und Via Balbi.

36. „Abbé" steht im französischen Sprachgebrauch des 18. Jahrhunderts für alle Geistlichen, nicht nur Äbte.

37. Louis Francois Armand Duplessis, Herzog von Richelieu (1696-1788), Großneffe des Kardinals, übernahm 1748 das Kommando zu Genua und hatte dort so großen Erfolg, dass die Genuesen beim französischen König seine Erhebung zum Marschall von Frankreich erwirkten. Im Manuskript verschrieben als „Richelien".

---

33. The Doria were one of the leading families of the merchant aristocracy of the republic of Genoa from about the 12th century on. From the middle of the 17th century they were excluded from the office of doge and dedicated themselves mostly to church careers and diplomatic service.

34. Andrea Doria (1466 – 1560), a famous condottiere as well as the foremost naval commander of his time, secured the city's independence from France and its alliance with Spain. He fought against the Turks and the Barbary pirates. He never became doge, but was the leader of a new oligarchic form of aristocratic government.

35. Today Via Garibaldi and Via Balbi.

36. In 18th century French usage, "abbé" meant any cleric, not just an abbot.

37. Louis Francois Armand Duplessis, duke of Richelieu (1696 – 1788), grand nephew of cardinal Richelieu, became commander of Genoa in 1748 and was so successful that the Genoese succeeded in getting him promoted to the rank of maréchal de France by the French king. In the mscr. misspelled as "Richelien".

In einer Nacht war ein solcher Sturm, daß man am Morgen in dem andern Hafen, die Darsenna genannt,[38] zwei Kauffarthey-Schiffe sah, von denen das eine gesunken war, so daß nur die Maste[n] aus dem Wasser ragten; das andere war von den Wellen aufgehoben und auf den steinernen Damm hingestellt worden.

Ich machte einen Spazierritt mit einigen Officiren nach einem Landgute der Familie Spinola[39] am Ufer westlich von der Stadt. Auch war ich zweimal in der Oper. Hier sah ich, wenn ich mich recht erinnere, einen italiänischen Prinzen in einer Loge, nebst einer Dame, die beide von ausgezeichnet schöner Gestallt waren. Er war masquirt [14] wie ein vornehmer Türke, doch ohne Masque vor seinem Gesichte. Die Dame wie eine Türkin. Das andere Mal stellte er sich zur Schau als preußischer Officier, mit großem Hute und kurzem spanischen Rohr; und die Dame hatte eine damit harmonirende Kleidung. – Auch einem masquirten Balle wohnte ich bei.

Am 13ten Februar segelten wir von Genua ab. Am 15ten sahen wir die Insel Gorgona[40], und Malora[41], einen Felsen mit einem Thurme, bei Livorno[42]. Wir ankerten auf der Rhede von Livorno, und nachdem wir mit 9 Schüssen salutirt hatten, wurde uns mit 9 gedankt. Wir fanden da ein holländisches Linienschiff „Rotterdam", Capitain Crull, welcher nachher anno 1782 zu St. Eustachius[43] gegen Admiral Rodney[44] blieb. Hiedurch wurde unsere Escadre 4 Linienschiffe stark. [15] Am 23ten segelten

One night we had a terrible storm. The next morning, we saw two merchant-marine ships in the next harbour, called "Darsenna".[38] One ship had sunk, so that only the masts were visible above the water. The other ship had been pushed by the waves and landed on top of a stone jetty.

With some other officers I rode out to visit the manor house of the Spinola family[39] on the coast, west of the city. Also I went to the opera twice. If I remember correctly, there I saw an Italian prince in his box with a lady, both were very good-looking. He was dressed up [14]as a noble Turk, but without a mask, and she was dressed like a Turkish lady. The second time he was decked out as a Prussian officer, with huge hat and short Spanish swagger-cane, and the lady was dressed to match. I also attended a masked-ball.

On February. 13th, we sailed out of Genoa. On the 15th, we saw the island of Gorgona[40], and Malora[41], a rock with a tower close to Livorno (Leghorn)[42]. We cast anchor in the Livorno roadstead, and after we had saluted with 9 shots, we were thanked with 9. There we found a Dutch ship of the line, "Rotterdam", and Captain Crull who later went down anno 1782, off St. Eustatius,[43] in battle when Admiral Rodney[44] carried the day. With this addition our squadron now numbered four ships of the line. [15]

---

38. Das Stadtviertel Darsena, wo zu Zeiten der Stadtrepublik die Galeeren gebaut wurden, befindet sich in unmittelbarer Nähe zum porto antico; http://de.wikipedia.org/wiki/Meeresmuseum_Galata.

39. Neben den Doria, Fieschi, Grimaldi und Durazzo gehörten die Spinola zu den einflussreichsten Familien der Republik Genua.

40. Felseninsel, 37 km südwestl. von Livorno, seit 1404 zu Florenz gehörig.

41. Felsenklippe mit Turm bei Livorno, auch Meloria genannt.

42. Livorno, italienische Hafenstadt, 1540-70 unter Cosimo I. Medici angelegt.

43. St. Eustatius, niederländische Insel in der Karibik, ein bedeutender neutraler Handelsplatz, der eine wichtige Rolle für den Nachschub von Waffen und Munition an die amerikanischen Kolonien spielte, war von Rodney bereits 1781 besetzt worden. Die Jahreszahl 1782 bezieht sich auf die „Battle of the Saintes", s. u. Anm. 44.

44. Sir George Brydges, erster Baron Rodney (1718-1792), britischer Seeoffizier, 1771 Konteradmiral, 1778 "admiral of the white", errang am 12. April 1782 seinen wichtigsten Sieg vor Dominica („Battle of the Saintes") gegen die Franzosen unter Admiral de Grasse. Rechteren verwechselt hier wohl Rodneys Einnahme von St. Eustatius im Februar 1781 mit diesem Sieg (s. u. Anm. 232 u. o. Anm. 43). Der Sieg vor Dominica rettete Großbritannien den Besitz von Jamaica, woraus höhere Einkünfte flossen als aus den 13 nordamerikanischen Kolonien, und schadete dem Ansehen Frankreichs als Seemacht. Rodney erhielt eine Pension von jährlich 2000 Pfund, eine damals sehr hohe Summe.

---

38. Darsena is the part of town where galleys were built at the time when Genoa was a republic; it is quite close to the "porto antico"; http://de.wikipedia.org/wiki/Meeresmuseum_Galata.

39. Next to the Doria, Fieschi, Grimaldi, and the Durazzo, the Spinola belonged to the most influential families in the republic of Genoa.

40. Rock island, approx. 23 miles southwest of Leghorn, became a Florentine possession in 1404.

41. Rocky cliff with a tower close to Leghorn, also named Meloria.

42. Italian harbour, built 1540 – 1570 under Cosimo Medici I.

43. St. Eustatius, a Dutch island in the Caribbean, a great entrepot of neutral trade and very important for the supply of arms and ammunition to the American colonies, was captured by Rodney in 1781. 1782 was the year of the „Battle of the Saintes"; cf. below fn. 44.

44. George Brydges, 1st Baron Rodney (1718 – 1792), English admiral, won his most famous victory on April 12th, 1782, off Dominica against the French admiral de Grasse, severely damaging French naval prestige. The author probably confuses this naval battle with Rodney's capture of St. Eustatius one year earlier (cf. fn. 43 and 238). His victory secured the possession of Jamaica for the British; at that time, Britain had more tax income from Jamaica than from the 13 North American colonies combined. Rodney was given a barony with a yearly pension of 2.000 L, a very large sum at the time.

wir von Livorno ab, und kamen bei Cap Negro vorbei, um in den Canal von Piombino[45], zwischen Elba und dem festen Lande, zu kommen. Als ich auf dem Halbdecke stand, hörte ich einen Angstschrei, und sah hinter dem Schiffe einen Matrosen, dessen Kopf aus dem Meere ragte. Er wurde in dem Strudel, der hinter dem Schiffe durch seinen Lauf entsteht (holländisch das Kielwasser, französisch „le Sillage" genannt) herumgedreht. Da das Schiff stark lief und das Meer unruhig war, dachte man gar nicht daran, ihm zu helfen.

Ich habe den Holländern den Vorwurf machen hören, daß sie sich gar nicht darnach umsähen, wenn Einer ins Meer fiele, weil sie auf so unvernünftige Weise wie die Türken an eine Praedestination glaubten. Die Ursache ist aber, weil es selten möglich ist, Einen zu retten. Was man [16] thun kann, ist, eine Chaloupe[46] auszusetzen. Wenn aber das Meer sehr hoch geht, ist dies nicht möglich und ist das Meer ruhiger, so dauert doch das Aussetzen so lange, bis der Mensch, der in seinen Kleidern schwimmen muß, nicht mehr zu sehen ist. Das beste ist, daß man ihm, wenn er anders ein guter Schwimmer ist, etwas zuwirft, z.B. einen der Hühner-Käfige, die hinten auf dem Schiffe stehen, woran er sich dann so lange halten kann und welches ihn von weitem sichtbar macht.

Ich erinnere mich, daß auf der französischen Flotte bei stürmischem Wetter und dunkler Nacht ein Signal durch einen Kanonenschuß und eine Laterne gegeben wurde, welches nach dem Signalbuche un homme à la mer (Mann über Bord) bedeutete. Dies konnte zu nichts helfen; es deutete aber doch an, daß man Werth auf ein Menschenleben setzte, – was immer zu loben ist. [17] Am 24ten passirten wir den Canal von Piombino zwischen Serboli[47] und Palmaria[48], sahen die Insel Giglio[49], und am 25. die Insel Palmerola[50]. Am 28. früh Morgens befanden wir uns ganz nahe bei der Insel Ischia, welche sehr hoch ist, und kamen am 1ten März bei Neapel[51] an. Wir thaten 21 Schüsse, welches eine königliche Salutirung ist. Die Zahl der Schüsse muß immer ungleich sein, und wenn sie beantwortet

---

45. Meerenge zwischen Piombino und der Insel Elba.

46. In deutscher Schreibweise: Schaluppe, kleines, einmastiges Segelschiff oder großes Beiboot eines Seeschiffs.

47. Felseninsel im Kanal von Piombino, zwischen Piombino und der Insel Elba.

48. Felseninsel im Kanal von Piombino, zwischen Piombino und der Insel Elba, auch „Palmziola" genannt.

49. Granitinsel, südöstl. von Elba, seit 1555/59 mit Siena zur Toskana gehörig.

50. Insel westlich von Neapel, auch „Palmarola" genannt.

51. Neapel, Hauptstadt des Königreichs N., seit 1735 von einer Nebenlinie der spanischen Bourbonen regiert.

On the 23rd we sailed out of Livorno, and sailed round Cape Negro, in order to enter the Channel of Piombino[45], between Elba and the continent. When I was standing on the bridge, I heard an awful scream, and then I saw the head of a sailor sticking out of the water behind the ship. He was lost in the wake that runs behind the ship (Kielwasser in Dutch; le Sillage in French). Because the ship was sailing so fast and the water was so turbulent, no one thought to rescue him.

I have heard some criticize that the Dutch do not even look back when somebody falls over board, because they supposedly have an unreasonable belief in predestination, just like the Turks. The real reason, however, is that it is almost impossible to rescue anybody. What can [16] be done, is to set out a sloop.[46] But when the waves are high, this is not possible; and even if the ocean is quieter, just putting out the life-boat takes so long, that the person trying to swim in wet clothes is usually no longer to be seen. The best thing to be done, if he is a good swimmer, is to throw him something – usually a chicken coop, rows of them are lined up at the back of the ship, and he can hold on to it till help arrives or climb up on it, which makes him more visible from far away.

I remember, that one dark stormy night, the French fleet gave a cannon and lantern signal which, according to our signal-book, meant "un homme à la mer" (man overboard). Nothing could be done; but at least it showed that they valued human life, which must always be praised. [17] On the 24th we passed the Channel of Piombino between Cerboli[47] and Palmaria[48], we saw the island of Giglio[49], and on the 25th the island of Palmerola[50]. At dawn on the 28th, we found ourselves quite close to the island of Ischia, which is very mountainous, and we arrived at Naples[51] on the first of March. We fired 21 shots, which is a royal salute. The number of cannon-shots must always be uneven, and they usually answer with the same number minus two shots, which was not the case here. 19 shots would

---

45. Straits between Piombino and the island of Elba.

46. The author uses the word "sloop" to describe a large ship's longboat.

47. Rock island in the channel of Piombino.

48. Rock island in the channel of Piombino, between Piombino and the isle of Elba, also named "Palmziola".

49. Granite island southeast of Elba, fell to Tuscany together with Siena in 1555/59.

50. Island west of Naples, also spelled "Palmarola".

51. Capital of Campania, then capital of the eponymous kingdom, governed by a side line of the Spanish Bourbons after 1735.

werden, was hier nicht geschah, so geschieht es mit 2 weniger. Hier wäre es mit 19 schicklich gewesen. Der französische Gesandte und der englische Lord Hamilton[52], kamen auf unser Schiff. Ich fuhr mit einigen Officiren nach Puzzuola[53]. Jeder bekommt eine Caleche für sich allein, auf der ein freier Sitz ohne Lehne für einen Menschen ist. Hinter ihm steht der Fuhrmann, wie auf einem Rennschlitten, und hält die Zügel und die Peitsche. Dieser muß nun in einem fort schreien, um bei dem großen Gedränge in den Stra- [18] ßen niemanden zu überfahren: „Guarda voi, guarda Signor Officiale", „Guarda Donna, Guarda Padre, guarda Signor tenente" etc. Wir fuhren den Weg dicht bei Neapel, welcher durch den Berg Pausilyp[54] durchgeht, 20 Schuh breit und 700 Schritte lang. In Puzzuolo wird das Amphitheater[55] gezeigt wo der h[eilige] Januarius den wilden Thieren vorgeworfen wurde, die ihn aber anbeteten, statt ihn zu zerreissen. Von da fährt man über den kleinen Meerbusen nach Baja[56] und kommt, indem man das Ufer verfolgt, an das Grab der Agrippina und zu den Bädern des Nero[57], welche viele unterirdische Gänge enthalten. Zuletzt geht man in einen schmalen Gang, wo die Hitze wie in einem Backofen ist. Am Ende davon ist eine siedende Quelle, worin man Eier siedet. Um dahin zu kommen, muß man sich ganz ausziehen. Denn in einer hal- [19] ben Minute läuft einem der Schweiß von allen Seiten herab. Wenige können es aushalten. Der Wasserbehälter des Agrippa[58] ist unter der Erde mit einer Menge Säulen, deren Bewurf so hart wie Marmor ist. Am See Avernus[59] ist die sogenannte Grotte der Sibille. Man geht da durch lange unterirdische Gänge bis zu einem Teiche, wo jeder der Führer einen Reisenden auf den Rücken nimmt und ihn eine weite Strecke durchs Wasser trägt, bis man wieder trocken stehen

have been proper here. The French envoy and the English [envoy], Lord Hamilton[52], came on board of our ship. Some officers and I went to Puzzuola[53]. Each officer got his own calash, the backless seat was just large enough for one person. The wagoner stood behind me, just like on a sleigh, and he held the reins and whip. He had to keep yelling, so that no one was run over with the huge crowds on the streets [18]: "Guarda voi, guarda Signor Officiale. Guarda Donna. Guarda Padre. Guarda Signor tenente etc." We took the road close to Naples, which led through the mountain Pausilyp[54], 20 shoes wide and 700 paces long. In Puzzuolo we were shown the amphitheater[55] where St. Januarius was thrown to the wild animals who worshipped him instead of tearing him to pieces. From there we crossed a small bay to Baja[56], and following the coast we arrived at the grave of Agrippina and Nero's[57] baths, which are full of underground passageways. At last one arrives in a narrow passageway, where it is as hot as a bake-oven. At the back is a water-source that can boil eggs. To reach and see this you have to undress because, after just half a minute, [19] you'll be dripping with sweat all over. Few people can stand it. The cistern of Agrippa[58] is underground with lots of pillars whose coatings are as hard as marble. At Lake Avernus[59] there is the so-called Sibyl's Grotto. You go through a long subterranean passageway to reach a pool, where each of the guides takes a tourist on his back and carries him a long way through the water until you reach dry land again. Since we had one more tourist than guides available, one of us had to stay behind and wait a while. This was my lot as I was the lowest-ranking officer. I could hear the others

---

52. Sir William Hamilton (1730 – 1803), Diplomat und Archäologe, der Ehemann von Lady Emma Hamilton, der Geliebten von Admiral Horatio Nelson, war von 1764 bis 1800 britischer Gesandter am Hof von Neapel.

53. Pozzuoli, Stadt westlich von Neapel am Golf von Neapel gelegen.

54. Der Posilippo trennt die Buchten von Neapel und Pozzuoli. Der Name des Bergrückens stammt von einer im Altertum hier gelegenen Villa Pausilypon (= ohne Sorge, „Sanssouci").

55. Eines der größten erhaltenen Amphitheater der Antike, gebaut zur Zeit Vespasians (2. Hälfte des 1. Jhs.n.Chr.).

56. Baia, Ort am Golf von Neapel, westlich von Pozzuoli. Das sog. Grab der Agrippina ist wahrscheinlich eine Theaterruine.

57. Die „Stufe di Nero" (Öfen des Nero) sind natürliche, aus vier Abteilungen bestehende Schwitzbäder.

58. Wahrscheinlich die Zisterne in der Villa Greco mit der Piscina Mirabilis, einem gewaltigen (72 m langen, 26 m breiten) unterirdischer Wasserbehälter für die Versorgung der römischen Flotte.

59. Am Lago d'Averno, einem ca. 3 km langen Krater, wurde in der Antike (Vergil) der Eingang zur Unterwelt vermutet. Ein 100 m langer Gang des antiken Militärhafens wurde auch als Grotte der Sibylle gezeigt.

52. Sir William Hamilton (1730 – 1803), diplomat and archaeologist, was the husband of Lady Emma Hamilton, the mistress of the British admiral Lord Horatio Nelson. From 1764 until his recall in 1800, he was the British envoy to the court of Naples.

53. Pozzuoli, town west of Naples on the gulf of Naples.

54. Posilippo mountain divides the bays of Naples and of Pozzuoli; its name derives from a villa situated here in antiquity called "Pausilypon" ("Sanssouci", "carefree").

55. One of the largest extant amphitheatres from antiquity, built at the time of emperor Vespasianus (2nd half of the 1st century A.D.)

56. Baia, town on the gulf of Naples, west of Pozzuoli. The so-called grave of Agrippina ist probably a ruined theatre.

57. The "stufe di Nero" (Nero's ovens) are natural steam-baths, consisting of four compartments.

58. Probably the cistern in Villa Greco with the "Piscina Mirabilis", a huge (72 x 26 meters) underground tank for the water supply of the Roman fleet.

59. In antiquity (Virgil), Lago d'Averno was considered to be the entrance to Hades. A 100 meter long covered walkway of the antique naval base supposedly was Sybil's grotto.

kann. Da nun ein Träger weniger als Reisende war, so mußte einer von uns zurückbleiben und warten. Dies wurde mir, als dem Untersten im Range, zu theil. Ich hörte die andern durchs Wasser plätschern; dieser Laut verlor sich aber bald, so daß alles todstill war und ich allein in der Mitte des Berges. Nach langem Warten hörte ich wieder einen Laut und es näherte sich einer, um mich abzuholen. Er wollte aber meine Lage benützen, und [20] weigerte sich, mich zu tragen, wenn ich ihm nicht noch über das Bedungene beschenkte. Ich sprang ihm aber auf den Rücken, und da er mich entschlossen sah, trug er mich fort. Von da kamen wir an die Grotte del Cane[60], wo 2 unglückliche Hunde wechselsweise gebraucht wurden, die Probe zu machen. Sobald sie mit dem Kopfe nahe an die Erde gehalten werden, bekommen sie Verzuckungen, und liegen dann wie todt. Nachher legt man sie hinaus an die frische Luft, wo sie allmählich wieder zu sich kommen. Brennende Fackeln gehen sogleich aus, wenn sie der Erde nahe gebracht werden. Allda sind auch die Schwitzbäder von St. Germano und der See Anagno, wo man das Wasser an vielen Orten kochen sieht. Der Berg Monte nuovo[61] ist i. J. 1538 in einer Nacht entstanden. – Solvaterra[62] dagegen ist ein eingesunkener Berg, der jetzt ganz eben ist. Rauch und Feuer strömt dort aus unterirdischen Löchern mit Geräusch und Schwefelgeruch hervor. Steine welche man an diese Oefnungen legt, werden alsbald cal- [21] cinirt[63] und voll Schwefels; und man präparirt dann Alaun[64] und Zinnober[65] aus denselben. Wenn man Papier an ein solches Loch legt, so verbrennt es nicht wegen des Windes, der beständig aus dem Loche bläst; ein eiserner Stab aber schmilzt alsbald.

Ein anderes Mal fuhren wir nach Portizi.[66] Vor dem Schlosse steht eine sehr schöne, ausgegrabene Reuterstatue. Das

splashing through the water; this noise soon became less and less audible, so that everything was deadly quiet and I was left alone in the middle of the mountain. After waiting for a long time, I finally heard a sound and somebody was coming to pick me up. But he wanted to take advantage of my situation, and [20] refused to carry me, if I didn't pay extra. But I jumped on his back and as he noticed my resolve, he carried me over. After this we came to the "Grotto del Cane" (dog's grotto)[60], where two hapless dogs were put to the test one after the other. When their heads were held down to the ground, they convulsed and lay there looking dead. Afterwards they put them out in the fresh air, where they gradually revive. Burning torches go out when they are put down near the ground. There is also the steam-bath of St. Germano and Lake Anagno where you can see several sources of boiling water. The mountain Monte nuovo[61] was created in one night, anno 1538. Solvaterra,[62] on the other hand, is a sunken mountain which is quite flat now. Smoke and fire, smelling of sulfur and making loud noises, spit out of subterranean holes. When rocks are put on these openings, they are soon calcified[63] [21] and covered with sulfur; and they use them to make alum[64] and cinnabar[65] (vermillion: a brilliant red pigment). If you hold paper over such an opening it won't burn because of the wind that always blows out of the hole, but an iron rod melts immediately.

One day we visited Portici.[66] In front of the palace is a very handsome excavated ancient equestrian statue. We did not get to see the Cabinet in the palace: they were very reserved, because recently some tourists had stolen

---

60. In der 8 m tiefen Grotte del Cane lagern bis in Kniehöhe Kohlensäuregase, so dass Hunde ersticken.

61. Der Berg ist ca. 149 m hoch.

62. Die Solvatara ist ein großer Vulkankrater von 770 m Durchmesser. Der Boden ist von einer weißlichen Kruste überzogen, auf der die Schritte widerhallen. Hier gibt es Erdspalten mit heißen Schwefeldämpfen, „Pseudo vulcanetti", die kochenden Schlamm auswerfen, Kohlensäure- und Mineralwasserquellen.

63. Kalzinieren bedeutet aus einer chemischen Verbindung Wasser oder Kohlendioxyd austreiben.

64. Alaun = Kalium-Aluminium-Sulfat, ein Mineral das u.a. bei der Herstellung von Farben, Leimen des Papiers, als Brotzusatz, fäulnishemmendes und blutstillendes Mittel Verwendung findet.

65. Zinnober ist ein Quecksilbererz, das zur Herstellung von roter Farbe dient.

66. Südöstlich von Neapel, bekannte Sommerfrische im 18. Jahrhundert. Das Schloss (Palazzo Reale) ließ Karl III. von Neapel 1738 als Sommerresidenz erbauen

---

60. Carbon monoxide stands knee-high in the grotto which extends 8 meters underground, so that dogs suffocate.

61. 149 meters (ca. 470 ft.) high.

62. Solvatara is a large sunken volcanic crater, 770 meters across. The ground is covered by a whitish thick crust, on which footsteps echo. There are crevices with hot sulfur gases, "pseudo vulcanetti" which throw up boiling mud, as well as sources of carbonic acid and mineral waters.

63. To calcify means to remove water or carbon dioxide from a chemical compound.

64. Alum, potassium aluminum sulfate, is a mineral used in the production of paints and paper, as a bread additive and as an antiseptic and styptic agent.

65. A mercury ore used to produce vermillion, a brilliant red pigment.

66. In the 18th century, a well-known summer resort southeast of Naples. Charles III had the Palazzo Reale built in 1738 as a summer residence.

Cabinet im Schlosse bekamen wir nicht zu sehen; man war sehr zurückhaltend damit, weil kurz vorher Reisende beim Beschauen Sachen daraus entwendet hatten. Die Stadt Herculan[e]um[67], die unter dem Flecken Portici begraben liegt, wurde anno 1711 beim Graben eines Brunnens entdeckt. Man steigt auf vielen Treppen hinab. Damals war das Theater völlig an den Tag gefördert. Von da gingen wir nach Pompeji[68], welches mehr befriedigt, als Herculan[e]um. Denn dieses ist von glühender Lava überströmt und verbrannt worden, Pompeji hingegen nur mit Asche und Erde bedeckt, so daß sich alles da erhalten hat. [22] Beim Eingang war die Caserne der Soldaten, in den Straßen geht man wie in tiefen Gräben, wo die Häuser auf beiden Seiten in der Erde stecken. Wir gingen von da den Vesuv[69] hinauf; jedoch ich konnte die andern nicht dazu bereden, weiter als ein Drittheil der Höhe zu erklimmen.

An einem andern Tage fuhr ich nach dem königlichen Schlosse Capo del Monte[70], wo die französische Gemäldegallerie ist. Diese rührt von des Königs Großmutter[71] her, die eine Prinzessin von Parma aus dem Hause Farnese war. Auch ein Medaillen-Cabinet ist da. Ich besah auch das Castell St. Elmo[72], welches Neapel beherrscht, und von dem aus man in der Ferne das Grab Virgil's[73] sieht. Etwas niedriger liegt das Ka[r]theuserkloster[74], von wo die schönste Aussicht über Neapel und das Meer mit seinen Inseln ist. Im Theater St. Carlo[75] wurde damals

things there. The city of Herculaneum[67] which lies buried beneath the village of Portici was discovered anno 1711 while they were digging a well. You have to go down many steps. There they discovered a whole theater. After this we went to Pompei[68] which was more interesting than Herculaneum because that was smothered with glowing lava and totally burned down; Pompei, on the other hand, was only covered with ashes and earth, thus everything was preserved. [22] At the entrance we saw the soldiers' barracks; the streets are like deep ruts, and the houses on both sides are planted deep in the ground. After this we began to walk up Mt. Vesuvius[69], but I could not inspire the others to make it further than one-third of the way up.

On another day, I went to see the French art gallery in the royal palace, Capo del Monte[70]. This was founded by the King's grandmother[71] who was a Farnese princess from Parma. They also had a cameo-cabinet (small private room). I also visited St. Elmo's Castle[72], which dominates Naples, and from which you can see Vergil's grave[73] in the distance. The Carthusian monastery[74], a bit lower down, affords the most beautiful view of Naples and the sea with its islands. The St. Carlo theater[75] was closed when we were there. But I got to see the church

---

67. Antike Stadt am Golf von Neapel, südöstlich von Neapel. 79 n. Chr. wurde die Stadt bei einem Ausbruch des Vesuvs unter einer 12 m hohen Schlammschicht, die mit der Zeit wie Tuffstein wurde, begraben. Das 1770 schon teilweise ausgegrabene Theater fasste 2000 bis 2500 Zuschauer.

68. Antike Stadt am Golf von Neapel, südöstlich von Neapel, am Fuße des Vesuvs, die bei dessen Ausbruch 79 n. Chr. von Lava und Asche verschüttet wurde.

69. Der 1282 m hohe Vesuv, ein bis heute tätiger Vulkan, liegt 12 km östlich von Neapel; einziger echter Vulkan auf dem europäischen Festland. Bis 1944 sah man über dem Krater eine „Rauchpinie" und nachts das Feuer.

70. Das Schloss Capodimonte wurde 1738 unter der Leitung von G. A. Medrano für König Karl III. von Neapel erbaut, aber erst ein Jahrhundert später vollendet; heute Nationalgalerie und Porzellansammlung.

71. Elisabeth, geb. Herzogin von Parma (und Toskana) (1692-1766).

72. Im Ostteil von Neapel liegt das die Stadt bekrönende Castel Sant'Elmo, das – um die Mitte des 14. Jahrhunderts angelegt – damals wie heute militärischen Zwecken dient.

73. Publius Vergilius Maro (70 – 19 v. Chr.) verfasste mit der „Äneis" ein Hauptwerk der römischen Antike.

74. Das Kartäuserkloster San Martino stammt aus dem 14. Jh. und wurde im 17. Jh. barockisiert.

75. Das berühmte Opernhaus San Carlo wurde 1737 von Carasale nach einem Entwurf von Giovanni Medrano errichtet.

67. Ancient city on the gulf of Naples, southeast of Naples. In 79 A.D., in an eruption of Mt. Vesuvius, the city was buried under a 36 ft. deep layer of mud which, in time, hardened to rock. The theatre which had been partially excavated in the 1770s could hold 2,000 to 2,500 spectators.

68. Ancient city on the gulf of Naples, southeast of Naples, at the foot of Mt. Vesuvius which was covered with lava and ashes by the eruption of 79 A.D.

69. Mt. Vesuvius, 1282 meters (4190 ft.) high, an active volcano situated 7 miles east of Naples, is the only real volcano on the European mainland. Up to 1944, a pine-cone shaped cloud was continually visible as was the fire at night.

70. The royal palace of Capodimonte was begun by G.A. Medrano for king Charles III. of Naples, but was only completed a century later. Today it houses the national gallery and a china collection.

71. Elizabeth, née duchess of Parma (and Tuscany) (1692-1766).

72. Castel Sant'Elmo is situated in the eastern part of Naples and towers above the city; it was built in the middle of the 14th century and has served military purposes ever since.

73. Publius Vergilius Maro (70 – 19 B.C.), author whose „Aeneis" is one of the most important works of roman antiquity.

74. Carthusian monastery, built in the 14th century and remodeled in the baroque style in the 17th century.

75. The famous opera house of San Carlo was built in 1737 by Carasale according to the plans of Giovanni Medrano.

nicht gespielt. Die Kirche des h. Januarius[76] aber besuchte ich, und sah die Capelle, [23] wo jährlich das Wunderwerk mit seinem Blute vorgeht, nämlich daß es flüssig wird.

Ein Holländer, der Kammerdiener beim Prinzen San Severino war, zeigte uns die Capelle[77] dieses Prinzen, in der die vorzüglichsten Statuen von Neapel sind, unter andern die eines Ritters, welcher im Begriff ist, aus einem Sarge zu steigen zum Andenken an einen aus der Familie, der im Kri[e]ge schon für todt im Sarge gelegen war, – und eine andere, welche „Il Desingannato" oder „Der Enttäuschte" heißt: eine Person ist in ein Netz verwickelt, sie zerreißt es und macht sich davon los.

Ein Institut vornehmer neapolitanischer Jünglinge besuchte unser Schiff mit ihren geistlichen Lehrern. Sie luden uns ein, sie wieder zu besuchen. Wir trafen sie gerade in einer Fechtstunde an. Der Fechtmeister war ein bejahrter Mann, von dessen Vater mir ein anwesender Neapolitaner [24] erzählte, derselbe sei ein ausgezeichneter Mann gewesen. Bei einem Duell habe er seinem Gegner zugerufen: „Sehet euch da vor hinter euch!" – und indem sich dieser umgesehen, habe er ihn durch eine Büffelshaut durch, womit seine Brust bedeckt war, durchbohrt. Der Ruhm dieser Heldenthat schien nach so vielen Jahren auf seinen Sohn zurückstrahlen zu sollen.

Ich hörte eine Predigt in einer Klosterkirche. Die Kanzel war an der Mauer befestigt und hatte eine Thüre in der Mauer, so daß man den Prediger nicht eher sah, als bis er auf der Kanzel stand. Zuerst kam einer, welcher das weibliche Geschlecht durchzuziehen schien. Denn zuweilen sprach er in einer feinen weiblichen Stimme mit vieler Ziererey, und dann fiel er wieder mit einer groben Baßstimme ein. In diesem Dialoge hielt er zuweilen inne, indem er durch das laute Gelächter unterbrochen wurde. Dieser verschwand durch die Thüre hinter der Kanzel, [25] und ein zweiter kam daraus hervor, welcher durch seinen melancholischen Ton jetzt die Gemeine in eine so traurige Stimmung versetzte, daß sie alle hätten weinen mögen, wie sie zuerst gelacht hatten.

Abends sieht man alles was Kutscher und Pferde hat, mit allen ihren Bedienten auf den Wagen und zu Fuß dabei in

of St. Januarius[76] and saw the chapel [23] where, every year, the blood miracle can be seen, meaning that it is liquefied.

A Dutchman, who was a servant to Prince San Severino, showed us the chapel of the prince[77], which contains some of the most remarkable statues in Naples; among them is one of a knight climbing out of his coffin, in memory of a family member, who, in a war, had already been put in a coffin for dead, and another one called "il Desingannato" or the disappointed one: a person caught in a net which he rips and walks away from.

Our ship was visited by a school class of aristocratic Neapolitan boys with their religious teachers. They invited us to return the visit. When we arrived they were in the middle of a fencing-lesson. The fencing-master was an older man. A Neapolitan there told us a story [24] about his father, who was an extraordinary man. During a duel he yelled at his opponent, "Watch out behind you!" and while he was turning around, the Neapolitan struck him through a buffalo hide that covered his chest. After all these years, the fame of this act was still reflected upon the son.

I listened to a sermon in a monastic church. The chancel was attached to the wall and there was a door in the wall, so that you did not see the preacher, before he appeared in the chancel. First, one preacher spoke, who seemed to be making fun of the female sex. Because sometimes he spoke with a high voice with lots of affectation (airs and graces), and then he used a low rough bass-voice. In the middle of this dialogue, he sometimes had to stop, because of the loud laughter. Then he disappeared through the door behind the chancel [25], and a second one came out who, using a very melancholy tone, had almost the whole congregation crying where they had been laughing just moments before.

In the evening, everyone who has a coachman and horses is seen driving through the city and round the

---

76. Dom San Gennaro. In der Kapelle San Gennaro steht die Statue des hl. Januarius, des Stadtpatrons von Neapel. In einem Silberreliquiar befinden sich das Haupt des Heiligen und zwei Gefäße mit seinem geronnenen Blut, das sich zweimal jährlich, am ersten Samstag im Mai und am 19. September, seinem Namenstag, wunderbarerweise verflüssigt.

77. In der Via De Sanctis steht die Capella Sansevero (S. Maria della Pietà dei Sangro), die 1590 als Grabkapelle der Familie Sangro errichtet wurde. Berühmt sind die Statuen von A. Corradini und Sammartini.

76. Cathedral of San Gennaro. The statue of Saint Januarius, patron saint of Naples, stands in San Gennaro chapel. A silver reliquiary contains the saint's head and two containers with his clotted blood which is miraculously liquefied twice annually, i.e. on the first saturday in May and on the 19th of September, his feast day.

77. The chapel of Sansevero (Santa Maria della Pietà dei Sangro) which was built in 1590 as burial chapel for the Sangro family is situated in the Via de Sanctis. The statues by A. Corradini and Sammartini are notable.

Processionen Schritt für Schritt durch die Stadt und um den Hafen fahren. Am 8ten März, als am Geburtstage S. Durchlaucht des Herrn Prinzen von Oranien[78], um 9 Uhr wurden auf allen Masten und Seegelstangen Wimpel und Flaggen aufgezogen und 24 Kanonenschüsse gethan, was um 4 Uhr und mit Sonnenuntergang wiederholt wurde.

Am 21ten ging die Escadre des nachts um 11 Uhr unter Segel, das Schiff „Rotterdam", Capitain Crul[l], blieb mit 150 Kranken zurück. Am 22ten passirten wir bei Ischia. Am 26ten bekamen wir so heftigen Wind, daß wir nur [**26**] die untersten Segel vermindert beibehalten konnten. Nämlich am großen Segel des großen und des Fockmastes ist 3 Schuh hoch unter der Segelstange wenn das Segel ausgebreitet ist, eine Reihe kurzer Stricke von beiden Seiten. Will man das Segel kleiner machen, so läßt man die Segelstange etwas herab und bindet dann diese an beiden Seiten des Segels hängenden Stricke an die Segelstange zusammen. Die Reihen Stricke heissen auf holländisch ein Rif, französisch: „un Ris. Refen oder ein Rif stecken (Rider la voile), prendre un ris dans la voile". Die hohen Segel haben 2 solche Riffe. Es ist schon ein Sturm, wenn man gereefde Untersegel haben muß. Wird er noch stärker, so müssen diese auch weg, und das Schiff treibt „voor Top en voor Takel", französisch: „à sec", wenn man nicht noch ein dreieckiges Segel, den Sturmfock, aufsetzt.

In solchem Sturme kamen wir durch die Gruppe von Inseln, die Le Formiche[79] heisen, dann durch die Meeren- [**27**] ge von Piombino, und am 31ten landeten wir auf der Rhede von Livorno. Am 9ten und 10ten wurde das Schiff kalfatert[80]. Hiezu muß das Schiff auf eine Seite überhängen, damit die Theile unter dem Wasser ausgebessert werden können. Ein Teil der Kanonen wurde von der einen Seite auf die andere gebracht; an die Segelstangen wurden auf einer Seite Fässer voll Wasser angehängt, und die Matrosen mußten sich auf die halbe Länge der Segelstangen setzen. (Sie hingen daran wie Vögel am Bratspieß.) Während man damit beschäftigt war, legte sich ein Schiff von Ragusa[81] nicht weit von uns vor Anker und fing an zu salutiren. Auf einmal fliegt während ich gerade mit dem Fernrohr hinsah, eine Kugel zwischen unsern Masten und den Matrosen, die da saßen, durch. Es wurde sogleich ein Officir

---

78. Wilhelm V. Batavus Prinz von Oranien, Fürst von Nassau (*Den Haag 8. März 1748, †1806), Erbstatthalter der Vereinigten Provinzen.

79. Nördlich von Giglio und südwestlich von Grossetto liegen die Klippen 'Formiche [Ameisen] di Grossetto`.

80. Kalfatern: Abdichten der hölzernen Außenhaut und des Decks eines Schiffes mit Werg, Teer oder Kitt.

81. Ragusa, heute Dubrovnik, seit 1718 unabhängige Republik, Hafenstadt in Süddalmatien.

---

harbor step by step in a grand procession with all their servants both on horse and on foot. On March 8th, the birthday of his highness the Prince of Orange[78], pennants and flags went up on all masts and yard-arms at 9am and 24 cannon shots sounded, which were repeated at 4pm and at sun down.

On the 21st, the squadron set sail at 11 o'clock at night. Capt. Crul with 150 sick sailors on the ship "Rotterdam" remained in port. We saw Ischia on the 22nd. We had such strong winds on the 26th that we could only keep reduced lower sails. [**26**] Namely, a row of short strings are attached about 3 ft. below the yards on both sides of the great sail of both the mainmast and the foremast when the sail is spread out. If you want to strike sail, then you lower the yard a bit and tie onto it the strings which are hanging down on both sides of the sail. These rows of strings are called "Rif" in Dutch, "Ris" in French. "Refen" or "ein Rif stecken" in Dutch, "Rider la voile" or "prendre un ris dans la voile" in French ("take in a reef" in English). The larger sails have two rows of such reefs. It is already a storm if you need your lower sail reefed. If the wind gets even stronger, these sails are taken off, and the ship drifts "voor Top en voor Takel" (Dutch), in French "à Sec" (English: "to scud with bare poles"), unless the triangular "storm foresail" is set.

In such a storm we sailed through the group of islands, called Le Formiche[79], then through the straits [**27**]of Piombino, and on the 31st we reached the Livorno roadstead. On the 9th and 10th, the ship was caulked[80]. For this, the ship had to lie on one side, so that the under-water portion could be repaired. Some of the cannon had to be moved from one side to the other; kegs full of water were hung on the yards, and the sailors had to sit half-way up on the yards. (They hung there like birds on a spit.) While we were busy with all these preparations, a ship from Ragusa[81] cast anchor close by us and started to salute (with gunshots). While I was watching this with my field-glass, a cannon ball suddenly

---

78. William V. Batavus, prince of Orange and Nassau (*at the Hague March 8th, 1748, died 1806), hereditary "stadhouder" (governor) of the "Staten General" (United Provinces, i.e. the Netherlands, more precisely: their central organ of political representation).

79. The cliffs "Formiche (ants) di Grossetto" are situated north of the island of Giglio and southwest of Grossetto.

80. Caulking a ship means to stop up the seams of its sides and decks with oakum and melted pitch; oakum is loose fibre from old ropes picked – at that time – by convicts and paupers.

81. Ragusa, today Dubrovnik, harbour in southern Dalmatia, independent republic after 1718.

mit einer Chalupe geschickt, um zu fragen, was das bedeute? Sie antworteten es sei ein Versehen des Canoniers („il Canoniere sara gastigalo").[82] Nicht lange nach dieser Zeit, kam in [28] einem englischen Hafen der Admiral Kempenfeld[83] um das Leben, da bei einer solchen Gelegenheit das Schiff das Uebergewicht bekam und umschlug, während er in seinem Zimmer war.

Am 14ten kam ein russisches Kriegsschiff von 60 Kanonen, und am 15ten das holländische Linienschiff „Zirkzee", Capitain Nebbens, hier an.[84] Am 21ten April wurden die Anker gehoben. Die Escadre segelte zwischen Palmaria und Serbolia durch, und kreuzte östlich von Sardinien, näherte sich der maurischen Küste gegen die Insel Galita[85] bei Tunis am 1ten Mai, von wo man Malta[86] und den Aetna[87] in Sicilien von ferne sah. Dann kreuzte die Escadre wieder südlich von Sardinien und ankerte am 15ten Mai auf der Rhede von Cagliari[88], der Hauptstadt von Sardinien. Der Vicekönig wurde mit 15 und die Stadt mit 9 Schüssen salutirt, worauf sie mit 13 und 7 dankten.

Es wurde gerade das Frohnleichnamsfest gefeiert. Die Mitglieder des Parlaments, alle in rothsammetner, mit Gold bordirter

flew between our masts and the sailors, who were sitting there. We immediately sent an officer in a sloop to ask what they were up to. They answered that it was a mistake of their gunner ("il Canoniere sara gastigalo").[82] Soon after this, [28] in some English port Admiral Kempenfeld was killed[83], while he was in his cabin, when during such an operation, the ship was too top-heavy and capsized.

On the 14th a Russian warship of 60 cannon came, and on the 15th, a Dutch ship-of-the-line arrived, the "Zirkzee" under Capt. Nebbens.[84] On April 21st we weighed anchor. The squadron sailed between Palmaria and Serbolia and cruised east of Sardinia, drew near the Moorish coast at the island of Galita[85], close to Tunis on May 1st, where we could see Malta[86] and Mt. Etna[87] on Sicily in the distance. Then we cruised south of Sardinia and cast anchor on May 15th in the roadstead of Cágliari[88], the capital of Sardinia. The Viceroy was saluted with 15 shots and the city with 9, to which they answered with 13 and 7 respectively.

We arrived on the feast of Corpus Christi. The members of Parliament followed the procession. They were dressed

---

82. Bei „gastigalo" liegt kein Lesefehler vor. Da Battaglias Wörterbuch der italienischen Sprache „gastigare" als Variante von „castigare" (bestrafen) nennt, ist anzunehmen, dass ein Abschreibfehler vorliegt, dass „castigato" gemeint war. Der Kanonier sollte also wegen seines Fehlschusses einen Verweis oder eine Strafe bekommen.

83. Richard Kempenfelt (1718-1782), 1780 Konteradmiral. Die 1756 gebaute „Royal George", mit 100 Kanonen eines der größten Schiffe ihrer Zeit, war 1782 sein Flaggschiff. Vor einer Reise erhielt die Mannschaft Landgang, um sich von ihren Angehörigen zu verabschieden. Da man aber Desertionen befürchtete, durften auch etwa 400 Personen das Schiff besuchen. Als zur gleichen Zeit das vollbeladene Schiff zu Reparaturarbeiten auf die Seite gelegt wurde, sank es innerhalb von Minuten. Nur 255 von 1 200 Menschen, die sich zu diesem Zeitpunkt auf dem Schiff befanden, überlebten. Unter den Toten war auch Kempenfelt.

84. Der Name lautet richtig wohl „Zierikzee", nach der gleichnamigen Stadt an der Osterschelde; der Kapitän war François Johan Nebben, der erst im Januar 1771 von Holland ausgelaufen war; s. van der Horst, Kinckel, S. 176.

85. Die heute zu Tunesien gehörende Insel Galita liegt 45 km nördlich von Cap Serrat.

86. Malta, südlich von Sizilien, Sitz des Malteserordens.

87. Vulkan auf Sizilien.

88. An der Südküste der Insel gelegene Hauptstadt des Königreichs Sardinien. 1297 belehnte der Papst das spanische Haus Aragon mit der Insel Sardinien, 1713/14 kam sie an Österreich und 1718/20 im Tausch gegen Sizilien an das Haus Savoyen.

82. "Gastigalo" is no deciphering error, but the verb "gastigare"is found in Battaglia's Grand Italian Dictionary only as a variant of "castigare (to punish or reprimand)". Maybe the copyist mistook the author's "t" for an "l"; he probably meant to say that the gunner was to be "castigato", i.e. reprimanded or punished for his mistake.

83. Richard Kempenfelt (1718 – 1782), vice admiral. In 1782, the "Royal George", built in 1756, with 100 guns one of the largest ships of its time, was his flagship. Before a new voyage, the crew was to be allowed to go ashore to say good-bye to their families. But as it was feared that many of them would desert the ship, about 400 visitors, women and children among them, were permitted to come aboard. When, at the same time, repair work was done on the fully laden ship and it was put on its side for this purpose, it sank within minutes. Only 255 of the 1200 people on board at that time survived. Vice admiral K. was among the dead.

84. The correct spelling of the ship's name should have been "Zierikzee" after the eponymous town on the Osterschelde; the captain was François Johan Nebben who had sailed from the Netherlands in January of 1771; cf. van der Horst, Kinckel, p. 176.

85. It today belongs to Tunisia and is situated 28 miles north of Cape Serrat.

86. South of Sicily, seat of the Order of Maltesian Knights.

87. Sicilian volcano.

88. Capital of the kingdom of Sardinia, situated on its southern coast. In 1297, the pope enfeoffed the house of Aragon with the island of Sardinia; in 1713/14 it fell to Austria, and in 1718/19 to the house of Savoy which bartered Sicily for it.

spanischer Kleidung, mit großen spanischen Perücken, folgten der Procession.

Man sieht hier viel dänische und [29] andere Schiffe welche hauptsächlich des Salzes wegen kommen. Man läßt das Meerwasser über die Felder hinfließen und dämmt diese d[...] die Sonnenhitze sie [...] sind. Di[...] Ihre Klei[...] schen, a[...] welchem[...] Hütten in[...] korbs und[...] als Gefäß[...] und Stück[...] der Kopfki[...] man absch[...] wie die ges[...]

Am 21ten M[...] her. Am 2ten[...] von Sardinie[...] 15ten Gargon[...] von Livorno. [...] terdam" nebs[...] Contre-Admir[...]

89. Cap Corse, N[...]
Korsika.
90. Die Insel Gorg[...]
34 km von der Stad[...]
91. Sir John Elphin[...]
in russischen Dienst[...] [...]lands Baltische Flotte.
Er war einer von drei britischen Seeoffizieren, die unter Katharina d. Gr. die russische Marine bei angestrebten Reformen berieten; er gehörte auch zum Stab Orlovs bei der Schlacht von Cesme. Die Familie E. gehört zum schottischen Hochadel.
92. Fürst Aleksej Grigorevic Orlov (1737-1807), russischer Admiral. Nach dem glänzenden Sieg bei Tschesme war die russische Flotte im Winter 1770/71 wieder in Livorno. Hofrat Johann Friedrich Reiffenstein und Graf Ivan Suvalov gewannen im Auftrag der Zarin den noch jungen Maler Philipp Hackert dazu, die Seeschlacht von Tschesme in zwölf großen Historienbildern festzuhalten. Orlov erschien die Darstellung der Verbrennung der osmanischen Flotte im Hafen von Tschesme nicht detailgetreu genug. Daher entschloss er sich mit Genehmigung der Zarin und des Großherzogs Leopold, dem Maler eine „wirkliche Vorstellung einer solchen Begebenheit" zu verschaffen und ließ bei Livorno vor einer riesigen Menschenmenge eine Fregatte beschießen und abbrennen. Hackert retuschierte sein Bild unter diesem Eindruck und lieferte den gesamten Zyklus termingerecht in St. Petersburg ab, wo zunächst in Peterhof, später im Winterpalais (heute in der Eremitage) aufgehängt wurde. S. Scharf, Katharina II.

in red velvet, gold-trimmed, Spanish attire, including large Spanish wigs.

You can see many Danish ships and those of other nations here [29] which come mainly for the salt. Sea water is directed to flood some fields and then these are dammed up until the sun dries them, after which they are covered with salt. The inhabitants that I saw on land were shepherds. Their clothing consists of a jacket, breeches, and [ga]iters, all made of black leather, with a wide belt, on [w]hich they carried the cartridges for their long guns. One [of] their huts in the woods, that I saw, was formed like a [be]e-hive, and stood about 12 feet high. There was noth[ing] to be seen inside except for a few vessels to keep milk [in,] small stools to sit on, and large pieces of cork about [a fo]ot square used as pillows. These are harvested from [cork]-oaks, which are peeled off, and then they grow a new [one], just as shorn sheep grow new wool.

May 21st, Capt. Nebbens arrived here with his ship [...]see". On June 2nd, we left Cágliari and sailed west of [Sardi]nia and Corsica. On the 14th we saw Cape Corso[89], [on the] 15th Gargona[90], [30] on the 16th we cast anchor [at] Livorno roadstead. Here we found the Dutch ship-[of-]line "Rotterdam" next to 5 Russian ships of war [under] the command of Vice-Admiral Elphinstone[91], [which, lat]er, July 1770 at Cesme, united with Orlow[92] and

[...] Corse, northern tip of the island of Corsica which has [belonged] to France since 1768.
[...] island, part of the Tuscan archipelago, 34 km outside of the [port of Livo]rno (Leghorn), to which it belongs today.
91. Sir John Elphinstone (1722 – 1785) was a lieutenant-general and vice-admiral in the Russian service and in 1769 commanded the Russian fleet in the Baltic. He was one of three British naval officers who advised the Russian navy on reforms in the reign of Catherine the Great. He was a member of Orlov's staff in the battle of Cesme. The Elphinstones belong to Scotland's high nobility.
92. Prince Aleksej Grigorevic Orlov (1737 – 1807), Russian admiral. After the grand victory at Cesme the Russian fleet lay at anchor at Leghorn through the winter of 1770/71. The Russian court councillor Johann Friedrich Reiffenstein and count Ivan Suvalov – at the tsarina's behest – succeeded in engaging the young painter Philipp Hackert to paint the battle of Cesme in 12 large historical tableaux. Orlov thought that the picture of the burning of the Turkish fleet in the port of Cesme was lacking in detail. Therefore he decided – with the tsarina's and grand duke Leopold's permission – to give the painter a "true idea of such an occasion": off Leghorn, he had a frigate shot and burned down in front of a huge crowd of people. Hackert retouched his picture under the impression of this "feu d'artifice" and delivered the whole cycle of pictures in good time to St. Petersburg where it was first hung at the "Peterhof" and later in the Winter Palace (today Ermitage). Cf. Claus Scharf, Katharina II, S. 191f.

Spiritow[93], 10 ships strong, to burn down the Turkish fleet of 15 ships-of-the-line leaving only one afloat[94]. Two Tuscan ships of war entered the roadstead, along with two Papal galleys. There is the Order of St. Stephen in this area.[95] The officers on these Tuscan ships are knights in this order, like the Maltese, they are obliged to fight the Turks. The soldiers and officers do things in the Austrian way. Every midnight, they have a drum ceremony where they appear armed. The Austrians call this "die Schaarwache" (police watch); it is to commemorate a drum miracle when a drum sounded all by itself to warn against an impending enemy attack. [31]

On June 30th, a supply ship arrived from Amsterdam for us. On July 9th, we sailed out of Livorno. On the Genua coast we saw Porto Fino[96], Oneglia[97] and Port Cros and Isle du Levant[98] on the French coast. The squadron consisted of 5 ships-of-the-line. On the 15th we saw Cape Sicie[99] close to Toulon; on the 21st the island of Minorca[100]. Here another sailor fell overboard on the 21st, from one of our other ships. He was a good swimmer, and I could see him taking off his jacket to be able to swim better. But the water was so choppy, that we could not set out a sloop. Just a bit later and he would have been saved. For we arrived at the island of Minorca, and since the wind came from there, it protected us, and the water

---

93. Spiritow, or Spiridov, Grigory Andreyevich (1713 – 1790), Russian admiral, joined the navy in 1723, became an officer in 1733, commander of ships in the Baltic fleet after 1741, rear admiral in 1762. During the Russo-Ottoman War 1768-1774 he was in charge of a squadron sent to assist the Greeks. In 1770, under Orlov, with him in charge of the avant-garde, the Russians drove the Turkish fleet into Cesme Bay and destroyed it there. He may have retired in 1774 because he resented the fact that Orlov was given all the credit for this victory.

94. Çeşme, Turkish harbour in the Aegean, opposite the island of Chios. Here the Russians destroyed the Turkish fleet in the night of the 5th/6th July 1770, the worst defeat for the Turks since the battle of Lepanto (1571).

95. Tuscan Order (both clerical and military) of St. Stephen, the pope and martyr, founded by Cosimo de Medici in 1562 to fight piracy and to defend the Christian faith, abolished in 1859 by the Italian king.

96. Harbour and peninsula southeast of Genoa.

97. Today a part of Imperia, west of Genoa.

98. The island of Port Cros and the island of Levant are situated southeast of Toulon; together with the island of Porquerolles they form the Hyères Islands.

99. Cape Sicié south of Toulon.

100. Menorca, second largest island of the Spanish Baleares, 1708 – 56 British, 1756 – 63 French, 1763 – 83 and 1798 – 1802 British again.

ger. Wir passirten nahe bei Port Mahon[101], und konnten die Festungswerke sehr deutlich unterscheiden. Am 23ten sahen wir die Insel Cabrera[102].

[32] Am 25ten kamen wir in die Bey von Majorca[103], salutirten die Stadt mit 11 Schüssen und wurde mit 7 bedankt. Wir schickten eine Chaloupe mit einem Officier an's Land, um unsere Ankunft beim Capitaingeneral der balearischen und pityu[s]ischen Inseln[104] zu melden und Pratica[105] zu holen, oder Erlaubniß, Communication mit dem Lande zu haben. Denn in allen Häfen muß man sich ausweisen, daß man von keinem mit der Pest angesteckten Orte kommt; widrigenfalls muß man Quarantaine[106] halten.

Hier tragen die Frauen das Haupt ganz umschleiert, und da der Haarwuchs in diesen Ländern sehr stark ist, so ist das Haar in zwey, mit einem seidenen Zopfe getheilt, welche bis auf die Waden hängen. Die sogenannten preußischen Zöpfe heißen auch queue de Catalogne, [was] eine Weibertracht ist. Abends sieht man beinahe die ganze Stadt sich am Meere baden. Die Knaben laufen aus dem Was- [33] ser und wälzen sich im Sande, so daß sie ganz mit Sand überzogen sind, und laufen dann wieder ins Meer. Doch wenn sie dieses auch noch so oft wiederholen, so verfehlen sie doch nie, sich die Stirne zu bekreuzigen, wenn sie ins Wasser gehen.

Es lag ein Regiment Cavalerie und ein Regiment Schweizer da. Ich war in einem Gasthofe, wo viele von den letztern speißten. Dort wurde der Bratspieß durch Hunde gedreht. Nämlich über dem Herde war eine Trommel mit der flachen Seite an der Mauer befestigt. Ein Hund wurde hinein gesper[r]t, und war, weil sich die Trommel drehte, genöthigt, immer fortzulaufen, wie in einer Tretmühle. Es waren 2 Mopshunde, welche abwechselten und dick und fett dabei waren.

was much calmer. We sailed close to Port Mahon[101], and could see the fortifications quite clearly. On the 23rd we saw the Island of Cabrera[102].[32]

On the 25th we arrived in the Bay of Majorca[103], saluted the city with 11 shots and were thanked with 7. We sent an officer in a sloop ashore to register our arrival with the Captain-general of the Balearian and Pitynian islands[104] and to pick up the "Pratica" or permission to have communication with the land.[105] For in all ports you have to prove that you have not been in any plague-infested place, you are put in quarantine[106] if you have been.

Here the women wear head-veils, and because they have such thick hair in these countries, they arrange their hair in two silky braids, which hang down to their legs. The so-called "Prussian braids" are the women's hair-do, here called "Queue de Catalogne". In the evening you see almost all the city bathing in the sea. The boys run out of the water [33] and roll around in sand, so that they are all covered with sand and then they run back into the water. Even if they do this over and over, they never forget to cross themselves on their foreheads, when they run into the water.

A cavalry regiment and a Swiss regiment were stationed there. I was in a tavern, where many of the latter were having their meal. There a roasting-spit was turned by dog-power. To wit, above the fire-place, a drum was attached to the wall on its flat side. A dog was locked inside, and since the drum kept turning, he was forced to keep running, just like on a treadmill. The two pug dogs had grown quite fat doing this. One spelled the other one off.

---

101. Mahón bzw. Puerto de Mahòn, Hauptstadt von Menorca, benannt nach dem karthagischen General Mago, 1535 von dem arabischen Piraten Haireddin Barbarossa eingenommen, von 1708 bis 1756 britisch, französisch bis 1763, wieder britisch, 1786 von den Spaniern zurückerobert und 1802 an Spanien abgetreten, wurde von den Briten wegen ihres guten natürlichen Hafens anstelle von Ciudadela zur Hauptstadt Menorcas gemacht.

102. Die Insel Cabrera liegt südlich von Mallorca.

103. Mallorca ist die größte Insel der spanischen Balearen.

104. Die Pityusen sind eine südwestliche Inselgruppe der Balearen mit den Hauptinseln Ibiza und Formentera.

105. Die Erlaubnis zu Landen, insbesondere wenn man aus einem Land kommt, in dem eine ansteckende Krankheit herrscht.

106. Quarantaine (franz. quarante = 40), üblicherweise 40 Tage Beobachtungssperre für Schiffe.

101. Mahòn or Puerto de Mahòn, capital of Menorca, is named for the Carthaginian general Mago. Captured by the Arab pirate Haireddin Barbarossa in 1535, it was British 1708 – 56, French until 1763, restored to the British in 1763, recovered by Spain in 1786 and finally ceded to Spain in 1802. It replaced Ciudadela as capital of Menorca during the Britsh occupation because of its fine natural harbour.

102. South of Mallorca.

103. Mallorca is the largest island of the Spanish Baleares.

104. The Pitynian islands form a southwestern group of the Baleares; Ibiza and Formentera are the main islands.

105. This permission to land was required for all ships coming from regions where there were contagious diseases.

106. The term is derived from the French word for forty, "quarante"; usually forty days of isolation to observe a ship.

Am 28ten Juli gingen wir unter Segel, steuerten gegen Süden und sahen am 31ten die Stadt Algier in einer Entfernung von 1 ½ Stunde. Sie liegt in einer großen Bey gegen die hohe Küste bergan gebaut, und gleicht einer [**34**] weisen, gegen den Berg der Länge nach ausgebreiteten Bettdecke. Man sah durch Ferngläser, daß die Erscheinung von 3 Kriegsschiffen Alarm machte, weil sie vielleicht in Erwartung der Dänen waren, die sie bombardiren wollten. Man sah Schiffe aus dem Hafen kommen, eine grüne Flache[107] aufziehen, und eine Kanone abfeuern. Wir zogen unsere Flaggen auch auf, erwiederten den Kanonenschuß und wendeten.

Am 6ten August sahen wir Corsica und Portcros auf den hyerischen Inseln[108], am 9ten die Insel Gorgona und am 10ten kamen wir zum vierten Mal bei Livorno vor Anker. Hier bekamen wir keine Pratica, sondern mußten 5 Tage Quarantaine halten. Am 27. segelten wir von Livorno ab, gingen nördlich und kamen am 30. August in die Bey von Spezia[109]. Diese ist ringsum von hohen Bergen umgeben. Die Einfahrt von der See ist durch die Insel Palmaria maskirt, an welcher der Hafen Porto Venere[110] liegt, so daß die größte Flotte da [**35**] vor allen Winden gesichert liegen kann. Da die Rhede von Genua äußerst unsicher und gefährlich ist, so würde Spezia zum Nachtheile der Haupstadt emporgekommen sein, wenn man es nicht auf alle Weise zu hindern gewußt hätte. Denn der Lage nach wäre Spezia einer der besten Häfen in der Welt. – Ich sah hier Trauben, deren Beeren so groß wie große Zwetschen waren. Am 1ten September stachen wir wieder in die See. Wir ließen Elba links von uns. Am 10ten fiel der 2te Segelmacher, der vorn am Bugspriet das Segel repariren wollte, in's Meer. Die Segel wurden gewendet, um den Lauf des Schiffes einzuhalten; doch er war schon untergesunken, ehe man helfen konnte. Wir fuhren südlich um Sardinien, ließen Sardinien, die Meerenge von Bonifacius[111] und Corsica rechts.

Am 21ten verließ uns Capitain Crul[l] und ging nach Marseille, weil sein Victualienschiff da war. Am 24ten sahen wir das Kriegsschiff „Zirksee", welches uns auf dem Kreuzposten nicht [**36**] getroffen hatte, hinter uns ankommen, und ankerten zum 5ten mal in Livorno.

---

107. Flagge; zum Zweck dieser Aktion gegen Algier s. Einleitung, S. 30 ff, Anm. 79.

108. S. Anm. 98

109. La Spezia, Hafenstadt, heute Italiens wichtigster Kriegshafen.

110. Portovenere, südlich von La Spezia, Hafenort mit einem mächtigen Kastell aus dem 12. Jahrhundert.

111. Die Straße von Bonifacio bildet die Meerenge zwischen Korsika und Sardinien.

On July 28th we sailed south, and saw the city Algiers about one half an hour away on the 31st. The city is situated in a bay, built up against the mountains and the high coast, and reminded me [**34**] of a white bed-cover, spread up against the mountains. Looking through our field-glasses, we saw that the appearance of 3 ships of war seemed to alarm them, perhaps because they were expecting the Danes who wanted to bombard them. We saw ships coming out of the port, hoisting a green flag[107] and heard a cannon-shot. We hoisted our flags, returned the shot, and put about.

On August 6th, we saw Corsica and Portcros on the Iles d'Hyeres[108], on the 9th the island of Gorgona and on the 10th we cast anchor at Livorno (Leghorn) for the 4th time. Here we received no "Pratica", but were put in quarantine for five days. On the 27th we left Livorno, sailed North and on August 30th we reached the Bay of La Spezia[109]. This is surrounded by high mountains. The entrance to the bay is masked by the island of Palmaria, opposite which is located the port city, Porto Venere[110]; so that the largest possible fleet can lie there [**35**] protected from all winds. The roadstead of Genoa is dangerous and unprotected, thus La Spezia would have flourished to the disadvantage of the capital city, if they had not contrived to stop this in all sorts of ways. For the location of La Spezia would make it one of the best ports in the world. – I saw grapes here that were individually the size of our larger plums. On September 1st we put to sea again, we could see Elba on our left. On the 10th, the second sail-maker fell overboard, while trying to mend the sail at the bowsprit. The sail was put about, to slow the course of the ship; but he had drowned before help could arrive. We sailed south around Sardinia, and left Sardinia, the Straits of Bonifacius[111] and Corsica on our right-hand side.

On the 21st Capt. Crul left us and went to Marseilles, because his supply ship was there. On the 24th we saw the warship "Zirksee", which had missed us at our cruising-position, [**36**] arriving after us and we cast anchor for the 5th time in Livorno.

---

107. The word "flag" is misspelled in the German text. For the purpose of this action against Algiers see Introduction, p. 30 ff, fn. 79.

108. Cf. fn 98.

109. Today Italy's most important naval base.

110. South of La Spezia, harbour with a large castle from the 12th century.

111. The straits of Bonifacius form the channel between Sardinia and Corsica.

Am 29ten September kam das englische Kriegsschiff „Liverpool" von 32 Kanonen hier an und am 12ten October 2 andere englische Kriegsschiffe, die „Venus" und „Alarm", welche den Herzog von Glo[u]cester[112] an Bord hatten. Sie paradirten und salutirten mit 21 Schüssen, als er von Bord ging.

Am 15ten kam Capitain Crul[l] wieder von Marseilles zurück. Am 16ten kam das holländische Linienschiff „Princess Maria Louisa", Capitain Berghuyss, welches zur Admiralitaet Herlingen [Harlingen] in Friesland gehörte, hier an. Unser Capitain van Goor van Hinlopen, welcher jetzt die Escadre von 6 Schiffen commandirte,[113] machte mit dem Capitain Nebbens vom Schiffe „Zirksee" eine Reise nach Florenz. Letzterer war sehr dick und fett, und mochte wohl beim Besehen der vielen Merkwürdigkeiten in den Marmorpalästen, wo viele Treppen zu steigen sind, sich sehr erhitzt und [37] wieder verkältet haben. Denn er wurde krank und starb.[114]

Am 27ten war das Begräbnis. Obwohl die Leiche am Lande lag, so ging die Cerimonie doch vom Schiffe aus. Mit Sonnenaufgang wurde auf des Commandanten Schiff „Nassau" die Flagge und Geus[115] bis zur halben Stange aufgezogen, die Spitze der Standarte an dem Maste festgemacht, welches dann die ganze Escadre mit Flagge und Wimpel nachmachte. In die Barkas, welche größer als die Chaloupen ist, wurde eine behängte Bahre gesetzt, und darauf von der großen Chaloupe bugsirt und an's Land geführt. Die Capitaine und alle Officiere der Escadre folgten in 13 Chaloupen. Sobald die letzte Chaloupe das Schiff verließ, fingen die Minutschüsse an. Jedes Schiff sollte 21 Schüsse thun, zuerst das Schiff des Verstorbenen, dann das des Commandanten und so weiter. Doch der englische Commandant hatte die Galanterie, gleich nach dem Commandanten zu feuern, [dann] das zweite [38] englische Schiff; Capitain Zoutman wollte aber diesem nicht nachgeben und schoß jedes mal mit ihm zugleich, was sich nicht gut ausnahm. Es fing um ½ 10 Uhr an und endigte um 12 Uhr. Jetzt wurde die Flagge und Geus

---

112. William Henry, Herzog von Gloucester und Edinburgh (1743-1805), Bruder des britischen Königs Georg III.

113. D.h., nunmehr den gesamten niederländischen Flottenverband, der 1770/71 ausgesandt worden war.

114. Zum plötzlichen Tod von Kapitän Nebbens s. auch van der Horst, Kinckel, S. 177; Ursache war evtl. der auf seinem Schiff wiederholt aufflackernde Typhus, der eine mehrwöchige Inkubationszeit haben kann; s. ebd.

115. Kleine, meist rechteckige Flagge, die von Marine- und Sportfahrzeugen zu besonderen Anlässen als Grußzeichen auf dem Steven oder Bugspriet geführt; die der niederländischen Marine zeigt die Nationalfarben in zwölf strahlenförmigen Segmenten; http://nl.wikipedia.org/Wiki/Geus_(vlag).

On September 29th the English warship "Liverpool" of 32 cannon arrived, and on October 12th, two other English warships, "Venus" and "Alarm", with the Duke of Gloucester[112] on board. They paraded and saluted with 21 shots as he left ship.

On the 15th Capt. Crul returned from Marseilles. On the 16th the Dutch ship-of-the-line, "Princess Maria Louisa" with Capt. Berghuyss, arrived, which belonged to the Admiralty of Herlingen in Friesland. Our Capt. van Goor van Hinlopen, who now commanded the 6 ship squadron,[113] went to visit Florence with Capt. Nebbens of the ship "Zirksee". The latter was very fat, and may have worked himself into a heat and then caught a bad cold, [37] climbing all the stairs in the many marble palaces trying to see all the sights. Soon after this he became very sick and died.[114]

His funeral was on the 27th. Even though the body was on land, the funeral ceremony began on the ships. At sunrise the flag and the jack[115] of the commander's ship "Nassau" were flown at half-mast, the tips of the standards were attached to the masts, which was then copied with flag and pennant by the whole squadron. A draped bier was set into the barque which is larger than a sloop and then towed by the big sloop and brought on land. The captains and all officers of the squadron followed in 13 sloops. As soon as the last sloop had left the ship, the shots started – one a minute. Every ship was to give 21 shots, first his own ship, then the commander's and so on down the line. But the English commander had the gallantry to fire right after the Commander, then the second [38] English ship. Capt. Zoutman did not want to yield to the English, and fired each time with him, which was not correct. This started at 9:30 am and ended at noon. Then the flag and the jack were fully hoisted and the funeral cortege was escorted to the so-called Dutch garden, the grave-yard reserved for the Netherlands. Even the Russian officers joined this

---

112. William Henry, Duke of Gloucester and Edinburgh (1743 – 1805), brother of king George III.

113. I.e., he now had command of the whole Dutch squadron which had sailed from Holland in 1770/71.

114. The sudden death of Capt. Nebbens is mentioned by van der Horst, Kinckel, p. 177, as well; it may have been caused by the typhoid fever endemic on his ship which can have an incubation period of several weeks; see ibid.

115. The author uses the Dutch term "geus" for this flag; cf. also http://nl.wikipedia.org/Wiki/Geus_(vlag).

wieder aufgezogen und der Leichenconduct, an den sich russische Officire anschlossen, ging nach dem sogenannten holländischen Garten, dem Begräbnißplatze der Holländer. Es ist ein Garten außer der Stadt am Ufer des Meeres, mit Blumen angelegt. Die Wege sind mit Steinen besetzt, auf welchen Grabschriften stehen. Auch ein Haus mit einer schönen Aussicht ist in diesem Garten, wo man Erfrischungen haben kann.

Am 30ten October kam das russische Schiff „Ritchislof" von 64 Stücken, Capitain Louw, hier an. Es kam von Paros[116]. Wir erfuhren, daß die Russen, welche den aufgestandenen Moreoten[117] beistehen sollten, geschlagen und dann die Moreoten von den Türken aufs grausamste ermordet, [39] dagegen die türkischen Schiffe bei Tschesme von den Russen verbrannt worden seyen.

Livorno ist eine sehr schöne Stadt, ganz regelmäßig gebaut, mit großen breiten Straßen, die geradelaufend auf dem Markte zusammen kommen. Die Häuser sind neu und gleichförmig gebaut. Ein Theil der Stadt, der von Kanälen durchschnitten ist, heiß[t] Klein-Venedig. Ich machte mit einigen Officiren eine Spacierfahrt nach Pisa[118]. Wir logirten Al Husaro, im Husaren. Ich stieg auf den um 13 Schuh[119] überhängenden, 140 Schuh hohen Thurm. Inwendig ist er ganz hohl. Die Treppe geht in der Mauer herum; jedoch oben, wo die Mauer dünner wird, geht die Treppe gegen die innere Seite nur an einem Geländer fort. Das Überhängen des Thurmes ist wohl daher entstanden, daß der Boden sich gesenkt hat. Denn wie könnte man einer Stadt einen so übeln Geschmack und Unsinn zutrauen, mit Fleiß so etwas Fehlerhaftes und Ungestaltes mit großen Kosten zu bauen? In [40] der Kathedralkirche sind die schönen Thüren von Bronze[120], welche aus Jerusalem gekommen sein sollen, merkwürdig. Wie mich däucht, sind sie in München im

procession. The Dutch garden is located on the coast, a bit outside of the city, and planted with flowers. The path is paved with stones, some of these had been grave markers with inscriptions. Also in the middle of this garden is a house with a nice view, where you can have some refreshments.

On October 30th, the Russian ship "Ritchislof", 64 cannon, under Capt. Louw arrived here. It came from Paros[116]. We learned, that the Russians, who were trying to aid the rebelling Moreans[117], were beaten and then the Turks killed the Moreans inflicting many atrocities, whereupon the Russians set fire to the Turkish ships at Cesme. [39]

Livorno is a very beautiful city, laid out according to a plan, with large wide streets that come together straight at the market-place. The houses are new and uniformly built. One part of town intersected by canals is called Little Venice. With some other officers, I took a trip to Pisa.[118] We lodged "Al Husaro" (at the hussar's). I climbed up the tower (140 shoes high, leaning 13 shoes[119] over). Inside it is quite hollow. The steps go round in the wall; but further up, where the wall is thinner, the steps are only guarded by a banister on the inside. The sinking ground has probably caused the tower to lean. For who would believe that the city could plan such nonsense and display such bad taste, not to mention the great cost of planning carefully such an off-kilter disaster? [40] The beautiful bronze cathedral doors[120], which are said to be from Jerusalem, are quite remarkable. If I recollect correctly, plaster-of-Paris copies of these are on display in the Art Cabinet in Munich. We also visited a spa[121], between Pisa and Lucca.

---

116. Eine der griechischen Kykladeninseln.

117. Moreoten sind die Einwohner des Peloponnes (Morea), der südlichen Halbinsel Griechenlands.

118. Die Universitätsstadt Pisa, im Mittelalter eine der bedeutendsten italienischen Städte, kam 1406 an Florenz. Durch die Versandung des Hafens und den Aufstieg Livornos (Ende 16.Jh.) verlor Pisa seine frühere Stellung.

119. 1 Schuh (Längenmaß), entspricht etwa 1 Fuß (ca. 30 cm).

120. Die Bronzetüren des Doms wurden nach einem Brand 1595 von Giambologna und Schülern nach dem Muster der alten Tür von Bonanno (1180) neu gegossen. Dieser, ein Bildhauer aus Pisa, soll 1174 zusammen mit einem Deutschen, Wilhelm von Innsbruck, den durch seine schiefe Stellung berühmten Glockenturm des Doms von Pisa erbaut haben. Ein Pisaner „Bonannus", doch wohl derselbe, hat 1186 eine Bronzetür am Dom von Monreale auf Sizilien gegossen; vgl. Fr. Müller, Die Künstler aller Zeiten und Völker, 1857.

116. One of the Greek Kyklades.

117. Moreans are the inhabitants of Peloponnesos (Morea), the southern Greek peninsula.

118. The university town of Pisa, one of the most important Italian cities in the Middle Ages, fell to Florence in 1406. Pisa lost its former position due to the silting up of its harbour and the rise of Leghorn (end of the 16th century).

119. A shoe probably equals one English foot.

120. The bronze doors of the cathedral were recast by Giambologna and his students in the mold of the „Bonanno" doors (1180) after a fire in 1595. Bonanno was a Pisan sculptor who, together with the German architect Wilhelm von Innsbruck, in 1174 supposedly constructed the campanile of Pisa cathedral, world famous for its leaning position. The Pisan "Bonannus", most probably identical with Bonanno, cast the bronze door of the cathedral of Monreale in Sicily in 1186; cf. Fr. Müller, Die Künstler aller Zeiten und Völker, 1857.

121. San Giuliano Terme.

Kunstcabinet von Gyps nachgeformt. – Wir gingen auch in das Bad[121], welches zwischen Pisa und Lucca liegt.

Am 9ten November entstand nach dem Retraite-Schuß Brand in der Krone des Löwen. (Dergleichen große Figuren sind an den Schif[f]sschnäbeln aller holländischen Schiffe ausgehauen.)[122] Wahrscheinlich war der Pfropf aus einer der 2 Kanonen, welche vorn stehen und die Jäger heißen (pièce de chasse) in das wurmstichige Holz dieser Figur gekommen. Es wurde ein Loch in die Krone gehauen und Wasser hineingegossen, auch mit der Feuerspritze hineingespritzt. Auch Capt. Crul sandte uns seine Feuerspritze. Nach einer Stunde war das Feuer gedämpft, und der Schif[f]szimmermann machte [41] einen andern, etwas unförmlichen Löwen. Es hätte aber leicht gefährlich werden können, da die Pulverkammer vorn im Schiffe nahe dabei war.

Als wir am 11ten November von Livorno absegelten, war unsere Escadre 6 Schiffe stark, und unser Commandant, ließ nach der in's Holländische übersetzten Seetaktik des H. v. Morogues[123], wie schon früher von Zeit zu Zeit, die Uebungen vornehmen, Schlachtordnung vornehmen u. s. w. Aber während wir diese Wendungen machten, zog Capitain Dedel auf einmal seine Flagge auf, salutirte uns mit 11 Schüssen und nahm den Weg nach Genua. Unser Commandant ärgerte sich sehr darüber.

Wir segelten nahe an der genuesischen Küste vorbei, und es war sehr unterhaltend, die Orte, wie Finale[124], Oneglia, Monaco[125] etc. deutlich zu unterscheiden, indem man auf den Schiffen Bücher hat, Portulane genannt, [42] in welchen die Küsten beschrieben sind. – Am 15. separirte sich Capitain Berghuis. Wir sahen die Insel Porquerolle[126] bei Toulon, am 18. den Berg auf der Insel Minorca am 19. die Insel Cabrera und Formentera[127], am 20ten Cap Palos[128] bei

On November 9th, after the "Retraite-shot" (taps), our lion's crown caught fire. (Such big figures, carved in wood, are attached to the prows of all Dutch ships.)[122] I guess the tamp from one of the two cannon located at the fore, which are called hunters ("piece de chasse"), had fallen into the worm-eaten wood of the lion's figure. We chopped a hole in the crown and poured water on it, and even used our fire-engines. Capt. Crul sent us one of his fire-engines, too. After about an hour, the fire was put out, and later the ship's carpenter [41] made another rather clumsy looking lion. But this could easily have ended disastrously, because the chamber in the bow of the ship containing the powder-kegs was close-by.

On November 11th, when sailing out of Livorno, our squadron was 6 ships strong. Our commander sometimes liked to have us practice the naval tactics of Mr. de Morogues[123], which had been translated into Dutch: taking up certain lines of battle, etc. But while we were practicing our turns, Capt. Dedel suddenly hoisted his flag, saluted us with 11 shots, and took off in the direction of Genoa. Our commander was very angry about this.

We sailed close to the coast near Genoa, and it was very entertaining to see the towns clearly; Finale[124], Oneglia and Monaco[125], etc., because we have books called portolanos on board [42] in which the coasts are described. On the 15th, Capt. Berghuis left us. We saw the island of Porquerolle[126], close to Toulon, on the 18th; the mountain on the island of Minorca, on the 19th the island of Cabrera and Formentera[127], on the 20th Cape Palos[128] close to Carthogena, on the 21st Velez Malaga[129], on the 22nd

---

121. San Giuliano Terme.

122. Solche Galionsfiguren führten nicht nur holländische, sondern auch viele andere Schiffe der Zeit am Bug.

123. Bigot de Morogues, Tactique navale; bei diesem Manöver tat sich die "Zierikzee" hervor, s. van der Horst, Kinckel, S. 176.

124. Finale Ligure, an der ligurischen Mittelmeerküste bei Savona, aus dem Zusammenschluss der Orte Finale Marina, Finale Pia und Varigotti entstanden.

125. Hauptstadt des gleichnamigen Fürstentums, seit 1297 von der genuesischen Familie Grimaldi beherrscht.

126. Porquerolles ist die westlichste Insel der Hyères-Inseln, südöstlich von Toulon.

127. Insel der spanischen Balearen, südlich von Ibiza.

128. Das Cabo de Palos liegt östlich der spanischen Hafenstadt Cartagena.

---

122. Not only Dutch, but most other ships had such figure-heads in the 18th century.

123. Bigot de Morogues, Tactique navale, Paris 1763; idem, Zee-tactick, Amsterdam 1767. The ship "Zierikzee" excelled in these maneuvers, cf. van der Horst, Kinckel, p. 176.

124. Finale Ligure on the Ligurian coast southwest of Savona combines the towns of Finale Marina, Finale Pia, and Varigotti.

125. Capital of the eponymous principality on the French mediterranean coast which has been ruled by the Grimaldi family of Genoa since 1297.

126. Porquerolles is the westernmost island of the Isles of Hyères, southeast of Toulon.

127. One of the Spanish Baleares islands, south of Ibiza.

128. Cabo de Palos is situated east of the Spanish harbour of Cartagena.

129. East of Malaga.

Carthogena, am 21. Velez Malaga[129], am 22. Maribella[130]. Als wir die Meerenge von Gibraltar passirten, hatten wir den Wind von hinten, und da die hohen Ufer von beiden Welttheilen sich dort einander nähern, so schien es mir, als wenn der Wind hier wie in einem Blasbalge zusammengepreßt mit desto größerer Gewalt uns forttriebe. Das Schiff lief mit der größten Geschwindigkeit (Die größte Geschwindigkeit eines Schiffes habe ich auf 12 ½ Meilen in einer Wagt[131] oder 4 Stunden angeben hören. Dies wäre in jeder Stunde 6 ¼ Stunde Wegs), und ein ungemein schönes Schauspiel war es, die unzählige Menge Delphine, Braunfische[132] und Tonnfische[133] zu sehen, die unser Schiff begleiteten und sich herumwälzten, als wenn sie unser Schiff für einen großen Fisch ansähen, dem sie die gebührende Achtung erzeigen wollten.

[43] Am 23. sahen wir Cap Vincent. Den 27ten bekamen wir einen Bo[o]tsmann, genannt Antonio Bibeiro von Cascaes[134]. Am 28. kamen wir an den Tagus[135], beim Ausfluß desselben sind viele Felsen, um welche das Meer bei der Ebbe und Fluth wie siedend aussieht. In der Mitte liegt das Fort du Bougie[136], und auf der rechten Seite des Flußes das Fort St. Julien[137]. Der Fluß hat 2 Einfahrten, an beiden Ufern, so daß man die Felsen in der Mitte läßt. Wir ankerten da, weil wir gegen die Ebbe nicht aufkommen konnten. Am 30ten segelten wir bis Belem[138]

Maribella[130]. When we were sailing through the Straits of Gibraltar, we had the wind from aft, and since the high cliffs of the 2 continents are so close here, it seemed to me to be a huge bellows that was blowing us along with a corresponding force. The ship was sailing at top speed. (The greatest speed I ever heard of on a ship was 12 and ½ miles in one watch[131] or 4 hours. This would mean 6 and ½ hr way, in an hour.) And it was a beautiful sight to see the schools of dolphins, brownfish[132], and tuna[133], which accompanied our ship and rolled and wallowed around as if they considered our ship to be a huge fish, to which they wanted to show the proper respect. [43].

On the 23rd we saw Cape Vincent. On the 27th we got a boatswain, named Antonio Bibeiro from Cascaes[134]. On the 28th we arrived at the Tagus[135]; at its mouth are many rocks, which make the water look like it is boiling at ebb and tide. In the middle the Fort du Bougie[136] is situated, and Fort St. Julien[137] on the right side of the river. The river has 2 channels close to the banks, so that you avoid the rocks in the middle. We cast anchor there, because we could not advance against the outgoing tide. On the 30th we sailed to Belem[138] (Bethlehem), where we also cast anchor. The monastery there contains the royal graves, and the royal palace, where the kings have lived ever

---

129. Östlich von Malaga.

130. Marbella, spanische Hafenstadt zwischen Malaga und Gibraltar.

131. Wagt = Wache. Der Autor dürfte sich hier auf die deutsche Landmeile zu 7,5 km beziehen. Dann hätte das Schiff ca. 90 km pro Wache bzw. 22,5 km/Stunde zurückgelegt, beachtlich für ein Segelschiff, das nicht in erster Linie auf Schnelligkeit gebaut war. Dazu passt die zweite Angabe des Autors mit dem Wegestunden-Maß. Eine Wegstunde entsprach üblicherweise einer halben Meile, also 3,75 km (dazu Wikipedia: „Wegstunde"); 6,25 Wegstunden hätten also 23,5 km/h bedeutet. Zum Vergleich: die schnellsten Tee-, Opium- und Goldrush-Klipper des 19. Jahrhunderts erreichten Stundengeschwindigkeiten um die 22 Seemeilen oder knapp 41 km/h.

132. Braunfische = Delphine (Tümmler).

133. Tonnfische = Thunfische.

134. Cascais, portugiesische Hafenstadt und Seebad, westlich von Lissabon.

135. Tagus, lateinischer Name des Rio Tejo, längster Strom der iberischen Halbinsel, der bei Lissabon in den Atlantischen Ozean mündet.

136. Bugio, Insel mit Leuchtturm an der Einfahrt in den Tejo.

137. Fort St. Julien, portugiesisch Fort Sao Juliao da Barra, wurde seit 1553 unter König Johann III. zum Schutz der Tejo-Mündung erbaut; eines der größten maritimen Bauwerke und größtes noch bestehendes Festungswerk in Vaubanscher Manier in Portugal; heute Sitz des Verteidigungsministeriums.

138. Belém, südwestlicher Vorort von Lissabon. Die Beschreibung des Einlaufens in Lissabon verweist auf die zeittypischen Probleme des Navigierens auf einem Fluss ohne Motorhilfe; so konnte z.B. auch die Fahrt von Travemünde nach Lübeck bis zu drei Tage in Anspruch nehmen.

---

130. Marbella, Spanish harbour between Malaga and Gibraltar.

131. The author probably refers to German land miles (of 7.5 km or 4.7 English miles) here. Thus, the ship would have covered 90 km (56.25 miles) in one watch or 22.5 km (14 miles) per hour, not bad for a ship not specially built for fast sailing. This fits well with the author's second statement about "hours of way" (half a German or 2.3 English miles); 6 ¼ of those would mean a speed of 14.3 miles per hour. By comparison, the fastest tea, opium, and gold rush clippers of the 19th century could attain speeds of 22 nautical or 25 English miles per hour.

132. Brownfish belong to the dolphin family.

133. The author uses an antiquated form of the modern German word for tuna.

134. Cascais, Portuguese harbour and resort town west of Lisbon.

135. Tagus or rio Tejo, the longest river of the Iberian peninsula, which flows into the Atlantic ocean at Lisbon.

136. Bugio, island with a lighthouse in the approaches to the Tejo.

137. In Portuguese "Fort Sao Juliao da Barra", built and enlarged several times from 1553 under king John III to protect the mouth of the Tejo river. It is one of the largest maritime buildings and the largest fortress built in the manner of Vauban in Portugal. Today it serves as seat of the defence ministry.

138. Belém, southwestern suburb of Lisbon. The description of the arrival in Lisbon points to the problem of sailing a river against the current without the help of an engine, a typical problem of 18th century navigation.

(Bethlehem), wo wir wieder ankerten. In dem dortigen Kloster ist die Begräbniß der Könige und der königliche Palast, in welchem die Könige seit dem Erdbeben[139] von Lissabon wohnen. Es ist sehr [44] groß, doch nur 1 Stockwerk hoch. Hier ist auch ein Schloß im Fluß. Wir salutirten dieses und schickten einen Officier um Pratica, um weiter vor die Stadt segeln zu dürfen. Da wir dies erhielten, segelten wir am 1ten Dezember bis vor die Stadt. Damals lag noch sehr viel in Ruinen; von großen Kirchen ragte oft noch ein Theil des Daches oder eines Giebels aus der Erde. Dagegen waren neue sehr lange Straßen nach der Schnur gebaut, die Häuser gleich hoch und mit Altanen.

Hier fanden wir die 2 dänische[n] Schiffe wieder, die wir vor einem Jahr in Malaga gesehen hatten. Sie kamen von ihrer Expedition gegen Algier zurück wo sie nichts ausgerichtet hatten. Am 12ten kam das holländische Schiff „Thetis", Capitain v. Braam,[140] aus Holland, und ging am 7. Januar wieder in die See. Am 6. Januar fuhr der König[141] den Fluß hinauf mit einer Chaloupe, die, wie mir däuchte, wohl 40 Ruderer hatte. Wenn der König darinnen ist, hält einer eine Fahne in der Höhe. Es wurde paradirt [45] und „Husee" gerufen, wie bei den Engländern „Hurra". Das Paradiren besteht darin, daß auf ein Commando die Flaggen aufgezogen werden und die Matrosen auf die Segelstangen hinauslaufen, wo Seile ausgespannt sind, an die sie sich anhalten.

Ich fand in Lisabon 2 holländische Leinwandhändler. Der eine hieß van der Aa und war von Almelo, der andere Beun von Tubbergen[142], 2 Stunden von Almelo. Diese luden mich zum Essen ein. Der Portowein, den wir tranken, ist sehr schwer und steigt in den Kopf. Nachmittags gingen wir in ein Kaffeehaus zu einem gewissen Rosendal. Als ich mit der Chaloupe wieder an Bord gehen sollte, fand ich mich so angegriffen, daß ich mich zur Ruhe begeben mußte. Um Mitternacht war ich wieder vollkommen wohl. Ich ging also mit dem Schreiber eines holländischen Schiffes, wel-

---

139. Am 1.11.1755 wurde Lissabon durch ein Erdbeben zerstört, das mehr als 30.000 Menschen das Leben kostete.

140. Jacob Pieter van Braam (1737 – 1803) trat 1748 in die „Admiralität van Amsterdam" ein, wurde 1751 durch Seeräuber gefangen genommen und blieb bis 1753 ihr Sklave, trat 1764 als Kapitän in die Dienste der Vereinigten Ostindischen Kompagnie; seit 1776 wieder Kapitän der Vereinigten Niederlande, 1793 Vizeadmiral. Er führte 1781 in der Schlacht auf der Doggerbank das Linienschiff „Admiraal Piet Heyn" von 54 Kanonen; s. http://home.arcor.de/thomas_siebe/dogger.html

141. José I., König von Portugal (1714-1777, regierte seit 1750).

142. Tubbergen (Provinz Overijssel), nordöstlich von Almelo. Die beiden Kaufleute stammten also aus der engeren Heimat Rechterens und luden ihn wohl als jungen Landsmann zum Essen ein.

---

since the Lisbon earth-quake[139]. It is very large [44], but just one storey high. There is also a palace in the river. We saluted and sent an officer to pick up the Pratica to proceed closer to the city. After receiving this on December 1st, we sailed up to the city. At that time there were still many ruins; some grand old church ruins, with only a part of the roof or gable sticking up above ground. On the other hand, the new streets were in good condition, very long and straight; the houses all built up to the same height and with balconies or galleries.

Here we saw the Danish ships again that we had met a year ago in Malaga. They were returning from their expedition against Algiers without having accomplished anything. On the 12th the Dutch ship "Thetis" arrived under Capt. v. Braam,[140] coming from Holland, and sailed out on January 7th. On January 6th, the king[141] went up river in a sloop, which if I remember correctly, had about 40 rowers. When the king is on board someone holds a flag up high. We paraded [45] and shouted "Husee", which is "Hurrah" in English. Parading means: at a command the flags are hoisted and the sailors run out on the sail-yards, where ropes are attached, which they hold on to.

In Lisbon I met two Dutch linen-cloth merchants. One was called van der Aa and was from Almelo, the other was Beun from Tubbergen[142], two hours distance from Almelo. These two invited me for a meal. The port-wine which we drank, is very heavy and made me dizzy. In the afternoon we visited a coffee-house to meet a certain Mr.Rosendal. When I was supposed to go back aboard with a sloop, I found myself so weak, that I had to take a rest. Around midnight I was feeling well again. I went down to the harbor with the clerk of a Dutch ship, who also happened to be there. We boarded a boat (called a frigate here), [46] along with the captain of an English

---

139. On Nov. 1st, 1755, Lisbon was destroyed by an earthquake which killed more than 30 000 people.

140. Jacob Pieter van Braam (1737 – 1803) joined the „Admiralty of Amsterdam" in 1748, was taken prisoner by pirates in 1751 and stayed their slave until 1753, entered into the service of the „Vereenigde Oostindische Compagnie" in 1764 as a captain, in 1776 captain of the Netherlands' Navy, vice-admiral in 1793. He commanded the ship-of-the-line "Admiraal Piet Heyn" of 54 guns in the Battle of the Doggerbank in 1781, cf. http://home.arcor.de/thomas_siebe/dogger.html

141. José I., king of Portugal (1714-1777, reigned 1750 – 1777).

142. Tubbergen (Prov. Overijssel), northwest of Almelo. These two merchants were from Rechteren's own region in the Netherlands and probably invited him for the meal because he was a young fellow countryman.

cher auch da war, an den Hafen. Wir stiegen nebst einem Capitain eines englischen Paquetboots in ein Boot (hier Fregatte [46] genannt), um auf unsere Schiffe zu kommen. Als wir an das holländische Kriegsschiff des Schreibers kamen, gab er den zweien die uns führten, das Geld in die Hände, und sprang geschwind in sein Schiff. Diese wurden wüthend, weil sie mehr erwartet hatten, warfen ihm das Geld nach, und weigerten sich, mich an mein Schiff zu bringen. Den englischen Capitain aber wollten sie an sein Schiff bringen. Ich machte mich auf eine gefährliche Scene in dieser Gesellschaft, um Mitternacht auf dem ungeheuren Fluße, gefaßt. Der englische Capitain aber zog mich aus der Noth; er sagte: "It is a very bad town. I will see you on your board". („Es ist eine böse Stadt; ich will sie auf Ihrem Schiffe wissen".) Sie hatten vor ihm Respect, und ich kam glücklich zurück.

Ich sah hier den holländischen Ministre, Herrn Saurin[143], den Sohn des berühmten Kanzelredners Saurin[144] im Haag. Ich war auch in einem Societäts-Hause, welches auf Englisch The long Room genannt [47] wird. Hier war ein Ceremonienmeister, der in Hofkleid mit Stock und Degen den ganzen Abend immer mit Empfangen und Begleiten beschäftigt war. Die Damen saßen in einem großen Halbzirkel. Wollte ein Herr tanzen, so wandte er sich an den Cerimonienmeister: Dieser forderte nach seinem Gutachten eine Dame auf und brachte sie dem Herrn. Hierauf wurde eine Menuet getanzt. Dann wurde die Dame auf ihren Platz, und eine andere an ihre Stelle gebracht. Wenn diese getanzt hatte, ging der Herr ab, und der Cerimonienmeister holte einen andern, – und so ging es fort, so daß jeder Herr mit 2 Damen und jede Dame mit 2 Herrn tanzte. Als dies vorbei war, wurde englisch getanzt.[145] – In einem andern Zimmer spielten die Herren Hazardspiele. Haufen Goldes wanderten von einer Stelle des Tisches zur andern. Der holländische Consul Kistemaker war eine Hauptperson dabei. Dieser hatte [48] dem König so viel

packet-boat in order to reach our ships. When we reached the clerk's Dutch warship, he gave the two who were rowing us, some coins and then quickly jumped onto his ship. These two threw a fit, because they had been expecting more money. They threw his money after him and refused to take me to my ship. But they wanted to take the English captain to his ship. I was preparing for a dangerous scene, alone with these two at midnight on this immense river. But the English captain helped me out of this difficult situation; he said, "It's a very bad town. I will see you on board your ship." They had respect for him and I returned safely on board my ship.

I saw the Dutch minister, Mr. Saurin[143], here, the son of the famous Preacher Saurin[144] in the Hague. I also visited an Assembly-House, which is called "The Long Room" in English [47]. We saw a Master of Ceremonies there, in court clothes with staff and sword, who was kept busy all evening long greeting and accompanying. The ladies were seated in a large semi-circle. If a gentleman wanted to dance, he first approached the Master of Ceremonies: who chose a lady at his discretion and then brought her to the gentleman. Then they danced a minuet. Then the lady was escorted back to her seat and a second one was chosen. When the second lady had danced, the gentleman was sent off and the Master of Ceremonies picked up another one, and so it went round and round, so that each gentleman danced with two ladies and every lady with two gentlemen. After this was over, they danced in the English style.[145] – In another room the gentlemen were gambling heavily. Piles of gold were pushed from one side of the table to the other. The Dutch Consul Kistemaker was a main figure here. He had loaned [48] the king so

---

143. Möglicherweise Philip Saurin, der auch 7 der 12 Bände gesammelter Predigten seines Vaters herausgab.

144. Jacques Saurin (1677-1730), musste nach der Aufhebung des Edikts von Nantes Frankreich verlassen, wurde Pfarrer in London, dann in Den Haag, wo er Prediger der reformierten französischen Gemeinde war.

145. Das Menuett war der im 18. Jahrhundert vielleicht beliebteste Tanz, meist ein Paartanz mit an sich einfachen Schritten (Schreittanz), aber schwer zu erlernender Haltung und Gestik; zugleich wurden die englischen Kontratänze, Gruppentänze, bei denen sich Herren und Damen gegenüber stehen, populär; s. Wikipedia unter „Historischer Tanz" und „Kontratanz".

---

143. Probably Philip S., who also edited 7 of the 12 volumes of his father's collected sermons.

144. Jacques Saurin (1677 – 1730) had to leave France after the repeal of the Edict of Nantes (1698), was a pastor in London, then at the Hague where he became the most renowned preacher of the reformed French church.

145. The minuet may have been the most costumary dance in the 18th century; it was usually danced in couples and had simple, small steps, but required postures which were difficult to learn; at the same time, English country dances where ladies and gentlemen usually start in opposite lines, became popular; see Wikipedia under "historical dances" and "country dance".

Geld vorgeschossen, daß er dafür die Diamantengruben von Brasilien[146] in Pacht hatte.

Am 19ten Januar 1772 hoben wir das Anker, passirten und salutirten das Schloß Belem; als sich aber der Wind änderte, ankerten wir wieder in der Catharinen-Bey. Erst am 24. erlaubte es der Wind und das Wetter, in die See zu gehen. Da sahen wir ein holländisches Schiff einlaufen, wahrscheinlich das des Capitain Dedel, welches uns an der genuesischen Küste verlassen hatte.

Am 3. Februar konnten wir mit dem Senkblei keinen Grund finden. Am 4. fanden wir Grund in der Tiefe von 110 Klaftern, was ein Zeichen ist, daß man sich dem Canal nähert. Am 7. hatten wir nach der Berechnung und Abmessung auf der runden Karte den Leuchtthurm bei Plymouth (genannt Eddistone,)[147] 13 Meilen von uns; nach der platten Karte waren wir nahe daran, und es dauerte sehr kurze Zeit, so sahen wir ihn wirklich vor uns. Am 8. Febr. sahen wir Point Peveral[148], bekamen einen Lootsee[Lotsen] mit Namen James Kock, und steuerten [**49**] auf die westlichen Nadeln von Wight.[149] So (The Needles) heißen die hohen, spitzigen Felsen bei der Insel Wight. Wir sahen die englischen Kriegsschiffe auf der Rhede von Spithead[150], salutirten sie mit 11 Schüssen und wurden mit 11 bedankt. Eine Chaloupe kam mit einem Officier vom englischen Commandanten zu uns. Die Mannschaft kam auf unser Schiff herüber, und deßungeachtet bekamen wir bald darauf Ordre, Quarantaine zu halten. Es war nicht zu begreifen, warum? Denn wir kamen von

much money, that in return he had been given a lease on the Brazilian diamond mines.[146]

On January 19th, 1772 we weighed anchor, passed and saluted Belem Castle; but since the wind changed, we cast anchor again in Catherine Bay. Only on the 24th the wind and weather allowed us to sail out to sea. Then we saw a Dutch ship coming into port, probably that of Capt. Dedel which had left us on the Genoese coast.

On February 3rd, we could not find ground with our sounding-lead. On the 4th we measured a depth of 110 fathoms, which is a sign, that the English Channel is near-by. On the 7th according to our measurements on the round map, we should be 13 miles from the Plymouth light-house (called Eddystone)[147]; according to the flat map, we should be close to it, and not very long afterwards, we actually did sight it. On February 8th, we saw Point Peveral[148], received a pilot on board, named James Kock (Cook), and navigated [**49**] towards the Needles, the western part of the Isle of Wight[149]. The Needles are the high, pointed cliffs on the Southwest corner of the Isle of Wight. We saw the English warships in the roadstead of Spithead[150], saluted with 11 shots and were thanked with 11 also. A sloop and officer came to us from the English Commander. The crew came over to our ship, and in spite of that soon afterwards we received the order to enter quarantine.

---

146. Im 18. Jahrhundert erschöpften sich die indischen und indonesischen Diamantenminen. Ein Portugiese entdeckte auf der Suche nach Gold in Brasilien die ersten Diamanten außerhalb Asiens; dieser Fund löste einen „Diamantenrausch" aus. – Ein Konsul Kistemaker konnte bisher in niederländischen biographischen Lexika nicht gefunden werden. Möglicherweise hat Rechteren sich beim Namen geirrt: Die Diamanten wurden in Brasilien gewonnen, aber der Diamantenhandel lief ausschließlich über Lissabon, wo die Aufkäufer aus Amsterdam und London zusammenkamen. Der wichtigste Käufer in den Jahren 1761 – 1771 war ein Daniel Gildemeester, der mehr als 925 000 Karat aufkaufte und dem König auch Geld vorstreckte. Dazu: Boxer, Golden Age, S. 204 – 225, zu Gildemeester bes. S. 224.

147. Die Eddystone Rocks liegen etwa 25 km südlich von Plymouth im Meer. Mit „runder Karte" dürfte ein Globus gemeint sein, auf denen im 18. Jahrhundert meist schon Schifffahrtsrouten und Tiefen markiert waren, mit der „platten Karte" eine für die Navigation geeignete Seekarte mit winkeltreuer Zylinderprojektion.

148. Vermutlich Peveril Point bei Swanage, Dorset (etwas südlich von Bournemouth).

149. The Needles sind der westlichste Ausläufer der Isle of Wight, einer Insel südlich von Southampton.

150. Spithead heißt die Meerenge zwischen Portsmouth und der Isle of Wight.

146. The Brasilian diamond mines replaced the Indian and Indonesian ones which had been exhausted in the 18th century. A Portuguese prospecting for gold in Brasil had found the first diamonds outside of Asia which led to a diamond rush. – A consul Kistemaker could not be found in any Dutch biographic dictionary. But maybe Rechteren did not remember the name right: The diamonds were mined or washed in Brasil, but traded only in Lisbon. The buyers from London and Amsterdam would come there to buy. In the years 1761 – 1771, a Daniel Gildemeester was the most important buyer who acquired over 925,000 carats and also loaned money to the Portuguese king; see Boxer, Golden Age, p. 204 – 225, for Gildemeester p. 224.

147. The Eddystone Rocks are situated approx. 15 mi. south of Plymouth in the English channel. The "round map" probably means a globe on which, in the 18th century, shipping routes and soundings were often marked, the "flat map" a chart with a cylindrical projection on which a course can be plotted as a straight line.

148. Presumably Peveril Point close to Swanage, Dorset (south of Bournemouth).

149. The Needles are the westernmost point of the Isle of Wight (Hampshire), an island south of Southampton.

150. Spithead is the name of the narrows between Portsmouth and the Isle of Wight.

Lisabon, wo ein beständiger Verkehr von Kaufartheyschiffen und Paquetboten nach England ist. Auch waren ja schon viele vom Lande bei uns gewesen, welche demnach alle hätten Quarantaine halten müssen. Am 9ten hoben wir das Anker und segelten nach der Modderbank oder dem Quarantainenplatz gegen Coues[151] auf der Insel Wight. Ein englisches Kriegsschiff lag da, um Acht zu geben, daß wir keinen Verkehr mit dem Lande hatten. Am 15. bekamen wir Pratica, hoben unser Anker und gingen mit Capitain Zoutman unter Segel nach der Rhede von Spithead bei Portsmouth[152]. [50] Capitain Krul und Kauw segelten nach Holland. Der englische Commandant Arbuthnot[153] kam auf unser Schiff. Wir salutirten ihn beim Weggehen mit 11 Schüssen und wurden mit 11 bedankt.

Eine fürchterliche Exekution bekamen wir hier zu sehen. Zwey Matrosen, welche desertirt waren, wurden in einer Barkas geführt, mit entblößtem Rücken an einen Querbalken, welcher durch 2 Pfeiler in Form eines Galgens gestützt war, mit gebundenen Händen aufgezogen und an den Füßen gebunden, so daß sie in der Luft hingen. An jedem Schiffe, wo sie hingeführt wurden, wurde ihr Urtheil verlesen und kamen ein Paar Unterofficire mit Knütteln (kurzen Stöcken, an welchen Stricke mit Knoten befestigt sind), und gaben ihnen eine vorgeschriebene Anzahl Hiebe, so daß jeder Hieb die Haut durchdrang. Dies ging so die ganze Flotte herum, und nach einigen Tagen sollte es von Neuem wiederholt werden. Es waren zwei Leute in den ersten Jünglingsjahren und Brüder. Der eine rief bei jedem Hiebe: „Ah my brother, my dear brother!" („Ach mein Bruder, mein lieber Bruder!") Beim Aussegeln erlebte ich beinahe eine ähnliche Scene, wie ich 8 Jahre [51] nachher zu Brest erlebte. Als wir das Anker gehoben hatten und das Schiff unter Segel war, während Commandeur van Loo commandirte, befand sich das Schiff des Capitain Zoutman quer vor uns vor Anker liegend. Wir waren so nahe daran, daß wir unfehlbar dagegen gerannt wären, da van Loo den Kopf verloren hatte. In dem Augenblicke kam Capitain v. Hinlopen und ließ augenblicklich die Segelstangen so wenden, daß der Wind das Segel rückwärts gegen den Mast drückte, wodurch der Stoß vermieden wurde.

We could not understand why? For we had just left Lisbon, which has continuous contact with England, both merchant ships and packet-boats. Also many Englishmen had been on our ship, all of whom, according to this, should have been put in quarantine. On the 9th, we weighed anchor and sailed to the mud bank, 'Modderbank', or the quarantine bed close to Cowes[151] on the Isle of Wight. An English man-of-war was stationed there to make sure we had no contact with land. On the 15th we received Pratica, weighed anchor and sailed under Capt. Zoutman into the roadstead of Spithead across from Portsmouth[152] [50]. Capt. Krul and Kauw sailed on to Holland. The English Commander, Arbuthnot[153], came on board our ship. We saluted him with 11 shots at his departure and were thanked with 11.

We saw a terrible execution here. Two sailors, who had deserted their ship, were displayed round in a barque. They were tied, bare-backed to the cross-bar, which was set up with two posts to look like a gallows, with their hands and feet tied up so that they were hanging in the air. At every ship where they were displayed, their sentence was read aloud and a couple of officers appeared with knouts (short sticks with strings in knots attached), and flogged them a prescribed number of lashes, so that each lash broke the skin. This went round the whole fleet, and after a few days it was to be repeated. They were two brothers, quite young. One yelled after each lash, "Ah, my brother, my dear brother!" When we sailed off, I experienced a similarly dramatic scene as I did at Brest 8 years later.[51] When we had weighed anchor and the ship was under sail, with Commander von Loo in charge, Capt. Zoutmann's ship was at anchor directly in front of us. We were so close, that we would definitely have rammed them, because van Loo had lost his head. Just at that moment, Capt. v. Hinlopen had the yard-arms turned, so that the wind pushed the sail back against the mast, thus avoiding a collision.

---

151. Cowes, Stadt an der Nordspitze der Isle of Wight; die Modderbank ist wohl eine Schlickbank.

152. Portsmouth, englische Hafenstadt ca. 100 km südwestlich von London.

153. Wohl der spätere Admiral Marriot Arbuthnot (1711 – 1794), vor 1775 Kommandant verschiedener Schiffe und meist in England eingesetzt, 1776 – 1778 stellvertretender Gouverneur von Neuschottland (Nova Scotia). Er befehligte bei der im Mskr., S. 80 – 86, beschriebenen Schlacht von Cape Henry am 16. März 1781 die englische Flotte beim Sieg über den französischen Verband unter Destouches.

---

151. Cowes, town at the northern point of the Isle of Wight.

152. Portsmouth, English port and naval base approx. 65 miles southwest of London.

153. Probably the later admiral Marriot Arbuthnot (1711 – 1794) who had been commander of several warships in British waters before 1775. 1776 – 1778 he served as vice-governor of Nova Scotia. He was the admiral who, in 1781, victoriously commanded the British fleet in the battle off Cape Henry (see mscr., p. 80 – 86).

Am 29ten Febr. gingen wir unter Segel durch die östliche Einfahrt zwischen der Insel Wight und dem festen Lande, sahen Bevesier, den Feuerthurm von den Cingels[154] und ankerten.

Am 1ten März hoben wir das Anker, passirten die Meerenge zwischen Dover und Calais, und sahen Nord Foreland[155], gingen wieder vor Anker wegen der Ebbe; denn wir mußten die Fluth erwarten, um weiter zu kommen; den 2. gingen wir wieder unter Segel. Am 3. sahen wir das Eck von Holland[156]. Am 4ten früh um ½ 2 Uhr sahen wir die Feuer von Egmond[157] und ankerten. Um 1 Uhr, [52] als die Ebbe aufhörte, gingen wir wieder unter Segel. Um ½ 4 liefen wir ein auf der Rhede bei Texel[158]. Am 7ten März ging der Commandeur v. Rechtern vom Schiff ab. Er wurde mit 7 Kanonenschüssen und 3 Hurrahs begrüßt. Ich begleitete ihn nach Amsterdam, von wo ich nach Almelo reißte.

Damals[159] hatte Holland wenige Kriegsschiffe in der See, so daß es schwer war angestellt zu werden. Da meine Familie mir nun in diesem Stücke mehr entgegen war, als daß sie meine Beförderung zur See suchte, weil es jedes mal viele Sollicitation[160] bei den Herren der Admiralitaet kostete, so oft man wieder auf einem Schiff angestellt werden wollte, so sah ich keine Gelegenheit, meinem Genie zu folgen, und um nicht müßig zu sitzen, übergab ich eine Suplik an den Herrn Stadthalter, er möchte mich zum Land-Officiren machen. Ich wurde Fähndrich unter dem Rechterschen Regiment, und ein Jahr nachher Fähndrich bei der Garde zu

---

154. Bevesier: s. o. Anm. 17; mit „Cingels" dürfte Dungeness, der als markantes Kap vorspringende südlichste Punkt der Grafschaft Kent bezeichnet sein. „Shingles" meint einen Strand aus Kieselsteinen; einen solchen hat Dungeness, seit 1615 auch einen Leuchtturm. Die Niederländer gaben wohl das englische Wort „shingles" als „Cingels" wieder; so erschien bspw. 1640 die Karte „De custe van Engellandt vandt Voorlandt tot de Cingels" (www.mapforum.com/15/col24.htm), womit – wie in unserem Text, nur umgekehrt – die Strecke von North Foreland bis Dungeness gemeint gewesen sein dürfte.

155. North Foreland, nordöstliche Spitze der Halbinsel Thanet, zwischen Margate und Ramsgate.

156. Eck von Holland = Hoek van Holland, kleiner Ort mit Leuchtturm westlich von Rotterdam, an der Mündung des Leks (eines Rheinarms) in die Nordsee.

157. Egmond aan Zee (Provinz Noord-Holland) mit Leuchtturm, westlich von Alkmaar.

158. Texel, die größte der westfriesischen Inseln in der Provinz Noord-Holland. Der im Osten der Insel gelegene Hafen Oudeschild war im 17./18. Jh. Ausgangspunkt für viele Seereisen in die niederländischen Kolonien.

159. Marginalnotiz: „Geschrieben im Jahr 179..". Im Text wird allerdings über die 1770-er Jahre berichtet.

160. Gesuche, Bitten.

On February 29th, we sailed East round the Isle of Wight, saw Bevesier, the light-house of the Cingels[154] and cast anchor.

On March 1st, we weighed anchor, reached the Straits between Dover and Calais, and saw North Foreland[155], cast anchor due to low tide; for we had to wait for high-tide to continue; on the 2nd we sailed on. On the 3rd we first caught sight of Hoek van Holland[156]. Early on the 4th at 1:30 a.m. we saw the light-house of Egmond[157] and cast anchor. When the low tide turned at one o'clock, we sailed on. [52] At 3:30 we reached the roadstead at Texel[158]. On March 7th, Commander v. Rechtern left our ship. He was greeted with 7 cannon-shots and 3 Hurrahs. I accompanied him to Amsterdam, then I travelled on to Amelo.

At that time[159], Holland did not have many warships under sail, so that it was difficult to find one to serve on. And my family was rather negative on the question of continuing my naval career, because this always implied much solicitation[160] at the doors of the gentlemen of the Admiralty, each time you wanted another job on a ship: so I saw no opportunity to follow my inclination; and not wanting to sit around idly, I submitted a supplication to the "Stadtholder" (governor), to make an army officer of me. I became a cadet in the Rechtern Regiment, and one year later a cadet in the Foot Guards (with the rank of Lieutenant), and after that Lieutenant (with the rank of Captain). My love

---

154. For "Bevesier" see fn 17. "Cingles" probably means the marked promontory of Dungeness, the southernmost point of Kent, and may be the Dutch rendering of the English word "shingles". Dungeness has Europe's largest shingle beach and has had a lighthouse since 1615. A Dutch chart published in 1640 describes "De custe van Engellandt vandt Voorlandt tot de Cingels" (www.mapforum.com/15/col24.htm), i.e. the same stretch as in our text, but the other way round.

155. Northeastern tip of the Isle of Thanet between Margate and Ramsgate.

156. Small town with a lighthouse, west of Rotterdam where the Lek (Rhine) flows into the North Sea.

157. Egmond aan Zee, west of Alkmaar, province of Noord-Holland.

158. Texel, the largest of the West Frisian islands in the province of Noord-Holland. The port of Oudeschild, situated in the east of the island, was where many ships in the 17th and 18th centuries left for the Dutch colonies.

159. Note on the margin: "written in the year 179."[last digit missing]; the time referred to is the 1770s, though..

160. Petitions, personal interviews with influential people.

Fuß, (mit dem Rang eines Leutnants), und später Leutnant (mit Capitains-Rang). Der Trieb aber, den ich hatte, mich zu unterrichten, vielleicht auch die Erinnerung an das Seeleben, mach- [53] te, daß das Garnisonsleben mir gar nicht anstand. Ich hatte gleich im Anfang gesucht, mit dem Regiment Fourgeaud nach Surinam[161] zu gehen. (Dieses Regiment wurde geschickt, um die Colonie gegen die Einfälle der entlaufenen Neger, welche eine zahlreiche Nation ausmachen, zu beschützen.) Als ich nicht dorthin mitkommen konnte, tröstete ich mich damit, daß ich im Haag war, wo ich vieles sehen und lernen konnte. Einmal machte ich eine kurze Reise nach Mastricht[162], Aaken und Spaa[163]. Im Jahr 1775 ging ich mit dem Directeur des prinzlichen Cabinets, Vosmaar, nebst 2 Officiren, nach Brüssel, Antwerpen[164] und Paris, wo wir 3 Wochen blieben, dann nach Lunéville, Nancy, Metz[165], Straßburg[166]. Damals kam gerade der König vom Sacre zu Rheims[167]. Von da ging Vosmaar nach Italien, ich aber nach Nürnberg[168], Würzburg[169] und Sommerhausen, besuchte auch meine Schwester[170] zu Ordruff[171]. Im Jahr 1776 ging ich nach dreivierteljähriger Abwesenheit wieder zum Regiment.

of learning and perhaps my memory of life at sea, had the effect [53] of making me dissatisfied with life in a garrison town. Right away I tried to join the Fourgeaud Regiment (which was sent to Surinam[161] to protect the colony from attacks by the fugitive negroes, who form a large population there). When I was not able to join them, I took consolation in being stationed in The Hague ('s Gravenhage), where I could see and learn many new things. Once I took a short trip to Maastricht[162], Aachen and Spa[163]. In the year 1775, I went to Brussels, Antwerp[164] and Paris with the Director of the Prince's Cabinet, Vosmaar, and two other officers. We stayed in Paris for 3 weeks, then went on to Lunéville, Nancy, Metz[165] and Strassburg[166]. At this time the king came from his coronation at Rheims[167]. After this Vosmaar went to Italy, but I went on to Nürnberg[168], Würzburg[169] and Sommerhausen (home), also I visited my sister[170] in Ordruff[171]. In 1776 after three quarters of a year's absence, I returned to my Regiment.

---

161. Surinam bzw. Niederländisch Guayana, niederländische Kolonie im Nordosten Südamerikas.

162. Maastricht (Provinz Limburg, Niederlande).

163. Die Reichsstadt Aachen und Spa waren im 18. Jahrhundert beliebte Kurorte, die Heilkräfte ihrer Quellen waren schon viel länger bekannt.

164. Brüssel, Hauptstadt, und Antwerpen, Handels- und Hafenstadt in den österreichischen Niederlanden.

165. Lunéville, Nancy und Metz, französische Städte in Lothringen.

166. Straßburg, Hauptstadt des Elsass.

167. Ludwig XVI. König von Frankreich bestieg am 10.5.1774 den Thron und wurde am 11.6.1775 in Reims gesalbt und gekrönt; vgl. Gazette de France, Nr. 48 (16.6.1775), 217, und 49 (19.6.1775), 221.

168. Reichsstadt in Franken, die am Ende des 18. Jahrhunderts viel von ihrer früheren Bedeutung als Zentrum von Handwerk und Handel verloren und damals etwa 40 000 Einwohner hatte.

169. Hauptstadt des gleichnamigen Hochstifts und Bistums in Franken, hatte um 1780 knapp 20 000 Einwohner.

170. Josina Elisabeth (1738 – 1804), aus der ersten Ehe seines Vaters, die 1754 den Grafen August Wilhelm zu Hohenlohe-Ingelfingen (†1769) heiratete; vgl. Anm. 3.

171. Die Stadt Ohrdruff und sechs Dörfer bildeten die Grafschaft Obergleichen, die 1631 an die Grafen zu Hohenlohe-Langenburg gefallen war und unter der Landeshoheit von Sachsen-Gotha stand.

---

161. Surinam or Dutch Guayana, Dutch colony in the northeast of South America.

162. Maastricht, province of Limburg, Netherlands.

163. The Imperial city of Aachen (in Germany) and Spa (in Belgium, province of Liège) were popular watering places in the 18th century, but had been known for their healing waters much longer.

164. Brussels, capital, and Antwerp, port and trading center of the then Austrian Netherlands.

165. Lunéville, Nancy and Metz, French cities in Lorraine.

166. Strasbourg (German: Straßburg), capital of Alsace.

167. Louis XVI., king of France, came to the throne May 10th, 1774, and was coronated at Reims on June 11th, 1775, cf. Gazette de France, no. 48 (June 16th, 1775), 217, and no. 49 (June 19th, 1775), 221.

168. Imperial city in Franconia which, at the end of the 18th century, had lost much of its former importance as a center of trade and industry; it had about 40.000 inhabitants then.

169. Capital of the eponymous see and principality in Franconia, in the author's day a town of about 20,000 inhabitants.

170. Josina Elisabeth (1738 – 1804), his half sister from his father's first marriage who, in 1754, married count August Wilhelm zu Hohenlohe-Ingelfingen († 1769).

171. Ohrdruff in Thuringia, south of Gotha. The town of O. and six villages formed the county of Obergleichen which had come into the possession of the counts of Hohenlohe-Langenburg in 1631 and was under the dominion of Sachsen-Gotha.

Im Jahr 1778 ging der Bayerische Erbfolgekrieg[172] an. Verschiedene hol- [54] ländische Officire, unter ihnen auch mein Bruder[173], begehrten Erlaubniß, dabei als Volontairs zu dienen. Doch man machte höheren Orts Schwierigkeiten und zeigte genug, daß man es nicht gern sehe. Ich hatte nun große Lust, mich auch dabei umzusehen. Um aber nicht lange vergeblich herumgezogen zu werden, machte ich den Anfang damit, daß ich meinen Abschied nahm und über Würzburg nach Ansbach ging, um mir des Herrn Markgrafen Durchlaucht[174] ein Vorschreiben an den Koenig von Preußen[175] auszubitten. Der Minister v. G[emmingen][176], zu dem ich erst ging, sagte mir, ich thäte besser, dem Herrn Markgrafen nichts davon zu sagen, er wolle es bei dem General Gö[r]tz[177] ausmachen. Nach langem Warten kam die Antwort vom General, Gr[af] v. Görtz, ich sollte selbst an den König schreiben. Doch war nun schon der Teschener Frieden[178] vor der Thür; ich entsagte also diesen Gedanken, und nahm mir vor, bei den Franzosen anzukommen zu suchen. Da die Landung in England vorgenommen werden

In the year 1778, the War of the Bavarian Succession[172] started. Several Dutch officers [54], among them my brother[173], asked for permission to serve as volunteers. But there were some difficulties with the higher ranks who made it quite clear that they did not approve of it. I also had a great desire to take part in this. Not wanting to be marched around in vain, I took heart and handed in my resignation. Then by way of Würzburg, I went to Ansbach, to ask his Grace, the Margrave[174] to write a letter to the King of Prussia[175]. Minister v. G[emmingen][176], whom I visited first, said it would be best not to mention this to his Grace, the Margrave, and that he would arrange it with General Görtz[177]. After a long wait, General v. Görtz answered that I should write to the King myself. But the Teschen Peace Treaty[178] was about to be signed, so I gave up this plan, and decided to try to get a position in the French army. As they

---

172. Nach dem Erlöschen der bayerischen Linie der Wittelsbacher 1778 ging Bayern an den aus der pfälzischen Linie stammenden Karl Theodor über, der ebenfalls ohne legitime Nachkommen war. Kaiser Joseph II. versuchte den Verlust Schlesiens zu kompensieren, indem er Ansprüche auf Teile Niederbayerns erhob und die bayerischen Reichslehen einzog. Dagegen protestierten u. a. König Friedrich II. von Preußen und der designierte Nachfolger Karl Theodors, Herzog Karl von Pfalz-Zweibrücken. Nach dem weitgehend ergebnislosen „Kartoffelkrieg" zwischen Preußen und Österreich wurde der Konflikt im Frieden von Teschen beigelegt.

173. Friedrich Ludwig Christian Graf von Rechteren-Limpurg-Speckfeld (1748 – 1814), Herr zu Almelo, Rechteren, Schulenborch und Eeze; vgl. Anm. 3.

174. Markgraf Alexander von Brandenburg-Ansbach und Bayreuth (1736 – 1806, reg. 1757 – 1791).

175. Friedrich II., König von Preußen (1712 – 1786, reg. 1740 – 1786).

176. Carl Friedrich Reinhard Freiherr von Gemmingen (1739 – 1822), Minister, Geheimer Rat, Präsident des Justizrats (II. Senat), trug dem Markgrafen die Bittschriften, Depeschen und Eingaben des Ministeriums vor und begleitete ihn auch häufig auf Auslandsreisen. S. Schuhmann, C. Fr. R. von Gemmingen.

177. Karl Friedrich Adam Graf Görtz, gen. v. Schlitz (1733 – 1797), seit 1771 in preußischen Diensten, 1777 preußischer Generalmajor, „verblieb in der königlichen Suite", General-Adjutant König Friedrichs II. von Preußen, 1795 Generalleutnant, s. ADB Band 9, S.395 – 396 (Graf Lippe). Sein Bruder war Johann Eustach Graf Schlitz gen. von Görtz (1737 – 1821), seit 1762 Prinzenerzieher in Weimar; 1778 bewog er als preußischer Gesandter Herzog Karl von Pfalz-Zweibrücken zum Einspruch gegen die geplante Abtretung eines Teils von Bayern an Österreich, s. ADB Band 9, S.393 – 395 (Bailleu).

178. Im Frieden von Teschen (13.5.1779) erhielten u. a. Österreich das Innviertel und Preußen die Sicherung seiner Ansprüche auf Ansbach und Bayreuth. Die bayerisch-pfälzischen Erbverträge von 1766, 1771 und 1774 wurden bestätigt und durch die Großmächte Österreich, Preußen, Frankreich und Russland garantiert.

---

172. After the extinction of the Bavarian line of the house of Wittelsbach in 1778, Bavaria fell to Karl Theodor of the Palatinate line who did not have any legitimate heirs, either. Emperor Joseph II. tried to compensate the loss of Silesia (which had been lost to Prussia) by laying claim to parts of Niederbayern (Lower Bavaria) and by annulling Bavaria's Imperial fiefs. However, king Frederick II. of Prussia and Karl Theodor's designated successor, duke Karl of Pfalz-Zweibrücken, protested against that. After the largely futile "potato war" between Prussia and Austria the conflict was resolved by the peace treaty of Teschen; cf. Introduction, fn.11.

173. Friedrich Ludwig Christian, count of Rechteren-Limpurg-Speckfeld (1748 – 1814), lord of Almelo, Rechteren, Schulenborch, and Eeze.

174. Margrave Alexander von Brandenburg-Ansbach and Bayreuth (1736 – 1806, reigned 1757 – 1791).

175. Friedrich (Frederick) II. („the Great"), king of Prussia (1712 – 1786, reigned 1740 – 1786).

176. Carl Friedrich Reinhard, baron of Gemmingen (1739 – 1822), minister, privy councillor, president of the judicial council (II. senate). He presented petitions, dispatches, and ministerial requests to the margrave and often accompanied him on his foreign travels; cf. Schuhmann, C. Fr. R. von Gemmingen.

177. Karl Friedrich Adam, count Görtz called von Schlitz (1733 – 1797), in Prussian service after 1771, 1773 Prussian Major General, „remained in the king's inner circle", Adjutant General to king Frederick II. of Prussia, 1795 Lieutenant General, cf. ADB, vol. 9, p. 395 – 396 (count Lippe). His brother Johann Eustach, count Schlitz called von Görtz (1737 – 1821), after 1762 tutor of the princes in Weimar; in 1778, as Prussian envoy, he convinced duke Karl von Pfalz-Zweibrücken to object against the planned cession of a part of Bavaria to Austria; cf. ADB, vol. 9, p. 393 – 395 (Bailleu).

178. Peace treaty between Austria and Prussia, May 13th, 1779. By this treaty, Austria received the so-called „Innviertel" (a stretch of territory on the river Inn) and Prussia's claims to Ansbach and Bayreuth were safeguarded. The Bavarian-Palatinate contracts of inheritance of 1766, 1771, and 1774 were reconfirmed and warranted by the great powers Austria, Prussia, France, and Russia.

wollte,[179] so suchte ich als Capitain à la Suite dabei zu sein. Der Fürst von Würzburg[180] **[55]** schrieb für mich an den französischen Gesandten am Reichstag, Marquis de Bombelles[181], und ich reißte nach Paris zu ihm. Der Hofrath Gilson[182] gab mir auch einen Brief an Herrn Herrmann[183], Agenten des Fürsten von Würzburg, mit, welcher mir sehr nützlich war. Der Marquis versicherte mich auf die höflichste Art, daß der Minister sich freuen würde, mich anzustellen, und ich dachte, daß ich vielleicht 14 Tage mich in Paris würde aufzuhalten brauchen. Jedoch es ging mir, wie sehr vielen Fremden: ich hielt die schmeichelhaften Versicherungen französischer Höflichkeit und Lebhaftigkeit für gangbare Münze. Ich wurde von einer Zeit auf die andere vertröstet. Zuletzt machte ich zufälliger Weise Bekanntschaft mit dem Grafen v. Forbach[184]. Damals wurde zu Vincennes[185] ein Wettrennen gegeben von Duc de Lauragay[186], Comte d'Artois[187] und Duc de Chartres[188], welchem ich beiwohnte.

were planning an invasion of England,[179] I tried to join up as "Captain à la Suite". The Prince Bishop of Würzburg[180] [55] wrote about me to the French envoy at the 'Reichstag' (Imperial Diet), Marquis de Bombelles[181], and I travelled with him to Paris. The Privy Councillor, Gilson[182], gave me a letter adressed to Herr Herrmann[183], the Agent of the Würzburg Prince-Bishop, which was very helpful. The Marquis assured me most politely, that the Minister would be very happy to employ me and I thought that I might be spending a couple of weeks in Paris. However my fate was similar to that of many other foreigners in Paris: I took at face value the charming assurances of French politeness and sprightliness. I was told to keep waiting. At last I happened to make the aquaintance of Count von Forbach[184]. I met him at the race-track at Vincennes[185], at a race given by the Duke de Lauragay[186], Comte d'Artois[187] and Duke de Chartres[188].

---

179. S. dazu u. Anm. 190.

180. Adam Friedrich Graf von Seinsheim (1708 – 1779), Bischof von Würzburg (1755 – 1779) und von Bamberg (1757 – 1779).

181. Marc-Marie Marquis de Bombelles (1744 – 1822), General, französischer Gesandter beim Reichstag, Bischof von Amiens.

182. Sieur Gilson, ein französischer Hofmeister, am Würzburger Hof als Erzieher des Grafen Max Clemens von Seinsheim angestellt, aber auch in diplomatischen Missionen nach Paris eingesetzt. Der Elsässer war sehr gebildet und sprach „ohnvergleichlich französisch und sehr gut teitsch", s. v. Roda, Seinsheim, S. 101, Anm. 549.

183. Wahrscheinlich Herr Harmant, Sekretär des Grafen von Eyck; er war Bischof von Seinsheims Kontaktmann in Paris und berichtete ihm ausführlich über Voltaires Tod; vgl. v. Roda (wie Anm. 182), S. 100.

184. Philipp Wilhelm Graf von Forbach (1754 – 1807), Vicomte de Deux-Ponts.

185. Vincennes, Stadt östl. von Paris, mit Residenzschloss der französischen Könige und großem Park. Bei dem Rennen handelte es sich wohl um ein Pferderennen, auch wenn die berühmte Trabrennbahn erst 1863 entstand.

186. Louis de Brancas, Duc (1731) de Lauragais (1714 – 1793), Ritter des Ordens vom Goldenen Vließ (1746).

187. Charles-Philippe de France, Comte d'Artois (1757 – 1836), Bruder Ludwigs XVI. und Ludwigs XVIII., 1824 bis 1830 als Karl X. König von Frankreich.

188. Louis-Philippe (1747 – 1793), Duc de Chartres (1752), Duc d'Orléans (1785) als „Philippe Égalité" ein Anhänger der Revolution, wurde schließlich auch guillotiniert. Sein ältester Sohn Louis-Philippe regierte 1830 – 1848 als König von Frankreich.

---

179. Cf. fn. 190 for an explanation of what the author is alluding to.

180. Adam Friedrich count von Seinsheim (1708 – 1779), bishop of Würzburg 1755 – 1779, bishop of Bamberg 1757 – 1779.

181. Marc-Marie marquis de Bombelles (1744 – 1822), French general, French envoy at the Imperial Diet, bishop of Amiens.

182. Sieur Gilson, a French private tutor, was employed as tutor of count Max Clemens von Seinsheim at the court of Würzburg, but was also sent on several diplomatic mission to Paris. This Alsatian was highly educated and spoke "French incomparably well and also very good German"; cf. v. Roda, Seinsheim, p. 101, fn. 549.

183. Probably Mr. Harmant, secretary of count von Eyck; he was bishop von Seinsheim's contact in Paris and reported to him at length on Voltaire's death; cf. v. Roda (see fn. 182), p. 100.

184. Philipp Wilhelm, count of Forbach and Deux-Ponts (1754 – 1807), is probably meant here; cf. fn. 189 below.

185. Town east of Paris with a royal palace and park. The race referred to was probably a horserace even though today's famous trotting race track only came into being in 1863.

186. Louis de Brancas, duke (1731) of Lauragais (1714 – 1793), knight of the order of the Golden Fleece (1746).

187. Charles-Philippe de France, comte d'Artois (1757 – 1836), brother of Louis XVI. and Louis XVIII., 1824 – 1830 king of France as Charles X.

188. Louis-Philippe (1747 – 1793), Duc de Chartres (1752), Duc d'Orléans (1785), a supporter of the revolution, known as "Philippe Égalité", later beheaded on the guillotine. His eldest son Louis-Philippe reigned 1830 – 1848 as king of France.

Der Comte de Deuxpont[189], welcher auf sein dringendes Anhalten, mit seinem Regiment eingeschifft werden sollte. (An die Expedition in England glaubte man nicht mehr.)[190] Der Graf schlug mir [56] vor, wenn der Minister mir das Brevet[191] als Hauptmann nicht geben wollte, so wollte er mich als Cadet gentilhomme[192] nehmen; denn anders könnte er mich nicht einschiffen; und nachher würde ich schon weiter employirt[193] werden. Man erzählte, 800 Personen hätten sich gemeldet, um freiwillig zu dienen, und der Ministre habe sich nicht anders zu helfen gewußt, als daß er erklärt, er würde keinen einzigen auf die Art anstellen. Ich nahm dieses Anerbieten mit Freuden an. Der Marquis de Bombelles sagte, er habe von mir bei der verwittweten Fürstin von Nassau-Saarbrück, einer gebornen Gräfin von[194] Erbach[195], gesprochen, und sie habe geäußert, ich sey ein Verwandter von ihr. Ich recommendirte dieser dann auch meine Sache. Denn sie hatte damals Einfluß, weil ihr Enkel[196] die Tochter des Ministre de la guerre, Prince de Monbarrey[197], heyrathete[198]. Sie speißte bei dem Minister mit dem Gra-

The Count de Deuxponts[189] (Zweibrücken) was hoping to be shipped out with his Regiment. (No one believed in the expedition to England any more.)[190] The Count [56] proposed to accept me as a "Cadet gentilhomme"[191], if the minister would not give me a brevet[192] rank (volunteer) as a captain, for otherwise he could not take me along; he assumed that I would continue to be employed afterwards. They said, 800 persons had signed up as volunteers, and the Minister did not know what else to do, except to explain that no one was to be employed[193] thus. I gladly accepted this proposal. The Marquis de Bombelles told me he had mentioned me to the widowed Princess von Nassau-Saarbrück, née (born) Countess[194] von Erbach[195], and she had said that I was related to her. I told her my whole story. For she had much influence, because her grandson[196] was married[197] to the daughter of the Minister of War, Prince de Monbarrey[198]. She dined at the house of the Minister

---

189. Christian Graf von Forbach, seit 1781 Marquis von Deux-Ponts (1752 – 1817), Sohn aus der morganatischen Ehe des Pfalzgrafen Christian IV. von Zweibrücken (1722 – 1775) und der Maria Johanna Camasse, Gräfin von Forbach (1734 – 1807). Er wurde 1775 Kommandeur des Regiments „Royal Deux-Ponts", das sein Vater 1757 für ihn begründet hatte.

190. Die Bemerkung bezieht sich auf den französischen Plan einer Invasion Englands im Bunde mit Spanien von 1778. Im Frühjahr 1779 warteten fast 40 000 Soldaten in Nordfrankreich darauf, nach England übergesetzt zu werden. Die englische Flotte vermied eine Schlacht mit den zahlenmäßig weit überlegenen verbündeten Flotten Frankreichs und Spaniens; diese mussten im Herbst, nicht zuletzt wegen der auf den Schiffen grassierenden Epidemien, das Unternehmen abbrechen; s. dazu Selig, Revolutionary Route, S. 33 f. Bei Selig als der jüngsten speziell auf den französisch-amerikanischen Feldzug von 1780/81 ausgerichteten Studie finden sich hilfreich zusammengefasst alle politischen Hintergründe und Planungen, die dazu führten.

191. Brevet: „Kurzer" Gnadenbrief des französischen Königs; Schutz-, Verleihungs-, und Ernennungsurkunde in Frankreich.

192. Cadet gentilhomme, ein junger Adeliger, der zu Kriegsdiensten ausgebildet wird, meist – wie auch Rechteren – unbezahlt (seine Militärakte erwähnt keine Soldzahlungen).

193. Employiren = anstellen, versorgen.

194. Nach „Gräfin von" gestrichen: „Nassau".

195. Sophie Christine Fürstin zu Nassau-Saarbrücken, geb. Gräfin zu Erbach-Erbach (1725 – 1795) , seit 1768 verwittwet.

196. Heinrich Prinz (seit 1794 Fürst) von Nassau-Saarbrücken (1768 – 1797) heiratete 1779 bzw. 1785 Marie de Saint-Mauris de Montbarrey (1761 – 1838), s. ADB, Band 11, S.553-554.

197. Alexandre Marie Léonor de Saint-Mauris, Prince de Montbarrey (1732 – 1796), französischer Kriegsminister vom 27.9.1777 bis 19.12.1780.

198. Vor „heyrathete" gestrichen: „und Beide sollten".

---

189. Christian count von Forbach and of Deux-Ponts (1752 – 1817), 1781 marquis of Deux-Ponts, son of the morganatic marriage of count palatinate Christian IV of Zweibrücken (1722 – 1775) and Maria Johanna Camasse, countess of Forbach (1734 – 1807).
In 1775, he became commander of the regiment Royal Deux-Ponts which his father had established for him in 1757; cf. fn. 184.

190. This alludes to the French plan of an invasion of England in alliance with Spain, proposed in 1778. In the spring of 1779, about 40.000 soldiers were waiting in Northern France to be transferred to England. The English fleet avoided being drawn into battle by the numerically superior allied fleets; those had to abort the operation in fall, not least because of epidemics ravaging the troops on these ships. Cf. Selig, Revolutionary Route, p. 33f. Selig's recent study of the French-American campaign of 1780/81 contains helpful information on its political and military background.

191. A young nobleman being trained as a soldier, usually unpaid, just like Rechteren (there is no mention of payment in his file at the army archive in Vincennes).

192. Short legal instrument issued by the French king: letter of protection, enfeoffment or appointment in France.

193. The original text uses the word "employiren" which is outdated in contemporary German.

194. "Nassau" deleted after "countess of".

195. Sophie Christine princess of Nassau-Saarbrücken, née countess Erbach-Erbach (1725 – 1795), widowed since 1768.

196. Heinrich prince (1794) of Nassau-Saarbrücken (1768 – 1797) married Marie de Saint-Mauris de Montbarrey (1761 – 1838) in 1779 or 1785; cf. ADB, vol. 11, p. 553 – 554.

197. Deleted before "married": "und Beide sollten (and both of them should)".

198. Alexandre Marie Léonor des Saint-Mauris, prince de Montbarrey (1732 – 1796), French minister of war from Sept. 27, 1777 to Dec. 19, 1780.

fen v. Monbarrey[199], und beide sollten sich vereinigen, um den Ministre auf gute Gedanken für **[57]** mich zu bringen. Der Graf v. Forbach erzählte mir, nachdem der unerbittliche Ministre mir auch keine Commission als Hauptmann geben wollte[200], so sey ich doch entschlossen mitzugehen, nämlich als Cadet gentilhomme. Als solcher erhielt ich bald darauf mein Brevet.

Anstatt 14 Tage, wie ich Anfangs gedacht, hatte ich 7 Monate warten müssen und war immer von einer Woche zur andern in der Ungewißheit gelassen worden. Deshalb kam ich nicht soviel in Gesellschaft, als wenn ich mir vorgenommen hätte, so lange da zu bleiben. Im Hotel D' Anjou[201], Rue Dauphine, wo ich war, logirten viele Teutsche. Mit diesen ging ich viel aus. Die Spaziergänge, Straßen und Environs von Paris waren mir zuletzt so gut bekannt, als wenn ich da geboren und erzogen wäre.

Wenige Tage, ehe ich von Paris wegging, war ich im Concert Spirituel[202], worin hauptsächlich geistliche Musik gemacht wird. Es wird an Tagen gehalten, wo keine Comedie seyn darf, und ist das Spectacle der Abbées. Der berühmte Musicus und **[58]** Schachspieler Filidor[203] führte gerade das Carmen seculare des Horaz[204] das er in Musik gesetzt, durch Chöre von Sängern und Sängerinnen auf. Die Ouverture waren die 4 Zeilen: Odi profanum vulgus etc. – Hinter mir sah ich einen alten Mann, den ich wegen seiner Brülle und aus seiner Gleichheit mit seinem gedruckten Bilde für Benj[amin]

with Count de Monbarrey[199], and both agreed to try to put the minister in a good mood [57] and to mention my name. Count von Forbach told me, the unrelenting minister could not be talked into commissioning me as captain[200], but that since I really wanted to take part, I could as "Cadet gentilhomme". As such I soon received my brevet.

Instead of waiting for two weeks, as originally expected, I had been kept waiting for seven months, and thus kept dangling from one week to the next. For this reason I did not meet as many people as I would have, if I had planned to stay that long. Many Germans lived at the Hotel d'Anjou[201], Rue Dauphine, which also was my lodging-house. We often went out together. The walks, streets, and environs of Paris I got to know as well as if I had been born and raised there.

A few days before leaving Paris, I went to a "Concert Spirituel"[202], where they played mostly religious music. This takes place on days when no comedy is allowed, and is the "entertainment of the clergy". The famous musician and [58] chess player, Filidor[203] was directing the "Carmen Seculare" (secular song) of Horace[204], which he had set to music for male and female choirs. The overture used the 4 lines: "Odi profanum vulgus" etc. Behind me I saw

---

199. Vermutlich Stanislas Graf von Montbarrey (1756 – 1794).

200. Im Manuskript steht hier: „nachdem sie den unerbittlichen Ministre mir auch keine Commission als Hauptmann geben wollte, [...]".

201. Im Manuskript: „Hotel D'Anjon".

202. Die Concerts spirituels wurden 1725 von Mitgliedern der Pariser Oper begonnen, um auch in der Fastenzeit, in der die Oper schließen musste, Aufführungsmöglichkeiten zu haben. Auf dem Programm standen meist große geistliche Oratorien. Die Konzertreihe wurde in vielen europäischen Städten (u.a. in Leipzig, Berlin, Wien, Stockholm) kopiert, in Frankreich aber nach dem Beginn der Revolution aufgehoben.

203. François-André Philidor (Filidor, 1726-1795), französischer Komponist, dessen Opern und Oratorien damals erfolgreich waren, einer der berühmtesten Schachspieler seiner Zeit, lebte in Paris und London. Im Manuskript verschrieben: „Tilidor".

204. Das Oratorium „Carmen saeculare" nach Horaz (Quintus Horatius Flaccus, 65 v.Chr. – 8 n.Chr., römischer Dichter) wurde 1779 in London uraufgeführt.

---

199. Probably Stanislas count of Montbarrey (1756 – 1794).

200. The manuscript seems to contain a grammatical mistake which renders it hard to make any sense of the clause; it says: "nachdem sie den unerbittlichen Ministre mir auch keine Commission als Hauptmann geben wollte (after she did not want to give me a commission as captain the unrelenting minister)".

201. "D'Anjon" in the manuscript.

202. The "concerts spirituels" constituted the earliest series of public concerts in Paris, inaugurated in 1725 by members of the Paris opera in order to be able to have musical productions in Lent when the opera had to close. The program contained mostly sacred oratorios. The concerts continued from 1725 to the French revolution (1791) when they were abolished. They were copied in many European cities as, e.g., Leipzig, Berlin, Vienna, and Stockholm.

203. Philidor, François André (1726 – 1795, London), French composer whose operas and oratorios were successful and widely known in his day, also one of the most famous chess players of his time; he lived in Paris and London. Misspelled in the manuscript as "Tilidor".

204. Quintus Horatius Flaccus (65 B.C. – 8 B.C.), Roman poet. The oratorio "Carmen saeculare" after his poem was first presented in London in 1779.

Franklin[205] erkannte, ein dicker Mann mit einer Glatze auf dem Kopfe und mit gerade herunterhängenden Haaren, mit einem schwarzen Rocke bekleidet. Adams[206] führte ihn. – Der nachherige König von Bayern, Max Joseph[207], war auch gegenwärtig.

Zuletzt lernte ich noch den Herrn von der Wisch[208], Hauptmann vom Zweibrückischen Regiment, kennen. Dieser sollicitirte auch, um Major zu werden, und wurde auf die nämliche Art wie ich vertröstet. Zuletzt mußte er zum Regiment reißen, ohne sein[en] Zweck erreicht zu haben. Mit diesem nahm ich die Post, um zum Regiment zu reisen; mein Bedienter ging mit einer Art von Landkutsche. Wir mach- **[59]** ten die zweiräderige Calesche[209] des Herrn v. d. Wisch, in der wir fuhren, immer ganz zu.

Einige Stunden von Rennes[210] in Bretagne geschah es vor Tagesanbruch, als wir beide schliefen, daß ich durch das Fallen der Calesche und meines Reisegefährten auf mich aufgeweckt wurde. Als wir aufhörten zu fallen, befand ich mich mit dem Gesicht in wasserweicher Erde, die Füße in die Höhe. Mein Reisegefährte, der sehr schwer und unbeholfen war, lag auf mir. In der Gefahr zu ersticken, that ich mein Aeußerstes, die

---

205. Benjamin Franklin (1706 – 1790), Mitunterzeichner der Declaration of Independence, 1776 amerikanischer Gesandter in Frankreich, erreichte ein Bündnis mit Frankreich (6.2.1778) und dessen Eintritt in den amerikanischen Unabhängigkeitskrieg. Erfinder des Franklin-Ofens, der bifokalen Brille und des Blitzableiters.

206. John Adams (1735 – 1826), Mitunterzeichner der Declaration of Independence 1776, kam Ende 1779 nach Paris, um mit England Friedensverhandlungen anzuknüpfen; Gesandter in den Niederlanden, 1782 wieder in Paris, wo er zusammen mit Franklin und Jefferson den Friedensvertrag mit England aushandelte; Vizepräsident unter Washington, 1797 – 1801 Präsident der USA. Sein Sohn John Quincy Adams (1767 – 1848), begleitete seinen Vater; 1794 Gesandter im Haag, 1797 Gesandter in Berlin, 1809 in St. Petersburg, 1817 amerikanischer Außenminister, 1825 – 1828 Präsident der USA. Beide Adams hielten sich damals in Paris auf.

207. Maximilian (I.) Joseph Pfalzgraf von Zweibrücken-Birkenfeld (1756 – 1825), 1795 Herzog von Pfalz-Zweibrücken, 1799 Kurfürst von Bayern und der Pfalz, 1806 König von Bayern, lebte häufig am Hof Ludwig XVI., wurde bereits 1770 Oberst und 1776 Kommandeur des französischen Fremdenregiments „Royal Alsace".

208. Johann Christoph von der Wisch entstammte einer adligen Familie in Schleswig-Holstein. 1739 geboren, trat er 1757 in das Regiment Deux-Ponts ein; 1768 Hauptmann. In Yorktown verwundet, mit dem militärischen Verdienstkreuz ausgezeichnet. 1793 schied er als General der französischen Armee aus dem Militärdienst aus; vgl. Bodinier, Dictionnaire, S. 561, sowie Acomb, Journal, S. 365.

209. Leicht gebaute, seitlich offene Kutsche mit Faltverdeck, von dem sich der Name des Fahrzeugs ableitet.

210. Rennes, Stadt in der Bretagne, westlich von Paris.

---

an old man, whom I recognized as Benjamin Franklin[205], because of his glasses and because of the likeness with his printed picture. He was a thick-set man with a bald spot on top of his head, wearing a black coat, and what hair he had, hanging down straight. Adams[206] was leading him round. – The future King of Bavaria, Max Joseph[207], was also present.

In the end I met Herrn von der Wisch[208], captain in the Zweibrücken Regiment. He was soliciting to become a major, and was consoled in the same way that I was. Finally he had to rejoin his regiment, without having reached his goal. We decided to travel together in a mail coach to reach our regiment; my servant went on ahead with a sort of rural conveyance. [59] We travelled in Herrn von Wisch's two wheeled calash[209], and always kept the top up.

At daybreak, a few hours distance from Rennes[210] in Brittany, I woke up suddenly, when our calash crashed and my travel companion fell on top of me. When we stopped falling, I found my face in the wet mud and my feet in the air. My travel companion, who was quite heavy and clumsy,

---

205. Franklin, Benjamin (1706 – 1790), signer of the Declaration of Independence, American envoy to France in 1776, was able to set up an alliance with France on Febr. 6th, 1778, and to secure France's decisive entry into the American War of Independence; he invented the Franklin stove, bifocal spectacles, and the lightning rod.

206. Adams, John (1735 – 1826), signer of the Declaration of Independence 1776, came to Paris at the end of 1779 in order to commence peace negotiations with England; envoy to the Netherlands, back in Paris in 1782, where he, together with Franklin and Jefferson, negotiated the peace treaty with England. First Vice President of the USA under Washington and second President of the US 1797 – 1801. His son, John Quincy Adams (1767 – 1848), accompanied his father to France, to the Netherlands and to England, 1794 envoy at the Hague, 1797 envoy in Berlin, 1809 in St. Petersburg, 1817 American Secretary of State, 6th President of the US 1825 – 1829. Both father and son were in Paris at this time.

207. Max I. Joseph (1756 – 1825), count palatinate of Zweibrücken--Birkenfeld, 1795 duke of Pfalz-Zweibrücken, 1799 elector of Bavaria and Pfalz, King of Bavaria 1806 – 1825. He often lived at the court of Louis XVI. and was made a colonel in 1770 and commander of the French foreign regiment "Royal Alsace" in 1776.

208. Johann Christoph von der Wisch, scion of a noble family in Schleswig-Holstein (then Danish), born 1739, joined the Deux-Ponts regiment in 1757, and was promoted to the rank of captain in 1768. In 1793, he was a general in the French army, retired in 1794; Bodinier, Dictionnaire, p. 561, and Acomb, Journal, p. 365.

209. Calash, a light and fast, usually two-wheeled vehicle with a leather or textile folding top.

210. Capital of the historic province of Britanny, west of Paris.

beschwerliche Bürde von mir abzuwälzen, welches mir auch so weit glückte, daß er von mir ab und mit dem Kopf unterwärts in ein Eck kam. So lange seine Lage erträglich gewesen war, d.h. so lang er auf mir lag, hatte er sich ganz ruhig verhalten und mich schreien lassen; jetzt aber fing er desto heftiger an, nach dem ich mich etwas auf die Seite gelegt hatte, so daß ich frei Athem schöpfen konnte. – Der Postknecht war sehr stark gefahren, und da die Chaussee in der Mitte hoch war, so wurde, als das Rad über einen Stein ging, die Caleche **[60]** von der Chaussée ab in einen Graben geworfen, welcher vielleicht 4 Schuh tief war. In diesem stack die Caleche nun ganz fest, die Räder in der Höhe. Die Eisen, durch welche die Haube gehalten wird, waren ganz voneinander gebrochen, so daß wir uns gar nicht rühren konnten. Ueberdieß war ein solches abgebrochenes Eisen, welches sehr spitzige Ecken hatte, mir gerade auf den Schläfen, so daß ich es mir bei der geringsten Bewegung in den Kopf drückte. Von außen hers[ch]te eine fürchterliche Stille. Der Postknecht war auch in den Graben gefallen, und lag unter dem Pferde. Nachdem er sich losgearbeitet hatte, hörten wir ihn sagen: „Ah mon Dieu je ne pourrai jamais vous tirer de là"; und so dringend wir auch unsere Noth vorstellten, so gab er doch mit Nichts als Weinen und Jammern Antwort. Endlich brachte er Bauern herbei, welche die Caleche zu bewegen anfingen, mir aber dadurch das Eisen in den Schlaf[211] drückten, so daß ich immer wieder schreien mußte, sie sollten aufhören. Ehe die Bauern kamen, konnte ich mir anfangs von unserer Lage keinen **[61]** Begriff machen; denn es war ganz finster um uns her. Doch konnte ich meine Hand in die Hosentasche bringen, aus der ich mit Mühe mein Messer nahm und durch das Leder schnitt. Nun sah ich daß Gras da stand, und freute mich darüber, denn zuvor hatte ich gemeint, wir wären in einen Morast gefallen, und gefürchtet, wir würden tiefer hineinsinken. Weil die Caleche zugemacht war, konnte man uns desto weniger helfen. Endlich wurden wir herausgezogen. Wie lange wir in dieser Lage gesteckt kann ich nicht bestimmen. Denn eine so zugebrachte Zeit mag sehr lang scheinen. Mein Reisegefährte behauptete, es habe eine halbe Stunde gedauert.

Von da ging es weiter nach Rennes, zu dem Seehafen Morlaix[212] und St. Pol de Leon[213], wo das II Bataillon lag. Das Land ist hier nicht sehr schön. Jeder Acker ist von einem lebendigen Zaun umgeben. Man verwundert sich in dieser Gegend nicht wenig, auf einmal in einem Lande zu sein, wo man mit der französischen Sprache nicht fortkommen kann. Das Bas

---

211. Gemeint: in die Schläfe.
212. Morlaix, Hafenstadt an der Nordküste der Bretagne.
213. St. Pol-de-Léon, Hafenstadt, nordwestlich von Morlaix.

was lying on top of me. Afraid of suffocating, I tried my utmost to push off the heavy load on top of me, and as luck would have it, I maneuvered him into a corner where he landed head down. But at least he was off my back. As long as his position had been tolerable for him, that means on top of me, he had kept quiet and let me yell: but now he started screaming even louder, after I had turned a bit on my side, so that I could catch a breath of air. – The coachman had been going very fast, and since the road was high in the middle, the calash was thrown into a ditch beside the road when one wheel hit a rock. [60] The ditch was about 4 shoes (feet) deep. The calash was now stuck in the mire with the wheels up on top. The iron ribs, which had held up the leather hood, were all broken off, so that we could not move at all. On top of all this, one of these broken iron rods, which had very sharp tips was too close to my temples, so that at every turn it was cutting my head. Outside it was terribly quiet. The coachman had also fallen into the ditch and lay under the horse. After he had worked his way free, we heard him say, "Ah mon Dieu, je ne pourrai jamais vous tirer de là!" (Oh my God, I'll never be able to get you out of there!); and the more we complained of our plight, the more he answered only with crying and lamenting. Finally he brought some farmers who started to move the calash, but they were pushing the iron rods into my temples,[211] so I kept yelling for them to stop. Before the farmers came, I had not been able to understand [61] our position, for it was very dark all around us. But finally I could get my hand in my pocket and with difficulty I reached my knife and could cut through the leather around us. Now I could see grass outside, which made me very happy, for I had imagined we might have landed in a marsh and feared we might keep sinking. Because the calash was closed, they could not do much to help us. At last they pulled us out. I still do not know how long we had been stuck in the mire. For if you are caught like this, it seems like a very long time. My travel companion maintained that this had lasted only half an hour.

After this we went on to Rennes, to the harbor Morlaix[212] and St. Pol de Léon[213], where we found the 2nd battalion. The country-side round here is not very pretty. Every field is bordered by hedges. You are very much surprised to suddenly find yourself in a place where French is not

---

211. The mscr. has a word form for „temples" which is unusual in modern German.
212. Harbour on the northern coast of Britanny.
213. Harbour northwest of Morlaix.

understood. The Low Breton[214] spoken here is quite different from French. [62] "Barat" means bread, "bara gwin" is white bread. The farmers wear their hair hanging straight down on their backs; they look pretty wild, like ours in Germany, that live deep in the woods.

The next day I rode, by way of Landivisiau, from St. Pol to Landernau[215]. None of these towns look pretty. Landernau, where the Colonel was with the 1st bataillon, has a small harbor; it is not situated on the coast; instead there is a canal leading to Brest[216], which is 4 hours distance away. After a few days, the regiment and I marched to Brest and then right through the town, past a house where the commander of the troops, General Comte de Rochambeau[217] was standing. We saw him there for the first time. Then we marched to the harbor and boarded vessels, which brought us to the warships and to the transport ships. We did not know our destination, but we guessed we would be going to North America. – The city of Brest does not show [63] her age; the lanes run straight as a string.

Our fleet consisted of 7 men-of-war; together with the transports we had a total of 40 vessels. The regiments Bourbonnois[218], Soissonnois[219], Saintonge[220], and Royal Deuxponts[221] together with a batallion of

---

214. The Breton language, "Bas Breton", together with Welsh in Wales and Cornish in Cornwall (disappeared in the 18th century), form the Brythonic group of the Celtic language.

215. The small towns of Landerneau and Landivisiau are situated between Morlaix and Brest.

216. Harbour in western Britanny, important French naval base.

217. Jean Baptiste Donatien de Vimeur, comte de Rochambeau (1725 – 1807), general who commanded about 6,000 French troops at Yorktown in 1781. He left America in 1783 and was appointed commander of Calais, later of the Alsace district. In the French revolution, he commanded the Army of the North in 1791. During the reign of terror he escaped the guillotine. Marshal of France in 1803; Bodinier, Dictionnaire, p. 555 f.

218. The Bourbonnois regiment was commanded by the marquis de Laval and vicomte de Rochambeau, son of comte de Rochambeau.

219. The Soissonnois regiment was commanded by comte de Saint Maisme and vicomte de Noailles, Lafayette's brother-in-law.

220. The Saintonge regiment was commanded by the comte de Custine.

221. The Royal Deux-Ponts regiment was commanded by count von Forbach, count of Deux-Ponts.

Bataillon Artillerie und einen Theil der Legion de Lauzun[222], aus Infanterie und Husaren bestehend. Im Ganzen wurden 5000 Mann eingeschifft. Es dauerte einen Monat, ehe man auslaufen konnte. Ich war auf dem Transportschiff „La Comtesse de Noailles". Der Capitain, ein Kauffarthey-Schiffer, war ein Gasconier, Namens Juisse[223], die zwei Officiere unter ihm Coquet und Pilotin. Endlich kam der Befehl zum Absegeln. Der Capitain, den wir noch gar nicht gesehen hatten, kam, und commandirte im Haarbeutel und weiß seidenen Strümpfen. Die Anker wurden gehoben und die Segel aufgezogen am 2. Mai. Man hatte aber nicht [64] beachtet, daß das Schiff mit einer, vielleicht 3 Zoll dicken, sehr langen Leine an ein Corps mort befestigt war. Dieß ist eine schwimmende Masse Holz, die mit einem Tau an einen Anker im Boden des Meeres angebunden wird und die Schiffe festhält fff, ohne daß diese selben einen Anker auszuwerfen brauchen. Als der Wind die Segel gefüllt hatte, hielt der Strick das Schiff zurück; und er mußte in dieser Verlegenheit durchhauen werden. Das angespannte Seil, welches über das Verdeck gezogen war, trennte sich nun wie mit einem Peitschenschlage, und würde, wenn es Jemanden getroffen hätte, ihn übel zugerichtet haben. Endlich war das Schiff im Gang, und Herr Juisse stand hinten beim Ruder, mit einem Sprachrohr commandirend; Pilotin hatte die Aufsicht am Vorderschiff. Während aber das Schiff im besten Laufe war, sahen wir den „Conquerant" (von 74 Canonen) quer vor uns vor Anker liegen. Juisse lenkte das Steuerruder, um links hinter dem Schiffe vorbeizukommen, was [65] aber nicht mehr thunlich war. Pilotin seinerseits dachte rechts vor dem Schiffe zu passiren, (er hatte ganz recht), und lies die Segel stechen, die das Vordertheil rechts abdrückten. Die Folge davon war, daß wir gerade auf den „Conquerant" anfuhren. Unser Bugspriet, (ein starker Mast, der vor dem Schiffe heraus ragt), zerbrach wie schwaches Rohr. Pilotin, der ein guter Seemann war, ließ geschwind einen Anker fallen, um mit diesem uns von dem andern Schiffe wieder loszuwinden. Wir mußten zurück in das Dock, um uns repariren zu lassen; und wir hatten die Hoffnung, nach Amerika zu kommen, beinahe verloren. Denn unconvogirt[224] würde man doch nicht in einem unbewaffneten

artillery and a part of the Legion de Lauzun[222], consisting of infantry and hussars, were all being taken on board. In all, 5000 men were taken aboard. We needed a month to prepare to sail. I was on the transport-ship "La Comtesse de Noailles". The merchant-marine captain came from Gascony[223] and was named Juisse, his two officers were named Coquet and Pilotin. Finally we got the order to set sail. The captain, whom we had not seen before, arrived and took command wearing a hair-net and white silk stockings. We weighed anchor and hoisted sails on May 2nd. [64]They had forgotten, that the ship was tied to a "Corps mort" by a very long line, almost 3 inches thick. The Corps mort is a swimming mass of wood, tied by rope to an anchor on the ocean floor, and holds the ships fast without their having to cast an anchor. When the wind had filled our sails, the rope held the ship back, and it had to be chopped off in this emergency. The taut rope, strung across our deck, tore apart like a whip-lash, and would have badly injured anyone caught in the way. Finally we were underway and Monsieur Juisse stood aft by the helm, giving his commands by speaking tube; Pilotin was in charge at the fore deck. When our ship was moving along nicely, we saw the "Conquérant" (of 74 guns) anchored right in our path. Juisse turned the helm, to pass behind the ship on the left, which [65] was no longer possible. Pilotin, on the other hand, wanted to pass in front of the ship to the right (he was right), and had the sail tacked, which pushed the foreship to the right. The result of this was that we ran straight into the "Conquerant". Our bowsprit (the thick mast, which sticks out in front of the ship) broke like a thin piece of straw. Pilotin, who was a good mariner, cast anchor quickly, to aid in unwinding ourselves from the other ship. We had to return to dock, to be repaired; and we almost lost our hope of ever arriving in America. For they would not send troops in an unarmed ship like

---

222. Die Legion de Lauzun wurde im März 1780 aus leichter Infanterie und etwa 300 Husaren aus verschiedenen französischen Truppenteilen der französischen Armee und Marine zusammengestellt und von dem Duc de Lauzun kommandiert.

223. Gasconier = Gascogner; die Gascogne, eine Region im Südwesten Frankreichs, war vom 12. Jahrhundert bis zum Ende des Hundertjährigen Kriegs ein Zentrum englischer Macht im südwestlichen Frankreich. Der typische Gascogner der volkstümlichen französischen Literatur ist ein heißblütiger Aufschneider. Nach Acomb, Journal, S. 8, lautete der Name Touisse; evtl. liegt in unserem Mskr. ein Lese- oder Schreibfehler vor.

224. Nicht im Konvoi, ohne Geleitschutz.

222. The legion de Lauzun was formed, in March 1780, from light infantry and about 300 hussars, taken from different parts of the French army and navy and was commanded by the duc de Lauzun.

223. Gascony, historic region in southwestern France. In the 12th century, Gascony passed to the English crown and remained the centre of English power in southwestern France to the end of the Hundred Years' War. The stereotyped Gascon of French popular literature is impetuous and hotheaded. The captain's name was Touisse according to Acomb, Journal, p. 8; there may be a spelling or reading mistake here.

ours without being convoyed.[224] But we need not have worried. For the weather was so bad, that the whole fleet was forced to return to port after 24 hours of bouncing around all night on the Brest roadstead; and in this time our ship was repaired. The Comte de Noaille[s][225] jested at a soirée at Brest, "que sa femme avoit voulu violer le Conquérant".[226] [66]

The fleet soon put to sea again; but a very strong wind scattered the transport ships towards the Spanish coast. We were lucky in that for this way we escaped the English fleet which was lying in wait for us at Plymouth. Near the latitude of Bermuda[227], we saw 6 English warships ready to attack our convoy. They must have been very surprised to see 7 men-of-war sailing out from behind our merchant vessels, and then forming a line between the English and our convoy. The English stayed at a distance, except for one ship, which sailed to the end of our line, then turned, in order to get at the other ships from behind and then passed our line so that it got a salvo from every ship and then returned fire. We learned that this squadron was coming from Jamaica[228], commanded by Capt. Cornwallis[229]. A few days earlier an enemy cutter had been captured[230], which was bringing over news of the capitulation of the Americans in Charlestown[231]. [67]

---

224. The mscr. says "unconvogirt" which is difficult to understand in current German.

225. Louis Marie vicomte de Noailles (1756 – 1804) served with his brother-in-law Lafayette in the War of Independence, deputy in the French "Etats Généraux" (Parliament) in 1789, emigrated to the US in 1792, but was killed in action in a French army operation in Haiti in 1803; see Acomb, Journal, p. 358.

226. "Violer" means to violate or rape; this would insinuate that "his wife had wanted to rape the ‚Conquérant'".

227. Bermuda Islands, approx. 33 degrees north, in the Atlantic Ocean, British colony since 1612.

228. Jamaica, third largest island of the Greater Antilles (Caribbean), British colony after 1655.

229. William Mann, count Cornwallis (1744 – 1819), British captain, admiral in 1799, brother of General C.

230. A single-masted vessel rigged like a sloop.

231. Charleston, South Carolina, in 1775 seat of the provincial congress that created South Carolina. In the spring of 1780, Sir Henry Clinton led a successful 45-day siege of Charleston by land and by sea. On May 12, the American general Benjamin Lincoln was forced to surrender the city and 5,000 troops; this opened the way to a further British invasion of the Carolinas. 1780 – 1782 C. was held by the British.

Beim Untergang der Sonne sah man 18 Schiffe, die für Kriegsschiffe gehalten wurden. Der Chevalier de Ternay[232] gab in der Nacht Befehl, fausse Route zu machen, nämlich einen andern, als dem vorher bestimmten Weg zu folgen. Man erfuhr aber nachher, daß es ein Convoy war, nur von einigen Fregatten[233] escortirt. Dies wäre eine schöne Beute gewesen. Der Chevalier de Ternay wurde von vielen getadelt, daß er das Gefecht nicht weiter engagiert hatte, weil wir wohl Sieger geworden wären. Man sagte sein Name sollte hinfort nicht Ternay sondern terni[234] seyn. Graf Rochambeau aber gab ihm großes Lob; denn seine Bestimmung sei gewesen, die Truppen wohlbehalten überzubringen. Der Comte de Grasse[235], welcher im folgenden Jahre geschickt wurde, um die Insel Guadeloupe[236] zu erobern ließ sich, um den „Jason" zu retten, den sein Vetter commandirte in ein Gefecht mit Admiral Rodney **[68]** ein, wurde (im April 1782) mit der „Ville de Paris" von 100 Canonen und noch 4 Linienschiffen der ersten Größe gefangen, und die Expedition scheiterte.[237] Nach einer Reise von 70 Tagen lief die Flotte am 12. Juli zu Newport[238] in Rhode Island ein. Sie hatte viele Skorbut-Kranke, das teutsche Regiment weit mehr, als jedes andere. Dies kommt wohl daher, daß der französische Soldat immer oben auf dem Schiffe in freier

At sundown, 18 ships were spotted on the horizon, which we took to be warships. The Chevalier de Ternay[232] gave the order at night to set "fausse route": this means to follow a new, not the previously determined route. But later we found out that it was a convoy escorted by only a few frigates[233]. This would have been a nice prize. Many criticized the chevalier de Ternay that he had not engaged the skirmish as we would probably have won. They said they wanted to rename him "terni"[234] instead of Ternay. Comte Rochambeau however praised him greatly, for his orders had been to transport the troops safely. The Comte de Grasse[235] who, a year later, was sent to conquer the island of Guadeloupe[236], took up combat with admiral Rodney[237] **[68]** in order to save the "Jason" which was commanded by his cousin. De Grasse lost the battle, ruined the expedition, and was taken prisoner (April 1782) with the "Ville de Paris" (100 cannon) and 4 other of the largest ships-of-the-line. The fleet sailed into Newport, Rhode Island[238] on July 12th, after a 70 day voyage. We had many down with scurvy, the German regiment hit harder than any other. I think it comes from the French eating less and always moving around

---

232. Charles Louis d'Arsac, Chevalier de Ternay (1722-1780), trat 1738 in die Marine ein, 1776 Commodore; er befehligte die Flotte, die die französischen Truppen nach Amerika brachte; starb im Dezember 1780 in Newport; s. Acomb; Journal, S. 363.

233. Fregatte: Kriegsschiff, etwas kleiner als ein Linienschiff, 28-60 Kanonen auf dem Hauptdeck, mit erhöhtem Achterdeck und Vordeck.

234. Terni: trüb, blind.

235. Francois Joseph Paul, marquis de Grasse-Tilly (1722-1788), 1781 Generalleutnant, seit 1762 Kapitän. Sein Seesieg in der „Battle of the Capes" am 5. September 1781 war entscheidend für den Erfolg der Belagerung von Yorktown; s. Acomb, Journal, S. 350.

236. Guadeloupe, größte Insel der kleinen Antillen, seit 1635 französische Kolonie, lange ein Zankapfel zwischen Frankreich und den Briten, die sich 1759-63, 1794, 1810-1813, 1815-16 in den Besitz der Insel setzen konnten.

237. Admiral Sir George Brydges, Baron Rodney (1718-1792) siegte im April 1782 in der „Battle of the Saintes" vor der Küste der Insel Dominica (s. dazu o. Anm. 44). Auf Befehl aus London hatte er im Februar 1781 die holländische Insel St. Eustatius eingenommen, einen wichtigen Stützpunkt für den neutralen Handel, v. a. aber für die Versorgung der amerikanischen Streitkräfte mit Waffen und Munition. Sein wahrscheinlich den Krieg entscheidender Fehler war es, sich dann auf das Beutemachen zu konzentrieren, denn deshalb entging ihm die französische Flotte, die am 5. September 1781 in der „Battle of the Capes" gegen Konteradmiral Graves siegte, sodass Franzosen und Amerikaner Yorktown unbehindert belagern konnten.

238. Newport, Rhode Island, wurde 1639 von Flüchtlingen aus Massachussetts gegründet, die den dortigen theologischen Querelen entgehen wollten. Der ausgezeichnete Hafen machte es bald zu einer der bedeutendsten Siedlungen in den amerikanischen Kolonien. 1784 zur Stadt erhoben.

---

232. Charles Louis d'Arsac, chevalier de Ternay (1722 – 1780) entered the French navy in 1738, commodore in 1776, commanded the fleet which took the French troops to America, died in Newport in December, 1780, see Acomb, Journal, p. 363.

233. Warship, somewhat smaller than a ship of the line, with 28 – 60 guns on the main deck, raised quarter deck and forecastle.

234. „terni": dim, dull, dreary.

235. Francois Joseph Paul marquis de Grasse-Tilly (1722 – 1788), French naval commander who engaged British forces during this war. His victory in the „Battle of the Capes" on Sept. 5th, 1781, was a decisive factor in the success of the siege of Yorktown; see Acomb Journal, p. 350.

236. Guadeloupe, largest island of the lesser Antilles (Caribbean), French colony after 1635, was often a bone of contention between France and the British who succeeded in wresting it from the French in 1759 – 63, 1794, 1810 – 13, and 1815 – 16.

237. Admiral Sir George Brydges, Baron Rodney (1718 – 1792), English admiral who captured the Dutch island of St. Eustatius (Statia) in 1781, a great entrepot of neutral trade, which was vital for the supply of arms and ammunition to the colonial American troops. His mistake – which probably decided the outcome of the war – of concentrating on the immense booty and its transport to England meant that the French and American troops could lay siege to Yorktown without intervention by his fleet after the French had beaten Rear Admiral Graves in the „Battle of the Capes"; cf. fn. 43, 44.

238. Newport, R.I., was founded in 1639 by refugees fleeing the theological disputes in Massachussetts. Its excellent harbour soon made it one of the most flourishing cities in colonial America. The British occupation 1776 – 1779 led to the flight of most of the leading merchants. Newport was incorporated as a city in 1784.

upon deck in the fresh air. If Capt. Juisse was lax about his duties in port, he was, on the other hand, very punctual in calling all the sailors together every evening for prayers and hymns, very often in Latin. Two French hymns, which he, of course, sang in his Gascon dialect, went like this:

I
"Je met, ma confiance
Vierge en Votre Secours
Servez moi de defence
Prenez garde de mes jours
Et quand ma dernire hure
Viendra fixer mon sort
Obtenez, que je mure
De la plus sainte mort. [69]

II
Notre Dame de bon secours
Nous vous prions tous agenaux
Quand la mort nous arrivera
Que nous puissions dire Ave Maria
Capt. Juisse:
Domine, salvum fac regem
Nostrum Ludovicum!
Choir of Sailors:
Et exaudi nos in die,
quo invocaverimus Te."[239]

---

[239]. I put my trust, virgin Mary, in your help, serve as my defence, take care of my days, and when my last hour arrives, make sure that I may die the most saintly death. Our lady of great help, we ask you on bended knees, when death comes to us that we can say „Ave Maria". Captain Juisse: God, protect our king Louis! Choir of sailors: And hear our prayer in the day when we will call upon you.

Auf unserem Schiffe waren Hauptmann Klook[240], Sundahl[241], v. Hake[242], Closen[243], und ein Dänischer Officier, Namens v. Löhnburg, der auch freiwillig als Capitain à la Suite mitging. (Capitain v. Hake lebt noch am Hofe zu Gotha); ferner die Lieut[e]n[ants] Pradellen[244], Sonntag[245], Zoller[246] (nachher

On our ship were the Captains Klook[240], Sundahl[241], v. Hake[242], Closen[243], and a Danish officer, named von Löhnburg, who also volunteered as a 'Capitain à la Suite' (Captain v. Hake is alive today at the court of Gotha); moreover the Lieutenants Pradellen[244], Sonntag[245], Zoller[246]

---

240. Wohl Bernhard Anton von Klock oder Klocker, geb. 1736 oder 1739, 1778 Hauptmann im Regiment Royal Deux-Ponts; Bodinier, Dictionnaire, S. 299 f. sowie Acomb, Journal, S. 353.

241. Christian Ludwig Philipp Sundhall oder Sundahl (1735 – 1787), seit 1754 in waldeckischem Dienst, 1779 Hauptmann im Regiment Royal Deux-Ponts, Militärverdienstkreuz 1781, vgl. Bodinier, Dictionnaire, S. 561, und Acomb, Journal, S. 362.

242. v. Hake: Entweder Freiherr Karl Ernst von Haacke, geb. 1744, Leutnant im Regiment Deux-Ponts 1760, Hauptmann 1777, unter Rochambeau in Amerika und 1781 mit dem „croix de mérite" ausgezeichnet, 1791 zum Oberst ernannt, 1792 in die Schweiz emigriert oder Friedrich Karl Ernst Ritter von Haacke, geb. 1752, Leutnant im Regiment Deux-Ponts 1768, Hauptmann 1779; auch er diente unter Rochambeau in Amerika, wurde ausgezeichnet und trat später in ein anderes Regiment ein; vgl. Bodinier, Dictionnaire, S. 270; s. auch Acomb, Journal, S. 351, und Tröss, Regiment, S. 64 f.

243. Ludwig Freiherr v. Closen-Haydenburg (1755-1830), Offizier im Regiment Royal Deux-Ponts, ausgezeichnet mit dem amerikanischen Cincinnatus-Orden, kgl. frz. Maréchal-de-camp, bayerischer Kammerherr und französischer Unterpräfekt. S. Baumann, Herzogtum Pfalz-Zweibrücken, S.45-64, hier 63; Gothaisches genealogisches Taschenbuch der freiherrlichen Häuser auf das Jahr 1863, 13.Jg., Gotha 1863, S.117; auch: Acomb, Journal (dies ist die Ausgabe seines Tagebuchs).

244. Wohl der Belgier Benoit van Pradelles, der wie Rechteren im Oktober 1781 den Dienst quittierte, aber in Amerika blieb; starb1809 in Baltimore; Bodinier, Dictionnaire, S. 543, sowie Selig, German Allies, T. IV, S. 46.

245. Philipp Wilhelm Sonntag, geb. 1745, im Regiment Deux-Ponts seit 1774, Kadett 1780, verließ das Regiment in den USA, s. Selig, Revolutionary Route 5.4.1. (www.hudsonrivervalley.net/AMERICANBOOK/right.html) sowie Bodinier, Dictionnaire, S.512.

246. Friedrich Freiherr v. Zoller (1762 – 1821), 1799 in bayerischen Diensten, 1814 kgl. bayer. Generalleutnant; ADB Band 45, S.410; s. auch Tröss, Regiment, S. 66.

240. Probably Bernhard Anton von Klocker (Klock), born 1736 or 1739, captain in the Royal Deux-Ponts regiment in 1778; Bodinier, Dictionnaire, p. 299 f., and Acomb, Journal, p. 353.

241. Christian Ludwig Philipp Sundhall or Sundahl (1735 – 1787), 1754 in the service of the counts of Waldeck; 1779 captain in the Royal Deux-Ponts regiment, decorated in 1781; Bodinier, Dictionnaire, p. 561 and Acomb, Journal, p. 362.

242. Either baron Karl Ernst von Haacke, born 1744, lieutenant in the Deux Ponts regiment in 1760, captain in 1777, who went to America under Rochambeau and was decorated with the "croix de mérite" in 1781, became a colonel in 1791 and emigrated to Switzerland in 1792, or Friedrich Karl Ernst Ritter von Haacke, who was born in 1752, lieutenant in the Deux Ponts regiment in 1768 and promoted to captain in 1779; he went to America with Rochambeau and later changed to an different regiment; decorated in America; Bodinier, Dictionnaire, p. 270; Acomb, Journal, p. 351, and Tröss, Regiment, p. 64 f.

243. Ludwig Freiherr v. Closen-Haydenburg (1755 – 1830), officer in the Royal Deux-Ponts regiment, awarded the American Order of Cincinnatus, French maréchal-de-camp, Bavarian chamberlain and French sous-prefect; cf. Kurt Baumann, Herzogtum Pfalz-Zweibrücken, S. 45 – 64; Gothaisches genealogisches Taschenbuch der freiherrlichen Häuser auf das Jahr 1863, Gotha 1863, S. 117; also Acomb, Journal (which is the printed edition of his American diary).

244. Probably the Belgian Benoit van Pradelles, who – like our author – left the regiment in 1781, but stayed in America and died in Baltimore in 1809; Bodinier, Dictionnaire, p. 449; Selig, German Allies, part IV, p. 46.

245. Philipp Wilhelm Sonntag, born 1745, soldier in the Deux Ponts regiment 1774, cadet 1780, left the regiment in the U.S.; Bodinier, Dictionnaire, p. 512; Selig, Revolutionary Route, ch. 5.4.1 (www.hudsonrivervalley.net/AMERICANBOOK/right.html).

246. Friedrich Freiherr (baron) von Zoller (1762 – 1821), in Bavarian service after 1799, 1814 royal Bavarian Lieutenant General; cf. ADB, vol. 45, p. 410; Tröss, Regiment, p. 66.

General), Verger[247] (jetzt General), Jschtersheim[248], Lutzan[249].

Am 12 Juli kam unsere Flotte in Rhode Island an; am folgenden Tage traf die Flotte des Admiral Grey[250], der uns verfolgte, in New York ein. Zehn Tage, nachdem wir debarquirt [70] waren, erschien die englische Flotte von 20 Segeln, worunter 10 Linienschiffe. Sie getrauten sich aber nicht, Etwas zu unternehmen; denn die französischen Truppen waren zu sehr verschanzt. Das Lager der Landtruppen war vor der Stadt und durchschnitt die Insel da, wo sie gegen das Meer zu eine schmale Landzunge bildet. Auf dieser waren zwei Batterien, die den Eingang zum Hafen mit Mörsern und glühenden Kugeln vertheidigten. Weiter lagen die 7 Kriegsschiffe embassirt, nämlich mit einem Anker vorn und einem hinten hinaus, so daß sie, unbewegt durch Strom und Wind, wie eben so viele Batterien da lagen und ein gekreuztes Feuer machten. Zwei kleine Inseln waren auch stark mit Canonen besetzt, und rückwärts wurde die Stadt und das Lager durch eine Reihe Redouten, die einander bestrichen, vertheidigt, so daß die Truppen sich auf dem kürzesten Wege auf jeden angegriffenen Punct begeben konnten.

(later General), Verger (now General)[247], Jschtersheim[248], Lutzan[249].

On July 12th, our fleet arrived in Newport, Rhode Island; the next day the fleet of Admiral Grey[250], who was pursuing us, arrived in New York. Ten days after our landing [70], the English fleet appeared with 20 sails, 10 of these ships-of-the-line. But they did not dare start any action; for our French troops were too well entrenched. The camp of the land troops was south of the city and cut the island at the point where it forms a narrow spit of land towards the ocean. At this spot we had two batteries stationed, who defended the entrance to the harbor with mortar and incendiary bombs. Moreover we had the 7 warships "embassirt", i.e. with 2 anchors, one at the bow and stern each so that they did not move with tide or wind, but were lying there like so many batteries and could deliver cross-fire. Two small islands were set up with many guns, and back behind them, the city and the camp were defended by a row of redoubts covering each other, so that the troops had the shortest route to any point of attack.

On August 25th, we celebrated St. Louis' Day[251] which was very festive, and each regiment fired [71] their cannon, one after the other, then the (artillery) batteries, and finally the ships-of-war round in a circle until they got back to the beginning. This was repeated three times without interruption.

---

247. Jean Baptiste Antoine de Verger (1762-1851), stammte aus der Schweiz, trat im Februar 1780 als „Cadet gentilhomme" in das Regiment ein, wurde noch 1780 zum Leutnant ernannt; er diente später in der Armee der Fürsten gegen das revolutionäre Frankreich, dann in Preußen und Bayern, wo er 1822 zum Generalleutnant aufstieg; er starb 1851 in München; s. Bodinier, Dictionnaire, S. 545 sowie Selig, Revolutionary Route, Kap. 6.1, Anm.118, (www.hudsonrivervalley.net/AMERICANBOOK/right.html); auch Tröss, Regiment, S. 69.

248. Franz Karl von Ichtersheim, geb. 1757, 1775 Leutnant, 1778 Oberleutnant im Regiment Deux-Ponts, quittierte den Dienst 1787, oder sein Bruder Franz Reinhard Hannibal von I., geb. 1754, Leutnant im Regiment Deux-Ponts 1773, Hauptmann 1785, der im selben Jahr das Regiment verließ; beide dienten in Amerika; vgl. Bodinier, Dictionnaire, S. 284; beide auch bei Tröss, Regiment, S. 64 f.

249. Wohl Wilhelm Friedrich Bernhard von Lutzau (Lützow) (1758 – 1787), Leutnant im Regiment Deux-Ponts 1775, verwundet bei Yorktown; Bodinier, Dictionnaire, S. 373; auch Tröss, Regiment, S. 69.

250. Admiral Grey: wahrscheinlich hat der Autor sich bei diesem Namen geirrt; er dürfte Konteradmiral Thomas Graves (1725 – 1802) meinen, der 1781 eine britische Flotte in den amerikanischen Gewässern befehligte.

247. Jean Baptiste Antoine de Verger (1762 – 1851) was born in Switzerland, joined the regiment as a ‚cadet gentilhomme' in 1780, lieutenant in 1780, later served in the princes' army against revolutionary France, then in Prussia and in Bavaria. He rose to lieutenant general in 1822 and died in Munich; Bodinier, Dictionnaire, p. 545; Selig, Revolutionary Route (as fn. 246), ch. 6.1. fn. 118; Tröss, Regiment, p. 69.

248. Ichtersheim, Franz Karl von (b. 1757), 2nd lieutenant in the Deux-Ponts regiment in 1775, 1st lieutenant in 1778, resigned in 1787, or his brother Franz Reinhard Hannibal (b. 1754), 2nd lieutenant in the Deux-Ponts regiment in 1773, captain in 1785, left the regiment in 1785. Both brothers served in America; cf. Bodinier, p. 284; Tröss, Regiment, p. 64 f.

249. Probably Wilhelm Friedrich Bernhard von Lutzau (Lützow) (1758 – 1787), lieutenant in the Deux Ponts regiment in 1775, wounded at Yorktown; Bodinier, Dictionnaire, p. 373; Tröss, Regiment, p. 69.

250. Admiral Grey: the author is most likely in error concerning the admiral's name; he probably means rear admiral Thomas Graves (1725 – 1802) who was in command of a British fleet in American waters in 1781.

251. August 25th is the feast-day of St. Louis and thus also of the reigning French king Louis XVI.

Es nahm sich sehr schön aus, als am 25. August das Ludwigsfest[251] gefeiert wurde, und jedes Regiment nebst seinen Feldstücken nacheinander ab- [71] feuerte, dann die Batterien, endlich die Kriegsschiffe im Zirkel herum bis dorthin, wo es angefangen hatte. Dies wurde ohne Unterbrechen dreimal wiederholt.

Ich war als Cadet zur Compagnie des Hauptmanns Sundahl gekommen, und campirte unter einem Zelte mit den Leutenants Verger und Zollern. Es überfiel uns einmal in der Nacht ein Orkan, wie sie in Amerika häufig sind, nämlich also, daß es auf eine völlige Stille plötzlich so wird, als wenn alle Elemente in Aufruhr wären. Wir standen auf einmal im Wasser, und da die Zeltstange brach, mußte jeder sie abwechselnd so lange halten, als seine Kräfte zuließen, damit man sich anziehen und seine Sache zurecht bringen konnte. Als es Tag wurde, sah man im ganzen Lager alle Zelte niedergeworfen und im Morast liegen. Ich bekam hierauf ein Qua[r]tier in der Stadt; die Soldaten blieben campirt; die Officiere ließen sich Baraquen machen. Gegen den Winter bekamen die Officiere Qua[r]tiere in der Stadt; die Soldaten wurden in leer gebliebene Häuser gelegt.

[72] Das Eigenthum wurde hier so heilig gehalten, daß Washington's Armee im Sommer nie anders als unter Zelten und im Winter in Baraquen wohnte. Auf etwas Aehnliches hatte sich einst der teutsche König Ariovist[252] so viel zu gut gethan, daß er dem Caesar sagen ließ, er könnte, wenn er wollte, wohl erfahren, was die Tapferkeit der Teutschen vermöchte, die in 14 Jahren unter kein Dach gekommen wären. „Quam vellet congrederetur; intellecturum, quid invicti Germani, qui intra annos quatuor decim tectum non subissend virtute possend."[253] In dieser Zeit starb der Chevalier de Ternay[254]; und der Chevalier de Touches[255], welcher den „Duc de Bourgogne" befehligte, übernam das Comando.

I had come as a cadet assigned to Captain Sundahl's company and shared a tent with the two lieutenants Verger and Zollern. One night, a hurricane hit us, such as are typical in America, namely at first it is completely quiet and then all the elements break loose. Suddenly we were standing in water, and as our tent stake broke, we had to take turns holding it up as long as physically possible while each one got dressed and packed his things. At daybreak, we saw that all the tents in our camp were blown down in the morass. After this, I was quartered in town, but the soldiers remained in camp; the officers had some barracks built. As winter came on, the officers were quartered in town, the soldiers got to share some empty houses. [72]

Property is considered so holy here that Washington's army was never quartered in private houses: in summer, they tented and in winter, they lived in barracks. Something similar is told about the Germanic king Ariovist[252]: that he had told Caesar that he could find out something about the bravery of the German troups by looking at their record: in 14 years they had not slept under a roof. "Quam vellet congrederetur, intellecturum, quid invicti Germani, qui intra annos quatuor decim tectum non subissend virtute possend."[253] At this time, the Chevalier de Ternay[254] died and Chevalier de Touches[255], who was captain of the "Duc de Bourgogne" took command of the whole fleet.

The General had a wooden hall built, as large as a medium-sized church, where the officers could meet and play cards,[256] also we met here before going on parade. One day we witnessed a terrible scene here.

---

251. Ludwigsfest: der 25. August ist der Festtag des hl. Ludwig und somit auch des französischen Königs Ludwig.

252. Ariovist, gest. 54 v. Chr., König des germanischen Suebenstammes; er wurde von Cäsar bei Mülhausen im Elsaß geschlagen; Cäsar erwähnt ihn in „De bello Gallico".

253. Gaius Julius Caesar, De bello Gallico I: Cum vellet, congrederetur: intellecturum quid invicti Germani, exercitatissimi in armis, qui inter annos XIIII tectum non subissent, virtute possent.

254. Er starb in Newport am 15. Dezember 1780 und liegt auf dem Trinity-Friedhof begraben; s. auch Anm. 232.

255. Charles Sochet Chevalier des Touches (1727 – 1793), trat 1743 in die Marine ein, 1780 Kommandant der „Neptun". Er löste Ternay als Flottenadmiral ab und befehligte den französischen Verband in der Schlacht von Cape Henry, in der er den Briten unter Arbuthnot unterlag und nicht, wie geplant, in die Chesapeake-Bay einfahren konnte; Acomb, Journal, S. 346.

---

252. Ariovistus, died 54 B.C., king of the Germanic tribe of the Suebi. Beaten by Caesar at Mulhouse in Alsace, Caesar mentions him in „De Bello Gallico".

253. The correct quotation from Gaius Julius Caesar, De Bello Gallico I, is: "Cum vellet, congrederetur: intellecturum quid invicti Germani, exercitatissimi in armis, qui inter annos XIIII tectum non subissent, virtute possent."

254. Died in Newport on Dec.15th, 1780, and was buried in the Trinity cemetery, cf. fn. 232.

255. Charles Sochet Chevalier des Touches (1727 – 1793), joined the French navy in 1743, commander of the "Neptune" in 1780. He took over as commander of the fleet after Ternay's death and led the French ships in the battle of Cape Henry in March, 1781, where he was beaten back by the English fleet under Arbuthnot and so was unable to enter Chesapeake Bay as planned; cf. Acomb, Journal, p. 346.

256. This building is also mentioned by von Closen; it was intended to give the officers a meeting place and a place where playing cards was permitted; gambling in the quarters was not allowed; Acomb, Journal, p. 55.

Der General hatte eine hölzerne Halle, so groß wie eine mittelmäßige Kirche bauen lassen, wo die Officiere sich unterhielten und ihre Parthie machten,[256] wo man sich auch versammelte, um auf die Parade zu gehen. Hier fiel eine furchtbare Scene vor.

Der Graf St. Germain[257], welcher [73] 20 Jahre von Frankreich abwesend und in Dänischem Dienst General geworden war, wurde zum Kriegsminister ernannt, und machte große Reformen in der Armee. Er wollte z. B. eine andere Disciplin einführen: Der Soldat sollte mit dem flachen Säbel gefuchtelt[258] werden. Dieß konnte aber in Frankreich nicht wohl Fuß fassen[259], da überall das Volk sich dagegen empörte. In Amerika aber glaubten die Obersten der Regimenter, welche junge Leute und vom Hofe waren, es ungehindert einführen zu können; aber – sechs Soldaten entleibten sich in kurzer Zeit wegen empfangener oder angedrohter Strafe.

So hatte auch der Oberst Graf Custine[260], ein großer Eiferer, – welcher ungeachtet seines Aristocratismus später General der Patrioten, endlich aber guillotinirt wurde, – einem Hauptmann befohlen, einen Soldaten auf diese Weise abstrafen zu lassen. Diesem aber, als einem ächten, alten Franzosen, war dieß äußerst zuwider; und er ließ die Strafe nur zum Schein vollziehen. Als dieß dem Custine berichtet wurde, fuhr er den Hauptmann mit den härtesten Worten an, und drohte, ihn geschloßen[261] nach [74] Frankreich zu schicken. Der Hauptmann ging nach Haus, und erschoß sich. Als die

---

256. Zweck des auch von Closen erwähnten Gebäudes war es, den Offizieren einen Treffpunkt zu geben, wo auch Kartenspiele erlaubt waren, um das Glücksspiel in den Unterkünften zu verhindern; Acomb, Journal, S. 55.

257. Claude Louis, comte de St. Germain (1707-1778), frz. General, organisierte die dänische Armee neu, frz. Kriegsminister 1775-1777. Sein Versuch, die preußische Diziplin in der frz. Armee einzuführen, stieß auf solchen Widerstand, dass er von seinem Amt zurücktreten musste; s. dazu Deflers, Militärreformen, auch zu den Gründen des Widerstands gegen die Reformen; vgl. auch Einleitung, S. 40 m. Anm. 125.

258. Fuchteln: das Schlagen mit der flachen Seite eines Degens, in der französischen Armee mit dem deutschen Wort (in französischer Schreibweise) „Schlague" bezeichnet.

259. Im Manuskript ist das Wort „fassen" doppelt geschrieben.

260. Adam Philippe, comte de Custine (1740/42 – 1793), war schon im Alter von fünf Jahren (!) Leutnant, mit 19 Jahren Hauptmann. Er war streng und tapfer, aber oft betrunken. Nach dem Dienst in Amerika Gouverneur von Toulon, 1788 Generalinspekteur der Kavallerie in Flandern. 1791 eroberte er mehrere deutsche Städte, verlor dann eine Schlacht und wurde daraufhin am 27. August 1793 hingerichtet; s. auch Acomb, Journal, S. 345.

261. D.h. als Gefangenen, evtl., aber weniger wahrscheinlich, sogar in Ketten.

Count St. Germain[257], who [73] had not been in France for 20 years, and had been made a general in the Danish army, had just been advanced to Minister of War and wanted to greatly reform the army. For example he wanted to introduce new discipline: hitting the soldier with the flat side of the sabre as punishment.[258] The French were not taking to this method,[259] and everywhere in France the people were openly rebelling against this. But in America, the colonels of the French regiments, who were young and straight from the court, thought they could get away with this; in a short period of time, however, six soldiers had committed suicide because of this punishment, received or threatened.

So Colonel Comte Custine[260], a true fanatic, who disregarding his aristocratic background and demeanor, became a Patriot General (in the French revolution) and ended up under the guillotine, had ordered a captain to punish a soldier in this way. This captain, a genuine old-style Frenchman, thought this was disgusting, and just gave the outward appearance of punishing him. When Custine got word of this, he reprimanded the captain in very harsh words and threatened to send him back to France in chains.[261] [74] The captain went home and shot himself. When the officers of his company, his own brother among them, came by on their way to the assembly-house, before going on parade with the Generals, they found him dead, slumped over his writing-desk, and as was related, holding a piece of paper on which was written: "Mes camarades, vengez-moi!"[262] You can imagine what sort of a mood they were in when they reached the parade grounds and started reproaching Custine.

---

257. Claude Louis, comte de St. Germain (1707 – 1778), French general, reorganizer of the Danish army, French minister of war 1775 – 1777. His attempt to introduce Prussian discipline into the French army met with such opposition that he had to resign; cf. Deflers, Militärreformen, for the political reasons of this resistance; cf. also Introduction, p.40 with fn 125.

258. The German verb for this form of punishment is "fuchteln"; in the French army it went under the term "schlague" which is the German word for "hit" or "beat" in French spelling.

259. The word "fassen" is mistakenly repeated in the German manuscript.

260. Adam Philippe, comte de Custine, born Feb 4th, 1742, became a lieutenant at the age of five (!), a captain at 19. He was a strict disciplinarian and valiant, but often drunk. After service in America, he became governor of Toulon, then Inspector general of the cavalry in Flanders in 1788. In 1791, he conquered several towns in Germany, was beaten once, recalled to Paris and executed Aug. 27th, 1793; cf. Acomb, Journal, p. 345.

261. The German verb "geschlossen" in the mscr. may mean "in chains" or simply "locked up".

262. "My comrades, take revenge for me!"

Officiere seiner Compagnie, unter denen auch sein Bruder war, ihn nach dem Versammlungshause abholen wollten, um von da mit der Generalität auf die Parade zu gehen, fanden sie ihn todt an seinem Schreibtisch, und, wie erzählt wurde, mit einem Papier vor sich, auf dem die Worte standen: „Mes camerades, vengez moi!"[262] Man kan sich denken, in welcher Stimmung sie auf den Paradeplatz kamen und über Custine herfielen. Sie belegten ihn mit derben Scheltworten und die Wuth war so groß, daß man alle Augenblicke fürchten mußte, es möchte mit gewaltthätigen Auftritten enden. Es ging aber damit aus, daß die Officiere sich verbanden, außer den Dienstverhältnissen ihm keine Aufwartung zu machen und keine Einladung von ihm anzunehmen. Jedoch wurde eine Ausnahme für zwei alte Officiere gemacht, denen es erlaubt sein sollte, weil sie ihre Retraite suchten. Solche Auftritte waren außerhalb Frankreich unerhört. So waren die Officiere vom Regiment Royal Comtois[263], welches in Isle de [75] France[264] in Garnison lag, gegen den obengenannten Chevalier de Ternay,[265] welcher da Gouverneur war, aufgestanden, und waren dafür alle cassirt worden, bis auf einige, die an der Verschwörung nicht hatten theilnehmen wollen. Dieses Regiment kam aber hiedurch in Verruf bei der ganzen Armee. In das Caffeehaus, welches jene Officiere besuchten, ging kein anderer. Wenn ein Regiment durch eine Stadt marschierte, gaben die Officiere der Garnison den Durchziehenden ein Repas de Corps[266], dem Regiment Royal Comtois aber nicht. – So machten die Officiere auch sogenannte Concordate, ungeachtet der König es verboten hatte. Nämlich, um alte Officiere, die nicht mehr dienen wollten, wegzubringen, verband man sich, jährlich so viel von seiner Besoldung abziehen zu lassen, als die Pension derselben betrage; und Alle, die nachher eintraten, mußten sich diesen Abzug gefallen lassen, so lang jene lebten.

They were throwing rough and abusive words at him and flying into a real rage that we all feared the scene might end in violence. But at last the officers agreed among themselves to only perform their official duties and beyond this not to give him any service and not to accept any invitation from him. But they made an exception for two old officers, for whom this was allowed, because they were preparing their retirement. Such scenes were unheard of outside of France. Once the officers of the Royal Comtois Regiment[263], which was garrisoned in the Isle de France[264],[75] rose in rebellion against the above mentioned Chevalier de Ternay,[265] who was governor there, and they were all cashiered (dismissed from service), except for a few, who had not wanted to participate in the conspiracy. Because of this the said regiment had a bad reputation throughout the army. No one else went into the coffee-house frequented by those officers. When a regiment marched through a town, the officers of the garrison gave the marchers a "Repas de Corps"[266], but not to the Royal Comtois Regiment. – Also the officers drew up so-called concordats, even though the king had forbidden them. Namely to replace the old officers, who did not want to serve any longer, the younger officers joined together and pledged to subtract from their own income enough money to pay the pensions of the old officers; and all who wanted to become officers had to agree to this plan, as long as the pensioners lived.

On September 13th, General Washington[267] and Comte Rochambeau travelled to meet each other in Hartfort for

---

262. „Meine Kameraden, rächt mich!"

263. Das Infanterieregiment Royal Comtois wurde 1673 unter dem Namen „Listenay" erstmals aufgestellt und 1685 in „Royal Comtois" umbenannt. 1781 diente auch es in Tobago und anderen Orten in der Karibik.

264. „Isle de France", alte Form von „Ile de France", ist die von niedrigen Höhen eingerahmte Gegend um Paris.

265. Hier könnte Rechteren sich irren, denn der oben genannte Chevalier de Ternay war wohl immer ein Angehöriger der Marine.

266. „Repas de corps", ein formelles Essen für das Offizierskorps.

---

263. The Royal Comtois infantry regiment was first set up as "Listenay" in 1673 and took the name "Royal Comtois" in 1685; it saw service in Tobago and other places in the Caribbean in 1781.

264. Isle de France (the archaic form of Ile de France) is the area around Paris, surrounded by low hill-chains.

265. The author is probably wrong here as de Ternay seems to have been in the navy through his whole life.

266. A formal meal for the officers of a military unit.

267. George Washington (1732 – 1799), general and first president of the USA, „father of his country". Born into a wealthy family of Virginia planters, he began work as a surveyor at the age of 14. He gained first military experience in the French and Indian War of 1754 – 1763. After an interval of 15 years during which he managed the family estate at Mount Vernon, VA, he took command of the American army encircling Boston in 1775. He took Boston by a vigorous siege. After his campaigns in the War of Independence he was overwhelmingly elected first president of the republic in 1789, re-elected in 1792. In his two terms in office, he established innumerable precedents and left a permanent stamp on the presidency.

Am 13ten September besprachen sich General Washington[267] und Graf Rochambeau zum ersten Mal in Hart- **[76]** fort[268], wohin sie, einander entgegengereißt waren. – General Arnold[269] commandirte in der Festung Westpoint[270], und war in Unterhandlung mit dem General Clinton[271], um sie ihm zu verrathen. – Der Zufall wollte aber, daß General Washington in diesem Orte war, als Major Andre[272], welcher die unterhan-

the first time[268][76]. – General Arnold[269] commanded Fort Westpoint[270], and was carrying on negotiations with General Clinton[271] to deliver it to him. By chance General Washington was there when Major Andre[272], the British contact, was captured by the militia in spite of his disguise. If General Washington had not been in Westpoint on that day, this most strategic point on the Hudson river[273] would have been lost, including all the American supplies. Arnold escaped and went over to the British.

---

267. George Washington (1732 – 1799), General, erster Präsident der USA, gilt als „Vater des Vaterlandes". Er entstammte einer wohlhabenden Pflanzerfamilie in Virginia und wurde mit 14 Jahren Landvermesser. Er machte erste militärische Erfahrungen im „French and Indian War" 1754 – 1763, verwaltete dann 15 Jahre den Familienbesitz bei Mount Vernon, Virginia; 1775 wurde er Kommandant der amerikanischen Truppen, die 1775 Boston eingeschlossen hatten. Er nahm Boston nach einer kraftvoll geführten Belagerung ein. Nach dem Unabhängigkeitskrieg wurde er 1789 zum ersten Präsidenten der neuen Republik gewählt, 1792 wiedergewählt. Während seiner zwei Amtszeiten schuf er zahllose Präzedenzfälle und formte dadurch das Präsidentenamt.

268. Hartford, Hauptstadt von Connecticut, liegt dort, wo der Connecticut-Fluss schiffbar wird. Holländische Händler erbauten 1633 ein Fort, die erste dauerhafte Besiedlung erfolgte 1635 durch 61 englische Siedler; 1637 nach der Stadt Hartford in England benannt. Das Versicherungswesen, bis heute wichtigster Erwerbszweig der Stadt, begann 1794 mit der Ausstellung der ersten Feuerversicherungspolice. Eine die Belagerung von Yorktown betreffende Besprechung zwischen Washington und Rochambeau fand etwas südlich von H. in Wethersfield statt.

269. Benedict Arnold (1741 – 1801) diente der amerikanischen Unabhängigkeit bis 1779, als er zu den Engländern überlief, und sein Name zum sprichwörtlichen Verräternamen in den USA wurde. Meldete sich 1775 freiwillig zum Kriegsdienst, erhielt nach dem siegreichen Angriff auf Fort Ticonderoga, New York, Truppenkommandos. 1778 wurde er Kommandant von Philadelphia, wo er bereits in englandfreundlichen Kreisen verkehrte. 1779 Kommandant des Forts West Point, New York, bot den Briten dessen Übergabe gegen 20 000,- Pfd. St. an. Als sein englischer Kontaktmann, Major John André, von den Amerikanern gefasst wurde, flüchtete Arnold auf einem britischen Schiff und überließ André seinem Schicksal – er wurde gehängt. Selbst die englandfreundlichen Kreise trugen ihm dies nach. Arnold ging 1781 nach England, wo er, von der Gesellschaft gemieden, verstarb.

270. Westpoint, New York, Sitz der 1802 gegründeten Militärakademie der USA, auf dem Westufer des Hudson. 1778/79 wurde der Ort von den Amerikanern unter der Leitung des polnischen Offiziers Tadeusz Kosciusko befestigt. 1780 misslang Benedict Arnold die verräterische Übergabe an die Briten.

271. Sir Henry Clinton (1738-1795), britischer Oberkommandierender während der amerikanischen Revolution. Sein Buch „Narrative of the Campaign of 1781 in North America" (Bericht über den Feldzug von 1781 in Nordamerika) rief eine verärgerte Antwort von Cornwallis in Bezug auf den Fall von Yorktown hervor.

272. John André (1751-1780), britischer Major, war der Sohn eines in London lebenden Kaufmanns aus Genf. Er diente als Adjutant der Generäle Grey und Clinton. Er war Benedict Arnolds Kollaborateur bei der geplanten Übergabe von Fort West Point an die Briten. Nach einem Treffen mit Arnold am 21. September 1780 wurde er von amerikanischen Milizen aufgegriffen und offenbarte den verräterischen Plan in einem Brief an Washington. Am 2. Oktober 1780 wurde er als Spion gehängt; in der Westminster Abbey wurde ihm ein Denkmal errichtet.

---

268. Hartford is the capital of Connecticut, at the head of navigation on the Connecticut river, 38 miles from the sea. Dutch traders built a fort in 1633, but first settlement was made in 1635 by 61 English settlers. 1637 it was named for Hartford, England. Insurance, the city's outstanding business, dates from 1794 (first fire insurance policy). – A later conference between Washington and Rochambeau concerning the Yorktown siege took place south of Hartford in Wethersfield, Connecticut, at the Joseph Webb house, 211 Main St.

269. Benedict Arnold (1741 – 1801) loyally served the cause of the American Revolution until 1779 when he went over to the British and made his name an epithet for traitor in the U.S. In 1775, Arnold, then a prosperous businessman in New Haven, Connecticut, immediately volunteered for military service and, after the successful attack on Ft. Ticonderoga, New York, rose to command. In 1778, he was placed in command of Philadelphia, Pennsylvania, where he began to move in loyalist (pro-British) circles. In 1779, he was put in command of West Point, New York, and asked the Britsh for L 20,000.- for the betrayal of that fort. When his British contact, Major John André, was captured by the Americans, Arnold managed to escape on a British ship, leaving André to be hanged as a spy. Even loyalists resented this. Arnold went to England in 1781, but never felt adequately compensated by the British. He died in London ostracized and ailing.

270. West Point, New York, military reservation and seat of the U.S. Military Academy, on the west bank of the Hudson river, was fortified in 1778/79 by the Americans under the Polish officer Tadeusz Kosciuszko. In 1780, Benedict Arnold's plot to turn West Point over to the British failed. The academy was founded in 1802.

271. Sir Henry Clinton (1738 – 1795), British commander-in-chief during the American revolution. His „Narrative of the Campaign of 1781 in North America" (1783) provoked an angry reply from Cornwallis concerning the fall of Yorktown.

272. John André (1751 – 1780), major in the British army, son of a merchant from Geneva living in London. Aide-de-camp to generals Grey and Clinton. He was Benedict Arnold's collaborator in the planned betrayal of Fort West Point to the British. He was picked up by American militiamen after a meeting with Arnold on Sept. 21, 1780, and admitted the character of his mission in a letter to Washington. Hanged as a spy on Oct. 2nd, 1780. A monument was erected to him in Westminster Abbey.

273. A major waterway of the eastern U.S. rising in the Adirondacks and situated in New York state for the whole length of its 315 miles. It was first explored in 1609 by Henry Hudson for whom it is named. It was of strategic importance during the revolution and was the scene of several battles. In 1807, steam navigation began on the river. It became a key factor in the opening of the American Midwest and for the growth of New York City.

delte Person war, trotz seiner Verkleidung von Milizen gefangen wurde. Wäre nicht General Washington gerade an diesem Tag in Westpoint gewesen, so wäre dieser sehr wichtige Punct am Hudsonfluß[273] mit allem Vorrath der Amerikaner verloren gewesen. Arnold entkam, und ging zu den Engländern über.

Um diese Zeit kam zu uns eine Gesandtschaft von den Stämmen der Cognuacas[274], Oneidas, Senecas, Cayugas, und Tuscaroras. Diese Wilden, waren, so lange die Franzosen Canada hatten, mit ihnen auf freundschaftlichem Fuß gewesen. Sie sagten zum General: „Wie kommt es daß unser Vater[275] seine Truppen zur Vertheidigung der Amerikaner sendet, welche gegen ihren Vater, den König von England[276], aufgestanden sind?" Der General den die Frage verlegen machte, wußte sich nicht an- [77] ders als mit philanthropischen Gründen zu helfen. Er sagte: „Euer Vater, der König von Frankreich, vertheidigt die Freiheit, die der Schöpfer allen Menschen gegeben hat, und hilft den Unterdrückten. Ich ermahne Euch aber, die vollkommenste Neutralität in diesem Streite zu beobachten."

---

273. Einer der größeren Flüsse der östlichen USA, entspringt in den Adirondacks und fließt über die gesamten 500 km seines Laufs durch den Staat New York. Benannt nach Henry Hudson, der den Fluss 1609 erforschte. Im Unabhängigkeitskrieg war er von großer strategischer Bedeutung, Schauplatz mehrerer Schlachten. 1807 begann die Dampfschifffahrt. Der Fluss wurde ein wesentlicher Faktor für die Besiedlung des mittleren Westens.

274. Indianerstämme, die um 1600 den sog. Irokesenbund bildeten, den langlebigsten Indianerbund. Er bestand ursprünglich aus den Stämmen der Mohawks, Oneidas, Onondagas, Cayugas und Senecas; 1722 schlossen sich die Tuscaroras als sechster Stamm an. Der Bund förderte „Frieden, zivile Regierung, Recht und Gesetz"; er hatte auch einige bedeutende Erfolge auf dem Schlachtfeld. Während der amerikanischen Revolution spaltete sich der Bund: die Oneidas und Tuscaroras schlossen sich den Amerikanern an, die übrigen den Briten. 1779 führte der amerikanische General John Sullivan eine Strafexpedition gegen die feindlichen Stämme, besiegte sie bei Elmira, New York. Das war das Ende des auch unter dem Namen der „fünf zivilisierten Völker" bekannten Bundes.

275. Ludwig XVI. (1754 – 1793), letzter König von Frankreich vor der Französischen Revolution. Seit 1770 war er verheiratet mit Marie Antoinette von Österreich. Er konnte die Parteiungen am Hof und den Widerstand der Aristokratie gegen Besteuerung nicht überwinden, berief 1788 die „Generalstände" und setzte so die Revolution in Gang; wurde 1793 mit seiner Familie wegen angeblicher Kollaboration mit auswärtigen Mächten hingerichtet.

276. Georg III. (1738-1820), König von England 1760-1820, ein umstrittener Herrscher. Politische Instabilität um 1770 entfremdete die amerikanischen Kolonien dem Mutterland und führte zu ihrem Verlust. 1788 erlitt er einen gesundheitlichen Zusammenbruch, wohl verursacht durch einen genetischen Defekt. Er war zuletzt nicht mehr in der Lage, die Herrschaft auszuüben; sein Sohn, der spätere Georg IV., übernahm 1811 die Regentschaft.

At this time, we were visited by some representatives of the Indian tribes of the Cognuacas, Oneidas, Senecas, Cayugas and Tuscaroras.[274] As long as the French had ruled Canada, they had been on a friendly footing with the savages. They said to our General: "How can it be that our Father[275] sends his troups to defend the Americans, who have revolted against their Father, the King of England[276]?" Our General, who was embarrassed by the question, could only help himself [77] with philanthropic reasoning. He said, "Your Father, the King of France, is defending freedom which our creator has given to all men and is helping the oppressed here. But I urge you to observe complete neutrality in this quarrel."

They were treated very well and given many gifts. In their language, rich in images, they answered: "Our Father, the King of France, has much milk in his breasts, as full as these are, so empty are our bellies." In the morning, we could watch them getting ready for their audience and dinner with the General. Some sat down in a row along the wall, sitting cross-legged on their heels, and they held little hand-mirrors in order to paint themselves properly with red and black colors. In the evening they performed a dance for us. One was sitting and beating on a drum, about seven were dancing with un-sheathed

---

274. Indian tribes which formed the Iroquois League shortly before 1600; the league was the most durable and effective of Indian federations. It originally consisted of the Mohawk, Oneida, Onondaga, Cayuga, and Seneca tribes; the Tuscaroras joined in 1722 as the sixth nation. The federation promoted "peace, civil authority, righteousness, and law", it also had some spectacular successes on the battlefield. The Iroquois became enemies of the French and dependent on the British for European goods. During the American Revolution, a schism developed; the Oneidas and Tuscaroras sided with the Americans, the others with the British. In 1779, U.S. general John Sullivan led a retaliatory expedition against the enemy tribes and defeated them near Elmira, NY. In 1784, the League, which was also known as the "five civilized nations" came to an end.

275. Louis XVI (1754 – 1793, king of France 1774 –1793. He was married to Marie Antoinette of Austria in 1770 and succeeded to the French throne on the death of his grandfather Louis XV. Unable to combat court factions and aristocratic opposition to financial reforms he was forced to summon the States General in 1788 and thus set in motion the revolution. He and his family were executed in 1793 for allegedly conspiring with foreign powers.

276. George III (1738 – 1820), king of Great Britain and Ireland 1760 – 1820, a controversial ruler. A period of political instability around 1770 alienated the American colonies and led to their loss in Lord North's ministry. In 1788, he suffered a breakdown probably caused by an inherited metabolic defect. In his final years he was completely incapacitated, his son, later George IV, became regent in 1811.

Sie wurden gut tractirt und reichlich beschenkt. In ihrer bilderreichen Sprache sagten sie: "Unser Vater der König von Frankreich, hat viele Milch in seinen Brüsten, so voll diese sind, so leer sind unsere Bäuche." Vormittags konnte man sie sehen, wie sie sich zur Audienz und zum Essen beim General anschickten. Einige saßen an der Wand nebeneinander, mit untergeschlagenen Beinen, so daß sie auf ihren Fersen saßen, und hatten kleine Spiegel in der Hand, um sich mit rother und schwarzer Farbe recht ordentlich zu bemahlen. Abends gaben sie einen Tanz zum besten. Einer saß, und schlug auf eine kleine Trommel, etwa sieben tanzten, mit bloßen Soldatensäbeln, die [sie] sich hatten geben lassen, mit äußerster Anstrengung [78] und Schnelligkeit, in allerhand kriegerischen Stellungen.

Um sie von der Macht des französischen Königs zu überzeugen, mußten alle Truppen paradieren. Sie zeigten aber keine Verwunderung über die Uebungen derselben, nicht einmal über die der Artillerie. Was ihnen gefiel, waren die großen Sappeurs[277] mit den großen Beilen, da ihre eigene Waffe ein kleines Beil ist, welches Tomahawk heißt. Dieß erinnert an die Erzählung Montaigne's[278], daß, als vor drithalbhundert Jahren[279] Wilde nach Paris kamen, diese nichts bewunderten als die großen Vorräthe von Fleisch und Wildprett in den Läden und die großen, bärtigen Schweitzer. Sie konnten nicht begreifen, wie diese bärtigen starken und wohlbewaffneten Leute einen Knaben bewachen und ihm gehorchen möchten, und nicht vielmehr einen aus ihrer Mitte zum Befehlshaber wählten. – Das einzige bewunderten die Wilden, die ich sah, daß die mit Früchten beladenen Obstbäume von den Soldaten unangetastet blieben.

---

277. Sappeure sind Pioniere, die Befestigungen unterminieren, Minen legen und entschärfen oder Schanzarbeiten übernehmen.

278. Michel Eyquem de Montaigne (1533 – 1592), bedeutender französischer Essayist und Philosoph, 1581 – 1585 auch Bürgermeister von Bordeaux. In seinem Essay „Über Kannibalen" (1580) beschreibt er brasilianische Indianer in Rouen im Jahr 1562.

279. Drithalbhundert = 250

army swords which had been given to them; they performed warlike steps with great exertion [78] and at a fast pace.

All of our troops were to parade, to show them the power of the French king. They were not amazed at our drills, not even by our artillery. What they really liked were the big "Sappeurs"[277] with their big hatchets, because their own weapon is a small war-axe called a "tomahawk". This reminded me of Montaigne's story[278], that when some savages came to Paris 250[279] years ago, they most admired the large supplies of meat and venison in the butchers' shops and the tall bearded Swiss guards. They could not understand, why these bearded, strong, and well-armed men would guard a boy (the king) and would obey him, and why they did not choose one of their own as chief. – The only thing that amazed the savages that I observed, was that our soldiers left untouched the fruit trees full of ripe fruit all around us. [79]

Soon after this I took a short trip to Boston[280], which is 30 miles from Rhode Island. I went with Lt. La Roche, son of the famous Mrs. von La Roche[281]. – I had signed up as a Cadet; but after some time General Rochambeau gave me

---

277. Sappeurs, English: sappers, are members of military engineer units who execute sapping (undermining fortifications) and other field fortification work and lay or disarm mines.

278. Michel Eyquem Montaigne (1533 – 1592), famous French essayist, mayor of Bordeaux 1581 – 85. In his essay "Of Cannibals" (1580) he describes Brazilian indians in Rouen in 1562.

279. The author renders this number in an antiquated way easily misunderstood in modern German.

280. Boston, founded by Puritan Englishmen in 1630, is named for Boston in Lincolnshire. It is the capital of Massachussetts. Shipping, shipbuilding, and maritime trade soon became the chief industries. The Boston Tea Party of 1773 (tea was destroyed because of the newly introduced customs duty on it) was the key incident which started the American Revolution. In 1775, Boston was besieged by Washington and in March of 1776, the British left the town. The city became the principal town of learning and education in the U.S.; Harvard University goes back to 1636. Boston had about 24,000 inhabitants at the time of the author's visit.

281. Frédéric von LaRoche was a lieutenant in the Hainaut company of the Deux-Ponts regiment; cf. Tröss, Regiment, p.68. His mother was Sophie von LaRoche, née Gutermann (1731-1807), writer whose first and most important work, "Geschichte des Fräuleins von Sternheim" (1771, Engl. Translation: "History of Lady Sophia Sternheim", 1776) was the first German novel written by a woman and is considered to be among the best works of a period in which English novels had great influence on German writers.

[79] Ich machte bald hernach eine kleine Reise nach Boston[280], welches 30 Meilen von Rhode Island entfernt ist, mit Lt. La Roche, dem Sohne der berühmten Frau v. La Roche[281]. – Ich war als Cadet übergeschifft; doch nach einiger Zeit gab mir der General Rochambeau eine Anstellung als Lieutenant; und etwas später bekam ich eine sogenannte Lettre de Service[282], vom König unterschrieben, um als Hauptmann à la Suite beim Reg. Royal Deuxponts zu dienen. In dieser Lage ist es, da man keinen bestimmten Dienst thut, nothwendig, daß man sich bei jeder Expedition oder Detachement freiwillig anbietet und ausbittet, mitzugehen, worauf man in jener Zeit, mit Flinte und Baionnet bewaffnet, sich in die Reihe der Unterofficiere stellte, welche das Serrefile[283] hinter der Front ausmachten. Auch war ich viel um die Person des Obersten, und stellte einen Gallopin[284] vor.

Der Anfang des Jahres 1781 war unglücklich für die Amerikaner. Die Linie von Pensylvanien[285], ein Drittheil der Armee, empörte sich, und marschirte unter Anführung eines [80] Sergeanten nach

a position as Lieutenant; and sometime later I received the so called Lettre de Service[282] signed by the King, to serve as "captain à la suite" in the reg[iment] Royal Deux-Ponts. In this position it is necessary to voluntarily offer assistance on any expedition or "Détachement", and, armed with musket and bayonet at that time, to accompany the non-commissioned officers, who formed a "Serrefile"[283] behind the front. Also I spent a lot of time around the colonel, and had the role of a "Gallopin"[284].

The beginning of 1781 was ill-fated for the Americans. The militia of Pennsylvania[285], one third of the army, revolted, and marched on Philadelphia[286], led by a sergeant, demanding their back-pay. [80] But they could not be enticed by British agents to go over to the enemy; and after many difficulties, they returned to their posts. At the same time General Arnold, who now was an English general and with whom the English generals served in spite of his betrayal, had invaded Virginia[287] with 2000 men. The Chevalier de Touches detached a warship with two frigates to obstruct Arnold's operations. They were not able to accomplish much, but captured the "Romulus", a ship of 44 cannon, and two transport-ships. Now it was

---

280. Boston, Hauptstadt von Massachussetts, 1630 von Puritanern gegründet, ist nach der gleichnamigen Stadt in Lincolnshire/England genannt. Schifffahrt, Schiffbau und Seehandel waren von Anfang an die hauptsächlichen wirtschaftlichen Aktivitäten. Die „Boston Tea Party" von 1773 (Vernichtung von Tee, weil er neuerdings verzollt werden musste) gehört zu den Vorfällen, die die amerikanische Revolution einleiteten. 1775 wurde B. von Washington belagert, 1776 verließen die Engländer die Stadt. B. wurde zu einer der wichtigsten Städte der Wissenschaft in den USA (die Harvard-Universität wurde 1636 gegründet); um 1800 ca. 24 000 Einwohner.

281. Frédéric von LaRoche, Leutnant in der Kompanie „Hainaut"; s. Tröss, Regiment, S. 68. Seine Mutter war die Schriftstellerin Sophie von LaRoche, geb. Gutermann (1730/31 – 1807), deren Hauptwerk, die „Geschichte des Fräuleins von Sternheim" (1771), der erste von einer Frau geschriebene deutsche Roman, als einer der besten Romane in einer Zeit gilt, in der v. a. englische Romane die deutsche Literatur stark beeinflussten.

282. Lettre de Service: Dienstbefehl.

283. Das Serrefile ist jeweils die letzte Reihe einer marschierenden Truppe.

284. Ein Galopin ist ein berittener Bote auf dem Schlachtfeld, im Frz. auch „galibot".

285. Pennsylvania, eine der 13 Kolonien, die gegen die englische Krone revoltierten, um 1643 zunächst von Schweden besiedelt, wurde 1655 zur niederländischen und 1664 zur englischen Kolonie. 1681 schenkte der englische König dem Quäker William Penn das Gebiet als persönlichen Besitz. Penn gab 1682 seiner Kolonie eine Verfassung, die bis zum Ende der Verwaltung durch Eigentümer 1776 in Kraft blieb. Um 1790 hatte P. etwa 434.000 Einwohner, neben den Quäkern v.a. Iren, Schotten und Deutsche.

---

282. Order of service in the French army.

283. The "serrefile" was the last line of a marching column of troops.

284. Galloper, battlefield messenger; French also "galibot".

285. Pennsylvania was first settled by Swedish immigrants around 1643, and in 1655 became part of the Dutch colony New Netherlands; this in turn became British in 1664. In 1681, the English king donated the land to the Quaker William Penn as a proprietary colony. Besides the Quakers, Irish, Scottish, and German immigrants predominated until the beginning of the 19th century. In 1790, Pennsylvania had about 434,000 inhabitants. The proprietary government was abolished in 1776.

286. Philadelphia was founded by William Penn as capital for his Quaker colony in 1683. It was the 2nd largest city of the British Empire in the 18th century and the political and cultural center of the American colonies at the time of the American Revolution. The 1st Continental Congress met here in 1774, the 2nd Continental Congress passed the Declaration of Independence in 1776. It was occupied by British troops from Sept. 1777 to June, 1778. The American constitution was promulgated here in 1787. From 1790 to 1800 it was the capital of the U.S.

287. Virginia is one of the 13 founding states of the U.S. The first failed settlement of 1584 – 1589, organized by Sir Walter Raleigh who named his colony for the "Virgin Queen" Elizabeth I., was followed by the founding of Jamestown in 1607, the first permanent English colony in America. Virginia soon prospered with tobacco and cotton as important export products. The capital is Richmond.

Philadelphia[286], um ihren rückständigen Sold zu fordern. Doch ließen sie sich nicht durch Unterhändler verführen, zum Feind überzugehen; und nach vielen Bemühungen wurden sie zurück gebracht. Zu gleicher Zeit war General Arnold, der jetzt englischer General war und mit dem die englischen Generale trotz seiner Verrätherey dienten, mit 2000 Mann in Verginien eingefallen. Der Chevalier de Touches dedaschirte ein Kriegsschiff mit zwei Fregatten, um die Operationen Arnold's zu stören. Sie konnten aber weiter Nichts ausrichten, als den „Romulus", ein Schiff von 44 Kanonen, und zwei Transportschiffe [zu] nehmen. Jetzt wurde beschlossen, daß Lafayette[287] mit 1000 Mann nebst 2000 Milizen von Virginien[288] gegen Arnold marschieren sollte; und die französische Flotte nebst 1200 Mann und Artillerie unter dem Baron de Viomenil[289] segelte zu eben diesem Zwecke im Anfang März 1781 von Newport ab. Sie bestand, mit Einschluß des neu eroberten „Romulus" aus 8 Kriegsschif-

decided that Lafayette[288], with 1000 men plus 2000 Virginia militia should march against Arnold; and the French fleet with 1200 men and artillery under Baron de Viomenil[289] sailed from Newport at the beginning of March 1781 for this very purpose. Including the recently captured "Romulus", it consisted of 8 warships. I volunteered to sail on the "Fantasque", a warship [81] which was being used as a transport-ship ("armé en flutte").[290] Leaving port, I had about the same luck as in Brest. The captain of the "Fantasque" was an "Officier auxiliaire", i.e. requisitioned from the merchant marine in order to serve for a time in the royal navy. Right out of the harbour, the ship ran aground on a sandbar. The general immediately sent an officer, who arrested our captain in his state-room, and with the help of an American pilot, he set the ship afloat again. The captain's name was de Vaudore.[291] A stormy sea and the different speeds drove the ships apart. We could

---

286. Philadelphia wurde 1683 von William Penn als Hauptstadt seiner Quäkerkolonie gegründet und war im 18. Jahrhundert die zweitgrößte Stadt des englischen Empire, zugleich das politische und kulturelle Zentrum der amerikanischen Kolonien. 1774 versammelte sich hier der 1. Kontinentalkongress, 1776 verabschiedete hier der 2. Kontinentalkongress die Unabhängigkeitserklärung, 1787 wurde hier die amerikanische Verfassung verkündet. Von September 1777 bis Juni 1778 war die Stadt britisch besetzt, von 1790 bis 1800 die Hauptstadt der USA.

287. Marie Joseph du Motier, marquis de Lafayette, auch: La Fayette (1757-1834), kämpfte 1777-1781 auf Seiten der Amerikaner gegen die Briten. 1777 schloss er gleich nach seiner Ankunft eine feste Freundschaft mit George Washington. Als Generalmajor kämpfte er im September 1777 mit Auszeichnung bei Brandywine, Pennsylvania. 1779 bewegte er die französische Regierung dazu, die amerikanischen Kolonien mit einem Expeditionskorps von 6 000 Mann zu unterstützen. Im April 1780 erhielt er das Kommando über eine Armee in Virginia. Er schloss Cornwallis mit seinen Truppen bei Yorktown ein. Nach dessen Kapitulation wurde er als „Held zweier Welten" gefeiert. 1789 legte er der französischen Nationalversammlung den Entwurf einer Erklärung der Menschenrechte vor, die – revidiert – angenommen wurde. Seine Popularität verflog, als 1791 die Nationalgarde (er war deren Kommandant) 50 Demonstranten erschoss. Er ging 1792 zu den Österreichern über, die ihn bis 1797 festsetzten. 1799 Rückkehr nach Frankreich, 1814-1824 Abgeordneter. 1824/25 besuchte er noch einmal die USA.

288. Virginia ist einer der 13 Gründerstaaten der USA. Der ersten von Sir Walter Raleigh organisierten, jedoch fehlgeschlagenen Ansiedlung von 1584 – 1589, benannt nach der „jungfräulichen Königin" Elizabeth I., folgte die Gründung von Jamestown im Jahre 1607, der ersten dauerhaften englischen Kolonie in Amerika. Virginia blühte bald mit der Ausfuhr von Tabak und Baumwolle als wichtigsten Produkten wirtschaftlich auf.

289. Antoine Charles du Houx, baron de Viomenil (1728 – 1792), entstammte einer lothringischen Adelsfamilie. Mit 12 Jahren Eintritt in die Armee, 1747 Hauptmann, 1762 Brigadegeneral, wirkte bei der Befriedung Korsikas 1768 – 1769 mit. 1780 wurde er unter Rochambeau nach Amerika entsandt. 1781 zum Generalleutnant ernannt, erhielt für seine Tapferkeit bei der Erstürmung von Yorktown das Große Ludwigskreuz. 1792 wurde er, den König beim Sturm auf die Tuilerien verteidigend, tödlich verwundet; s. auch Acomb, Journal, S. 364.

---

288. Marie Joseph du Motier, marquis de Lafayette (or: la Fayette, 1757 – 1834), fought with the American colonists against the British 1777 – 1781. Arriving in America in 1777, he immediately struck up a lasting friendship with George Washington. Appointed a major general he fought with distinction at Brandywine, PA, in Sept. 1777. Returning to France he convinced the French government to support the American colonies with an army corps of 6000 men. In April 1780, he had command of an army in Virginia and encircled Cornwallis' troops at Yorktown. After Cornwallis' capitulation he was celebrated as the "hero of two worlds". He submitted the draft of a declaration of the rights of man to the French national assembly. His popularity was destroyed when the National Guard (which he commanded) killed 50 demonstrators in 1791. He defected to the Austrians in 1792 who took him prisoner until 1797. He returned to France in 1799 and was a member of the Chambre des Députés 1814 – 1824. He visited the U.S. 1824 – 1825.

289. Antoine Charles du Houx, baron de Viomenil (1728 – 1792), was the scion of a noble family of Lorraine. He joined the French army at the age of 12 and rose to the rank of brigadier general in 1762. He was instrumental in the pacification of Corsica 1768 – 1769. In 1780, he was sent to America under Rochambeau's command to support the colonies' struggle for independence. In 1781, he was made lieutenant general and received the cross of St. Louis for his valor at the storming of the Yorktown defences. In 1792, he was severely wounded defending the king at the storming of the Tuileries palace and died a few weeks afterwards; cf. Acomb, Journal, p. 364.

290. The author explains this term correctly, but too briefly. Most of the guns of such ships were removed and the decks were then used to transport goods, people, or to serve as floating hospitals.

291. A M[onsier] de Vaudoré is, however, mentioned as commander of the "Fantasque" in the Wikipedia article on the battle of Cape Henry.

fen. Ich fuhr freiwillig auf dem „Fantasque" mit, [81] einem Kriegsschiff, das als Transportschiff gebraucht wurde („armé en flutte").[290] Beim Auslaufen ging es mir nicht viel besser, als in Brest. Der Capitain des „Fantasque" war ein Officier auxiliaire, d. h. aus der Kauffartei-Schiffahrt requirirt worden, um einige Zeit bei der königlichen Marine zu dienen. Gleich vor dem Hafen blieb das Schiff auf einer Sandbank sitzen. Der General schickte sogleich einen Officier, welcher unseren Capitain in seiner Cajute in Arrest setzte, und mit Hülfe eines Amerikanischen Piloten das Schiff wieder flott machte. Der Capitain hieß de Vaudore.[291] Die ungleiche Fahrt der Schiffe und eine stürmische See trennte die Schiffe. Es hätte großes Unheil daraus entstehen können, wenn die Escadre sich zur rechten Zeit wieder vereint hätte.[292] Am 16. März, in der Nähe der Chesapeak-Bai[293], entdeckte man bei starkem Nebel, eine Fregatte, und machte auf sie Jagd. Bald hierauf sah man durch den Nebel einige große Schiffe; und auf ein gegebenes Signal richteten sich die Schiffe [82] in Schlachtordnung.[294] (Der Abstand der Schiffe in der Linie ist gemeiniglich eine Kabel-Länge oder 60 Klafter[295]. Die Länge eines großen Kabeltaues ist 360 Schuh.) Im Nebel verschwanden die feindlichen Schiffe wieder; man hörte aber immer Signale von Kanonenschüssen. Endlich klärte sich die Luft auf; und die zwei Escadres lagen einander gegenüber. Die Franzosen hatten auf allen Schiffen die englische Flagge, und die Engländer die französische. Dieß war aber unnütz; denn jeder wußte recht gut, wer der andere war. Den ganzen Morgen wurde gegenseitig manoevrirt, bis die Engländer hinter die Escadre, in die Verlängerung der Linie

---

290. Der Begriff wird vom Autor richtig, aber zu knapp erklärt: der größte Teil der Geschütze wurde auf solchen Schiffen ausgeräumt, die Decks dann für Fracht, Personentransport oder oft auch als Lazarett genutzt. Anders als heute üblich spricht Rechteren von Schiffen überwiegend in männlicher Form.

291. M. de Vaudoré wird jedoch im Wikipedia-Artikel über die Schlacht von Cape Henry als Kommandant der „Fantasque" genannt.

292. Oder meint der Autor: wenn die Escadre sich *nicht* zur rechten Zeit wieder vereint hätte ?

293. Chesapeake Bay: Größte Bucht (ca. 311 km lang, 5 – 40 km breit) in der atlantischen Küstenebene der USA. Ihr südlicher Teil grenzt an Virginia, der nördliche an Maryland. 1607 siedelten hier die ersten Europäer in Jamestown. 1608 kartierte John Smith die Bucht. Baltimore ist hier der größte Hafen; die Fischerei ist bedeutend.

294. Bei der hier beschriebenen Seeschlacht handelt es sich um die Schlacht bei Cape Henry vom 16. März 1781, nicht um die für den Ausgang der Belagerung von Yorktown entscheidende Schlacht von Chesapeake Bay bzw. „battle of the Virginia capes" vom 5. September 1781 zwischen den Flotten des französischen Konteradmirals de Grasse-Tilly und des britischen Konteradmirals Graves.

295. Klafter, entspricht einem englischen „Faden", d.h. 6 Fuß bzw. ca. 1,8 m; die Schiffe hielten also ca. 100 m Abstand voneinander in der Linie.

---

have met with disaster, if the squadron had joined[292] up at the appointed time. On March 16th, close to Chesapeake Bay[293], we discovered a frigate in heavy fog and gave chase. Soon afterwards we saw several large ships through the fog; and after a signal was given, the ships lined up for battle.[294] [82] (The distance between the ships in the line is usually one cable length or 60 fathoms[295]. The length of a large cable-rope is 360 feet.) The enemy ships disappeared in the fog, but we could still hear gunshot signals. Finally the fog lifted and the two squadrons faced each other. The French were flying an English flag on every ship, and the English were flying the French flag. But this did not help, for everyone knew well enough who the other one was. All morning long both sides maneuvred around each other, until the English came behind the squadron, in the extension of the line. Now the front-most ship put about, and the whole line followed, so that both lines were sailing toward each other. The first two ships pulled down the decoy flags, when the first shot was fired, and hoisted their original ones. The English, in addition to their own flag, also hoisted a large red flag on the mast of each ship. The "Fantasque", which until then [83] had been in the line, in order to impress the English, now pulled back and positioned herself behind the "Romulus". The French had the wind from starboard, and the English from port. Since the wind was very strong, the ships were listing to the side away from the wind. On this side the gunports of the lower battery had to be closed, this means the lower row of guns could not be used. On the other side, which was exposed to the wind, the lower battery towered up high above the surface of the water. Whereas it is usual in such sea battles to gain the wind or to lie above the wind, because the wind

---

292. Thus in the original text, but does the author mean "had not joined up"?

293. Largest inlet (193 miles long and 3 – 25 miles wide) in the Atlantic coastal plain of the eastern U.S. Its southern part is bordered by Virginia, the northern part by Maryland. The first European settlement, Jamestown, was founded in this area in 1607. One year later, Captain John Smith explored and mapped the bay. In the War of 1812, the British invaded through Chesapeake Bay. Baltimore is the chief port; the fisheries are important.

294. The naval battle described here is the Battle of Cape Henry of March 16th, 1781 (or 1st Battle of the Virginia Capes), not the more important battle of Chesapeake Bay or 2nd Battle of the Virginia Capes of Sept. 5th, 1781, between the fleets of the French rear-admiral de Grasse-Tilly and the English rear-admiral Graves in the same waters which was decisive for the outcome of the American War of Independence.

295. A fathom, German "Klafter", corresponds to 6 English feet or a little more than 1.8 meters.

kamen. Nun wendete sich das vorderste Schiff, und die ganze Linie folgte, so daß die zwei Linien gegeneinander segelten. Die zwei Vordermänner zogen bei der ersten Kugel, die sie schoßen, die falsche Flagge nieder und die ihrige auf. Die Engländer zogen außer ihrer Flagge auf jedem Schiff eine große rothe Flagge am Mast auf. Der „Fantasque", welcher bis [**83**] dahin in der Linie gelegen war, um zu imponiren, zog sich jetzt zurück und legte sich hinter den „Romulus". Die Franzosen hatten den Wind von der rechten und die Engländer von der linken Seite. Da der Wind sehr heftig war, hingen die Schiffe sehr nach der Seite, welche vom Winde abgewendet war. Von dieser Seite mußten die Schießlöcher der unteren Batterie geschloßen bleiben, und man konnte also die untere Reihe der Kanonen nicht brauchen. An der Seite hingegen, die gegen den Wind stand, ragte die untere Batterie weit über die Wasserfläche hervor. Wie man sich nun sonst streitet, um den Wind zu gewinnen oder über dem Winde zu liegen, weil man dann sich von dem Winde gegen den Feind treiben lassen und ihn verfolgen kann, so suchte jetzt jeder, unter den Wind zu kommen.[296] Die Folge hievon war, daß beide Theile mit dem Wind auf dem Rücken in trichterförmiger Gestallt nebeneinander fortsegelten. Hinter der Linie lag eine Fregatte, welche die Signale des Generals (Bei den Franzosen nennt man den Commandanten einer Escadre auch General.) [**84**] repetirte, weil in der Linie ein Schiff das andere deckte, die Fregatte aber von allen gesehen wurde.

Die vorderen Schiffe kamen sehr nahe aneinander. Der „Romulus" von 44 Kanonen, welcher kein Linienschiff war, mußte doch jetzt mit in der Linie liegen; hinter ihm lag der „Fantasque", und gegen ihm über der Dreidecker „London" von 98 Kanonen. Dieser feuerte aber nicht, sondern segelte in gerader Richtung auf ihn zu um die Linie zu durchbrechen. Weil aber der „Romulus" unablässig feuerte, so wurde der „London" zuletzt an seinen Masten beschädigt. Er stand also von seinem Vorhaben, die Linie zu durchbrechen, ab, drehte sich und zeigte seine drei Reihen Kanonen. Jetzt mußte man denken, daß es dem „Romulus" bei dem ungleichen Kampf übel ergehen würde. Aber von den zwei Lagen, die er empfing, war zu seinem Glück eine zu hoch und die ande[re] zu niedrig gerichtet. (Dieß kam vom Schwanken des ungestümen Meeres her.) Hierauf waren sie vonein- [**85**] ander entfernt.

---

296. Rechteren beschreibt die Standardtaktik bei einer Seeschlacht zwischen Segelschiffen: wegen der für eigene Segelmanöver günstigeren Position sucht man normalerweise auf die Luvseite der gegnerischen Linie zu gelangen; in diesem Fall war es wegen des starken Windes und der so entstandenen Schräglage der Schiffe aber vorteilhafter, auf der Leeseite des Gegners zu sein, um volle Breitseiten schießen zu können.

will blow you towards the enemy and you can give chase, so now both sides tried to move below the wind.[296] The result was that both sides were sailing in a funnel-shape beside each other driven by a tail-wind. A frigate was sailing behind the line, which repeated the signals of the general [84] (the French call the squadron commander a general); because in the line one ship covered the other, and the frigate could be seen by all.

The foremost ships got very close to each other. The "Romulus" of 44 cannon, which was not a ship-of-the-line, now had to take up a position in the line; behind it lay the "Fantasque", and across from it the triple-decker "London" of 98 guns. This one did not fire, but sailed straight at him [the „Romulus"] in order to break through the line. Because the "Romulus" continued firing, at last they hit the masts of the "London". He gave up his intention of breaking through our line, put about, and showed his three rows of guns. Now one would assume, that the "Romulus" would experience an ugly finish in this unequal battle. But of the two volleys which it took, one was aimed too high and the other too low, as luck would have it. (This was caused by the rocking of the ships on the tumultous sea.) After this they drifted apart from each other.[85]

---

296. The author describes the standard tactics of a naval battle in the age of sail; it was usually more advantageous to be to the windward of the opposing line because manoeuvers were much easier this way, but in this case it was better to be on the leeside because the ships were listing heavily and full broadsides could only be fired from the leeward position.

Von den Engländern war das vordere Schiff der „Robust". Dieser hatte kaum das Feuer des sechsten Schiffes, des „Neptun", ausgehalten, als er sich wendete, und alsdann auf einen Pistolenschuß weit zwei Lagen von hinten der Länge nach von dem „Neptun" erhielt, so daß er von einer Fregatte begleitet, sich entfernte. Nicht besser ging es auf unserer Seite dem „Conquérant", welchem sein Steuerruder beschädigt wurde, so daß er nicht in der Linie bleiben konnte und unter das Feuer des „London" kam. Der „Neptun" aber gab dem „London" im Vorbeigehen eine Lage, so daß er vom „Conquérant" ablassen mußte.

Dieses sehr heftige Gefecht dauerte 5/4 Stunden. Von französischer Seite wurde der Verlust auf 80 Todte und 120 Verwundete angegeben.[297] Es war dieß das zweite Seetreffen, von welchem ich, ohne im Mindesten die Gefahr zu theilen, Augenzeuge war. Abends passirte uns der „Conquérant" in der Nähe; eine traurige Stille herrschte auf dem durchlöcherten und fast zertrümmerten Schiffe; unzählige [86] Löcher waren in den Segeln. Am folgenden Morgen sah man von Weitem unaufhörlich nackte Leichen durch die Geschützlöcher in das Meer werfen, so daß man denken konnte, der „Conquérant" allein habe so viele Todte gehabt, als für die ganze Flotte angegeben wurden.

Der Entzweck, in der Chesapeak-Bay zu landen, war nun verfehlt, weil die englische Escadre sich gleich nach dem Gefechte dahin zog, und unsere Schiffe zum Theil hergestellt werden mußten. Man kehrte also nach Rhode Island zurück; und die Generale beschlossen, zu Land auf New-York loszugehen. Der Admiral Graf Barras[298], der mit einer Fregatte aus Frankreich kam, übernahm jetzt das Commando der Escadre. 500 Franzosen und 1000 Mann Milizen blieben unter N. de Choisy[299] zurück, um die Forts zur Vertheidigung der Flotte zu besetzen. Die Truppen

The foremost English ship was the "Robust" which had just been fired on by the "Neptune", the 6th ship, when they put about, and immediately received two volleys from the "Neptune" fired from behind the whole length of the ship at a distance of about a pistol shot; after this he withdrew accompanied by a frigate. The "Conquérant" on our side did not fare much better, because its rudder was damaged, so that it could not remain in the line and moved into the path of fire of the "London". The "Neptune" gave the "London" a volley while passing so that he had to leave off firing at the "Conquérant". This very heavy combat lasted about one and ¼ hours. On the French side the casualties were listed as 80 dead and 120 wounded.[297] This was the second naval battle that I witnessed, without ever being in danger myself. In the evening we sailed past the "Conquérant"; a somber silence emanated from the ruined ship shot full of holes; [86] the sails hung in tatters. The next morning from afar, we could see corpse after naked corpse being thrown into the sea through the gun ports, so many that we thought the "Conquérant" alone had had as many casualties as were reported for the whole fleet.

The goal of landing in Chesapeake Bay had thus been missed, because the English squadron moved there right after this battle, and many of our ships had to be repaired. Therefore we returned to Rhode Island, and the generals decided to march on New York. Admiral Comte Barras[298], who arrived on a frigate from France, took command of the squadron. 500 French and 1000 militia remained there under N. de Choisy[299] in the forts

---

297. Diese Angaben Rechterens stimmen recht genau mit denen überein, die auch sonst in der Literatur zu dieser Schlacht gemacht werden.

298. Admiral Jacques-Melchior de Saint-Laurent, comte de Barras (1719 – 1793), erzwang im August 1778 die Öffnung des Hafens von Newport für die französische Flotte, die im September 1781 die Belagerungswaffen und -geräte nach Yorktown brachte. 1782 nahm er den Briten die Insel Montserrat ab; s. Acomb, Journal, S. 340.

299. N. de Choisy, nach Bodinier, Dictionnaire, S. 113 f.: Claude Gabriel, marquis de Choisy (1723 – 1799(?)), aus bürgerlicher Familie (?), seit 1741 in der französischen Armee. 1772 Brigadegeneral, trat als solcher auch in Rochambeaus Expeditionskorps ein. Nach Meinung des Herzogs von Lauzun war er ein tapferer, jedoch zu cholerischer Mann; 1791 Generalleutnant, schied 1792 aus dem Heeresdienst aus; s. Acomb, Journal, S. 343.

297. Our author's count of the dead and wounded corresponds closely to that of most other reports on this battle.

298. Jacques-Melchior de Saint-Laurent, comte de Barras (1719 – 1793), had forced the opening of the port of Newport, R.I., for the French fleet in August, 1788; in 1782, he had taken the then British island of Montserrat; cf. Acomb, Journal, p. 340.

299. Probably Claude Gabriel, marquis de Choisy (1723 – 1799(?)), originally from a bourgeois family (?). He had joined the French army in 1741. In 1772, as a brigadier general, he was a member of Rochambeau's expeditionary corps. According to Lauzun he was a valiant man, but too choleric. Lieutenant general in 1791, he left the army in 1792 for health reasons; cf. Bodinier, Dictionnaire, p. 113 f., and Acomb, Journal, p. 343.

wurden auf das feste Land nach Providence[300] übergeschifft. Von da marschirten die Truppen in größter Geschwindigkeit durch Connecticut[301] bis an den Hudsons-Fluß, und fasten Posten zu Philipsburg[302], wo das [**87**] Corps d'armée des General Washington, welches mit den französischen Truppen 9000 Mann ausmachte, sich mit ihnen vereinigte. Die Absicht des General Washington war gewesen, New-York anzugreifen, – was auch geschehen wäre, wenn General Clinton außer den 3000 Man[n], die er zur Verstärkung des Gen. Arnold nach Virginien schickte, seine Garnison noch mehr geschwächt hätte, und die französische Flotte unter Admiral Grasse[303] da gewesen wäre, um zur See mitzuwirken. Dieser sollte aus den Inseln[304] kommen, um die Escadre des Admiral Barras beim Abzug von New Port zu schützen, und bei der sehr kurzen Zeit, die er da bleiben sollte, dem General Rochambeau zu einer von demselben zu bestimmenden Expedition beizustehen. Der Admiral Grasse hatte die Insel Tobago[305] erobert, und war jetzt in St. Domingo[306].

to guard the fleet. The troops were shipped to the mainland at Providence[300]. Then they marched very quickly through Connecticut[301] and on to the Hudson River, and took up position at Philipsburg[302], where they united [**87**] with General Washington's "corps d'armée" (main army) which, counting the French troops, numbered 9000 men. It had been General Washington's intention to attack New York, which would have happened if General Clinton had weakened his garrison beyond the 3000 men, whom he had sent to Virginia to reinforce Gen. Arnold and if the French fleet under Admiral Grasse[303] had been there to aid in a naval operation. He was to sail up from the islands[304], in order to protect Admiral Barras' squadron during their departure from Newport, and during the very short time that he was to remain there to aid General Rochambeau in an expedition he was planning. Admiral Grasse had captured the Island of Tobago[305], and was now in St. Domingo[306].

---

300. Providence, seit 1900 Hauptstadt von Rhode Island, liegt am oberen Ende der Narragansett-Bucht am Providence-Fluss; 1639 von Roger Williams gegründet. Die Stadt wuchs rasch auf der Basis eines blühenden Dreieckshandels mit Molasse, Rum und Sklaven. Der britische "Sugar Act" von 1764 fügte diesem Handel erheblichen Schaden zu, viele Händler wurden Schmuggler. Die Verbrennung des Zollschiffes "Gaspee" 1772 hier war der erste Gewaltakt gegen die britische Herrschaft. Französische Truppen seit 1778 hier stationiert.

301. Connecticut, eine der ursprünglichen 13 britischen Kolonien in Amerika. Holländer errichteten die ersten Faktoreien am Connecticut-Fluss, dauerhafte europäische Besiedlung begann jedoch erst mit Siedlern aus der Massachussetts-Bay-Kolonie 1633 – 1635. Nach der Gründungsurkunde besaß C. einen Landstreifen, der sich in west-östlicher Richtung vom Atlantik bis zum Pazifik erstreckte. Eine königliche Urkunde – von 1662 bis 1818 in Kraft – sah die Selbstregierung der Siedler vor.

302. Philipsburg, New York, einige Kilometer nördlich der heutigen Stadtgrenze von New York City etwa bei Dobbs Ferry am Hudson gelegen; Philipsburg Manor ist ein historisches Denkmal. S. die Kartenskizze bei Selig, German Allies, T. 3.2, S. 39.

303. François Joseph Paul marquis de Grasse-Tilly (1722 – 1788), französischer Konteradmiral; sein Sieg am 5. September 1781 in der Seeschlacht um die Beherrschung der Chesapeake Bay war der einer der entscheidenden Faktoren für den Erfolg der Belagerung von Yorktown und somit für den Ausgang des Amerikanischen Unabhängigkeitskriegs; s. auch o. Anm. 284.

304. Gemeint sind die karibischen Inseln.

305. Tobago ist die nördliche Insel der Inselrepublik von Trinidad und T. und liegt nahe am südamerikanischen Festland. Von Kolumbus auf seiner dritten Reise im Jahre 1498 entdeckt, seit der Mitte des 16. Jahrhunderts von Spanien kolonisiert, in der Folge Stützpunkte von Piraten. 1797 wurde Trinidad, 1814 auch T. britisch.

306. St. Domingo, die Hauptstadt der Dominikanischen Republik, liegt an der Südküste der Insel Hispaniola. 1496 gegründet, somit die älteste dauerhafte europäische Siedlung in Amerika; 1509 Sitz des (spanischen) Vizekönigs.

300. Providence, Rhode Island, capital of that state since 1900, at the head of Narragansett Bay, was founded by Roger Williams in 1639. The community grew fast after having become a base for a thriving triangular trade in rum, slaves, and molasses. The Sugar Act of 1764 had severely damaged the triangular trade and many traders took to smuggling. The burning of the British customs ship "Gaspee" close to Providence in 1772 was the first act of violence against the British rule. French troops were quartered in Providence in 1778.

301. Connecticut is one of the original 13 English colonies in America. The Dutch established the first trading posts on the Connecticut River, permanent settlement by Europeans began with settlers from the Massachussetts Bay Colony in 1633 – 35. The original charter gave residents a claim to a strip of land westward all the way to the Pacific. A royal charter of 1662 which provided for self-government remained in power until 1818.

302. Philipsburg, New York, on the Hudson river close to Dobbs Ferry, a few miles north of the present city line of New York City. Philipsburg Manor is a historic site; cf. the map in Selig, German Allies, pt. 3.2, p. 39.

303. François Joseph Paul marquis de Grasse-Tilly (1722 – 1788), French admiral whose victory in the battle of the Virginia Capes in the fall of 1781 was instrumental in the success of the siege of Yorktown; cf. fn. 284.

304. This means the Caribbean Islands.

305. Tobago, northern island of the island republic of Trinidad and T., discovered by Columbus on his 3rd voyage in 1498. Colonized by Spain from the middle of the 16th century, the islands became pirate bases. In 1797, the British conquered Trinidad, in 1814, Tobago became British, too.

306. St. Domingo, capital of the Dominican Republic, on the southern coast of the island of Hispaniola, is the oldest permanent European settlement in America, founded in 1496, seat of a viceroy in 1509.

Es wurde also beschlossen, nur eine Demonstration gegen New-York zu machen, um Clinton abzuhalten, mehr Truppen nach Virginien zu schicken, und dann zu Land den Marsch dahin anzutreten. General Rocham- [88] beau schrieb an den Admiral Grasse und an den Gouverneur von Domingo und den spanischen Admiral Solano[307]. Diese genehmigten alle den Plan. Der Gouverneur versprach, die 3000 Mann französische Truppen unter dem General St. Simon[308] auf 3 Monate zu schicken; und der spanische Admiral besorgte, daß 1 200 000 Franken übermacht wurden, deren die Armee bedurfte.

Der Englische General Cornwallis[309] hatte die Amerikaner in Nord-Carolina zurückgeschlagen, und war in Verginien mit 8000 Mann eingedrungen. Lafayette mit 1000 Mann konnte sich nur so behaupten, daß er von einem Fluß zum andern auswich, um dem General Waine[310], der mit der Linie von Pensulvanien zu Hülfe kam, entgegen zu gehen. Nun lag die Armée auf der Linken des Hudson-Flußes, die französische links, die Amerikanische rechts, durch eine breite Schlucht getrennt, mit der rechten Flanke gegen den Fluß. Damals hatte

It was decided to stage a diversionary attack on New York, in order to detract Clinton from moving troops to Virginia, and then to start marching south. General Rochambeau [88] wrote to Admiral Grasse and to the Governor of Domingo and to the Spanish Admiral Solano[307]. They all authorized this plan. The Governor promised to send General St. Simon[308] with 3000 French troops for 3 months; and the Spanish Admiral saw to it that 1,200,000 francs which the army needed were transferred.

The English General Cornwallis[309] had beaten the Americans back in North Carolina, and had advanced into Virginia with 8000 men. Lafayette, with 1000 men, was just dodging from one river to the next, trying to link up with General Waine[310], who was coming to his aid with the Line of Pennsylvania. Now the army was encamped on the left

---

307. José de Solano y Bote, marqués del Socorro (1726 – 1806), seit 1770 Gouverneur und Generalkapitän von St. Domingo, trug durch seine Erlaubnis, Truppen nach Virginia zu bringen, und durch die Bereitstellung einer großen Geldsumme in Edelmetall statt dem wertlosen Papiergeld der verbündeten Kolonien zur Soldzahlung an die Soldaten wesentlich zum Sieg der amerikanischen Revolutionäre bei.

308. Claude Anne de Rouvroy, marquis de Saint Simon Montbléru (1743 – 1819), trat mit elf Jahren in die französische Armee ein, 1756 Leutnant im Regiment Auvergne, 1770 Brigadegeneral, 1780 maréchal-de-camp. Er kommandierte die Truppen, die die Flotte von de Grasse-Tilly nach Yorktown brachte. Da er auch dem spanischen Adel angehörte, nahm er 1790 spanische Nationalität an und kämpfte gegen die französischen Invasionstruppen. Er wurde bei der Einnahme von Madrid gefangen genommen, zum Tode verurteilt, aber von Napoleon begnadigt; vgl. Bodinier, Dictionnaire, S. 484, auch Acomb, Journal, S. 361.

309. Charles Cornwallis, erster Marquess Cornwallis (1738 – 1805), entstammte einer prominenten Familie. Er war Politiker und Soldat, Abgeordneter im britischen Unter- und Oberhaus; Militär im Siebenjährigen Krieg. Nahm freiwillig Dienst in den amerikanischen Kolonien, errang mehrere Siege, bevor er am 19. Oktober 1781 bei Yorktown kapitulieren musste. Trotz der Niederlage behielt er das Vertrauen der Regierung und wurde 1786 als Generalgouverneur nach Indien entsandt, wo er erfolgreiche Feldzüge führte und wichtige Verwaltungs- und Justizreformen durchsetzte. 1793 nach Großbritannien zurückbeordert und 1798 als Lord Lieutenant nach Irland geschickt, wo er eine Rebellion unterdrückte. 1802 handelte er mit Napoleon den Frieden von Amiens aus. 1805 als Vizekönig nach Indien entsandt, starb er kurz nach der Ankunft.

310. Anthony Wayne (1745 – 1796), aus Waynesboro, Pennsylvania; 1777 Brigadegeneral und Kommandeur der Einheiten aus Pennsylvania. Er kämpfte bei Brandywine, Germantown und Monmouth, nach Yorktown unter General Greene in Georgia. 1783 verließ er den Militärdienst; Abgeordneter in Pennsylvania und in Georgia.

307. Admiral José de Solano y Bote, marqués del Socorro (1726 – 1806), contributed greatly to the victory of the American colonies, by permitting troops to be transported to Virginia and also by supplying a large sum of money in precious metals instead of the worthless paper money of the colonies, for the payment of the troops.

308. Claude Anne de Rouvroy, marquis de Saint Simon Montbléru (1743 – 1819), joined the army at the age of 11, lieutenant in the Auvergne regiment in 1756, brigadier general in 1770, "maréchal de camp" in 1780. He commanded the troops landed by Admiral de Grasse-Tilly who took part in the siege of Yorktown. As he was a Spanish nobleman as well, he took Spanish nationality in 1790 and left France. He fought the invading French and was taken prisoner when the French took Madrid, condemned to death, but pardoned by Napoleon; cf. Bodinier, Dictionnaire, p. 484 f., also Acomb, Journal, p. 361.

309. Charles Cornwallis, 1st marquess Cornwallis (1738 –1805), was born into a very well connected family. He was a politician and soldier, whose career included times in the House of Commons and House of Lords as well as army service in the Seven Years' War. He volunteered for service in the American colonies and led his troops to several victories before being forced to surrender at Yorktown on October 19th, 1781. Despite this defeat he retained the confidence of the government and was sent as governor-general to India in 1786, where he led successful military campaigns and enacted administrative and judicial reforms. In 1793, he was called back to Britain and, in 1798, was appointed Lord Lieutenant of Ireland where he succeeded in suppressing a rebellion. In 1802, he negotiated the peace of Amiens with Napoleon. He was sent as viceroy to India in 1805, but died shortly after his arrival.

310. Anthony Wayne (1745 – 1796), born at Waynesboro, PA, brigadier general in 1777, commander of the Pennsylvania line. He fought at Brandywine, Germantown, and Monmouth. After Arnold's defection, he prevented the British occupation of West Point. After Yorktown, he served under Gen. Greene in Georgia. Retired from active service in 1783, elected to the Pennsylvania General Assembly, later to Congress as a representative of Georgia.

ich mir 2 Pferde angeschaft, und der Oberst hatte [**89**] mir ein Soldaten-Zelt für mich allein zugestanden. Das eine Pferd hatte einem Englischen Dragoner-Unterofficier[311] gehört, welcher damit desertirt war.

Am 15. Juli segelte eine Escadre von 5 kleinen Schiffen (das Admiralschiff hatte 16 Kanonen) den Fluß aufwärts, um die Zufuhr der Lebensmittel zu Wasser zu unterbrechen. Ein Unterofficier von Soissonais mit einem Detaschement von 12 amerikanischen Dragonern hinderte die Landung. Dieser Unterofficier wurde sehr ausgezeichnet, und hatte die Ehre, an der Tafel des Generals zu speißen. Jedoch ein Fahrzeug, welches Brod für 4 Tagen bei sich hatte, wurde genommen. (Der Soldat wurde auf 4 Unzen[312] Brod reducirt) Man gab dem Soldaten dafür Reiß und etwas mehr Fleisch. Er war aber immer fröhlich bei diesen Entbehrungen. Darin gingen die Officiere ihm voran, die diesen mühsamen Marsch zu Fuß machten und dieselbe Kost, wie der gemeine Soldat, hatten. Jeder durfte 150 Pfund an Bagage haben, die Matratze und alles mit eingerechnet. So viel wurde auf dem Compagnie-Wagen aufgenommen.

Dieser Unfall geschah bei Nacht. Da man in großer Entfernung das Feuer hinter der Front sah und schießen hörte, so geschahen Allarm-Schüsse, und das Lager mußte sogleich abgebrochen werden. Mein [**90**] Dragoner-Pferdt hatte ich einem Bauern von holländischer Abkunft, deren es hier sehr viele giebt, anvertraut, daß er es auf seiner Wiese weiden ließ. Als wir nun aufbrechen mußten, gab ich dieses Pferd für verloren. Denn es war wohl ¾ Stunden weit entfernt. Doch ich war noch nicht mit Allem fertig, als ich es zu meiner Verwunderung schon an dem Piquet-Pfahl stehen sah. Es wußte aus Erfahrung, was diese Schüsse bedeuteten, und war sogleich über den Zaun gesprungen und in vollem Rennen nach seinem, ihm bekannten Platze gelaufen.

Als man von dem Vorgang unterrichtet war, blieb das Lager auf seiner Stelle; es wurde aber am Ufer, wo der Fluß am schmalsten ist, eine Batterie von Zwölfpfündern und Haubizen errichtet, um die feindlichen Schiffe bei der Rückkehr zu [**91**] empfangen. Sie hielten aber, so viel als möglich, das entgegengesetzte Ufer des sehr breiten Flußes.[313] Doch wurde ein Schiff

---

311. Dragoner: Kavalleristen, ursprünglich berittene und mit einem Gewehr ausgerüstete Infanteristen (der Name spielt darauf an, dass sie wie Drachen Feuer spien).

312. Unze: ca. 30 Gramm.

313. Es könnte sich hier um die „Tappan Zee" genannte seeartige Ausbuchtung des Hudson etwas nördlich von New York City handeln; dies wird bestätigt durch die Angabe bei Selig, Revolutionary Route, S. 104, dass der Angriff bei Tarrytown, N.Y., erfolgte, und zwar in der Nacht des 16.07.1781.

---

bank of the Hudson River, the French on the left, the Americans on the right, divided by a wide ravine, with the right flank towards the river. At that time I had supplied myself with 2 horses, and the colonel [**89**]had granted me a military tent for myself alone. One of the horses came from an English NCO of Dragoons[311] who had deserted with it.

On July 15th, a squadron of 5 small ships (the admiral's ship had 16 guns), sailed up the river trying to cut off our supply line on water. An NCO of Soissonais, with a detachment of 12 American dragoons, obstructed the landing. This NCO was highly honored and was invited to dine at the general's table. Unfortunately one ship, which carried the bread supply for 4 days was seized. (The soldiers were reduced to 4 oz.[312] of bread). They were given some rice and a bit more meat. But the soldiers were all cheerful on this slim diet. The officers set a good example during this difficult march on foot and took the same diet as the soldiers. Each man was allowed 150 lbs. of baggage, including the mattress, all things weighed together. So much was allowed on the company-wagon.

This attack happened at night. Since we could see the fire behind the front and heard gun-fire from afar, alarm shots were given and we had to break camp instantly.[**90**] I had left my Dragoon-horse with a Dutch farmer – there are quite a few Dutch farmers in New York – who agreed to put it to pasture on his meadow. When we had to leave, I thought that the horse would be lost, because it was a ¾ hour ride away. But I was just finishing up, when to my amazement, I saw my horse standing at the picket-stake. He knew from experience what these shots meant and must have jumped over the fence and run at a gallop to reach his well-known tether-spot.

When we were told about the operation, the camp was rebuilt in the same place; but a battery of 12-pounders and howitzers was set up along the river bank, where the river was narrowest, to meet [**91**] the enemy ships upon their return. But they held as closely as possible to the opposite bank of the very wide river.[313] However, one ship went up in flames. 20 men jumped overboard. One

---

311. Dragoon: cavalry man, originally mounted infantry man, armed with a gun (so named as breathing fire like a dragon).

312. 1 ounce equals appr. 30 grams.

313. This may refer to the wide stretch of the Hudson River named "Tappan Zee", north of New York City. This idea is confirmed by Selig's statement that the attack happened close to Tarrytown, N.Y.; Revolutionary Route, p. 104.

angezündet. Zwanzig Mann sprangen über Bord. Einer wurde auf der anderen Seite des Flußes gefangen, und erzählte, eine Haubizgranate habe das Schiff in Brand gesteckt, es sei von mehr als 20 Kugeln durchlöchert gewesen.

Das Regiment Royal-Deuxpont exercirte vor einigen Mitgliedern des Congresses[314]. So wie das Regiment ankam, ließ der Oberst jede Division beim Einschwenken auf der Stelle feuern und alsdann im Attaquiren reteriren, mit veränderter Front in Collonne, und in quarré, immer mit Begleitung der Canonen. Zuletzt kam ein langes, ununterbrochenes Rotten- oder Bataille-Feuer, welches am Rand eines engen Thals, wo die gegenüberstehende, mit Wald bewachsene Seite einen Widerhall gab, sich vortreflich ausnahm. Zur großen Verwunderung der Amerikaner. Denn das französische Exercit[i]um [Exerziermethode] war durch den Grafen St. Germain so zweckmäßig und vernünftig eingerichtet worden, wie es [92] später auch in anderen Diensten überall angenommen wurde.

Am 21. Abends wurden 5000 Mann, wobei 2500 französische Truppen, unter dem Marschal de Campo, Chevalier de Chatellux[315], dedaschirt. Man marschirte die ganze Nacht durch auf Kingsbridge[316] bei New-York, und deployirte[317] in eine Achtung gebietende Stellung, wo wir 48 Stunden blieben und bivauquirten. Die Generale recognocirten und nahmen den Plan allen Werken auf. Ich begleitete den Obersten, als er die Stellung der Engländer besichtigte, und ritt nachher mit dem Hauptmann v. Esbeck[318] hin, wo die Generale Washington und Rochambeau mit ihrer Umgebung standen. Von einer entfernten Schanze, wo man jedoch mit bloßen Augen Hessische oder Ansbachische Soldaten in der blauen Uniform unterscheiden konnte, wurde

soldier was captured across the river, and he told that a howitzer grenade set the ship afire. More than 20 shots had riddled it.

The Royal-Deuxponts Regiment performed some drills for some members of Congress[314]. When the regiment arrived, the colonel had each division fire at the pivot (about-face), and then retreat during an attack with a change of front into a column, and in "quarré" (square), always accompanied by cannon. At the end came a long uninterrupted firing in platoons or battlefield-firing, which sounded very impressive because we were standing in a narrow valley across from a thick forest which produced a fine echo – much to the amazement of the Americans. Count St. Germain had arranged the French "Exercit[i]um" (drill) in such a practical and reasonable fashion [92] that it was later adopted by other armies everywhere.

On the evening of the 21st, 5000 men were detached – 2500 of them French troops – under the Marshal de Campo, Chevalier de Chatellux[315]. We marched all night long to Kingsbridge[316] close to New York, and deployed[317] in an imposing position, where we stayed 48 hours, and bivouacked. The generals reconnoitered and sketched the plan of all fortifications. I accompanied the colonel, when he inspected the position of the English, and afterwards I rode with Captain von Esbeck[318] to assist the Generals Washington and Rochambeau and their entourage. From a distant entrenchment, where, with the naked eye, we could distinguish the Hessian and Ansbach soldiers

---

314. Wohl Mitglieder des im März 1781 aus Angehörigen des 2. Kontinentalkongresses gebildeten, in Philadelphia tagenden sog. Verfassunggebenden Kontinentalkongresses, der bis 1789 regierende Körperschaft der USA war.

315. François Jean Beauvoir, chevalier und später marquis de Chastellux (1734 – 1788), 1747 Leutnant, 1754 Hauptmann, 1761 Oberst, 1769 Brigadegeneral, seit März 1780 maréchal-de-camp und Generalmajor in Rochambeaus Expeditionskorps, seit 1774 Mitglied der Académie Francaise; vgl. Bodinier, Dictionnaire, S. 38 f. sowie Acomb, Journal, S. 343.

316. Nördlich von Yonkers am Hudson im Westchester County.

317. Deployiren: aus der Marschordnung in die Kampfordnung übergehen, aufmarschieren.

318. Heinrich Ludwig Eberhard v. Esebeck (1740 oder 1743 – 1809) war einer von drei Brüdern, die im Regiment Deux-Ponts dienten, zwei davon unter Rochambeau in Amerika. Da sein älterer Bruder seit 1779 bereits Oberstleutnant war, H.L.E. aber 1778 zum Hauptmann befördert worden war, dürfte er hier gemeint sein; s. Bodinier, Dictionnaire, S. 209, sowie Acomb, Journal, S. 348, und Tröss, Regiment, S. 69.

314. It must have been members of the Congress of the Constitution which was formed on March 1st, 1781, from the 2nd continental congress and was the governing body of the U.S. until 1789. It met in Philadelphia.

315. François Jean Beauvoir, chevalier, later marquis de Chastellux (1734 – 1788), lieutenant in the Auvergne regiment in 1747. He was a "maréchal de camp" and major general in Rochambeau's corps as of March, 1780; member of the Académie Francaise in 1774; cf. Bodinier, Dictionnaire, p. 38 f., and Acomb, Journal, p. 343.

316. North of Yonkers on the Hudson river, Westchester County.

317. To take a battle position coming out of a marching order.

318. Three brothers of this noble family served with the Royal Deux Ponts regiment, at least two of them under Rochambeau in America: Henry Louis Eberhard (1743 – 1809) and Louis Eberhard (1740 – 1817). The younger brother was made captain in 1778, the elder was a lieutenant colonel in 1779. Either one of them could be the one mentioned here, but since the author talks of captain von E. he probably means the younger one; cf. Bodinier, Dictionnaire, p. 209; Acomb, Journal, p. 348, and Tröss, Regiment, p. 69.

auf die Generale, die auf einer Erhöhung standen, gezielt. Etwa 30 Schritte vor ihnen war ein Pferd angebunden. Zu dessen Füssen schlug eine Kugel in die Erde, worüber das Pferd sehr wild wurde. Nicht lange darauf schlug eine ganz nahe hinter den Generaln in die [**93**] lockere Erde, so daß der Koth haushoch spritzte. Eine dritte ging wieder bei ihnen vorbei. Ich weiß nicht, wie lange sie dies fortgetrieben haben. Doch so viel ist gewiß, daß Niemand getroffen wurde.[319]

Washington, obwohl es ihm nicht an Muth fehlte, würde doch, wenn er allein gewesen wäre, sich aus Grundsätzen, wie ich glaube, nicht ohne Noth exponirt haben. Da er aber diese Bravade mitmachen mußte, so schien es doch, als ob er sich mit Fleiß quer gegen den Feind stellte, um eine schmählere Front anzubieten. – Auf diese Art wurde der Marschall Turenne bei Sasbach[320] erschossen.

Wir bezogen hierauf wieder das Lager. Am 19ten August aber setzten sich die zwei Armeen wieder in Bewegung. Sie gingen über den Hudson-Fluß. Ein Theil der Armee näherte sich New-York bis ins Angesicht von Statenisland[321], errichtete Oefen, und gab sich den Schein, als wollte man Magazine errichten, so daß General Clinton, der [**94**] jetzt 12 000 Mann in New-York hatte immer glaubte er werde belagert. Plötzlich marschirte die Armee auf den Delaware[322] zu, (durch New-Yersey) und passirte den Fluß zu Trenton[323], wo die Pferde ihn durchwaten konnten. Jetzt sah Clinton wohl, was wir vorhatten. Aber es war zu spät. Der Admiral Grasse war, seinem Versprechen gemäß, in der Chesapeak-Bay angelangt. Endlich kamen

by their blue uniforms, shots were fired at our generals who were standing on an elevation. A horse was tethered about 30 paces away. A cannonball hit the ground near its hooves which drove the horse quite wild. Not long after this one, another cannonball hit into soft earth close behind the generals [93], so that clods shot up very high. A third one flew past them. I do not know how long this lasted, but this I know for sure, that no one was hit.[319]

Washington, who was not lacking in bravery, would, on principle, not have positioned himself in this manner, if he had been alone, in my opinion. But since he was forced into this bravado, it seemed that on purpose he stood with his side towards the enemy, in order to present a narrower front. In a similar position, Marshal Turenne was shot and killed by a cannonball at Sasbach[320].

After this we returned to camp. But on August 19th the two armies were set in motion. We crossed the Hudson River. Part of the army approached New York within view of Staten Island[321], built ovens and pretended to be building storage depots, so that General Clinton [94], who now had 12000 men in New York, continued to believe that we were laying siege. Suddenly the army marched to the Delaware[322] (through New Jersey) and crossed the river at Trenton[323], where the horses could wade across. Now Clinton saw what we were planning. But it was too late. Admiral Grasse had reached Chesapeake Bay, as he had

---

319. Zu diesem Vorfall auch Selig, Revolutionary Route, S. 107 f., wo als Datum der 22.07.1781 genannt ist.

320. Henri de Latour d'Auvergne, vicomte de Turenne (1611 – 1675), 1643 Maréchal de France, einer der bedeutendsten französischen Heerführer vor Napoleon, wurde am 27. Juli 1675 vor der Schlacht von Sasbach (Baden) gegen die kaiserliche Armee bei der Geländeerkundung von einer Kanonenkugel getötet.

321. Staten Island, eine Insel in der Mündung des Hudson, heute einer der fünf Stadtteile (boroughs) von New York City.

322. Insgesamt 660 km langer, schiffbarer Fluss, Grenze zwischen New Jersey und Pennsylvania bzw. zwischen New York und Pennsylvania. Die Gezeiten machen sich bis Trenton bemerkbar. Der Fluss spielte vor dem Bau der Eisenbahnen im Kanalsystem der östlichen USA eine bedeutende Rolle.

323. Seit 1790 Hauptstadt von New Jersey, seit 1679 permanent besiedelt. Der Name geht auf einen der ersten großen Landbesitzer, William Trent, zurück. Am 26.12.1776 errang Washington hier seinen ersten großen militärischen Sieg, als er überraschend den vereisten Delaware überquerte und die in T. stationirten hessischen Söldner schlug. 1784 war T. kurzzeitig Hauptstadt der USA, doch wünschten die südlichen Staaten für diese Funktion eine weiter südlich gelegene Stadt. Seit 1792 Stadtrecht.

319. This incident also reported by Selig, Revolutionary Route, p. 107 f., where July 22nd, 1781, is given as its date.

320. Before the beginning of the battle of Sasbach on the Swiss border on July 27th, 1675, where the Imperial army beat the French, Henri de Latour d'Auvergne, vicomte de Turenne (1611 – 1675), maréchal de France since 1643, one of the most important French military leaders before Napoleon, was killed by a cannonball when reconnoitering the area.

321. Island in the mouth of the Hudson, one of today's five boroughs of New York City.

322. Navigable river in New Jersey and Pennsylvania, about 400 miles long. It forms the border between New Jersey and Pennsylvania as well as – for a shorter stretch – between New York and Pennsylvania. Before the railroads came up the river played an important role in the system of waterways of the eastern U.S.

323. Capital of New Jersey since 1790. Permanent settlement goes back to the year 1679. In 1719, the settlement was named for one of the major landowners, William Trent. On Dec. 26th, 1776, George Washington won his first major military victory at T., when he surprised and routed the Hessian mercenaries stationed there by crossing the frozen Delaware river. In 1784, T. was the capital of the U.S. for several weeks, but the southern states wanted a capital city further south. T. was incorporated as a city in 1792.

die Truppen am 4. September nach Philadelphia, wo sie am Staatenhause[324], vor dem versammelten Congreß defilirten. Wir waren von Newport bis Philadelphia 136 Stunden weit marschirt, und hatten 26 mal das Lager aufgeschlagen. Ich machte von Philadelphia einen Ausflug nach dem etwa 2 Stunden entfernten Germantown[325], welches Pastorius[326] aus Sommerhausen (wo das Haus seiner Eltern noch zu sehen ist) gegründet hat. Der Ort ist 2 Stunden lang, die Häuser sind weit auseinander gebaut. Als ich eine Stunde weit gegangen war, sah ich die Kirche des Ortes. Damit hatte ich genug, und kehrte wieder um.[95] Er hat auch einem Orte, dessen Lage mit der von Sommerhausen Aehnlichkeit hat, den Namen Neu-Sommerhausen[327] gegeben.

Philadelphia selbst ist ein langes Viereck (1/3 Meile lang und halb so breit), dessen eine schmale Seite vom Delaware, die andere von dem kleinen Fluße Schuylkil[328] begränzt ist. Die Stadt ist gleich von Anfang nach einem Plane gebaut worden, nach welchem immer fortgefahren wird. Damals war ¾ davon gebaut, und wir campirten auf dem noch leeren Platze, welcher aber gegenwärtig auch angebaut seyn mag.

---

324. Das State House von Philadelphia wurde in den Jahren 1752 – 1753 im georgianischen Stil für den Staat Pennsylvania erbaut. Sitz des 2. Kontinentalkongresses; Unabhängigkeitserklärung und Verfassung der USA hier unterzeichnet. Heute heißt das Gebäude Independence Hall; es liegt in der Chestnut Street in Philadelphia.

325. Germantown ist ein historischer Stadtteil von Philadelphia; erste Besiedlung 1683 durch deutsche Pietisten aus Krefeld unter Leitung von F.D. Pastorius. Gewerbe wie Weberei, Gerberei und Wagnerei, führten rasch zu wirtschaftlichem Wohlstand. William Rittenhouse errichtete hier 1690 die erste Papiermühle in den Kolonien, 1737 entstand hier eine der größten Druckereien des damaligen Amerika. Im Oktober 1777 konnte Washington in der Schlacht von G. den britischen Verteidigungsring um Philadelphia nicht durchbrechen. G. wurde 1854 nach Philadelphia eingemeindet.

326. Franz Daniel Pastorius (1651-1719) aus Sommerhausen bei Würzburg führte 1683 die erste Gruppe deutscher Siedler nach Amerika. Er legte den Grundriss der neuen Siedlung fest, diente als erster Bürgermeister und unterzeichnete 1688 die erste Petition gegen die Sklaverei in den britischen Kolonien.

327. Neu-Sommerhausen, kleines Städtchen nördlich von Germantown.

328. Schuylkill, etwas über 200 km langer Fluss, dessen gesamter Lauf im Staat Pennsylvania liegt; benannt von seinem holländischen Entdecker. – Mit „Meile" dürfte Rechteren eine deutsche Landmeile zu 7,5 km meinen, wonach die Stadt sich auf 2,5 km Länge und 1,25 km Breite erstreckt hätte. Dies widerspricht der gleichzeitigen Beschreibung von Georg Flohr, der die Stadt auf 3 englische Meilen (4,8 km) in der Länge und Breite schätzte; s. Selig, German Allies, T. 3.1, S. 34. Wahrscheinlich liegen die Schätzungen so weit auseinander, weil 1781, wie Rechteren ja auch ausführt, noch nicht die gesamte Fläche eine städtische Bebauung hatte.

---

promised. On September 4th, the troops finally arrived in Philadelphia, where they passed in review in front of the assembled Congress at the State House[324]. We had marched for 136 hours from Newport to Philadelphia, and had encamped 26 times. From Philadelphia I took an excursion to Germantown[325] which is about two hours distant and which was founded by Pastorius[326] from Sommerhausen (where his parents' house can still be seen). Germantown stretches over a distance of two hours; the houses are built far apart from each other. After I had hiked for about an hour, I could see the church tower. That was enough for me and I turned back. [95] He (Pastorius) gave the name Neu-Sommerhausen[327] to a village whose position is similar to that of Sommerhausen.

Philadelphia itself is a long square (one third of a mile long and about half as wide), the one narrow side is bordered by the Delaware River, the other one by the little river Schuylkil (Schuylkill)[328]. This is a planned city, built on a square grid that can be extended. At this time about ¾ of it was built up, and we camped on the empty blocks, which today may be built up, too.

---

324. The Pennsylvania State House was built for the province of Pennsylvania in Georgian style in the years 1752-1753. It became the seat of the second Continental Congress, and both the Declaration of Independence and the Constitution of the United States were signed here. Today it is named Independence Hall; it is situated on Chestnut Street in Philadelphia.

325. Germantown, historic residential area of Philadelphia, PA, first settled by German pietists from Krefeld, led by F.D. Pastorius of Sommerhausen, in 1683. Trades such as weaving, tanning, and wagon building soon led to prosperity. William Rittenhouse built the first papermill in the colonies in 1690; in 1737, one of the colonies' largest printing presses was established here. On Oct. 4th, 1777, Washington's Continental Army did not succeed in breaking the defenses of British-occupied Philadelphia there. G. was annexed to Philadelphia in 1854.

326. Franz (Francis) Daniel Pastorius (1651 – 1719) of Sommerhausen in Franconia led the first German settlers to the American colonies in 1683. He laid out the settlement of Germantown, served as its first mayor, and signed, in 1688, the first antislavery petition in the British colonies.

327. New Sommerhausen, north of Germantown, Pennsylvania.

328. The whole length – about 120 miles – of the Schuylkill river is situated in Pennsylvania. It was named by its discoverer. The author again seems to refer to the German landmile of about 7.5 km (or 4.5 English miles); the city thus would have had about 1.75 English miles in length, 0.8 miles in width. This is contradicted by George Flohr, a soldier in the Deux-Ponts regiment who was there at the same time; according to him it was about 3 English miles long and wide; cf. Selig, Washington's German Allies, pt. 3.1, p. 34. This discrepancy can probably be explained by the fact that not all of the laid-out area was built up at the time, as our author indicates.

Von hier marschirte die Armee zu Land durch Virginien. Die Grenadiere und Jäger unter Befehl des Obersten und Brigadiers, Grafen Custine, wurden auf kleinen Schiffen zu Head of Elk[329] eingeschifft, um so die Bay von Chesapeak hinunter zu fahren, und die Festung Yorktown[330], wo Cornwallis sich verschanzt hatte, zu berennen (investir.) Der Oberst G[raf] Zweibruck war mit eingeschifft, **[96]** und [ich] in seiner Begleitung. Gleich im Anfang hatten wir starken Nebel, und als er sich aufklärte, war der Graf Custine, unser Commandant, verschwunden. Da man nun nicht wußte, ob nicht die Engländer an der Mündung der Chesapeak-Bay wären, getraute man sich nicht, weiter zu segeln, und wir liefen in Annapolis[331] ein. Nach kurzem Aufenthalt allda segelten wir weiter, und liefen in den James-Fluß[332] ein, und kamen nach Williamsburg[333], 3 Stunden von Yorktown. Unser Corps war schon angekommen, vermehrt durch 3 Regimenter aus den Inseln, Touraine[334], Agenois[335] und Gatinois[336], und die Volontairs vom General St. Simon. Die französische Armee belief sich auf 7000 und die Amerikanischen Continental-Truppen auf 4000, wozu noch

From here the army marched through Virginia. The grenadiers and riflemen under the command of Colonel and Brigadier Count Custine boarded small ships at Head of Elk[329] in order to sail down Chesapeake Bay and attack the fortress of Yorktown[330], where Cornwallis had dug his entrenchments. Colonel Count von Zweibruck[en] was on board [96] and [I] was with him. At the beginning we were fogbound, and when it lifted, our commander, Count Custine, had disappeared. Since we suspected that the English were waiting at the mouth of Chesapeake Bay, we were worried about sailing on, so we put into Annapolis[331]. After a short time there, we sailed on and put into the James River[332], and came to Williamsburg[333], 3 hours distance from Yorktown. Our Corps had already arrived, plus the addition of 3 regiments from the islands: Touraine[334], Agenois[335], and Gatinois[336], and the volunteers of General St. Simon. The French army numbered 7000 and the American Continental Troops 4000; added to this were 2000 men of the Virginia

---

329. Head of Elk, heute: Elkton und Elk Neck, gegenüber Havre de Grace im nördlichen Maryland.

330. 1691 als Exporthafen für Tabak gegründet und bis heute – obwohl es nur etwa 200 Einwohner hat – die Kreisstadt des gleichnamigen County, das wiederum zu den acht ältesten von Virginia gehört.

331. Hauptstadt von Maryland seit 1695, 1649 von Puritanern gegründet. 1783/84 trat hier der Kongress der USA zusammen. Das „State House" wurde 1772–1779 errichtet. Seit 1845 ist A. Sitz der Marineakademie der USA.

332. Fluss im Staat Virginia, der im Allegheny-Gebirge entspringt und über 547 km im Wesentlichen nach Süden in die Chesapeake-Bucht fließt.

333. Selbstständige Stadt auf der Halbinsel zwischen dem James- und York-Fluss, 1633 erstmals unter dem Namen „Middle Plantation" besiedelt, diente zunächst als Fluchtort bei Indianerüberfällen. Das College „William and Mary", eines der ältesten in den USA, wurde schon 1639 gegründet. Als 1699 Jamestown niederbrannte, wurde W. Hauptstadt von Virginia, benannt nach König William III. Im Mai 1776 forderte hier die Versammlung von Virginia den Kontinentalkongress auf, die Unabhängigkeit zu erklären. 1780 wurde Richmond Hauptstadt und W. verlor rasch an Bedeutung. – „Colonial W.", eine restaurierte Stadt, wurde nach 1926 erbaut.

334. Regiment Touraine, gegründet 1625 als Regt. du Plessis Joigny, 1781 in Yorktown eingesetzt; s. http://xenophongroup.com/mcjoynt/regts.htm

335. Regiment Agénois, gegr. als Regt. Balagny 1595, 1762 Béarn benannt; 1780/81 eingesetzt in Savannah, Yorktown und Pensacola; vgl. o.

336. Regiment Gatinois = Gatinais, Auvergne; gegr. 1606 als Regt. du Bourg, 1635 Auvergne; 1780/81 eingesetzt in Savannah, Yorktown und Pensacola; vgl. o.

---

329. Today Elkton and Elk Neck, across from Havre de Grace, northern Maryland.

330. Yorktown, VA, was founded in 1691 for the export of tobacco and – even though it only has about 200 inhabitants – it is the county seat of Yorktown county, one of Virginia's eight oldest counties.

331. Annapolis, capital of Maryland since 1695, was founded by Puritans in 1649. In 1783/84, Congress met here. The State House was built 1772–1779. It has been the seat of the Naval Academy since 1845.

332. River in Virgina which rises in the Allegheny mountains and flows mainly south into Chesapeake Bay. It is 340 miles long and is tidal almost to the state capital, Richmond.

333. Williamsburg, VA, an independent city on the tidewater peninsula between the James and York rivers. It was first settled in 1633 as Middle Plantation and served as a refuge from Indian attacks. The college of William and Mary, one of the oldest in the U.S., was founded in 1693. In 1699, after Jamestown had burned down the town became the capital of Virginia and was renamed in honour of king William III. In the Capitol building, Patrick Henry presented his protest against the Stamp Act in 1765. In May 1776, the Virginia Convention urged the Continental Congress to declare independence. In 1780, the state government was moved to Richmond and W.'s importance declined. – Colonial W., a restored town, was set up after 1926.

334. The Touraine regiment was founded in 1625 as du Plessis Joigny regiment and was deployed at Yorktown in 1781; cf. http://xenophongroup.com/mcjoynt/regts.htm

335. The Agénois regiment was founded in 1595 as Balagny regiment, in 1762 renamed Béarn; deployed at Savannah, Yorktown, and Pensacola in 1780/1781; cf. above.

336. The Gatinois regiment was founded in 1606 as du Bourg regiment, renamed Auvergne in 1635, deployed the same way as Agénois in 1780/1781; cf. above.

2000 Virginische Milizen unter Obrist Nelson[337] kamen. Diese marschirten alle auf Yorktown um die Belagerung zu beginnen.

Die Stadt Yorktown liegt an dem breiten Fluß York; gegenüber liegt Glo[u]cester[338]. Dieses **[97]** wurde durch die Legion von Lauzun und 1500 amerikanischen Milizen unter General Choisy berannt. Die Festung Yorktown war eigentlich ein verschanztes Lager. Die Werke liefen in Gestallt eines Halbmondes, dessen zwei Spitzen bis an den Fluß reichten. Vor der Spitze, welche, vom Fluß aus gesehen, die rechte war, lag eine Schlucht, welche parallel mit der Festung lief. Diese war durch Schanzen und ein Verhau vertheidigt. Wo diese Schlucht aufhörte, waren zwei Redouten[339] und eine Batterie. Es schien jedoch, daß der Feind sich nicht getraute, diese äußere Linie zu vertheidigen, und fürchtete, tournirt zu werden. Denn man fand sie des Morgens verlassen. Sie wurde gleich besetzt, und der Feind in einen viel engeren Zirkel eingeschlossen. Als wir ankamen, sah man nur eine einzige Schießscharte, für den Retraite Schuß-Abends[340]. General Viomenil wollte, man sollte gleich stürmen, was Cornwallis erwartete. Es hätte da- **[98]** bei gehen können, wie kurz zuvor dem Grafen D'Estaing[341] bei Savannah, der mit Verlust von ein Paar tausend Mann abgeschlagen wurde. Außer den Kanonen, Mörsern[342] und Haubitzen[343] auf den Wällen waren noch die Steinstücke

militia under Colonel Nelson[337]. These all marched together in order to begin the siege of Yorktown.

Yorktown is situated on the wide York river, opposite is the town of Glocester (Gloucester)[338]. [97]This was besieged by the Lauzun Legion and 1500 American militiamen under General Choisy. The fortress of Yorktown was actually an entrenched camp. The trenches ran in the form of a half-moon, with the two tips reaching to the river. In front of the tip, which seen from the river was on the right-hand, lay a ravine, which ran parallel to the fortress. This was protected by trenches and a barricade. Where this ravine ended there were two redoubts[339] and a battery. It seemed that the enemy did not dare defend this outer line, and feared to be beaten back . For we found it empty on the next morning. It was occupied right away to pull a much tighter circle around the enemy. When we arrived we saw only one single embrasure (crenel) for the "Retraite" (tattoo) shot at sundown.[340] General Viomenil wanted us to attack right away which Cornwallis was expecting. That could have turned out [98] as it recently had for Comte d'Estaing in Savannah[341], who was beaten back with the loss of several thousand men. Apart from the cannon, mortars[342] and howitzers[343] on the ramparts

---

337. Thomas Nelson (1738 – 1789), 1781 Gouverneur von Virginia, führte die Miliz von Virginia bei Yorktown. Gab danach das Gouverneursamt auf und zog sich auf ein kleines Gut zurück; s. Acomb, Journal, S. 358.

338. Gloucester, county (Kreis) in Virginia, besteht seit 1651, benannt nach dem dritten Sohn von König Karl I., der Herzog von Gloucester war. Es liegt ca. 120 km östlich von Richmond am York-Fluss und an der Chesapeake-Bucht. Es war der Hauptort des indianischen Powhatan-Bundes, wo 1607 der englische Siedler John Smith von der Prinzessin Pocahontas vor der Hinrichtung bewahrt wurde. Der Unabhängigkeitskrieg endete in Yorktown, das direkt gegenüber dem Gloucester Point liegt; nur die Anwesenheit einer französischen Flotte verhinderte, dass Cornwallis sich mit seinen Truppen dorthin zurückziehen konnte.

339. Befestigung in der Form eines vorgelagerten Vorwerks, meist eckig und ohne Flankenverteidigung.

340. Kanonenschuss, meist um 22 Uhr als Signal für die Soldaten, in die Quartiere zurückzukehren, im Englischen oft „tattoo" (nach niederländisch „tap toe", d. h. Ende des Ausschanks).

341. Charles Hector, comte d'Estaing (1729 – 1794), 1777 Konteradmiral, wurde beim Angriff auf Savannah, Georgia, 1779 schwer verwundet; er wurde während der Herrschaft des „terreur" 1794 in Paris hingerichtet. – Savannah, Georgia, 1733 von General James Oglethorpe und britischen Siedlern gegründet. 1751 wurde Georgia königliche Kolonie, S. deren erste Hauptstadt und, nach 1763, ein Zentrum des Pelzhandels. 1779 gelang es einer amerikanisch-französischen Armee nicht, das von britischen Loyalisten gehaltene S. einzunehmen.

342. Kurzes Geschütz für steile Schusswinkel.

343. Geschütz für steiles Feuer mit geringeren Geschossgeschwindigkeiten als reguläre Kanonen.

---

337. Thomas Nelson (1738 – 1789), governor of Virginia in 1781, commanded the Virginia militia at Yorktown. He then renounced the governor's office and retired to his small property; cf. Acomb, Journal, p. 358.

338. Gloucester county in Virginia was founded in 1651 and named for the third son of king Charles I. of England who was duke of G. It is situated east of Richmond, the capital of Virginia, and borders on the York river and Chesapeake Bay. It was the seat of the Powhatan confederacy where, in 1607, the English settler John Smith was saved by the Indian princess Pocahontas. The American War of Independence ended in Yorktown, directly opposite of Gloucester Point; only the presence of a French fleet prevented Cornwallis from retreating there.

339. Fortification in the form of an outwork or field work usually square and without flanking defences.

340. Cannon shot at 10 p.m. recalling soldiers to quarters, often called „tattoo" from the Dutch „taptoe" (closing the tap of the cask, i.e. end of the sale of liquor).

341. Charles Hector, count d'Estaing (1729 – 1794), was seriously wounded in an attack on Savannah, Georgia, Sept – Oct. 1779. Guillotined in Paris during the reign of terror. – Savannah, Georgia, was founded by General James Oglethorpe and a group of 113 English settlers in 1733. In 1751, Georgia was made a royal colony, S. became the first capital and , after 1763, an important center of the fur trade. In 1779, an American-French army failed to take S. which was under the sway of British loyalists.

342. Short piece of ordnance for throwing shells at high angles.

343. Ordnance for firing shells at high angles at lower velocities than a regular cannon.

there now were the stone-pieces ("pirriers") taken from the ships, ready to greet the enemy. In the night of October 7th, the first "tranchée" (trench) was opened, at a distance of 450-500 "toise"[344] on the right, where the enemy had projecting earth-works, on the left at only 300 toise. These stretched out for 600-700 toise (the toise at 6 shoes), with 4 fine redoubts. – The reason that the generals chose this distance was the reputation of General Cornwallis and the strength of the garrison.

From the 8th to the 9th, the regiments Gatinois and Royal Deuxponts under St. Simon and Custine relieved the regiments Bourbonnois and Saintonge. The regiment marched in the flank [99]by squads, so that only two men were in the front. For in this American war, the infantry was never deployed other than in twos, because the cavalry, against which you need more strength, was not so considerable there.

General Vioménil was reviewing as the troops marched past him. Our Colonel said to him: "Mon Général, je vais mener mon Régiment aux coups de Canon pour la première fois." – "Avec gloire sans doute," was the general's answer.[345] Right after this, two cannonballs, looking just like bowling balls came bouncing over a little hill, which protected us. And since the regiment formed a hook at right angles and the front part was arranged towards the city, the balls flew past this and flew straight into the latter, whereby an adjutant named Ruf lost his arm, and a soldier lost his life. The enemy had heard the sound of [100]our drums and howitzers, and directed some ricochet-shots[346] over there. Washington to whom our colonel told this, replied, "It's only inviting a shot!" ("daß heißt nur einen Schuß herbeilocken"). From this time on we marched into the trenches very quietly.

On the 10th all the batteries were ready, andv heavy firing with cannon and bomb-throwing began. The "Charon", an English warship which hampered the left wing of

---

344. French linear measure equalling approx 1.95 meters (6' 6").

345. "General, I am about to lead my regiment into cannon fire for the first time." – "With glory, doubtlessly", was the answer.

346. Shooting indirectly, hoping to hit a goal, which cannot be hit directly, with ricocheting cannon balls. – There seems to be a mistake in the mscr. here, probably made by the copyist. The German text says that the "blowing of our howitzers and drums" was heard, but Rechteren who often uses French terms probably wrote "our haut-bois" were heard. Unlike today's orchestral oboes, "haut-bois" (as the French word indicates) produced a very loud tone; they were the woodwinds most used by the military bands of that time.

„Charon", ein englisches Kriegsschiff, welches den linken Flügel der Attaque incommandirte, ward mit glühenden Kugeln in Brand geschossen. Am Abend waren die Batterien des Feindes zum Schweigen gebracht. In der Nacht antwortete er nur mit leichten Stücken. Vom 11ten bis 12ten rückte Gatinois und Deuxpont wieder in die Tranchée.

Jetzt wurde zur zweiten Parall[e]le, in der Entfernung von 180 Toisen, oder 1080 Schuh, geschritten. Die linke Seite fing beim Ende der Schlucht an; auf der rechten Seite waren aber noch 2 feindliche [101] Schanzen vorwärts der Festung, wo die Parallele nicht bis an den Fluß gezogen werden konnte, sondern mit einem Epaulement[347] gegen die Schanze endete. Da in dem Reglement steht, daß die Officiere, die auf den gefährlichsten Posten bei den Arbeitern sind, Cuirasse[348] anlegen sollen, was aber außer Brauch ist, so standen am Eingange der Tranchée zwei Fässer mit Cuirassen und Pickelhauben als Antiquitäten da, deren sich Niemand bediente. Dieß kam den Amerikanern, die als ganz neue Völker Nichts von Ueberlieferungen aus den Ritterzeiten wissen sehr wunderlich vor.

Vom 14ten bis zum 15ten kam Gatinois und Royal Deuxponts wieder in die Tranchée[349]. Die 2 Schanzen vor der Festung, welche in der Continuation unserer zweiten Parallele lagen, sollte mit Sturm genommen werden. Der Marquis de la Fayette mit der amerikanischen leichten Infanterie wurde mit dem Angriff auf die Redoute auf der rechten Seite an dem Fluß, [102] und der Baron de Viomenil mit den französischen Truppen gegen die nächste Schanze beauftragt. Um 8 Uhr marschirten die 4 Compagnien Grenadiere und Jäger von Gatinois und Royal Deuxponts, soutenirt[350] von den Regimentern Gatinois und Bourbonnois, in größter Stille gerade gegen die erste Redoute, und die Amerikaner eben so gegen die andere. Die Gewehre wurden nicht geladen. Die Dispositionen des B[aron] de Viomenil und des Grafen Guillaume de Deuxponts, des Bruders von unserem Obersten und des Lt. Colonel de l'Escadre von Gatinois waren so gut genommen, daß die Schanze mit dem Bayonnet erobert wurde. Es waren blos Hessen in der Schanze. Sie feuerten eine Zeitlang; doch als die Hindernisse des Grabens und Verhaues und der Palisaden beseitigt waren, half kein Widerstand mehr. Ein großer Theil blieb oder ward verwundet. Ein Major, 6 Subaltern-Officiere und 68 Mann wurden gefangen genommen,

our attack was set afire by our incendiary bombs. In the evening, the enemy batteries had been silenced. During the night they answered only with light artillery. From the 11th to the 12th, the Gatinois and the Deuxpont regiments took the trench duty again.

Now a second line of parallels [trenches] were drawn, at a distance of 180 "toise", or 1080 "shoes" (feet). The left side began at the end of the ravine; on the right side there were 2 enemy earth works [101]in front of the fortress, where the parallels could not be drawn up to the river, but ended with a parapet or breast-work[347] against the entrenchment. Since our regulations state that the officers, who are with the workers at the most dangerous posts, are to wear cuirasse[348] which are no longer used, two barrels with suits of armor and spiked helmets were standing as antiques at the entrances to the trenches; nobody put them on. This must have looked most amazing to the Americans, who being a very new nation, knew little about the traditions from the bygone age of knights.

From the 14th to the 15th the Gatinois and the Royal Deuxponts took to the trenches[349] again. The two entrenchments in front of the fortress, which lay in the continuation of our second parallel, were to be taken by storm. The Marquis de la Fayette with the American light infantry was charged to attack the redoubts on the right side close to the river [102], and the Baron de Viomenil with the French troops,was to attack the next redoubt. At 8 p.m. the 4 companies grenadiers and riflemen of Gatinois and Royal Deuxponts, assisted[350] by the regiments Gatinois and Bourbonnois marched quietly up to the first redoubts, and the Americans up to the other one. The guns were not loaded. The dispositions of Baron de Vioménil and of Count Guillaume de Deuxponts, the brother of our colonel and the Lt. Colonel de l'Escadre of Gatinois, were so well thought out (or: complied with ?) that the redoubt was captured with the bayonet alone. There were only Hessians in the redoubt. They fired for a while; but when the obstacles of the trench, the barricade and the palisades had been overcome, they gave up their resistance. A large number were killed or wounded. One major, six subordinate officers, and 68 soldiers were taken prisoner, and two

---

347. Epaulement: Brustwehr mit Sandsäcken
348. Küraß: lederne Brustwehr
349. Tranchée: Laufgraben bei einer Belagerung
350. Soutenieren: unterstützen

347. Often fortified only by sandbags.
348. Leather suit of armor.
349. The author again uses the French word for "trench" here.
350. The author uses a French loanword for "assist" unusual in present-day German.

und 2 kleine Haubitzen erobert. Nach dem Feuern wurde es auf einmal stille, und [103] darauf hörten wir 3 mal „Vive le Roi!" rufen.

Dieses verursachte nun ein fürchterliches Feuer aus der Festung; alle Kanonen waren auf diese Werke gerichtet. Es war als wenn Alles in Feuer von dieser Seite stände. Wir glaubten, sie wollten aus der Festung ausfallen und die Tranchéen angreifen. Deshalb mußten Alle aus der Tranchée heraus und sich auf den inneren Rand stellen. Ein Hagel von Kugeln ging über die Köpfe weg und zwischen den Bayonetten, durch. Wir machten uns gefaßt, wenn der Feind auf der äußeren Brustwehre stände, die Gewehre abzufeuern und zugleich mit dem Feind in die Tranchée zu springen.

Als endlich alles ruhiger wurde, hörten wir wieder ein Geplänkel vom linken Flügel. Der Graf Custine hatte einen falschen Angriff von dieser Seite veranstalten sollen, um die Aufmerksamkeit des Feindes von dem Haupt- [104] punct abzuziehen. Jetzt kam dies aber hinterdrein, nachdem alles vorbei war, um ½ 9 statt ½ 8, wie bestimmt worden war, und kostete 9 Menschen das Leben. Auch wurde dadurch wieder ein allgemeines Musketen- und Kartätschenfeuer aus der Festung veranlaßt, wo man einen neuen Angriff vermuthete. Man glaubte, daß Custine wieder einmal zu viel ins Glas gekuckt.[351]

Der Oberst, welcher heute mich hatte um sich haben wollen, war um seinen Bruder besorgt, und befahl mir, mich nach ihm zu erkundigen. Ich ging gegen die Redoute, wo ich gleich dem Chevalier Alexander la Methe[352] begegnete, welcher auf einem branquard[353] getragen wurde. Eine Musketenkugel hatte ihm die linke Kniescheibe zerschmettert, und eine andere das rechte Knie durchbohrt. Er wurde gut curirt, und ich sah ihn 30 Jahre nachher, anno 1811 in Würzburg als Commandanten der französischen Garnison.

Ich konnte im Dunkeln den näch- [105] sten Weg nicht finden, und aus der Stadt schnurrten noch immer Kugeln vorbei. In

small howitzers were captured. After the firing, it was suddenly very quiet, [103] and then we heard someone shout "Vive le Roi" for three times.

This resulted in a terrible cannonade out of the fortress: all of their guns were directed against these entrenchments. It seemed that everything was under fire from that side. We expected them to sally out of the fortress and attack the trenches. For this reason all were ordered out of the trenches and had to position themselves on their inner edge. A hail-storm of bullets flew over our heads and between the bayonets. If the enemy should appear on the outer breastworks, we were prepared to fire our guns and jump into the trench at the same time as the enemy.

When things finally quieted down, we again heard a skirmish from the left wing. Comte Custine was supposed to have staged a decoy attack from this side, in order to attract the attention of the enemy [104] away from the central point. But now it came way too late, when all the shooting was over – at 8:30 instead of 7:30, as had been agreed upon, and lost us the lives of nine men. Also the fortress where they assumed that a new attack was being started answered again with general musket and shrapnel fire. We suspected that Custine, once again, had been deep in his cups.[351]

The colonel, who wanted me to be around him today, was worried about his brother, and ordered me to check on him. I went to the redoubts, where I met Chevalier Alexander la Methe[352], who was being carried on a stretcher[353]. A musket-ball had smashed his left knee-cap, and another one had shot through his right knee. He received good medical treatment, and I saw him 30 years later in Würzburg, anno 1811, where he was commander of the French garrison. [105]

I could not find my way in the dark, and from the city some shots were still flying around. In this predicament,

---

351. S. o. Anm. 260.

352. Alexandre, comte de Lameth (1760 – 1829), nahm mit seinem Bruder Charles François (1757 – 1832) am Feldzug in Amerika teil. Nach Acomb, Journal, S. 353, war es Charles, der in Yorktown verwundet wurde; Alexandre wurde geschickt, um ihn zu ersetzen. Beide Brüder machten danach bedeutende Karrieren als Militärs, Abgeordnete in der Nationalversammlung und in der Staatsverwaltung unter Napoleon.

353. Branquard: Tragbahre

---

351. Cf. above, fn. 260.

352. Alexandre Theodore Victor, comte de Lameth (1760 – 1829), took part in the American revolution together with his brother Charles François (1757 – 1832). According to Acomb, Journal, p. 353, it was Charles who was wounded at Yorktown and Alexandre was sent to replace him. Both brothers later had notable careers as military officers, representatives in the "Assemblée Nationale", and as administrators after Napoleon had come to power.

353. The author uses the French term "branquard".

dieser Verlegenheit begegnete ich dem Hauptmann von Stack[354], der Adjudant bei einem General war, und eben so im Dunkeln irrte. Wir kehrten also beide zurück, denn der Graf Zweibruck war nicht mehr da. Es hatte ihm eine Kugel beim Ersteigen des Walles, in welchen sie hineinschlug, die Erde mit solcher Gewalt in die Augen gespritzt, daß man für sein Gesicht fürchtete.

Als es Tag wurde, sah ich die Schanze, die einen empörenden Anblick darbot. Denn die Todten lagen nackt ausgezogen da. Von da ging ich in die andere Schanze, wo Lafayette als Sieger auf einer Trommel saß. Ich ließ mich ihm vorstellen.

Die eroberten Redouten wurden nun gleich in die Parallele gezogen. Der Hauptmann von Mühlenfels[355], welcher, wie ich glaube, noch am Leben ist, und in Stut- **[106]** gardt mit dem Titel als General pensionirt ist, commandirte die Compagnie Jäger, und der Hauptmann von Hake[356], dessen Bruder noch kürzlich in Gotha lebte, die Grenadiere.

Am 16ten mit Tagesanbruch machten die Engländer einen Ausfall mit 600 Mann leichter Infanterie unter Oberstleutnant Abercromby[357]. Sie überfielen einen Hauptmann von Agenois mit 50 Mann in einer Redoute und vernagelten 4 Kanonen. Sie wurden aber verhindert, weiter in die Tranchée einzufallen; und die Kanonen konnten denselben Abend wieder gebraucht werden. Nun wurden die neuen Batterien von der II. Parallele mit schwerem Geschütz versehen.

I met Captain von Stack[354], who was a general's adjutant, and was also wandering around in the dark. We both returned together, for Count Zweibrucken was no longer there. When he had been scaling the wall, a cannonball hit close-by and had hurled some soil into his eyes with such great force that all were afraid for his eyesight.

At daybreak, I saw the entrenchments which presented a shocking scene, for naked dead bodies were strewn all about. From there I went to the other redoubt where I found Lafayette, as the victor, sitting on a drum. I asked to be introduced to him.

The conquered redoubts were immediately pulled into the parallels. Captain von Mühlenfels[355], who, I believe, is still alive and lives in Stuttgart **[106]** as a retired general, commanded the company of riflemen ("Jäger"), and Captain von Hake[356] whose brother lived in Gotha not too long ago, commanded the grenadiers.

At daybreak on the 16th, the English attempted a sortie under Lt. Col. Abercromby[357] with 600 light infantry. They attacked an Agénois captain with 50 men in a redoubt and boarded up 4 cannon. But they were repulsed and did not get any further in the trench; and the cannon could be used again that very evening. Now the new batteries of the second parallels were equipped with heavy artillery.

---

354. Da vier Offiziere dieses Namens 1781 in Amerika dienten, ist nicht klar, welcher von ihnen hier gemeint ist: evtl. Johann Franz Anton von Stack, 1740 in Sarreguemines (Saargemünd) geboren, 1769 Hauptmann und Adjutant Vioménils; er war wohl 1801 noch am Leben; oder: Eloy François Joseph de Stack, geboren 1763 (?) in Fénétrange (Lothringen), Kommandant der Chasseurs im Regiment Royal Deux-Ponts; s. Tröss, Regiment, S. 68.

355. Vermutlich Karl Adam (1828 Graf) v. Mühlenfels (1748-1838), k.u.k. Geh. Rat, kgl. württemb. Kammerherr und Reisemarschall, s. Gothaisches genealog. Taschenbuch der Gräflichen Häuser auf das Jahr 1868, 41. Jg., S. 1076; Gothaisches genealog. Taschenbuch der Briefadeligen Häuser 1907, 1. Jg., S. 547-551; auch Acomb, Journal, S. 357.

356. Hauptmann v. Hake: s. o. Anm. 242.

357. Sir Robert Abercromby (1740 – 1827), in der Schlacht von Ticonderoga 1758 zum Fähnrich ernannt, nahm an den Schlachten von Brooklyn, Brandywine und Germantown sowie an der Kapitulation von Yorktown teil, 1782 Oberst und Adjutant des Königs. Er machte in Indien seit 1788 eine bedeutende militärische Karriere, wurde 1798 Abgeordneter im Parlament, 1801 Kommandant der Burg von Edinburgh und 1802 General. Er starb 1827 als ältester General der britischen Armee in Airthrey in Schottland; s. auch Acomb, Journal, S. 339.

354. Of the four officers of this name serving in America at the time the one mentioned here was probably Johann Franz Anton von Stack, born at Sarreguemines Jan. 17th, 1740. He served in several French regiments from 1758, had the rank of captain in 1769, and was Vioménil's adjutant in America. He was probably still alive in 1801, but it may have been Eloy François Joseph de Stack, born 1763 (?) in Fénétrange, Lorraine, commander of the "chasseurs" in the regiment; cf. Bodinier, Dictionnnaire, p. 514, and Tröss, Regiment, p. 68.

355. Probably Karl von Mühlenfels (1748 – 1838, created count in 1828), Imperial and Royal Privy Councillor, Royal Württemberg chamberlain and travelling marshal, cf. Gothaisches genealogisches Taschenbuch der Gräflichen Häuser auf das Jahr 1868, 41. year, p. 1076, or Gothaisches genealogisches Taschenbuch der briefadligen Häuser 1907, 1. year, p. 547 – 551; also: Acomb, Journal, p. 357.

356. Cf. above, fn. 242.

357. Sir Robert Abercromby (1740 – 1827), brother of the more famous Sir Ralph A., appointed ensign at the battle of Ticonderoga in 1758. Present at battles of Brooklyn, Brandywine, and Germantown as well as at the capitulation at Yorktown. Colonel and aide-de-camp to the king in 1782. Member of Parliament 1798, governor of Edinburgh castle in 1801, full general in 1802. Died at Airthrey, Scotland, in 1827 as the oldest general in the British army; cf. Acomb, Journal, p. 339.

Am 17ten besetzte das Regiment Bourbonnais und Royal Deux Ponts die Tranchée. Das Feuer der Batterien, denen der Feind nichts als leichte Stücke und Haubitzen entgegensetzen konnte, war jetzt so furchtbar, daß man erwarten mußte, auf die Nacht würde [107] gestürmt werden.

Da kam um 1 Uhr Nachmittags ein Officier herüber, der ein weißes Schnupftuch schwenkte. Cornwallis erbat sich einen Waffenstillstand von 24 Stunden. Es wurden aber im Anfang nur 2 gestattet. Als diese abgelaufen waren, wurde der Waffenstillstand von neuem verlängert, so daß man sich von beiden Seiten ruhig auf die Brustwehr stellte, bis zur bestimmten Minute, wo es zu Ende ging und jeder wieder herunterstieg, weil man glaubte, das Feuern werde sogleich wieder angehen. Dies geschah einige Male. Der Waffenstillstand wurde am 18ten fortgesetzt, und am 19ten wurde die Capitulation unterzeichnet.

Da es nun Sitte ist, daß die Truppen, die in der Tranchée sind, wenn der Feind zu capituliren anfangt, drinnen bleiben, bis der Feind die Festung übergiebt, wie auf dem Ehrenposten, „poste d'honneurs", so blieb das Regiment jetzt 52 Stunden unter freiem Himmel.

[108] Am 19. October um Mittag besetzte ein Detachement Amerikaner und die Grenadiere von Bourbonnais 2 Schanzen der Festung nach der Capitulation. Um 2 Uhr defilirte die Garnison von Yorktown vor der combinirten Armee, die in 2 Linien stand, so daß die Engländer die Franzosen auf der rechten, die Amerikaner auf der linken Seite hatten. Cornwallis war zum Schein krank, und General Ohara[358] an seiner Stelle. Gleich wo die Linie anfing, war General Rochambeau vor seinen Truppen, und Washington gegenüber mit Lafayette bei den Amerikanern. Die Kränkung sich vor den Amerikanern demüthigen zu müssen, war zu groß für die Engländer. General Ohara, an der Spitze der Garnison, wendete sich an General Rochambeau, indem er seinen Hut abzog. (Denn daß er seinen Degen überreichte, habe ich nicht gesehen.) Dieser wies ihn aber an General Washington. [109] Hierauf defilirte das ganze Corps durch die Linie, stellte sich auf einer Ebene in Front und nahm das Gewehr bei Fuß. Dann wurden alle Gewehre in Haufen

On the 17th, the regiments Bourbonnais and Royal Deux-Ponts occupied the trenches. The fire of our batteries, to which the enemy could only respond with light artillery and howitzer fire, was now so heavy that we had to expect that we would storm at [107] night.

Then at 1 o'clock in the afternoon, an officer came over waving a white handkerchief. Cornwallis asked for a 24 hour truce. But at first he was only allowed two hours. When this time was up, the truce was extended again, so that on both sides the soldiers quietly leaned against the breast-works, up to the minute when the time ran out and then everyone climbed down again, because we believed that the firing would start up again right then. This was repeated several times. The truce was continued on the 18th, and then on the 19th the terms of capitulation were signed.

As it is the custom that the units which are in the trenches when the enemy starts negotiations on the capitulation stay there until the enemy surrenders the fortress, so the whole regiment remained outdoors for 52 hours on the "poste d'honneurs" (post of honor). [108]

On October 19th, at noon after the capitulation, a detachment of Americans and the Bourbonnais grenadiers occupied two redoubts of the fortress. At 2 p.m., the Yorktown garrison marched past the two combined armies, which stood in two lines, so that the English had the French on their right and the Americans on their left. Cornwallis pretended to be sick, so General O'Hara[358] replaced him. Right where the line began, General Rochambeau stood in front of his troops, and opposite him was Washington with Lafayette and the Americans. It was too much of a slight for the English to have to humiliate themselves before the Americans. General O'Hara, at the head of the garrison, turned to General Rochambeau, as he took off his hat. (For I did not see that he gave him his sword.) Rochambeau, however, passed him on to General Washington. [109] After this the whole corps marched through the lines, stood in a front on level ground and held their

---

358. Charles O'Hara (um 1740 – 1802), unehelicher Sohn von James O'Hara, Lord Tyrawley, trat 1752 als Kornett in die britische Armee ein, stieg schnell zum Oberstleutnant auf; 1766 war er Kommandant in Goree in Senegal. Von Oktober 1780 an Brigadegeneral in Amerika, in der Schlacht von Guilford courthouse schwer verwundet. Er war Gefangener in Amerika und von 1793 bis 1795 in Frankreich, gegen General Rochambeau ausgetauscht. Seit 1798 General und Gouverneur von Gibraltar, wo er 1802 starb.

358. Charles O'Hara (ca. 1740 – 1802) was the illegitimate son of James O'Hara, 2nd lord Tyrawley; he joined the British army as a cornet in 1752 and quickly rose to the rank of lieutenant colonel. He commanded troops at Goree/Senegal in 1766. As of October 1780, he served as a brigadier general in America, seriously wounded in the battle of Guilford courthouse. Prisoner in America until 1782 and in France 1793 – 1795, exchanged with General Rochambeau. Full general and governor of Gibraltar in 1798, died there in 1802.

(faisceaux) gestellt und, nebst 22 Fahnen, von dem Generalstab (Etat-Major de l'armée) in Empfang genommen. Endlich defilirte das Corps ohne Gewehr auf dem nämlichen Weg in die Stadt zurück. Die englischen Officiere wußten nicht genug, wie sie ihre Verachtung gegen die Amerikaner zeigen sollten. Kein Officier hatte seinen Degen gezogen. Die Amerikaner um sich zu rächen, setzten in die Zeitung, sie hätten sich betragen wie Knaben, die in der Schule Schläge bekommen haben, die Teutschen aber (Hessen und Ansbacher) wie Männer von Tapferkeit. ("They behaved like boys, who had been whip[pe]d in school, but the Germans like men of true fortitude.")

Die Amerikaner stachen freilich im Aeußerlichen sehr ab. Ihre Officiere hatten Uniformen, die übrigen aber gingen in kleinen, leinenen, vielmals schmutzigen und zerrissenen [109a] Westen. Das Einzige, was sie auszeichnete, war ein lederner Casque[359]. Sie waren aber um so mehr zu bewundern, daß sie bei so vielen Entbehrungen noch so viel getan hatten.

Die Stadt gewährte einen sehr traurigen Anblick der Verheerung. Cornwallis hatte 3000 Sclaven aus den Plantagen in Virginien mitgenommen und diese waren jetzt mit ihm eingeschlossen gewesen. Dazu kamen die Blattern unter sie, so daß sie wie Heerden Schafe auf der Straße lagen. Die am Leben gebliebenen wurden nun von ihren Herren zurück gefordert.

Als die Garnison von Glo[u]cester sich ergeben hatte, ereignete es sich, daß der Obrist Tarleton[360] mit einem französischen Aide de Camps[361] an einen Ort ritt, wohin er zum Essen eingeladen war. Da kam ein Amerikaner, welcher des Obristen Pferd als sein ihm geraubtes Eigenthum reclamirte, und Tarleton hatte die Erniedigung vom Pferde steigen zu müssen. [109b] Obrist Tarleton war Advocat gewesen, hatte aber eine Legion[362] leichter Cavallerie errichtet. An seiner rechten Hand hatte er den Daumen und den vorderen Finger verloren, so daß er keinen Säbel halten konnte; er hielt deshalb nur einen

guns at their feet. Then all guns were put in piles ("faisceaux") and next to them 22 flags, all accepted by the general staff ("Etat-Major de l'armee"). Finally the corps marched back into town without their guns, along the same route. The English officers could not show enough disdain for the Americans. No officer drew his sword. The Americans, getting their own back, printed in the paper, that the English were acting like school-boys, who had been beaten during recess, the Germans (Hessians and Ansbachers) had conducted themselves bravely. ("They behaved like boys, who had been whip[pe]d in school, but the Germans like men of true fortitude.")

The Americans presented a starkly contrasting picture by their outer appearance. Their officers had uniforms[359], all others wore small, linen vests often dirty and torn;[109a] what they all wore, were leather helmets. They were all the more to be admired, considering how much they accomplished with so much deprivation.

The city was in a very sad state of devastation. Cornwallis had taken 3000 slaves from Virginia plantations and these had been locked in with him. Then a plague of small-pox befell them, so that many lay in the streets like herds of sheep. Those still alive were now demanded back by their masters.

After the Gloucester garrison had surrendered, an odd thing happened, when Colonel Tarleton[360] was riding with a French aide-de-camp[361] to a place where he had been invited to dine. An American happened to meet them who claimed the colonel's horse as his stolen property, and Tarleton was humiliated by having to get off this horse. [109b] Col. Tarleton had been a lawyer, but had put together a legion[362] of light cavalry. He had lost the thumb and index finger on his right hand, this meant that

---

359. Casque(t): Helm. Nach den Memoiren von Sir Nathaniel Wraxall, trug Charles James Fox, der Politiker, der seit 1781 in Opposition zur Regierung Georgs III. stand, „… ständig einen blauen Frack und eine gelbliche Weste, die beide im Allgemeinen nicht neu und sogar abgetragen aussahen … Diese Farben … bildeten das Uniformmerkmal Washingtons und der amerikanischen Aufständischen."

360. Sir Banastre Tarleton (1754–1833), britischer Offizier, Oberstleutnant der Kavallerie, der am 17. Jan.1781 bei Cowpens, Südkarolina, fast seine ganze Kolonne an General Daniel Morgan verlor, war vom 28. September bis 19. Oktober 1781 in Gloucester bei Yorktown; s. Acomb, Journal, S. 363.

361. Aide de Camp: Adjutant

362. Legion meint hier eine privat aufgestellte Truppe von etwa 1 200 Mann. In der Antike hatte eine Legion eine Truppenstärke von 3 000 – 6 000 Mann.

359. According to the memoirs of Sir Nathaniel Wraxall, Charles James Fox, the English politician who opposed George III's government in 1781 "constantly wore a blue frock coat and a buff waist coat, neither of which appeared in general new and sometimes appeared to be threadbare … These colors … then constituted the distinguishing badge or uniform of Washington and the American insurgents." – A casque(t) is a helmet.

360. Sir Banastre Tarleton (1754 – 1833), British officer who lost almost all of his column at Cowpens, SC, on Jan. 17th, 1781, to General Daniel Morgan; he was at Gloucester, opposite Yorktown Sept. 28th – Oct. 19th, 1781; cf. Acomb, Journal, p. 363.

361. This term has the same meaning in French and in English.

362. In Roman antiquity, a legion comprised 3,000 – 6,000 men. The legion mentioned here was a privately raised unit of about 1,200 men.

dünnen Stock in der Hand, und so ritt er an der Spitze seiner Soldaten. Er machte sich durch Bravour aber auch durch Excesse berühmt.

An dem Tage, da die Batterien gegen Yorktown zu schießen anfingen, stieß er mit seinem Corps auf den Herzog von Lauzun[363]. Dieser mit seinen Husaren warf ihn. Ein Husar brannte seine Pistole ihm ganz nahe auf den Leib ab; zu seinem Glück war aber die Kugel in die Pistolen-Halfter gefallen. Hierauf verfehlte ein Lancier[364] seinen Stoß auf ihn. Durch den Choc des Pferdes ward er hiebei zu Boden geworfen, von seinen Leuten aber gerettet.

Merkwürdig war bei dieser Belagerung eine Hündin, welche im Lager der Engländer vor der Stadt [110] Junge hatte. Da die Engländer sich zurück in die Festung zogen, kam das Nest der Hündin hinter die französischen Verschanzungen. Diese aber lief täglich durch das heftige Feuer von beiden Seiten zu ihrem Herrn in die Stadt, und kam dann wieder zurück, um ihre Jungen zu säugen.

Jetzt da der Feldzug beendigt war, und die Aussicht auf mein Vermögen meine Gegenwart in Deutschland erford[e]rte, bat ich um Erlaubniß, nach Hause zu gehen. Der General gab mir einen Paß, um daheim meine Privatgeschäfte zu versehen, „pour vaquer à mes affaires particuliaires"[365]; und der Oberst Graf Zweibruck gab mir ein Zeugniß seiner Zufriedenheit. Ueberhaupt kann ich nicht genug die Güte und Freundschaft rühmen, die er mir erwiesen hat. Ich reißte also mit den Lieutenants Baron Bibra[366] aus Franken und La Roche, welche auch von der Armee abgingen, ab. Wir ritten auf unse- [111] ren eigenen Pferden. Diese Herren überlegten aber nicht, daß wir eine Reise von 120 Stunden zu machen hatten, und strengten um die Wette ihre Pferde so an, daß sie mir weit vorkamen.

he could not hold a sabre; for this reason he just held a thin cane in his hand, and rode thus when leading his soldiers. He was quite famous for his bravado, but also for his excesses.

On that day, when the batteries began to fire on Yorktown, he and his corps faced the Duke of Lauzun[363], who defeated him with his hussars. One hussar sent a shot very close to his body; as luck would have it the bullet fell into his pistol-holder. Right after this a lancer's[364] thrust missed him. By the shock of his horse, he was thrown to the ground, but saved by his men.

Another curious thing during this siege was a bitch that gave birth to a litter of pups in the English camp outside the city. [110] Because the English retreated into the fortress, the litter remained behind in the French entrenchments. Every day she ran through heavy fire from both sides to reach her master in the city, and then always ran back to suckle her pups.

Now that the campaign was over and the prospect of my inheritance demanded my attention in Germany, I asked for permission to return home. The General gave me a passport, to arrange my affairs at home ("pour vaquer à mes affaires particuliaires")[365]; and Col. Count Zweibrucken gave me a favorable reference. In general, I cannot praise enough the favor and friendship that he has shown me. Then I set out with two Lieutenants, Baron Bibra[366] from Franconia and La Roche, who were also leaving the army. We were all riding our own horses[111]. These two, disregarding the fact that we had a journey of 120 hours ahead of us, competed to ride their horses so fast that I was

---

363. Armand Louis de Gontaut Biron, duc de Lauzun (1747 – 1793), trat 1761 ins Militär ein, diente 1779 mit Auszeichnung im Senegal, wurde zum Oberst befördert, war dann unter Rochambeau in Amerika mit einer privat aufgestellten, überwiegend aus Deutschen bestehenden Truppe. Kommandierte Truppen am Rhein und in Italien, bevor er 1793 zum Tode verurteilt wurde. Acomb, Journal, S. 354.

364. Lancier: Lanzenreiter, Ulan

365. Wörtliches Zitat aus dem Schreiben des Generals in Rechterens Personalakte Yb 346 beim Militärarchiv in Vincennes, mit dem einen Unterschied, dass dort statt „à mes affaires" von „à ses affaires" die Rede ist.

366. Ferdinand Johann Ignaz Freiherr von Bibra, geb. 1756, war 1773 Leutnant im Regiment Deux-Ponts, 1777 Oberleutnant, 1784 Hauptmann; 1786 quittierte er den Dienst; s. Bodinier, Dictionnaire, S. 57. Wenn er mit dem hier Genannten identisch ist, müsste er später zum Regiment zurückgekehrt sein; s. auch Tröss, Regiment, S. 66.

363. Armand Louis de Gontaut Biron, duc de Lauzun (1747 – 1793), joined the French army in 1761, campaigned in Senegal 1779, served in America under Rochambeau with a privately raised legion consisting mostly of Germans. He held commands in Belgium, on the Rhine, and in Italy before being sentenced to death in 1793. Morally dissolute, but with military ambitions; cf. Acomb, Journal, p. 354.

364. The author uses the French word for lancer in the German text.

365. Almost literal quote from the general's letter in Rechteren's army file Yb 346 at Vincennes; there, of course, it says "à ses affaires" instead of "à mes affaires".

366. Ferdinand Johann Ignaz Freiherr von Bibra, born July 31, 1756, was a 2nd lieutenant in the Royal Deux-Ponts regiment in 1773, 1st Lieutenant in 1777, Captain in 1784, left army service in 1786; cf. Bodinier, Dictionnaire, p. 57; Tröss, Regiment, p. 66. If he was the person mentioned here he must have returned to the regiment later.

Bei der Ueberfahrt über den Potowmak[367] aber fand ich sie wieder. Das P[f]erd des la Roche konnte gar nicht mehr fort: er mußte also zurück bleiben. Bibra hinkte mit dem seinigen zur Noth bis Philadelphia. Die Reise ging beinahe durch lauter Wald. Auf den Abstand einer Tagesreise aber fand man immer wieder ein Wirthshaus, und eines für die Mittagsruhe, wo dann alle Reisenden in Gesellschaft zusammen frühstückten und zu Mittag und Abend aßen. Wir kamen durch Alexandria[368] und Baltimore[369].

In Philadelphia machte ich dem französischen Gesandten, Marquis de la Luzerne[370], meine Aufwartung; und sein Secretair, Monsieur de Marbois[371], der nachher in Frankreich ansehnliche Posten versehen hat, und vielleicht noch lebt, (wenigstens ließt man den Namen noch in Zeitungen,) gab mir einige Depeschen an den Grafen Monbarrey [112] mit. Sie müssen aber von keiner besondern Wichtigkeit gewesen sein. Denn als ich ihn fragte,

left far behind. But crossing the Potomac[367] I caught up with them again. La Roche's horse could not go on and he had to stay behind. Bibra just barely limped his into Philadelphia. Almost the whole journey was through dense woods. But every evening we always found an inn, and another one for a noon-time rest, where all travellers sat together and took their meals – be it breakfast, dinner or supper. We came through Alexandria[368] and Baltimore[369].

In Philadelphia I paid a visit to the French envoy, Marquis de la Luzerne[370]; and his secretary, Monsieur de Marbois[371], who later held very high positions, and may be still alive (at least I see his name in the newspapers): he gave me some dispatches for Comte Monbarrey [112]. They cannot have been very important. For when I asked him, whether I should throw them in the ocean

---

367. Potomac, hier irrig „Potowmak", Fluss an der mittleren Ostküste der USA, entspringt in den Appalachen und fließt in die Chesapeake-Bucht. Der District of Columbia, der der amerikanischen Bundesregierung direkt untersteht, liegt an der Stelle, bis zu der die Gezeiten fühlbar sind; bis dorthin ist der Fluss auch schiffbar. Mount Vernon, Washingtons Familiengut, liegt unterhalb des District of Columbia. Der Name P. wurde zuerst 1608 von Kapitän John Smith aufgezeichnet.

368. Alexandria, Virginia, südlich des District of Columbia am Potomac gelegen, wurde erstmals 1695 besiedelt, 1748 als Stadt ausgebaut, nach John Alexander benannt. Einzige Stadt der USA, die keinem „County" angehört. Washington trug zur Festlegung der Straßenverläufe bei. 1791 – 1847 Teil des District of Columbia.

369. 1729 gegründet, nach einer englischen Hochadelsfamilie benannt. Um 1780 wurde B. zu einem wichtigen Hafen und Schiffbauplatz; 1797 lief hier das erste Kriegsschiff der USA vom Stapel. Der Kontinentalkongress tagte hier von Dezember 1776 bis März 1777. 1827 wurde hier die erste Eisenbahnlinie der USA (Baltimore & Ohio) begonnen. Heute ist B. die größte Stadt von Maryland.

370. Anne-Césare, chevalier de la Luzerne (1741 – 1791), Offizier und Diplomat, zeichnete sich im Siebenjährigen Krieg aus, war schon 1762 Generalmajor und Kommandant der kgl. Grenadiere. Als Diplomat diente er zuerst in Bayern, ab 1779 in Amerika. Als Gesandter war er 1779 – 1783 in Philadelphia, wo er durch eine persönliche Geldanleihe die Versorgung der amerikanischen Truppen ermöglichte. Im Gegenzug wurde ihm garantiert, dass der Kongress keinen Friedensvertrag mit Großbritannien ratifizieren würde, bevor ein Frieden zwischen England und Frankreich geschlossen war. Kehrte 1783 nach Europa zurück, starb 1791 als Botschafter in London.

371. François, marquis de Barbé-Marbois (1745 – 1837), 1783 in der Nachfolge de la Luzernes französischer Geschäftsträger in den USA; im selben Jahr heiratete er die Tochter eines Gouverneurs von Pennsylvania. Kehrte 1789 nach Frankreich zurück, während der Revolution mehrmals verhaftet, aber 1801 zum Staatsrat und Direktor der Staatsbank ernannt. 1803 handelte er in dieser Funktion den „Louisiana Purchase", den Verkauf großer Teile des heutigen Mittelwestens und Südens der USA, an die junge Republik aus. 1808 – 1834 Präsident des Rechnungshofes. 1815 Ernennung zum Justizminister, 1816 Rücktritt von diesem Amt.

367. Misspelled "Potowmak" in the German text; river in the east central U.S. It rises in the Appalachian mountains and flows into Chesapeake Bay. The District of Columbia lies on the left bank at the head of the tidewater; the river is navigable to Washington, D.C. Mt. Vernon, George Washington's home, is on its bank below D.C. The name was first recorded by John Smith in 1608.

368. Alexandria, Virginia, on the Potomac river, south of D.C. The site was first settled in 1695, organized as city in 1748 and named for John Alexander who had originally been granted the land. A. is the only city without any county affiliations in the U.S. George Washington helped lay out its streets. 1791 – 1847 part of D.C.

369. Baltimore, Maryland, established in 1729, named for the English barons Baltimore, was an important seaport and shipbuilding centre at the time of the American revolution. In 1797, the first U.S. navy ship was launched here. The Continental Congress met here from Dec., 1776, to March, 1777. In 1827, the first U.S. railroad (Baltimore & Ohio) was started here. Today it is Maryland's largest city.

370. Anne-César, chevalier de la Luzerne (1741 – 1791), second French minister to the United States 1779 –1783. Distinguished himself in the Seven Years' War and rose to the rank of major-general, then served as a diplomat, first in Bavaria, then in America. He guaranteed a personal loan the the young republic and in return obtained the agreement that Congress would not ratify a peace treaty with Great Britain before peace had been agreed upon between France and Britain. He died as French ambassador in London.

371. François, marquis de Barbé-Marbois (1745 – 1837) became the French chargé d'affaires in the U.S. after de la Luzerne had returned to France. In the same year, he married the daughter of a former governor of Pennsylvania. He returned to France in 1789, was arrested several times during the years of the Revolution, but was made director of the treasury in 1801. In this function he negotiated the Louisiana Purchase of 1803 by which the U.S. acquired the land west of the Mississippi to the Rocky Mountains. In 1808, he became president of the Cour des Comptes and held this post until 1834. 1815 Attorney General, renounced that office in 1816.

if we were taken prisoner, he answered that this was not necessary.

Baron Bibra and I made arrangements for our crossing with the owner of a small two-masted ship laden with Virginia tobacco. The ship was named "Betsy", under Captain Gallagher from Cork, Ireland[372]; the two other officers' names were Tillinghast and MacDoughal. The sailors were English, who had mutinied; when their captain, armed with a pistol, tried to resist them, they had thrown him overboard and had then defected with the ship to the Americans.

(In Philadelphia, I visited a botanist, Master Bertram[373], and bought two crates full of American plant seeds.)

The ship was anchored quite a long distance away from Philadelphia; we went there in a small boat [113], and it was already dark when we arrived. We heard some loud yelling, and saw that Tillinghast was standing on deck, holding a gun, and threatening to shoot the sailors down below. This beginning was not very auspicious. Beside Lt. von Bibra, there were two other passengers on board: a merchant mariner from Marseille, and a surgeon, whose ship had been captured by the English. The officers and passengers of us had to stick together. Only one sailor, Peter, an Italian, sided with the captain.

One night about half-way through our voyage, after a quiet crossing, we ran into the most violent storm imaginable. The waves broke over the ship, so that water ran down the hatch, where the stairs led down to the cabin. In a panic I jumped out of my berth, which was attached to the wall, about 3 shoes (feet) up from the floor. But a crate, which was not tied to the wall, hit my leg [114] so hard, that I decided to get back into my berth. Now while everything was clattering around, some burning coals fell out of the little stove, which was heated with hard coal, and started rolling along on the floor. The hatch, which led down below, where the gun-powder

---

372. Cork, Irish Corcaigh (swamp), county seat of Cork County, one of the best natural harbors in Europe.

373. William Bartram (1729 – 1823), son of John B., the first American botanist and founder of the Philadelphia Botanical Gardens. William B.s book *The Travels of W.B.* (1791) first described the flora and fauna of the Carolinas, Georgia, and Florida. This book was very popular in Europe and influenced Wordsworth, Coleridge, and Chateaubriand, but it was largely ignored in the U.S. until 1928.

nach dem Platze hinabstieg, wo auch das Pulver war, stand offen, weil man etwas da geholt hatte. Die Matrosen waren ganz entmuthigt, verkrochen sich und riefen: „Ah we are lost souls!" (Ach, wir sind verlorene Seelen!) Der Capitain allein war oben auf dem Schiff, wo er an einem herabhängenden Strick sich haltend und auf den Knien rutschend, herumgeschleudert wurde. Endlich gelang es ihm mit heftigen Schreien und Toben, die Mannschaft wieder in Thätigkeit zu bringen. Jetzt zerriß der Wind das Segel am Mast mit einem fürchterlichen Schlag. Dieß war unser Glück. Denn wenn der Wind länger auf das Segel gedrückt hätte[374], waren wir verloren. Der eine Officier Master Tillinghast, nahm seine Zuflucht zu einem Flaschenkeller mit Rum oder Brandwein, der unter mir stand, und [**115**] trank brav darauf los. Der andere, Master Mac Doughal, hatte von einer Rolle an einem Strick einen solchen Schlag gegen die Rippen bekommen, daß er in seine Hangmatte neben mir mußte gebracht werden. Jetzt kam eine Welle, welche das Schiff so auf die Seite warf, daß die Kiste, in der die Gewehre waren, sich gegen meine Lagerstätte aufrichtete. Nun fing Master Mac Doughal an zu seufzen: „Now I believe, she will go down": (Nun glaube ich geht das Schiff zu Grunde; es hat so viel Wasser bekommen, daß es nicht wieder aufstehen kann.) Es erhob sich aber; und allmählich bekamen wir mehr Hoffnung. Jedoch wenn der Capitain fragte, wie es an der Pumpe stände, hieß es immer einige Zoll hoch mehr Wasser, als vorher.

Als die schreckensvolle Nacht vorüber war, blieb das Wetter noch immer sehr stürmisch. Die Jahreszeit, es war um Weihnachten, brachte es so mit sich. Einmal zerbrach die Stange, womit das Steuerruder [**116**] regiert wird. Die Matrosen aber, welche überhaupt vortreffliche Seeleute waren, wußten es, unbefohlen, gleich wieder herzustellen.

Nachdem wir nun an 6 Wochen bei immer stürmischem Wetter gesegelt waren, bekamen wir gegen Abend von Weitem Land zu sehen. Es war da gar nicht die Rede davon, die Höhe der Sonne zu messen, und Abends aus dem Laufe des Schiffes und dem Cours, den man gehalten hatte, auf der Charte das Besteck zu machen, oder den Platz zu berechnen, wo das Schiff sein möchte. Wir segelten dreist gegen Sonnenaufgang; und als man Land sah, wurde ein Atlas aufgeschlagen und berathschlagt, ob dieses die französische, die spanische oder die englische Küste sey. Es blieb unentschieden; der Atlas wurde wieder zugemacht, und wir segelten auf das Land zu.

was also stored, had been left open, because somebody had fetched something. The sailors were at their wits' ends, they were only trying to hide and kept screaming: "Ah, we are lost souls!" Only the captain was up on deck, tumbling around, where he was holding on to a rope, that was hanging down, and he was slipping along on his knees. At long last he succeeded with much screaming and bluster in bringing the crew back to work on deck. Next the wind tore the sail from the mast with a terrible blow. This was lucky for us, for if the wind had pushed[374] on the sail much longer, we would have gone down. One of the officers, Master Tillinghast, retreated into the wine cellar, where rum and brandy were stored, which was just below us, [**115**] and set right to drinking. The other one, Master MacDoughal, had been hit so hard in his chest by a block attached to a rope, that he had to be put in his hammock, which hung next to mine. Then came a wave which threw the ship on her side, and the crate which held the guns turned over against my berth. Now Master MacDoughal began to moan: "Now I believe, she will go down." (She has taken so much water, that she cannot righten herself again.) But she slowly did right herself, and gradually we regained our hope. But whenever the captain asked how the pumps were doing, they reported a few inches more water than before.

After this horrible night was over, the weather remained very stormy. It was usual for this time of the year, around Christmas. One day the rod which governs the rudder broke. [**116**] But the sailors, who in general were excellent mariners, knew how to repair it right away, without being ordered to.

After sailing through 6 weeks of stormy weather, we sighted land far off one evening. We could not even try to measure the angle of the sun or, in the evening, compare the path of the ship to the set course, by reckoning on the chart with the compass and fixing the ship's position. None of this, we just sailed to the East; and when we saw land, an atlas was opened and we wondered whether this was the French, Spanish or English coast. It was left undecided; we just shut the atlas, and sailed for shore.

---

374. Im Manuskript steht: „hatte".

374. The German text erroneously has the indicative instead of the subjunctive.

Mit Tagesanbruch sahen wir, daß wir nahe an einem Felsen so groß wie eine Kathedralkirche waren. Schnell wurde das Schiff gewendet; und nachdem wir vielleicht eine Stunde diesen Cours gehal- [117] ten hatten, sahen wir wieder Felsen vor uns. Es blieb Nichts übrig, als so hin und her zusegeln, wodurch wir aber immer mehr an's Land kamen. Endlich sahen wir, daß es sich in einen Halbzirkel von Felsen endete, die wie eine Stadt mit Thürmen aussahen. Es waren die so genannten Penmarcs[375] an der Küste von Bretagne. M. Tillinghast kam herunter und sagte mir: "It will be a bitter night for us; we will have a pretty look out in the other world." (Es wird eine bittere Nacht sein; wir werden eine hübsche Aussicht in die andere Welt haben.) Auf meine Frage warum? – sagte er: Gehen sie nur hinauf und sehen sie: wir sind von Felsen umringt. Er wollte wieder aus der Rum Boiteille sich Trost holen; aber der französische Kauffartheyschiffer und sein Wundarzt zerschlugen sie. Jetzt fingirte er eine heftige Kolik, mischte Essig mit Pfeffer, als Surrogat, und trank dieses hinein. [118] Es war ein schlimmes Dilemma. Lavirte man so hin und her, so konnte das Schiff nicht aushalten; und zuletzt kam [es] doch auf die Küste. Wollte man nachgeben, und das Schiff stranden lassen, so war die Ladung und das Schiff verloren, und die Menschen auch noch nicht gerettet. Ich fragte den Capitain, was er zu thun gesonnen sei? Er antwortete: „Ich werde das Schiff und die Ladung für meine Rheder zu erhalten suchen; und wenn dazu keine Möglichkeit ist, auf unsere Rettung bedacht sein."

Die Wellen schlugen mit solcher Gewalt in das Schiff, daß ein Theil vom Bord abgeschlagen wurde. Der Capitain ließ die Kanonen, deren wir 8 hatten, bis auf zwei ins Meer werfen, um das Schiff zu erleichtern. Diejenigen, welche dieß thaten, standen dabei fast mit dem halben Leib im Wasser. Dieses läuft zum Theil wieder durch Abzüge heraus, weil es von oben mit den Wellen hinein- [119] gekommen ist. Wenn aber das Schiff vom Wind sehr auf die Seite gedrückt wird, so hilft das Wasser dazu, daß das Schiff sich nicht erhebt. Es wurden also die Beilen herbeigeschaft; und wenn es so lag, dann hieß es wieder: „Where are the hatchets?" (Wo sind die Beile?) Das Abhauen eines Mastes geht leicht, wenn man auf die Seite einhaut, von welcher der Wind drückt, weil er die getrennten Theile von einander reißt. Hingegen auf der anderen Seite drückt der Wind die durch das Beil getrennten Theile fest zusammen. Ohne Mast aber ist das Schiff ein Spiel der Wellen.

---

375. Penmarcs, eine Felsenformation an der Küste der Bucht, die sich von der Stadt Penmarc'h nach Norden bis Audierne (oder von der Pointe de Penmarc'h bis zur Pointe du Raz) erstreckt. P. ist eine kleine Ortschaft im Département Finistère, einige Kilometer südlich von Quimper.

At daybreak, we saw that we were close to a rock as large as a cathedral. Quickly the ship was put about, and after sailing for about an hour in this direction,[117] we saw more rocks ahead of us. There was nothing else to do but to sail back and forth, which brought us closer and closer to the shore. At last we saw that it ended in a half-circle of rocks looking like a city with towers. It was the so-called Penmarcs[375] on the coast of Brittany. Master Tillinghast came down and told me, "It will be a bitter night for us; we will have a pretty look out into the other world." When I asked him why? – he answered, "Go up on deck and have a look round, we are surrounded by rocks." Once again he was looking for comfort in his bottle of rum, but the French merchant-skipper and the surgeon smashed his bottle. Then he feigned a severe colic, mixed pepper and vinegar together, as a substitute cordial, and drank it down. [118] We were caught on the horns of the dilemma. If we tacked back and forth, the ship would not last long and would be wrecked on the coast. If we gave up and stranded the ship, both the ship and cargo would be lost, and the people on board might not be saved. I asked the captain, what he intended to do? He answered, "I shall try to save the ship and cargo for my ship's owner, and if this should prove impossible, then I will think of saving ourselves."

The waves broke over the ship with such a force, that some parts were broken off. The captain had all but two of our eight original guns thrown into the ocean, in order to lighten our load. The sailors working on this, were standing almost up to the waist in water. Part of this water ran out through the scuppers because it came in with the high waves.[119] When the ship was pushed onto its side by the wind, the weight of the water was part of the reason the ship could not righten herself. Then the hatchets were brought out; and when the ship was in this position we always heard, "Where are the hatchets?" ("Wo sind die Beile?"). Cutting down the mast is quite easy if you chop on the side from which the wind is blowing, because this helps to rip it off. But if you chop on the lee side, the wind just presses the two parts back together again. Without the mast the ship is at the mercy of the waves.

---

375. Penmarcs, a rock formation on the coast of the bay which extends north from the town of Penmarc'h to Audierne (or from the Pointe de Penmarc'h to the Pointe du Raz). P. is a small town in the département Finistère, a few miles south of Quimper.

Als die Kanonen in das Meer geworfen waren, wollten die Matrosen den Capitain nöthigen, das Schiff stranden zu lassen; denn da das Schiff sich nicht mehr vertheidigen ließ, würden sie gefangen und alle hingerichtet werden.

Zu bewundern war die Fassung des Herrn von Bibra. Obwohl [**120**] er, wie ich glaube, nicht schwimmen konnte, so hatte er doch seine Kleider ausgezogen und stand, in den Mantel gehüllt, da. Er verabschiedete sich mit dem Italiäner Peter, um, wenn das Schiff scheiterte, nach abgeworfenem Mantel, eine bewegliche Treppenleiter, womit man in die Cajute stieg, zu ergreifen, und sich beide im Meer daran zu halten. Peter äußerte sich aber gegen die Anderen, daß er keine Lust habe, sich zu dieser Parthie zu engagieren.

Beim Untergang der Sonne sahen wir auf einmal unserer Errettung entgegen. Der Wind drehte sich ein wenig, so daß wir über die äußersten Felsen, die uns umgaben, in das offene Meer konnten. Wir waren wohl noch nicht ganz sicher. Doch um Mitternacht, als wir berechnen konnten, daß wir im offenen Meere seien, war alle Furcht verschwunden. Am folgenden Tage liefen wir in Belle Isle[376] ein. Die Reise [**121**] hatte 36 Tage gedauert.

Ich ging von da über Aurai, Henebon[377] nach l'Orient[378], um den amerikanischen Consul zu sprechen, weil der Schiffcapitain, ungeachtet wir mit dem Eigenthümer des Schiffes accordirt hatten, für meinen Bedienten noch mehr haben wollte. Da ich dies nicht schuldig zu sein glaubte, ließ er mir die zwei Kisten mit Sämereien, welche ich in Philadelphia gekauft hatte, nicht verabfolgen. Ich fand den Consul nicht. Von Belle Isle fuhr ich über nach Quiberon[379], einer Landspitze, wo später die

---

376. Belle-Ile-en-mer, Insel etwa 13 km südwestlich der Halbinsel Quibéron im Département Morbihan, Bretagne, 1761 – 1763 unter britischer Besatzung, wurde in demselben Vertrag an Frankreich zurückgegeben, in dem Nova Scotia an Großbritannien fiel.

377. Aurai: Auray, bretonisch Alre, Städtchen im Département Morbihan südwestlich von Rennes. Das 1558 zerstörte Schloss war ein Sitz der Herzöge der Bretagne. – Hennebont, Ortschaft im Département Morbihan, einige Kilometer nordöstlich von Lorient.

378. Lorient, Stadt im Département Morbihan, bedeutender Hafen im 17. und 18. Jahrhundert. Der mittelalterliche Flecken Blavet bekam nach der Errichtung der Zitadelle unter Ludwig XIII. (1610–1643) den Namen Port-Louis. Ludwig XIV privilegierte die Niederlassung einer Handelsgesellschaft, der Name L. (l'Orient) leitet sich vom Orienthandel ab. Nachdem Frankreich seine Besitzungen in Indien verloren hatte, ging L.s Handel stark zurück.

379. Quibéron, Département Morbihan, Städtchen und Halbinsel an der Südküste der Bretagne. Ein britischer Seesieg hier im Jahre 1759 kam einer drohenden französischen Invasion Englands zuvor.

When the cannon had been thrown overboard, the sailors wanted to force the captain to abandon the ship; for the ship could no longer be defended, and they feared they would all be captured and put to death.

Herr von Bibra's composure was most admirable. Although, [120] as I believe, he could not swim, he had taken off his clothes and stood there covered only by his coat. Together with the Italian, Peter, he said good-bye to us, and planned, after the wreck of the ship, to throw off his coat and grab the wooden ladder which we used to climb down into the cabin, and that these two would hold on to it in the ocean. Peter told the others, however, that he did not want to have anything to do with this plan.

At sunset we suddenly saw that we would be saved. The wind turned a bit, so that we could sail out into the open sea around the furthest of the high rocks that surrounded us. But we were not completely safe yet. However at mid-night, when we could reckon on the map that we were in the open ocean again, we lost all fear. The next day we arrived at Belle Isle[376]. The voyage had taken 36 days.[121]

I went to l'Orient (Lorient)[377] by way of Aurai and Henebon[378], to speak with the American Consul, because the ship's captain, disregarding my agreement with the owner of the ship, wanted to charge more for the passage of my servant. Because I did not think I owed him this, he took possession of my two crates of seeds, which I had bought in Philadelphia. I did not find the consul. From Belle Isle

---

376. Belle-Ile-en-mer, island about 8 miles southwest of the Quibéron peninsula, département Morbihan, Brittany. Its citadel was important from the 16th to the 19th centuries. Occupied by the British 1761 – 1763, returned to France by the same treaty which yielded Nova Scotia to Britain.

377. Lorient, city in the département Morbihan, Brittany, important harbor town in the 17th and 18th centuries. It was named Port-Louis when the citadel was built under Louis XIII (1610 – 1643). Louis XIV authorized a merchant company to settle here, the name „l'Orient" (Lorient) derives from the trade with eastern countries. After France lost its Indian possessions, trade declined.

378. Aurai: Auray, Breton Alre, town in the département Morbihan, southwest of Rennes. Its chateau was a residence of the dukes of Brittany, destroyed in 1558. – Henebon: Hennebont, town in the dép. Morbihan, Brittany, a few miles northeast of Lorient.

aus England geschickten Emigranten eine Niederlage erlitten. Diese Gegenden hat Julius Caesar, der gegen die Veneti Krieg führte, treffend beschrieben, Lib. III. Cap. 12-16.[380] Von den Venetis hat die Stadt Vannes[381] ihren Namen. – Hier wird das Bas Breton gesprochen, das alte Celtische[382], welche Sprache sich in Biscaya[383], Niederbretagne, in Wales, in Irland und bei den Bergschotten erhalten hat.

[122] Die Dörfer auf der Halbinsel von Quiberon sind nur kleine Gruppen von Häusern, die in die Runde gebaut sind und alle aneinander hängen. Man muß sich zwischen diesen Häusern durch die engsten, winkelichten Stege und über Düngerhaufen durchwinden. Solche Dörfer sieht man wie Maulwurfhaufen auf der Halbinsel zerstreut. Von ihren Häusern sieht man viele geziert mit vergoldetem und farbigem Schnitzwerk als Ueberbleibseln von gescheiterten Schiffen, auch mit den Namen dieser Schiffen. Ich traf manche Namen in holländischer Sprache an. Ein Beweis, wie gefährlich die Küste ist.

Da die Engländer Meister auf der See waren, war beinahe alle Zufuhr aus Frankreich abgeschnitten. Allen fehlte es an Geld. Ich war genöthigt, bei einem Unterofficier, dessen Frau [123] Marketenderey trieb, gegen 25 und 30 Procent Geld zu lehnen, wofür ich eine Anweisung an meinen Banquier in Paris gab. Ich hatte nicht viel mehr übrig; aber statt liegen zu bleiben und Geld von Paris kommen zu lassen, entschloß ich mich, mit meinem Bedienten die Reise zu Fuß zu machen. Dazu konnte ich die Kosten noch bestreiten. Ich nahm den Weg über Vannes, Rennes, Laval[384], Mayenne[385],

(Ile) I took a boat to Quiberon[379], situated on a peninsula, where later the emigrants sent over from England suffered a defeat. Julius Caesar, who fought a war against the Veneti, fittingly described this area Lib.III Chap. 12-16.[380] The capital city, Vannes[381], takes its name from the Veneti. Here Low Breton is spoken, the old Celtic language[382] which can still be heard in the Bay of Biscay[383] region, Lower Brittany, in Wales, in Ireland, and among the Highland Scots.[122]

The villages on the Quiberon peninsula are only small groups of houses, which are built in a circle all attached to each other. To get around these houses you have to wind your way over the most narrow and crooked lanes and past manure piles. Such villages look like molehills strewn over the whole peninsula. You can see many of their houses decorated with gilded or colored carved woodwork, the remains of shipwrecks. Some show the names of these ships. I saw some names in the Dutch language, which proves how dangerous this coast can be.

Because "Britannia ruled the waves" almost all French harbors were blocked. No one had any money. I was forced to borrow money at 25 and 30 per cent from a petty officer whose wife ran an army canteen store ("Marketenderey"), [123] for this I gave them a draft on my banker in Paris. I did not have much left over, but instead of hanging around and waiting for my money to arrive from Paris, I decided to undertake the journey on foot with my servant. For this I had just enough funds. I went by way of Vannes,

---

380. Caius Julius Caesar, De Bello Gallico, III. Buch, Kap. 12 – 16.

381. Vannes ist der Vorort des Départements Morbihan und liegt etwa 2 km vom Golf von Morbihan entfernt. Es gehörte seit 990 zum Herzogtum Bretagne. Seine großartigen Gärten sind berühmt.

382. Keltische Sprachen sind neben dem Bretonischen die walisischen, irischen und schottischen Mundarten, die teilweise bis heute gesprochen werden.

383. Bucht des Atlantischen Ozeans an den Küsten Spaniens und Frankreichs, die nicht zuletzt durch ihr stürmisches und regnerisches Wetter bekannt ist.

384. Vorort des Départements Mayenne, östlich von Rennes. Die Grafen von L. spielten eine wichtige Rolle in der französischen Geschichte.

385. Städtchen im Dép. Mayenne, einige Kilometer nördlich von Laval.

---

379. Quibéron, dép. Morbihan, a small town and peninsula on the southern cast of Brittany. A British naval victory here in 1759 ended the threat of a French invasion of Britain.

380. Caius Julius Caesar, De Bello Gallico, lib. III, ch. 12 – 16.

381. Vannes is the capital of Morbihan département, Brittany, about 1 mile inland from the Golfe du Morbihan. It is famous for its gardens.

382. Celtic languages are still spoken in Wales, Ireland, and Scotland as well as in Brittany.

383. Atlantic bay between the coasts of France and Spain, notorious for its bad weather.

Alencon[386], Mortaigne[387], Verneuil[388], Nonencoart[389], Dreux[390], Versailles[391] nach Paris, wo ich in den ersten Tagen des Jahres 1782 ankam.

Rennes, Laval[384], Mayenne[385], Alencon[386], Mortagne[387], Verneuil[388], Nonencoart[389], Dreux[390], Versailles[391] to Paris where I arrived in the first days of the year 1782.

---

386. Dép. Orne, am Zusammenfluss der Flüsse Sarthe und Briante. A. ist bekannt für die im 17. Jahrhundert aus Venedig hierher gebrachte Produktion von Tüll und Spitze. A. war der Hauptort eines gleichnamigen Herzogtums, das 1549 an die französische Krone fiel. 1873 wurde hier die hl. Therese von Lisieux geboren.

387. Mortagne au Perche, Ortschaft im Dép. Orne zwischen Alençon und Chartres.

388. Verneuil-sur-Avre, Vorort des gleichnamigen Kantons im Département Eure, Region Haute-Normandie.

389. Nonancourt, Dép. Eure in der Normandie, einige Kilometer westlich von Dreux.

390. Dép. Eure-et-Loir, Städtchen am Fluss Blaise nordwestlich von Chartres, nach einem keltischen Stamm benannt. Die Hugenotten wurden hier 1562 geschlagen, was den Beginn der Religionskriege bedeutete.

391. Hauptstadt des Départements Yvelines, südwestlich von Paris, entwickelte sich um einen von Ludwig XIV. erbauten Palast, der etwa ein Jahrhundert lang Hauptresidenz der französischen Könige und Regierungssitz war. Etwa 20 000 Menschen waren mit dem Hof verbunden; ca. 1000 Adlige mit 4000 Bediensteten lebten im Palast selbst, etwa 14 000 Soldaten und Diener wohnten in der Stadt. Die „Assemblée Nationale" trat hier 1790 zusammen.

---

384. Capital of Mayenne département, east of Rennes. The counts of L. played an important role in French history.

385. Small town in the département Mayenne, a few miles north of Laval.

386. Dép. Orne, on the juncture of the Sarthe and Briante rivers. It is known for tulle and lace manufacture, introduced from Venice in the 17th century. Capital of the duchy of A., it passed to the French crown in 1549. Sainte Thérèse of Lisieux was born here in 1873.

387. Mortagne-au-Perche, small town in dép. Orne, between Alençon and Chartres.

388. Verneuil-sur-Avre, seat of the eponymous canton in the dép. Eure, Haute-Normandie region.

389. Nonancourt, dép. Eure, Normandie, a few miles west of Dreux.

390. Dép. Eure-et-Loir, on the Blaise river northwest of Chartres. Named after a Gallic tribe. The Huguenots were defeated here in 1562, marking the beginning of the Wars of Religion.

391. Capital of Yvelines département, southwest of Paris. The city developed around the palace built by Louis XIV, which was the principal residence of the kings of France and the seat of government for more than 100 years. About 20,000 people were attached to the court, about 1,000 noblemen with 4,000 attendants lived in the palace itself, 14,000 soldiers and servants in the town. The „Assemblée Nationale" met here in 1790.

Bildanhang / Illustrations

Friedrich Reinhard von Rechteren im Uniformrock mit dem französischen Militärverdienstorden eines Chevaliers, etwa im Alter von 66 Jahren; unbekannter Maler; Privatbesitz; (Foto: Michael Hettler).

Friedrich Reinhard von Rechteren in a uniform coat with a chevalier's cross of the French military order of merit, about 66 years of age; unknown painter; privately owned; (photo: Michael Hettler).

Schloss Sommerhausen um die Mitte des 19. Jahrhunderts, also fast noch zu Rechterens Lebenszeit; unbekannter Künstler; Gemeinde Sommerhausen.

Sommerhausen castle in the middle of the 19th century, as it might have appeared at the end of Rechteren's life; unknown artist; town of Sommerhausen.

Die Sommerhäuser Bürgerwehr um 1800 trug ähnliche Uniformen wie diese Mitglieder des Sommerhäuser Burschenvereins in den 1950er Jahren;
Foto: Gemeinde Sommerhausen.

The Sommerhausen militia around 1800 wore uniforms quite similar to those of these members of the Sommerhausen „Burschenverein" (Young Men's Association) in the 1950s; photo: town of Sommerhausen.

Die Hafeneinfahrt von Brest, von der Königlichen Batterie aus gesehen (um 1770); von Louis-Nicolas van Blarenberghe (1716 – 1794); Schloss Versailles (Wikimedia).

The entrance to the port of Brest, seen from the Royal Battery (ca. 1770); by Louis-Nicolas van Blarenberghe (1716 – 1794); Palace of Versailles (Wikimedia).

Das Linienschiff „Conquérant" am 1. Aug. 1798 in der „Battle of the Nile"; von Thomas Luny; Wikimedia.

The ship-of-the-line „Conquérant" on Aug. 1st, 1798, in the „Battle of the Nile", by Thomas Luny; Wikimedia.

Die vorzüglich befestigte Stellung der französischen Streitkräfte in Newport, Rhode Island, die auch Rechteren ausführlich erwähnt; aus: Plan de Défense de New-Port dans l'isle Rhode … aux ordres de Monsieur le chevalier de Ternay; Archives Nationales.

The well-fortified positions of the French armed forces in Newport, Rhode Island which are mentioned in detail by Rechteren; from: Plan de Défense de New-Port dans l'isle Rhode … aux ordres de Monsieur le chevalier de Ternay; Archive Nationales.

Füsilier, Jäger (Chasseur) und Grenadier des Regiments Royal Deux-Ponts; aus: J.M. Petzinger: „Regimenteraufstellung"; Hessische Hausstiftung, Schlossmuseum Darmstadt, Inv.-Nr. B 21710.

Fusilier, Rifleman (Chasseur), and Grenadier of the Royal Deux-Ponts regiment; taken from: J.M. Petzinger: „Regimenteraufstellung"; Hessische Hausstiftung, Schlossmuseum Darmstadt, Inv.-Nr. B 21710.

Copie.

Nous Jean Baptiste Donatien de Vimeur Comte de Rochambeau, Lieutenant Général des armées du Roi, grand'croix de l'ordre Royal et militaire de St Louis, Gouverneur de Villefranche, en roussillon, commandant un Corps de troupes de Sa Majesté très-Chrétienne.

Il est permis à Monsieur frederich Reynhard, Comte de Rechteren, Comes Sancti Imperii officier à la suite du Régiment de Royal deux Ponts infanterie allemande et Capitaine au service de Hollande de passer à Philadelphie. C'est un officier d'un mérite reconnu qui a mérité l'estime de tous ses Camarades.

signé Le Comte de Rochambeau

fait à Newport en rhode Island, le 14 août 1780

Par Monsieur Le Comte
signé De Sibille
Pour Copie Conforme
Le Commissaire de guerre
en l'Ecole Royale M[ilitai]re de St Cyr.

Sur le refus de M. le Commissaire des guerres, de signer la Copie Conforme aux originaux, que je dui presenterai... Sur le refus de me donner acte motivé de ce refus.... Je soussigné, Colonel, Commandant en second l'école Royale militaire de St Cyr, déclare, Sur ma parole d'honneur, La dite Copie Conforme aux originaux, qui existent entre mes mains, et que Je promets representer quand bon semblera.
St Cyr le 26 Xbre 1816.
Le Ch[evali]er Athenais de Trijou=incoudalembert

Rochambeau stellt Rechteren einen Urlaubsschein für eine Reise nach Boston aus (im Schreiben heißt es zwar: Philadelphia, aber nach dem zeitlichen Ablauf des Feldzugs und Rechterens Erinnerungen müsste Boston gemeint sein), Newport, Rhode Island, 14. Aug. 1780; aus Rechterens Personalakte beim Service historique de la Défense, Vincennes.

Rochambeau issues a permit to Rechteren for a visit to Boston (in the letter, it actually says "Philadelphia", but according to the course of the campaign and Rechteren's own memoirs, it should have said Boston), Newport, Rhode Island, Aug. 14th, 1780; taken from Rechterens personal file at the Service historique de la défense, Vincennes.

George Washington als General der Kontinentalarmee in der typischen Uniform in Blau und Gelb, 1776; von Charles W. Peale (1741 – 1827); Wikimedia.

George Washington in the blue-and-buff uniform of a general of the Continental Army, 1776; by Charles W. Peale (1741 – 1827); Wikimedia.

Der Marquis de Lafayette als Generalleutnant der Französischen Nationalgarde (also einige Jahre nach dem Amerikanischen Unabhängigkeitskrieg); von Joseph-Désir Court (1797 – 1865); Schloss Versailles.

The marquis de Lafayette as Lieutenant-General of the French National Guard, i.e. several years after the American War of Independence; by Joseph-Désir Court (1797 – 1865); Palace of Versailles.

Modell des als Transport- oder Hospitalschiff umgerüsteten Kriegsschiffs „Fantasque", auf dem Rechteren die erste Schlacht der „Virginia Capes" miterlebte; Wikimedia.

Model of the warship „Fantasque" which had been modified to serve as a transport or hospital ship; Rechteren witnessed the „First Battle of the Virginia Capes" on board this ship; Wikimedia.

Am 16. März 1781 wurde Rechteren an Bord der „Fantasque" Augenzeuge der „Battle of Cape Henry" oder „First Battle of the Virginia Capes", die er lebhaft und recht genau beschreibt; Maler: V. Zveg (1962); Hampton Roads Naval Museum, Norfolk, VA.; Foto: US Navy Naval History and Heritage Command (Wikimedia).

On March 16th, 1781, Rechteren became an eye-witness of the „Battle of Cape Henry" or „First Battle of the Virginia Capes" on board the „Fantasque"; he gives a lively and fairly accurate description of this naval engagement; painter: V. Zveg (1962); Hampton Roads Naval Museum, Norfolk, VA.; photo: US Navy Naval History and Heritage Command (Wikimedia).

Schlacht von Yorktown: Washington und Rochambeau geben letzte Befehle vor der Schlacht; gemalt 1836 von A. Couder (1789 – 1873); Schloss Versailles (Wikimedia).

Battle of Yorktown, showing Washington and Rochambeau giving last orders before the battle; painted 1836 by A. Couder (1789 – 1873); Palace of Versailles (Wikimedia).

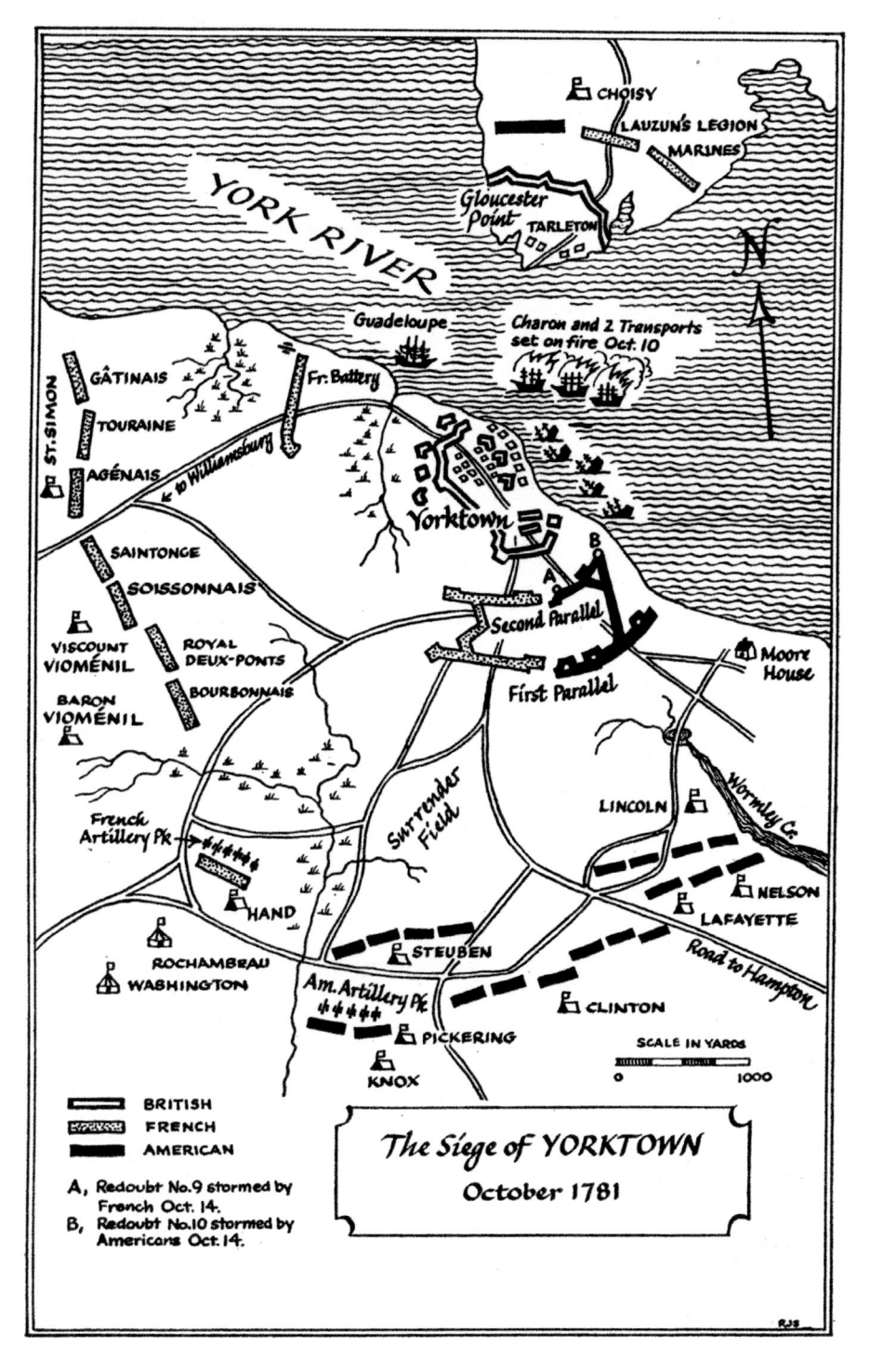

Plan der Belagerung der Festung Yorktown im Herbst 1781; „A" bezeichnet die Schanze 9, die von Rechterens Regiment „Royal Deux-Ponts" unter dem Befehl von Oberstleutnant Wilhelm von Zweibrücken gestürmt wurde, „B" die Schanze 10, die amerikanische Truppen unter Marquis de Lafayette eroberten; aus: Acomb, Journal.

Plan of the siege of Yorktown fortress in the fall of 1781; „A" indicates redoubt No. 9 which was stormed by Rechteren's regiment „Royal Deux-Ponts" under the command of Lt.-Colonel Guillaume de Deux-Ponts, „B" redoubt No. 10 which was taken by American troops under the command of marquis de Lafayette; from: Acomb, Journal.

Oberstleutnant Wilhelm von Zweibrücken (Deux-Ponts), noch mit dem Verband seiner beim Sturm auf die Schanze 9 der Festung Yorktown erlittenen Kopfverletzung, nimmt im Namen seines Regiments die Glückwünsche der Generale Washington (rechts, mit gezogenem Hut) und Rochambeau (links, mit dem Rücken zum Betrachter) zu dem den ganzen Feldzug entscheidenden Erfolg entgegen; Zeichnung von George C. Woodbridge (1931 – 2004);
aus: Tröss, Regiment.

Lt.-Colonel Wilhelm von Zweibrücken (Deux-Ponts), with his head still in bandages from the wound suffered in storming redoubt No. 9 of the fortress of Yorktown, receives the congratulations of generals Washington (on the right, with his hat taken off) and Rochambeau (on the left, showing his back) for this success which decided the outcome of the whole campaign; sketch by George C. Woodbridge (1931 – 2004); taken from: Tröss, Regiment.

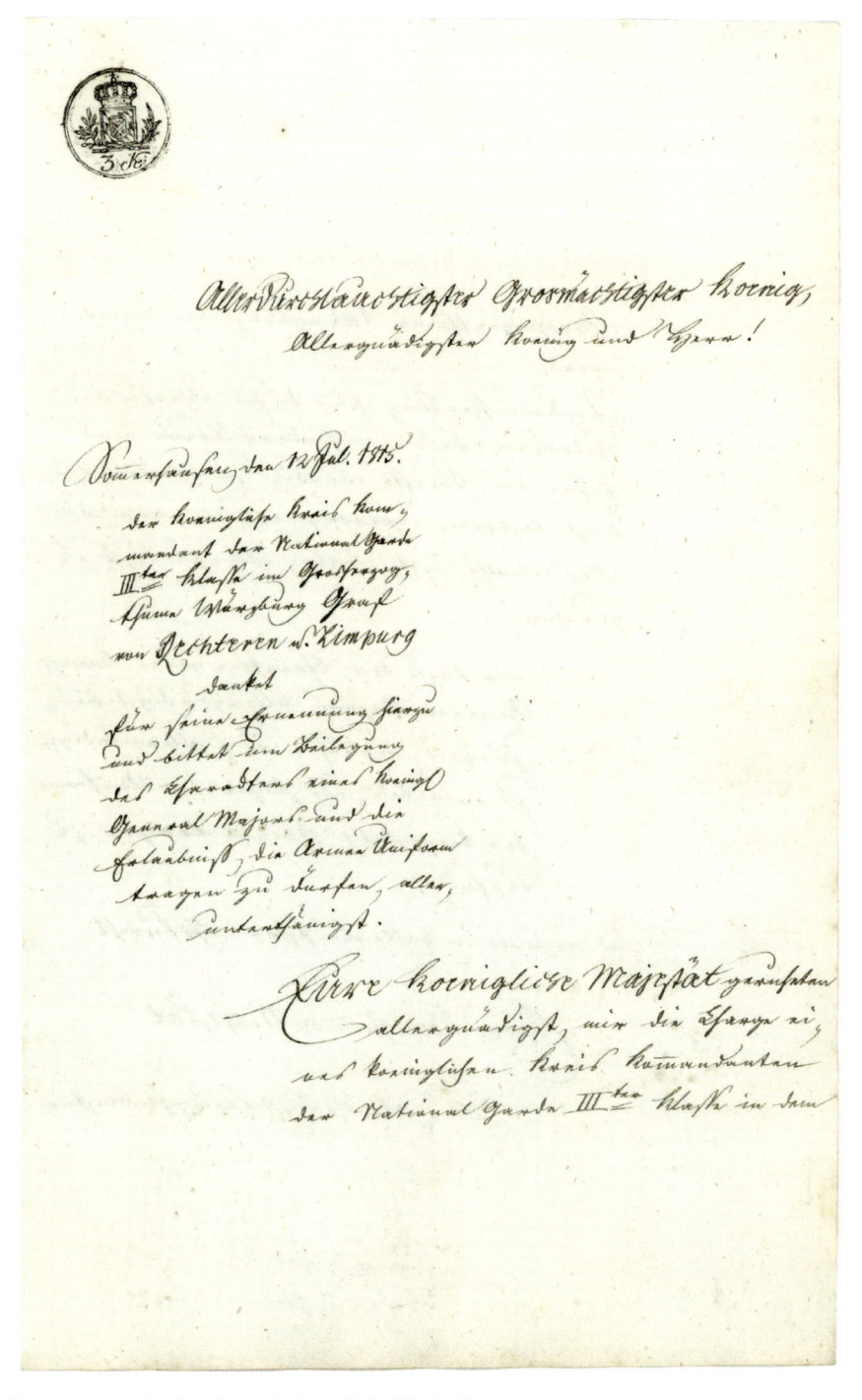

Rechteren dankt dem bayerischen König für die Ernennung zum Kommandanten der Nationalgarde im Großherzogtum Würzburg und bittet zugleich um Verleihung des Titels eines Generalmajors, Sommerhausen, 12. Juli 1815, mit eigenhändiger Unterschrift Rechterens; BHStA, Kriegsarchiv, OP 81367.

Rechteren thanks the King of Bavaria for having been appointed commander of the national guard in the Grand-Duchy of Würzburg and asks to have the title of major general conferred on him, Sommerhausen, July 12th, 1815, signed in Rechteren's own hand; BHStA, Kriegsarchiv, OP 81367.

Großherzogthum Würzburg zu übernehmen,
habe.

Indeme Handlung für dieses allerhöchste
Zutrauen, daßer mich durch Treue und
Eifer im Dienste würdig zu machen äußerst bestreben werde, erlaube mir die
allerunterthänigste Bitte, allergnädigst zu
geruhen,

  mir sogar den Character eines Königl.
  General Majors allergnädigst bei-
  zulegen, imgleichen auch allergnädigst
  zu erlauben, als solcher die Uniforme
  des königlichen Armee tragen zu
  dürfen,

und ersterbe in allertiefster Ehrfurcht

  Eurer koeniglichen Majestät

    allerunterthänigst treuergebenster

      Friedrich Heinrich Eberhard Rudolph
      Graf von Zastrow u. Lonperg.

Rechteren in der Uniform eines Generalmajors à la suite der Bayerischen Armee, wohl 1817, also im Alter von ca. 66 Jahren, mit dem französischen Militärverdienstorden und einer Armbinde in den bayerischen Farben, vor dem Hintergrund der Festung Marienberg in Würzburg; die vor den Festungswerken am Main paradierende Truppe ist wohl Teil der ihm unterstehenden Nationalgarde im Großherzogtum Würzburg; unbekannter Maler; Privatbesitz; (Foto: Michael Hettler).

Rechteren in the uniform of a major-general à la suite of the Bavarian army, probably in 1817, about 66 years of age, with a chevalier's cross of the French military order of merit and a brassard in the Bavarian colours, visible in the background is Marienberg fortress in Würzburg; the troops parading in front of the fortress walls on the banks of the river Main probably belong to the Bavarian National Guard in the Grand-Duchy of Würzburg which he commanded; unknown painter; privately owned; (photo: Michael Hettler).

Graf Rochambeau, der Oberkommandierende der französischen Truppen im Amerikanischen Unabhängigkeitskrieg 1780 – 1782; Maler: Charles-Philippe Larivière (1789 – 1876), Öl auf Leinwand (1834);
Foto: PHGCOM (Wikimedia), Schloss Versailles.

Count Rochambeau, the commander-in-chief of the French forces in the American War of Independence 1780 – 1782; painter: Charles-Philippe Larivière (1789 – 1876), Oil on canvas (1834); photo: PHGCOM (Wikimedia), Palace of Versailles.

Quellen und Literatur / Bibliography

Ungedruckte und gedruckte Quellen:

Fürstlich Castell'sches Archiv, Castell (FCA)

FCA HA XIV c 138: Fragment aus der Lebensgeschichte des Herrn Grafen (Friedrich Reinhard) zu Rechteren-Limpurg, von dem Herrn Grafen geschrieben im Jahr 17 …; zitiert (quoted as): Mskr., mscr.

FCA HA I d II 7: Umsetzung des Abteilungsvertrags vom 6.11.1819 mit den bayerischen Behörden und dem Vormund in Castell, 1820 – 1822.

FCA HA IV 55: Geburtsanzeige von Friedrich Reinhard von Rechteren-Limpurg

FCA HA IV 118: Personalia des weiland Erlauchten … Herrn Friedrich Reinhard Burkhard Rudolph Grafen von Rechteren zu Limpurg … (Nachruf auf Rechteren von 1842), zitiert (quoted as): Nachruf (Obituary).

Darin auch: Lebensbeschreibung von Friedrich Reinhards Sohn Ludwig (Louis) 1811 – 1909.

Bayerisches Hauptstaatsarchiv, München (BHStA)

MA 5783: Die Differenzen in Hinsicht der zur Reichsgrafschaft Limpurg-Speckfeld gehörigen Orte Sommerhausen …, 1803/04; darin: Beurkundete Darstellung der den beyden regierenden Herren Grafen Friedrich Ludwig Christian und Friedrich Reinhard … von Rechteren-Limpurg von Seiten des Kurbayerischen Fürstenthums Würzburg widerfahrnen Eingriffe und harten Kränkungen … und erlittenen unerhörten Vergewaltigungen und Mißhandlungen auch Schäden und Kosten, 1803 (Druckschrift); zitiert (quoted as): Beurkundete Darstellung (Documentary Record).

MA 5784: Die Eingriffe des Grafen von Rechtern-Limpurg in die diesseitigen Territorial-Gerechtsame …, 1804

MA 74554: Die Reise des Grafen von Rechtern-Limpurg nach Holland, 1809

MInn 47716: Besitz-Ergreifung der durch die rheinische Bundes-Acte unter k. Souverainität gekommenen Grafschaft Limpurg-Speckfeld …, 1806

MInn 47717: Familienverträge und Verhältnisse des Herrn Reichsrats Grafen Rechtern zu Einersheim, 1822 – 1911

MInn 47246: Reichsratswürde des Hauses Rechtern-Limpurg, 1818 – 1909

Bayerisches Hauptstaatsarchiv, Abt. IV: Kriegsarchiv

OP 81367: Personalakt (der bayerischen Armee) über Friedrich Reinhard von Rechteren-Limpurg, 1815 – 1842

Bayerisches Staatsarchiv Würzburg (StAW)

Reg.v.Ufr. 1943/45, Nr. 1871: Staatsrechtliche Angelegenheiten des Innern: Graf von Rechteren-Limpurg, standesherrliche Gutsherrschaft …, 1834 – 1848

Reg.v.Ufr. 1943/45, Nr. 12563: Staatsrechtliche Angelegenheiten des gräflichen Hauses Rechteren-Limpurg …, 1803 – 1842

Service historique de la Défense, Vincennes

Yb 346: Personalakte von Friedrich Reinhard Comte de Rechteren bei der französischen Armee

Stadtarchiv Würzburg (StadtAW)

Grundliste (nach Häusern geführtes Einwohnerverzeichnis) Herrngasse 2 (District II, Nr. 578)

Adressbücher der Stadt Würzburg 1806, 1829, 1833, 1838

Literatur:

Vorbemerkung: Um den Anmerkungsapparat zu entlasten, enthalten zahlreiche Fußnoten in der vorliegenden Ausgabe von Rechterens Memoiren und in der Einleitung nur Sachinformationen ohne eine Quellenangabe. Es handelt sich in allen diesen Fällen um Informationen, die der Wikipedia, der Encyclopaedia Britannica (15. Ausgabe von 1974) oder Meyers Großem Taschenlexikon in 24 Bänden, 5. Aufl. 1995 entnommen sind und dort ohne große Mühe nachgeprüft werden können, weil zu den erläuterten Namen oder Begriffen ein eigener Artikel vorliegt, oft sogar in allen drei Nachschlagewerken. Wo aber ein weiterführendes Werk der Sekundärliteratur zitiert wird oder wo der Leser Mühe haben könnte, den einschlägigen Artikel bzw. die zitierte Quelle in den genannten Nachschlagewerken zu finden, sind die üblichen Titelangaben gemacht worden.

Preliminary note: In order to limit the volume of the annotations in this edition – and in the introduction as well – many footnotes contain only factual information without identifying its source. In all of these cases, the information is taken either from Wikipedia, the Encyclopaedia Britannica (15th ed. of 1974) or Meyers Großes Taschenlexikon in 24 vols., 5th ed. 1995, and can easily be checked there because the reader will find individual articles (often enough in all three of these encyclopedias) for the persons, places or events being discussed directly under their own names. But where it would be difficult to find the pertinent article in those encyclopedias or where secondary literature is quoted, the reader will find the usual quotations.

Aa, A[braham]J[acob] van der (Hg.): Biographisch Woordenboek der Nederlanden …, 10 Bde., Haarlem 1858 ff.

Acomb, Evelyn M[artha] (ed.): The Revolutionary Journal of Baron Ludwig von Closen 1780 – 1783, translated and edited with an introduction by E.M. Acomb, Chapel Hill (1958); zitiert (quoted as): Acomb, Journal.

Allgemeine Deutsche Biographie (ADB), 56 Bde., hg. durch die Historische Commission bei der kgl. (bayer.) Akademie der Wissenschaften 1875 – 1912, unveränd. ND Berlin 1967 – 1971.

Battaglia, Salvatore (Gründer): Grande Dizionario della Lingua Italiana, 21 Bde., 1961 – 2002.

Baum, Hans-Peter: Lehenswesen in Franken, in: Historisches Lexikon Bayerns (http://www.historisches-lexikon-bayerns.de), 2014; zitiert (quoted as): Baum, Lehenswesen.

Baumann, Kurt: Das Herzogtum Pfalz-Zweibrücken. Umrisse einer Landesgeschichte, in: ders./idem: Von Geschichte und Menschen der Pfalz. Ausgewählte Aufsätze, hg. von Kurt Andermann, Speyer 1984, S. 45 – 64, hier 63; zitiert/quoted as: Baumann, Herzogtum Pfalz-Zweibrücken.

Bigot de Morogues, Sébastien François: Tactique navale ou traité des evolutions et des signaux, Paris 1763; zitiert (quoted as): Bigot de Morogues, Tactique navale.

ders./idem: Zee-tactick, of Grond-regulen der krygskunde ter zee […], vermeerdert met […] anmerkingen , en […] veranderingen […] met veele bygevoegde figuuren opgehelderd. Als mede eene verhandeling van de voordeelen eener groote zeemagt […]. Gedeeltelyk uit vreemde taalen by een verzameld en vertaald, door Lodewik Grave van Byland, Amsterdam 1767.

Bodinier, Gilbert: Dictionnaire des officiers de l'armée royale qui ont combattu aux Etats-Unis pendant la guerre d'indépendance, 1776 – 1783, Vincennes 1983; zitiert (quoted as): Bodinier, Dictionnaire.

Boxer, C.R.: The Golden Age of Brasil 1695 – 1750. Growing Pains of a Colonial Society, Berkeley/CA, 1962.

Dansk Biografisk Leksikon, begonnen und hg. von C[arl] F[rederik] Bricka, 27 Bde., Kopenhagen 1933 – 1944.

Deflers, Isabelle: Die Militärreformen des Comte von Saint-Germain, in: Zeitschrift für Historische Forschung 42 (2015), S. 411 – 431; zitiert (quoted as): Deflers, Militärreformen.

Dohna, Jesko Graf zu (Hg.): Emma Fürstin zu Castell-Rüdenhausen. Erinnerungen (Veröffentlichungen der Gesellschaft für fränkische Geschichte, R. XIII, Bd. 50), Würzburg 2014.

Europäische Stammtafeln Neue Folge, hg. von Detlev Schwennicke, Bd. IV: Standesherrliche Häuser I, Marburg 1981.

Fränkisches Volksblatt, Nr. 256 vom 8. November 1963.

Freeden, Max H. von: Aus den Schätzen des Mainfränkischen Museums Würzburg. Ausgewählte Werke mit 156 Bildtafeln, 2. Aufl., Würzburg 1972; zitiert (quoted as): von Freeden, Schätze.

Gazette de France, gegr. 1631 als „La Gazette", seit 1762 Gazette de France. Organe officiel du gouvernement royal, Jg. 1775, Nr. 48 (16.06.1775) und Nr. 49 (19.06.1775), (abrufbar im Internet).

Gebhardt, Bruno: Handbuch der deutschen Geschichte, 8. Aufl., hg. von Herbert Grundmann, Stuttgart 1960 (hier benutzt: verb. Nachdruck, 1962); zitiert (quoted as): Gebhardt, Deutsche Geschichte.

Gothaisches genealog. Taschenbuch der Gräflichen Häuser auf das Jahr 1868, 41. Jg.,

Gothaisches genealog. Taschenbuch der Briefadligen Häuser 1907, 1. Jg.

Greene, Jerome A.: The Guns of Independence. The Siege of Yorktown, 1781, New York, N.Y. 2005; zitiert (quoted as): Greene, Guns of Independence.

Gutmann, Friedrich: Sommerhausen in Wort und Bild. Geschichtliche und kulturgeschichtliche Darlegungen nach Quellen, 2. Aufl., berichtigt, ergänzt und erweitert von Georg Furkel, Sommerhausen 1970; zitiert (quoted as): Gutmann/Furkel, Sommerhausen.

Horst, Frank C. P. van der: Biografie eines herausragenden Bürgers von Heilbronn: Heinrich August Freiherr von Kinckel (1747 – 1821), in: Christhard Schrenk/Peter Wanner (Hgg.): heilbronnica 5. Beiträge zur Stadt- und Regionalgeschichte = Quellen und Forschungen zur Geschichte der Stadt Heilbronn 20 bzw. Jahrbuch für schwäbisch-fränkische Geschichte 37, Heilbronn 2013; zitiert (quoted as): van der Horst, Kinckel.

Israel, Jonathan J.: The Dutch Republic. Its Rise, Greatness, and Fall 1477 – 1806 (The Oxford History of Early Modern Europe), Oxford 1998; zitiert (quoted as): Israel, Dutch Republic.

Kann, Beate: Würzburger Ehrenbürger 1819 bis 1837 (Stadtarchiv Würzburg, Hinweise – Informationen Nr. 19), Würzburg 1994; zitiert (quoted as): Kann, Ehrenbürger.

Kissinger, Henry A.: Weltordnung, München 2014 (Orig.: World Order, New York, 2012).

Kneschke, Ernst Heinrich (Hg.): Neues Allgemeines Deutsches Adels-Lexikon, 9 Bde., unveränd. ND der Ausg. Leipzig 1859 – 1870, Leipzig 1929/30; zitiert (quoted as): Kneschke, Adelslexikon.

Lexikon des Mittelalters, 9. Bde., München und Zürich 1980 – 1998; zitiert (quoted as): LexMA mit Bandnr. (with no. of vol.)

Metzler Goethe-Lexikon. Personen – Sachen – Begriffe, 2. verb. Aufl., Stuttgart/Weimar 2004.

Müller, Fr.: Die Künstler aller Zeiten und Völker, 1857.

Napoleon und Bayern. Katalog zur Bayerischen Landesausstellung 2015 in Ingolstadt, hg. von Margot Hamm, Evamaria Brockhoff, Volker Bräu, Stefanie Buchhold und Uta Lerche, Augsburg 2015; zitiert (quoted as): Napoleon und Bayern.

Prescher, H.: Geschichte und Beschreibung der zum fränkischen Kreis gehörigen Reichsgrafschaft Limpurg, 2. Teil, Stuttgart 1790; zitiert (quoted as): Prescher, Reichsgrafschaft Limpurg.

Redelberger, Richard: Herrschaftsgericht Sommerhausen vor 125 Jahren, in: Die Mainlande, 16. Jg. Nr. 15 vom 14. August 1965; zitiert (quoted as): Redelberger, Herrschaftsgericht.

Roda, Burkhard von: Adam Friedrich von Seinsheim. Auftraggeber zwischen Rokoko und Klassizismus. Zur Würzburger und Bamberger Hofkunst anhand der Privatkorrespondenz des Fürstbischofs (1755 – 1779) (Veröffentlichungen der Gesellschaft für fränkische Geschichte VIII, 6) Neustadt/Aisch 1980; zitiert (quoted as): v. Roda, Seinsheim.

Scharf, Claus: Katharina II., Deutschland und die Deutschen (Veröffentlichungen des Instituts für europäische Geschichte Mainz, Abt. Universalgeschichte, Bd. 153), Mainz 1995; zitiert (quoted as): Scharf, Katharina II.

Schuhmann, Günther: Carl Friedrich Reinhard von Gemmingen (1739 – 1822), in: Fränkische Lebensbilder, 16. Bd., hg. von Alfred Wendehorst (Veröffentlichungen der Gesellschaft für fränkische Geschichte VII A, 16), Neustadt/Aisch 1996.

Selig, Robert A.: Georg Daniel Flohr's Journal: A New Perspective, in: Colonial Williamsburg, vol. 15, No. 4, 1993, p. 47 – 53 (www.americanrevolution.org/flohr1.html)

Selig, Robert A.: The Washington – Rochambeau Revolutionary Route in the State of New York, 1781 – 1782. An Historical and Architectural Survey, Hudson River Valley Institute, Poughkeepsie, N.Y. 2001; zitiert (quoted as): Selig, Revolutionary Route.

Ders. (idem): Deux-Ponts Germans. Unsung Heroes of the American Revolution, in: German Life, vol. 2 (16.2.1995), S. 50 – 53

Ders. (idem): François Joseph Paul Comte de Grasse, the Battle off the Virginia Capes, and the American Victory at Yorktown (www.americanrevolution.org/degrasse.html)

Ders. (idem): George Washington's German Allies. Das deutsche königlich-französische Infanterie Regiment von Zweybrücken or Royal Deux-Ponts, Teile II, III und IV, in: Journal of the Johannes Schwalm Historical Association, vol. 7, Nr. 1 (2001), Nr. 2 (2002), Nr. 3 (2003); zitiert (quoted as): Selig, German Allies.

Ders. (idem): Unruhige Tage am Main: Die Revolution kommt nach Winterhausen/Restless Days along the Main: The Revolution Comes to Winterhausen, in: German Life, December/January 2014, S. 2 – 4, 4 – 5; zitiert (quoted as): Selig, Unruhige Tage/ Restless Days.

Ders. (idem): Wenn die Katze aus dem Haus ist … Mehr wahre Geschichten aus Winterhausen/ When the cat's away … More true stories from Winterhausen, in: German Life, August/September 2011, p. 47 – 47, 47 – 49; zitiert (quotes as): Selig, Wenn die Katze … /When the cat …

Ders. (idem): 6. August 1787 – 3. June 1814: Vier Herren in 27 Jahren in der Reichsgrafschaft Rechteren-Limpurg-Speckfeld/6 August 1787 – 3 June 1814: Four Masters in 27 Years for the Imperial County of Rechteren-Limpurg-Speckfeld, in: German Life, August/September 2012, p. 32 – 33, 34 – 34; zitiert (quoted as): Selig, Vier Herren in 27 Jahren.

Johann Siebmachers großes und allgemeines Wappenbuch, neue, reich vermehrte Auflage … Bd. 1, 3. Abt.: Hoher Adel, II. Reihe: Die erlauchten Grafengeschlechter Deutschlands, bearb. v. A. Maximilian Gritzner, Nürnberg 1878; zitiert (quoted as): Siebmacher, Wappenbuch.

Simon, Ernst Otto: Hans Christoph Ludwig von Closen, aus niederbayerischem Adel, französischer General, Teilnehmer am Unabhängigkeitskampf der USA und dann Unterpräfekt in Simmern, o.O [Simmern] o.J. [1986] (Schriftenreihe des Rhein-Hunsrück-Kreises, Nr. 3)

Spindler, Max (Hg.): Handbuch der Bayerischen Geschichte, 3. Bd.: Franken, Schwaben, Oberpfalz bis zum Ausgang des 18. Jahrhunderts, München 1971; zitiert (quoted as): Spindler, Handbuch.

Tröss, Rudolf Karl: Das Regiment Royal-Deux-Ponts. Gesammelte Beiträge zur Geschichte des Regiments, hg. von der Stadverwaltung Zweibrücken, 1983; zitiert (quoted as): Tröss, Regiment.

Weiss, Wolfgang: Übergang an Bayern (1795 – 1814), in: Geschichte der Stadt Würzburg, Bd II: Vom Bauernkrieg 1525 bis zum Übergang an das Königreich Bayern 1814, hg. von Ulrich Wagner, Stuttgart 2004; zitiert (quoted as): Weiss, Übergang an Bayern.

Whaley, Joachim: Das Heilige Römische Reich Deutscher Nation und seine Territorien, 2 Bde., Darmstadt 2014 (engl. Originalausgabe: Germany and the Holy Roman Empire; Oxford 2012); zitiert (quoted as): Whaley, Hl. Röm. Reich.

Winterhäuser Kalenderblatt, Januar 2012, hg. vom Geschichtsverein Winterhausen.

Wunder, Gerd/Schefold, M./Beutter, H.: Die Schenken von Limpurg und ihr Land, Sigmaringen 1982; zitiert (quoted as): Wunder/Schefold/Beutter, Schenken von Limpurg.

Register / Index
von Jesko Graf zu Dohna und Hans-Peter Baum

Das Register enthält die im Quellentext und in der Einleitung erwähnten Personen, Orte, Institutionen, bes. Regimenter, und Schiffe, nicht jedoch Sachbegriffe. Nicht nachgewiesen werden der Autor der hier veröffentlichten Memoiren, Friedrich Reinhard von Rechteren-Limpurg, selbst sowie seine Grafschaft Limpurg-Speckfeld. Das Register richtet sich bei den Seitenangaben nach dem deutschen Text, im englischen Text gibt es (aufgrund verschiedener Satzstellung) an einigen Stellen geringfügige Verschiebungen von nicht mehr als einer Seite nach vorn oder zurück. Auch die Schreibformen der Namen sind nach der deutschen Orthographie aufgenommen; nur gelegentlich werden englische Formen zusätzlich genannt. Da alle Personen in den Fußnoten mit Lebensdaten, sämtlichen Vor- und Nachnamen und Titeln erläutert werden, da dort auch reichliche Informationen zu Orten und Institutionen vorliegen, wird im Register auf genaue Angaben dazu verzichtet. Geklammerte Seitenzahlen stehen dort, wo ein Lemma nur indirekt genannt wird. So wird z. B. Kapitän Gallagher von der „Betsy" auf S. 113 namentlich genannt, auf S. 114 – 116 nur als „der Kapitän" erwähnt.

The index contains the names of all persons, places, institutions, especially regiments, and ships mentioned in the text of the memoirs published here and in the introduction, except for Friedrich Reinhard von Rechteren-Limpurg himself and his county Limpurg-Speckfeld. The index is basically German and has the German name forms; the English forms are mentioned only in a few cases. The indication of page numbers corresponds to the German text; in a few places, there are differences between both texts of one page forward or back. The reason for that is the different word order in German and English sentences, especially of adverbial phrases. As family and personal names, life dates, titles, and functions have been fully listed in the footnotes as well as detailed information on places and institutions, it was thought unnecessary to duplicate that information in the index. Page numbers in parentheses indicate that the person or place in question are mentioned only indirectly. Thus, Captain Gallagher of the ship „Betsy" is mentioned by name on page 113, but only as „the captain" on pages 114 – 116. The frequently used German abbreviation „frz." stands for „French", an „Oberst" or „Obrist" is a colonel.

Aa, van der (Leinwandhändler) 67
Aachen 72
Abercromby (engl. Oberstleutnant) 108
Adams 77
Aetna 58
Affenberg (in Afrika) 47
Agenois (Regiment) 103, 108
Agrippa 53
Agrippina 53
Aix en Provence 48
Alarm (engl. Schiff) 63
Alençon (Dept. Orne) 118
Alexandria (Virginia) 112
Algier 47, 62, 67
Alkmaar (Niederlande) 46
Almelo (Prov. Overijssel) 9, 10, 13, 23, 45, 46, 67

Amerika 32, 33, 37, 39, 41 – 43, 50, 80, 86, 87
Amsterdam 46, 60
Anagno-See 54
André (engl. Major) 89
Annapolis (Maryland) 103
Ansbach (Bayern) 9, 18, 27, 45, 73
Antwerpen 72
Arbuthnot (engl. Kommandant) 70
Ariovist (german. König) 38, 86
Arnold (amerikan. dann engl. General), 89, 93, 97
d'Artois, Comte 74
Atlantik 33
Aurai (Bretagne) 116
Avernus-See 53

Baja (bei Neapel) 53
Balearen und Pityusen (Inseln) 61
Baltimore (Maryland) 112
Bamberg (Bayern) 27
Barras, Graf (franz. Admiral) 96, 97
Barbareskenstaaten 30, 31
Bas, de, (Leutnant auf der „Nassau") 46
Bayern (Kurfürstentum, dann Königreich) 14, 15, 17, 21, 24
Belem (Portugal, „Bethlehem") 66, 69
Belle Isle (en Mer, Bretagne) 116

Berghuyss/Berghuis (Kapitän der „Princess Maria Louisa") 63, 65
Bermuda-Inseln 37, 81
Bertram, Master (Bartram, amerik. Botaniker) 41, 113
Betsy (Schiff) 113
Beun (holl. Leinwandhändler) 67
Bevesier (Cap Béveziers, Beachy Head) 46, 71
Bibeiro, Antonio (Bootsmann) 66
Bibra, von (Leutnant) 111 – 113, 116
Bigot de Morogues, Sébastien François (Verfasser einer Seetaktik) 65
Binker (Kadett auf der „Nassau") 46

Biscaya 117
Bombelles, Marquis de (frz. Gesandter am Reichstag) 74, 75
Bonifacius (Meerenge, straits of) 62
Boreel de Moregneau (Leutnant auf der „Nassau") 46
Boston (Massachusetts) 92
Bourbon (frz./span. Königshaus) 22
Bourbonnois (Regiment) 79, 105, 106, 109
Braam, van (Kapitän der „Thetis") 67
Brandenburg-Ansbach, Markgraf von 73
Brasilien 69
Breslau 13
Brest (frz. Kriegshafen) 35, 36, 43, 70, 79, 81, 94
–, Rade de (Reede, „Rat") 81
Bretagne 43, 77, 115
Brock, Georg Ignaz (Würzb. Bürgermeister) 23
Brüssel 72

Cabrera (Insel) 61, 65
Caesar, Caius Julius 38, 86, 117
Cágliari (Sardinien) 58,59
Calais 46, 71
Cap Corso 59
Cap Negro 52
Cap Palos 65
Cap Sicié (bei Toulon) 60
Cap St. Vincent (Portugal) 47, 66
Capo del Monte (Schloss b. Neapel) 55
Cartagena ("Carthogena", Spanien) 66
Cascais (Portugal, "Cascaes") 66
Castell (Grafen von, Grafschaft) 13, 19
Castell St. Elmo (bei Neapel) 55
Catharinen-Bey (b. Lissabon) 69

Cayugas (Indianerstamm) 90
Cerboli ("Serboli", "Serbolia") 52, 58
Cesme s. Tschesme
Ceuta (Marokko) 47
Charleston (South Carolina, "Charlestown") 81
Charon (engl. Schiff) 106
Chartres, Duc de 74
Chateau d'If (bei Marseille) 48
Chatellux, Chevalier de (Marschal de campo) 100
Chesapeake Bay 94, 96, 101, 103
Choisy, N. de (General) 96, 104
"Cingels" (Dungeness) 71
Clinton (engl. General) 89, 97, 98, 101
Closen, Ludwig von (Leutnant, Adjutant Rochambeaus) 34, 35, 37, 39 – 42, 84
Columbus, Christoph 50
Cognuacas (Indianerstamm) 90
Compiègne 49
Comtesse de Noailles, La (frz. Transportschiff) 33, 35, 80
Connecticut 97
Conquérant (frz. Linienschiff) 36, 80, 81, 96
Coquet (Offizier auf der „Comtesse de Noailles") 80
Cork (Irland) 113
Cornwallis (Kapitän, Bruder des Generals) 81
Cornwallis (engl. General) 39, 98, 103 – 105, 109, 110
Corsica s. Korsika
Cowes („Coues", Isle of Wight) 70
– „Modderbank" (Quarantäneplatz bei Cowes) 70
Crull/Krul (Kapitän der „Rotterdam") 51, 57, 62, 63, 65, 70
Custine, Graf (frz. Oberst, später General) 87, 88, 103, 105, 107

Darsenna s. Genua
Dedel, Salomon (Kapitän der „Kennemerland") 46, 65, 69
Delaware (Fluss) 101, 102
Deux-Ponts (Regiment) s. Royal Deux-Ponts
Deuxpont(s), (Christian) Comte de (Oberst) 40, 75, 103, (107), 111
Deuxponts, Guillaume Comte de (Oberstltn.) 40, (105), 106, 108 s. auch Forbach, Graf von
Doria, Andrea 50
Doria, Familie 50
Dover 71
Dresden 13
Dreux (Dept. Eure et Loir) 118
Duc de Bourgogne (frz. Schiff) 86
Dull (Hauslehrer, Advokat) 10, 45

„Eck von Holland" (Hoek van H.) 71
Eddystone (Leuchtturm vor Plymouth) 69
Egmond (an Zee) 71
Eibelstadt (Unterfranken) 27
Elba 52, 62
Elphinstone (Contre-Admiral) 59
England 73, 75
Erthal, Franz Ludwig von (Fürstbischof von Würzburg) 12
Esebeck, v. (Hauptmann) 100
L'Escadre (Lt. Colonel im Regiment Gatinois) 106
D'Estaing, Graf 104
Europa 39, 41, 42, 50

Fantasque (frz. Schiff) 93 – 95
Farnese (Adelsfamilie) 55
Filidor (Philidor, „Tilidor") 76
Finale Ligure 65
Florenz 63

Flohr, Franz Daniel (Soldat) 34, 35, 37, 39, 41, 42
Fontainebleau 49
Forbach, Graf v. 74, 76 s. auch Deuxpont(s), Guillaume Comte de (identisch)
Formentera (Insel) 65
Formiche di Grossetto (Inselgruppe) 57
Fort du Bougie (Tejo-Mündung) 66
Fort Notre-Dame de la Garde (b. Marseille) 48
Fort St. Julien (Tejo-Mündung) 66
Fourgeaud (Regiment) 72
Franken (Region) 9, 10, 11, 19, 20, 45, 111
Franklin, Benjamin 77
Frankreich (France) 10, 12, 14, 15, 87, 96
Franz I. Stephan, röm.-dt. Kaiser 11
Friesland 63
Fürth (Bayern) 12

Gaibach (Unterfranken, Konstitutionssäule) 23
Galita (Insel bei Tunis) 58
Gallagher (Kapitän der „Betsy") 113, (114 – 116)
"Gargona" s. Gorgona
Gatinois (Regiment) 103, 105, 106
Gemmingen, von (Minister in Ansbach) 73
Genua 49 – 51, 62, 65
– Darsenna (Teil des Hafens von Genua) 51
– Molo 49
Germantown (Pennsylvania) 39, 102
Gibraltar 31,66
Giech, Friedrika Antoinetta Gräfin von (Rechteren erste Ehefrau) 11, (13)
Giech, Graf von (Rechterens Schwager) 12

144

Giglio (Insel) 52
Gilson (Hofrat) 55
Gloucester, Stadt (Virginia) 104, 110
Gloucester, Herzog von 63
Gö(r)tz (General) 73
Goor van Hinlopen, Jan van (Kapitän der „Nassau") 46, 63, 70
Gorgona ("Gargona", Insel b. Livorno) 51, 59, 62
Gotha (Thüringen) 84, 108
Grasse, Comte de (frz. Admiral) 82, 97, 98, 101
Graves, Thomas ("Grey", engl. Konteradmiral) 85
Grotto di Cane (b. Neapel) 54
Guadeloupe (Insel) 82

Haag (den Haag) 68, 72
Hake, v. (Kapitän) 84
Hake, v. (Hauptmann) 108
Hamilton, Lord 53
Haren, van (Leutnant auf der "Nassau") 46
Hartford ("Hartfort", Connecticut) 89
Head of Elk (Maryland) 103
Heffner (bayer. Landeskommissär) 16, 17, 19
Helder (den, Niederlande) 46
Hellmitzheim (Unterfranken) 24
Hennebont („Henebon", Dept. Morbihan) 116
Herculaneum 55
Herlingen (Admiralität) 63
Herrmann (Agent des Fürstbischofs von Würzburg in Paris) 74
Hohenlohe-Kirchberg, Auguste Eleonore Prinzessin von (Rechterens 2. Ehefrau) 21
Holland 70, 71
Holländischer Garten (Friedhof bei Livorno) 64
Hompesch, Freiherr von (kurbayer. Landeskommissär) 14
Horaz 76
Hudson (Fluss) 39, 90, 97 – 99, 101
Hyerische Inseln 62

IJsselstein (Niederlande) 10, 46
Inseln (karibische) 97, 103
Irland 113, 117
Ischia (Insel) 52, 57
Ischtersheim (Leutnant) 85
Isle de France (Region) 88
Isle du Levant 60
Italien 72

Jamaika 81
James-Fluss (Virginia) 103
Januarius, Hl. (San Gennaro) 53, 56
Jason (Schiff) 82
Jefferson, William (3. US-Präsident) 42
Jerusalem 64
Juel (dän. Kapitän) 47
Juisse (Kapitän der „Comtesse de Noailles") 80, 83

Kaas (dän. Admiral) 47
Kanada 90
Karthäuser-Kloster S. Martino (bei Neapel) 55
Kauw (holländ. Kapitän) 70
Kempenfeld (engl. Admiral) 58
Kennemerland (holländ. Schiff) 46
Kingsbridge (bei New York) 100
Kistemaker (holländ. Konsul) 68
Kitzingen (Unterfranken) 27
Klein-Venedig (Ortsteil von Livorno) 64
Klook (Hauptmann) 84
Kock, James (Lotse) 69
Kohlhaas, Michael (Romanfigur) 18
Korsika 59, 62
Kroon (Leutnant auf der „Nassau") 46

Lafayette, Marquis de (frz. General u. Politiker) 93, 98, 106, 108, 109
La Methe, Chevalier Alexandre de 107
Landernau (Bretagne) 79
Landivisiau (Bretagne) 79
La Roche, v. (Leutnant) 92, 111, 112
La Roche, Sophie v. 92
Lauragay, Duc de 74
Lauzun, Herzog von 111
Lauzan, Legion de 80, 104, (111)
Laval (Dept. Mayenne) 117
Levante (Region) 48
Lindelbach (Unterfranken) 15, 16, 24
Lissabon (Lisbon) 67 – 70
– Gesellschaftshaus "The Long Room" 68
Livorno (Leghorn) 30, 51, 52, 57, 59, 60, 62, 64, 65
Liverpool (engl. Schiff) 63
Löhnburg, v. (dän. Offizier) 84
Loo, van (Kommandeur auf der „Nassau") 46, 70
London (engl. Schiff) 95, 96
Lorient („l'Orient", Westfrankreich) 116
Louw (russ. Kapitän der „Ritchislof") 64
Lucca 65
Ludwig XVI. König v. Frankreich (72), 83, 90, (91)
Lunéville (Lothringen) 14, 72
Lutzau (Lutzau, Lützow, Leutnant) 85
Luzerne, Marquis de (frz. Gesandter in Philadelphia) 112

Maastricht 72
Mac Doughal (Offizier auf der „Betsy") 113, 114
Main (Fluss) 18
Mainz 12
Malaga 47, 48, 67
Mallorca ("Majorca") 61
Malora s. Meloria
Malta 58, 60
Marbois, de (Sekretär) 112
Marbella („Maribella") 66
Marktbreit (Unterfranken) 27
Markt Einersheim (Unterfranken) 14, 15, 24, 25, 28
Marseille 39, 48, 49, 62, 63, 113
Max I. Joseph, König v. Bayern 77
Meloria (Insel) 51
Metz (Lothringen) 72
Minorca 60, 65
Mittelmeer (Mediterranean) 10, 29, 30, 35, 37, 43
Molo s. Genua
Monaco 65
Monbarrey, Prince de 75
Monbarrey, Graf 76, 112
Montaigne (Literat, Bürgermeister von Bordeaux) 91
Monte Nuovo 54
Morlaix (Bretagne) 78
Morogues, de s. Bigot de Morogues
Mortagne („Mortaigne", Dept. Orne) 118
Mühlenfels, v. (Hauptmann) 108
München 21, 22, 25, 64

Nancy 72
Napoleon Bonaparte, frz. Kaiser 21
Nassau (holländ. Linienschiff) 33, 46, 63
Nassau-Saarbrücken, Fürstin von, geb. Gräfin v. Erbach 75

Nassau-Weilburg (holländ. Linienschiff) 46
Neapel (Naples) 32, 52, 55, 56
Nebbens, François (Kapitän der „Zierikzee") 58, 59, 63
Needles, the (Felsen auf der Isle of Wight) 69
Nelson (amerikan. Oberst) 104
Neptun (frz. Kriegsschiff) 96
Nero, stufe di 53
Neu-Sommerhausen (Pennsylvania) 102
Neundorf (Mittelfranken) 24
New Jersey 101
Newport (Rhode Island) 34, 82, 93, 97, 102
New York 38, 85, 96 – 101
Niederbretagne 117
Niederlande (Netherlands) 9, 12, 13, 23
Noailles, Comte de 36, 81
Nonancourt ("Nonencoart", Dept. Eure) 118
Nordamerika 79
North Foreland ("Nord Foreland") 71
North Carolina 98
Nürnberg 27, 72

Oberlaimbach (Mittelfranken) 24
Oberthür, Prof. Franz (Würzburger Theologe) 23
Ochsenfurt (Unterfranken) 14, 16, 19, 23
O'Hara ("Ohara", engl. General) 109
Ohrdruff (Thüringen) 72
Oneglia 60, 65
Oneidas (Indianerstamm) 90
Oranien, Prinz v. 57
Orlow (russ. Admiral) 59
Overijssel/Oberissel (niederländ. Provinz) 9, 13, 45

Palmaria 52, 58, 62
Palmerola (Insel) 52

Paris 29, 43, 72, 74, 91, 117, 118
Parma, Prinzessin von 55
Paros (Insel) 64
Pastorius, Franz Daniel 39, 102
Pausilyp (Posilippo, Berg bei Neapel) 53
Penmarcs (Felsenformation an der Küste der Bretagne) 115
Pennsylvania 39, 41, 92, 98
Peter (italien. Matrose auf der "Betsy") 113, 116
Pfalzbayern s. Bayern
Philadelphia 41, 93, 102, 112, 113, 116
– State House 102
Philipsburg (New York) 97
Pilotin (Offizier auf der „Comtesse de Noailles") 80
Piombino, Kanal von 52, 57
Pisa 64, 65
– Al Husaro (Gasthaus in Pisa) 64
Plymouth (England) 69, 81
Point Peveral 69
Pompeji 55
Porquerolles (Insel bei Toulon) 65
Port Cros 60, 62
Port Mahon 61
Porto Venere 62
Portizi 54, 55
Porto Fino 60
Portsmouth (England) 70
Potomac (Fluss) 112
Pradellen (Leutnant) 84
Preußen, Friedrich II., König von 73
Princess Maria Louisa (holländ. Schiff) 63
Providence (Rhode Island) 97
Puzzuoli („Pozzuola") 53

Quibéron (Halbinsel und Städtchen, Dept. Morbihan) 116, 117

Ragusa 27
Rechteren (Schloss in Overijssel) 9, 45
Rechteren-Limpurg-Speckfeld, Eberhard Ludwig Graf von (Vater des Autors) 9, 45
Rechteren-Limpurg-Speckfeld, Graf (Kommandeur auf der „Nassau", Vetter des Autors) 46, 71
Rechteren-Limpurg-Speckfeld, Ludwig Christian Graf von (Bruder des Autors) 11, 73
Rechteren-Limpurg-Speckfeld zu Almelo, Sophia Gräfin von (Mutter des Autors) 9, 12
Reims („Rheims", Champagne) 72
Reintjes (Kommandeur auf der „Nassau") 46
Rennes (Hauptstadt der Bretagne) 77, 78, 117
Rhode Island 34, 82, 85, 92, 96
Richelieu (Marschall) 50
Ritchislof (russ. Schiff) 64
Robust (engl. Schiff) 96
Rochambeau, Graf v. (frz. General) 34, 37, 38, 41, 42, 79, 82, 89, 92, 97, 98, 100, 109, (111)
Rodney (engl. Admiral) 51, 82
Romulus (engl., dann frz. Schiff) 93, 95
Rosendal 67
Rotterdam (holländ. Linienschiff) 32, 51, 57, 59
Royal Comtois (Regiment) 88
Royal Deuxponts (Regiment) 11, 33, 77, 79, 92, 100, 105, 106, 109
Ruf (Adjutant) 105

Saintonge (Regiment) 79, 105
San Severino, Prinz 56
Sardinien 58, 62
Sasbach (Baden) 38, 101
Saurin (holländ. Minister) 68

Saurin (Kanzelredner) 68
Savannah (Georgia) 104
Schenk von Limpurg, Karl 27
Schuylkill (Fluss bei Philadelphia) 102
Schwab (Hauslehrer) 9, 45
Seneca (Indianerstamm) 90
Sibille, Grotte der 53
Sizilien 58
Soissonnois (Regiment) 79,
Solano (span. Admiral) 98
Solvaterra 54
Sommerhausen (Unterfranken) 9, 13, 15 – 18, 24 – 28, 39, 45, 72, 102
Son, van (Kadett auf der „Nassau") 46
Sonntag (Leutnant) 84
Spa (Belgien) 72
Spanien 32
Spengler (Leutnant auf der „Nassau") 46
Spezia, La (Hafenstadt in Ligurien) 62
Spinola (Genueser Patrizierfamilie) 51
Spithead 69, 70
Spiritow (russ. Admiral) 60
Stack, v. (Hauptmann, Adjutant) 108
Staten-Island (New York) 101
St. Carlo (Theater in Neapel) 55
St. Domingo 97, 98
St. Eustachius (Eustatius, karibische Insel) 51
St. Germain, Graf (frz. General und Kriegsminister) 40, 87, 100
St. Germano 54
St. Paul (Pol) de Leon (Bretagne) 78, 79
St. Simon (frz. General) 98, 103, 105
St. Stephan (ritterlicher Orden) 60
Straßburg 72
Stupp (bayer. Direktionsrat) 24
Stuttgart 108

Sundahl/Sumdahl (Hauptmann) 84, 86
Surinam 10, 72

Tabago s. Tobago
Tagus (Tejo, Tajo, Fluss) 66
Tarleton (engl. Obrist) 110, (111)
Ternay, Chevalier de (frz. Admiral) 37, 82, 86, 88
Teschen, Frieden von 73
Texel (niederländ. Insel) 71
Thetis (holländ. Schiff) 67
Tilidor s. Filidor
Tillinghast (Offizier auf der „Betsy") 113 – 115
Touches, Chevalier des 86, 93
Toulon (frz. Kriegshafen) 49, 60, 65
Touraine (Regiment) 103
Trenton (New Jersey) 101
Tschesme ("Cesme") 30, 60, 64
Tubbergen (Overijssel) 67
Tunis 58
Turenne (frz. Marschall) 38, 101
Tuscarora (Indianerstamm) 90

Unterfranken (Bayern) 21, 27
Utrecht 10, 46
Versailles 49, 118

Van der Aa s. Aa, van der
Van Goor van Hinloopen s. Goor van Hinlopen
Van Haaren S. Haren, van
Van Loo s. Loo, van
Van Son s. Son, van
Vannes (Stadt in der Bretagne) 117
Vaudore (frz. Kapitän der „Fantasque") 94
Velez Malaga 66
Venus (engl. Schiff) 63
Verger (Leutnant, später General) 22, 85, 86
Verneuil (Dept. Eure) 118

Versailles 118
Vesuv 55
Ville de Paris (frz. Linienschiff) 37, 82
Vincennes 74
Vioménil, Baron de (frz. General) 93, 104 – 106
Vergil 55
Virginia 42, 93, 97, 98, 103, 110
Vosmaar (niederländ. Kabinettsdirektor) 72
Vries, de (Leutnant auf der „Nassau") 46

Wayne („Waine", amerik. General) 98
Wales 117
Washington, George (1. Präsident der USA, General) 38, 41, 42, 86, 89, 90, 97, 101, 105, 109
Wenlerswyk (Kadett auf der „Nassau") 46
Westfalen („Westphalen") 13
Westpoint (New York), Festung 89, 90
Wetzlar, Reichskammergericht 11
Wien 12
Wight, Isle of 69 – 71
Williamsburg (Virginia) 103
Winterhausen (Unterfranken) 16, 18, 24, 26 – 28
Wisch, von der (Hauptmann) 43, 77, (78)
Würzburg, Stadt 13, 17, 22, 23, 25, 27, 72, 73, 107
– Hof Weinsberg (zeitweilig in Rechterens Besitz) 22
Würzburg, Fürstbischof von 12, 74
Würzburg, (kur)bayerisches Fürstentum 14, 18
Würzburg, Großherzogtum 18, 21

York (Fluss in Virginia) 104

Yorktown (Virginia), Festung 11, 29, 40, 41, 43, 103, 104, 109 – 111
Ysenburg, Graf (Stadtkommandant von Würzburg) 16

Zierikzsee („Zirksee", holländ. Kriegsschiff) 58, 59, 62
Zoller(n) (Leutnant, später General) 22, 84, 86
Zoutman (Kapitän der „Nassau-Weilburg", später Admiral) 46, 63, 70
Zweibrücken, s. Deuxponts

www.spurbuch.de